John O'Donovan, Irish Archaeological and Celtic Society

Annals of Ireland. Three fragments, copied from ancient sources by Dubhaltach MacFirbisigh; and edited, with a translation and notes, from a manuscript preserved in the Burgundian Library at Brussels

John O'Donovan, Irish Archaeological and Celtic Society

Annals of Ireland. Three fragments, copied from ancient sources by Dubhaltach MacFirbisigh; and edited, with a translation and notes, from a manuscript preserved in the Burgundian Library at Brussels

ISBN/EAN: 9783337156879

Printed in Europe, USA, Canada, Australia, Japan

Cover: Foto ©ninafisch / pixelio.de

More available books at **www.hansebooks.com**

ANNALS OF IRELAND.

THREE FRAGMENTS,

COPIED FROM ANCIENT SOURCES

By DUBHALTACH MAC FIRBISIGH;

AND EDITED,

WITH A TRANSLATION AND NOTES,

FROM A MANUSCRIPT PRESERVED IN THE BURGUNDIAN LIBRARY AT BRUSSELS,

BY

JOHN O'DONOVAN, LL.D., M.R.I.A..

PROFESSOR OF CELTIC LANGUAGES, QUEEN'S COLLEGE, BELFAST;
CORRESPONDING MEMBER OF THE ROYAL ACADEMY OF SCIENCES, BERLIN.

DUBLIN:
Printed at the University Press,
FOR THE IRISH ARCHÆOLOGICAL AND CELTIC SOCIETY.
1860.

THIS COPY WAS PRINTED FOR

W F SKENE, ESQ

MEMBER OF THE SOCIETY.

DUBLIN:
PRINTED AT THE UNIVERSITY PRESS,
BY M. H. GILL.

THE
IRISH ARCHÆOLOGICAL AND CELTIC SOCIETY.

MDCCCLX.

Patron:

HIS ROYAL HIGHNESS THE PRINCE CONSORT.

President:

HIS GRACE THE DUKE OF LEINSTER.

Vice-Presidents:

THE MOST NOBLE THE MARQUIS OF KILDARE, M. R. I. A.
THE RIGHT HON. THE EARL OF DUNRAVEN, M. R. I. A.
THE RIGHT HON. LORD TALBOT DE MALAHIDE, M. R. I. A.
VERY REV. CHARLES W. RUSSELL, D. D., President of Maynooth College.

Council:

EUGENE CURRY, ESQ., M.R.I.A.	PATRICK V. FITZPATRICK, ESQ.
REV. THOMAS FARRELLY.	JOHN C. O'CALLAGHAN, ESQ.
REV. CHARLES GRAVES, D.D., F.T.C.D., M.R.I.A.	JOHN O'DONOVAN, ESQ., LL.D., M.R.I.A.
	GEO. PETRIE, ESQ., LL.D., M.R.I.A.
REV. JAMES GRAVES, A.B.	REV. WILLIAM REEVES, D.D., M.R.I.A.
THOMAS A. LARCOM, Major-General R.E., M.R.I.A.	WM. R. WILDE, ESQ., F.R.C.S.I., M.R.I.A.

Secretaries:

REV. J. H. TODD, D.D., Pres. R.I.A. | J. T. GILBERT, ESQ., M.R.I.A.

INTRODUCTORY REMARKS.

HE following Three Fragments of Annals, never before published, were copied in the year 1643 for the Rev. John Lynch, author of "Cambrensis Eversus," by Dubhaltach Mac Firbisigh, or, as he anglicized his name, "Dudley Firbisse"[a], from a vellum MS., the property of Nehemias[b] Mac Egan, of Ormond, chief Professor of the old Irish or Brehon Laws; but the MS. from which the present text has been obtained, and which is now preserved in the Burgundian Library at Brussels (7, c. n. 17), is not in Mac Firbis's hand, but in that of a scribe who copied immediately from his MS., as appears from several marginal remarks.

The name of this second transcriber nowhere appears. It is quite clear,

---

[a] *Dudley Firbisse.*—For some account of Dudley Firbisse the reader is referred to "Genealogies, Tribes, and Customs of Hy-Fiachrach."—Introduction, p. vii. to xii. Mr. O'Conor, of Belanagare, informs us, in a letter published by Dr. Ledwich in his "Antiquities of Ireland" (2nd ed., Dublin, 1804), p. 303, that Duald Mac Firbis was instructed by the Mac Egans of Ormond, who were hereditary Brehons, and professors of the old Irish laws. It would also appear that he studied for some time with the O'Davorans of Thomond. For his Translations from Irish Annals for Sir James Ware, the reader is referred to the "Miscellany of the Irish Archæological Society," vol. i. p. 198 to 263.

[b] *Nehemias* is the usual Latinized form of Gilla-na-naemh, as appears from a Gloss in Lib. T. C. D., H. 2, 13.

clear, from his marginal observations, that he was a classical scholar, and a critic of considerable acumen; and that he had carefully compared these Fragments with the "Annals of the Four Masters." He also made an Index to the whole, in which he gives the dates from the "Annals of the Four Masters," which dates Lynch has adopted in his "Cambrensis Eversus" without any attempt at correcting them, although they are sometimes two and three years before the true years.

In the present edition of these Fragments the chronology of the Annals of Ulster is generally followed, with the addition of one year. The original Fragments exhibit the Anno Domini in very few instances; and even where they do, their dates are almost invariably incorrect.

Of the age or nature of the MS. from which Mac Firbis copied these Fragments of Annals, we have no clue to form any correct opinion, as he, or the later transcriber who followed him, has evidently modernized the orthography. He tells us, in several places, that the MS. was effaced, and that he could not read some important passages in consequence of the shattered condition of the old book.

The first Fragment relates chiefly to the Northern Ui Neill, and was, probably, compiled in Ulster originally; but the other two evidently belong to Ossory, or Laeighis (now Leix), and must have been compiled in some monastery in either of these territories. This is evident from the first lengthened notice in these Fragments: namely, of Feradhach, son of Duach, King of Ossory, whose death is entered in the "Annals of the Four Masters," at the year 582. It is also very evident, from the detailed accounts given of the renowned deeds of Cearbhall, King of Ossory, and of Cenneidigh, son of Gaethin, King of Laeighis. The Comharba, or successor, of Molua of Cluainferta-Molua, is also referred to as having composed poems in praise of this Cearbhall.

It

It is a very curious fact, that while these Fragments dwell with particular emphasis upon the achievements of the princes of the territories of Ossory and Leix, and of those of their relatives, the Ui-Neill, not a single reference is made to the Dal gCais, who soon afterwards eclipsed, not only the princes of those territories, but the more powerful and royal Ui Neill themselves; and, what is still more remarkable, in the account of the Battle of Bealach Mughna, in which Cormac Mac Cullinan was killed, A.D. 908, there is not one word said about the claim of the Dal gCais to the kingdom of Munster, although the work called "Cath Bealaigh Mughna," quoted by Keating, dwells upon it with remarkable emphasis. The inference to be drawn from this fact is, either that the Dal gCais had not risen to any remarkable point of power or celebrity before 908, or that the writers of these Annals were hostile to them.

The more lengthened stories and details of battles, in these Fragments, are curious specimens of Irish composition. Some of them have evidently been abstracted from long bardic descriptions of battles, and are interspersed with the wonderful and wild, the supernatural and incredible.

In the translation of the present Fragments nothing has been changed or modified; but the originals are given with scrupulous fidelity, as specimens of the manner in which our ancestors intermingled the wildest fiction with historical facts. The reader will remark this in the legend of Donnbo, in the description of the Battle of Almhain, as well as in the account of the shout of the King's Jester at the same battle, which continued to be heard in the sky for an incredible period of time.

The account of the battles between the Aunites, or Danes, and Norwegians, in Carlingford Lough, and elsewhere in Ulster, has probably been taken from an Ulster work on the Wars of the Danes and Norwegians in Ireland, now unfortunately lost or unknown. The account of these wars, now in progress of printing by Dr. Todd, is a Munster and Dalcassian production, and dwells almost exclusively upon the achievements of the men of Munster, especially upon the renowned deeds of the Dalcassian race of Thomond, who are panegyrized in glowing bardic eloquence. The present Fragments, however, make no mention whatever of any opposition given by the Dal gCais, or other Munster tribes, to the Danes, from which it is sufficiently obvious that they were extracted from local Annals preserved by the Ui Neill, and other tribes who were adverse to the Munstermen.

The account of the Gall-Gaels of Ireland who had joined the Danes, and lapsed into Paganism, is very important, as our previous ideas about them were very confused. O'Flaherty thought that these Gall-Gadelians were confined to the western islands of Scotland ("Ogygia," Part iii., c. 75); but it is clear from these Annals that they were also in Leinster and various parts of Ireland.

The account of the attack on Chester, in the third Fragment, was, probably, taken from some English or Welsh annalist, but no narrative exactly like it has been found in Geoffrey of Monmouth, or any English chronicler.

The account of the battle between the Norwegians and Moors in Mauritania, and of the Blue-men brought by the former into Ireland, has not been found in any other writer.

As already observed, the spelling has been modernized by the later scribes, but very old words and phrases, with some idioms now obsolete, will be observed throughout; such as ꝼopuaiꞃlıġ, acacomnaıc, ꝼoꞃ maꝑb, &c. The spelling of the MS. has been carefully preserved throughout, though it is evidently not as old as the language in which these Fragments are written.

J. O'D.

FRAGMENTA ANNALIUM HIBERNIÆ.

FRAGMENTA ANNALIUM HIBERNIÆ.

RAGMENTA tria Annalium Hiberniæ extractum [*sic*] ex codice membraneo Nehemiæ mac Ægan senis, Hiberniæ Juris peritissimi, in Ormonia, per Ferbissium ad usum R. D. Joannis Lynch.

Ab anno Christi circiter 571 ad annum plus minus 910.

[FRAGMENTUM I.]

[α. ↄ. 573.] Ƙl. Caṫ Ḟeiṁin in quo uiccuṗ eṗc Colman beg mac Diaṗmaḋa eċ iṗṗe euaṗic. bṗénann ḃioṗoṗ quieuiṫ in Chṗiṗco, cl**ṗṗ**. anno aecaciṗ ṗuae, uel ccc°.

Ƙ. Ƙ. Ƙ. Ƙ. Ƙ. Ƙ. Léiṡim na ṗeċċ Ƙallanḋa ṗin ṗeaċam.

[581.] Ƙal. Caṫ Manann in quo Aoḋan mac Ṡaḃṗain uiccoṗ eṗaċ.

[582.] Ƙal. Maṗḃaḋ Ḟeaṗaḋaiṡ Ḟinn, mic Duaċ, ṗi Oṗṗaiṡe. Aṗ é ṗo imuṗṗo an cṗeaṗ ṗí ṗe ṗé Colaim cille ḋo ċuaiḋ ḋo ċum niṁe,

---

ª *Feimhin,*—otherwise Magh Feimhim, a large plain in the barony of Iffa and Offa, in the county of Tipperary. The dates printed within brackets are added by the Editor. F. M. signify Four Masters.

ᵇ *Brenann of Biror.*—i. e. St. Brendan of Birr, in the King's County, of whom, see Four Masters, A. D. 571, p. 206; and Adamnan's "Vita Columbæ," lib. iii. c. 2; Colgan's Acta SS., p. 193; also Lanigan's

FRAGMENTS OF ANNALS OF IRELAND.

HREE fragments of Annals of Ireland, extracted from a vellum manuscript [the property] of Gilla-na-naemh Mac Egan, senior, a man most learned in the Irish laws, in Ormond, by Mac Firbis, for the use of the Rev. Mr. John Lynch.

From about the year of Christ 571 to about the year 910.

[FRAGMENT I.]

[A. D. 573.] Kal. The battle of Feimhin[a], in which Colman Beg, son of Diarmaid [chief of the southern Ui-Neill] was defeated, but he himself escaped. Brenann of Biror[b] quievit in Christo, in the 180th year of his age, vel ccc.

K. K. K. K. K. K. K. I leave these seven years vacant.

[581.] Kal. The battle of Mannan[c], in which Aodhan MacGabrain [King of Scotland] was victorious.

[582, F. M.] The killing of Feradhach Finn[d], son of Duach, King of Osraighe. He was the third king, who, in the time of Colum Cille, went

---

" Ecclesiastical History of Ireland," vol. ii. p. 38, *sq.*

[c] *Manann.*—i. e. the Isle of Man. See

Annals of Tighernach, and of Ulster, A. D. 581.

[d] *Feradhach*, King of Osraighe, or Os-

ninṁe, ┐ aṛ é ṛo an ḟáṫ aṁail ṛo innir Colam Cille o'Qoḋ mac
Ainmiṛeċ.

Tṛeblaio móṛ oo ġaḃáil an Ḟeaṛaḋaiġ. Clann Conla oo ṫoi-
ġeaċṫ oo ġabail ṫaiġe ṛaiṛ: uaiṛ oo Choṛca Laoiġḋe o'Ḟeaṛa-
ḋaċ mac Ouaċ, uaiṛ ṛeaċṫ ṛíġ oo ġaḃṛao Oṛṛaiġe oo Coṛco
Laoiġḋe, ┐ ṛeaċṫ ṛiġ oo Oṛṛaiġiḃ ṛo ġaṛ ṛiġe Choṛċa
Laoiġḋe.

Coccaḋ iaṛaṁ ooṛoṁ ṛe Cloino Conla, ┐ aṛ ann ṛo baoiṛium
'na ṫulġ, aġuṛ a ṛeoio uile aiġe ann; aṁail ba béṛ oo na ṛiġaiḃ
ṫuilġ umṛa o'ioḃaṛ .i. ṛoiall aṛ ċaṛuṛ a ccṛann ┐ a ccṛannoca
aiṛġio, ┐ a ccoṛáin, ┐ a n-eṛġṛaḋa, oo ṫaḃaiṛṫ oṛoġnam 'ṛan
oíoċe; a mbṛanouiḃ, ┐ a ḟṛiṫcealla, ┐ a ccamáin cṛéouma ṛa
ṛoġnum an laoi.

Rob iomḃa imuṛṛo ṛeoio aġ Ḟṛaḋaċ, ṛaṛa móṛ a nġṛaḋ laiṛ, ┐
ooná aṛ olc ḟṛiṫ iao, óiṛ ní ċualaṛom a ḃíġ nó a ṁóṛ óiṛ no aiṛġio,
oġ ṫṛén no aġ ṫṛuaġ a n-Oṛṛaiġiḃ, na hiṛġaḃéa aiġiṛioṁ oo ṫaṛ-
ṛaiṅġ a inmuṛ ṛin uaḋ oo ċuṁoaċ na ṛéo ṛain. Tanġaṫṫaṛ ṫṛa
a meic o' ionnṛoiccio Ḟṛaḋaiġ coniġe an ṫolcc oo ḃṛeiṫ na ṛéo
leó. Cṛéo aṛ áil ouiḃ, a ṁaca, ol Ḟṛaoach? Na ṛeoio oo
ḃṛeiṫ linn, ol na mic. Ní bḟṛéaoi, aṛ Ḟṛaḋaċ, uaiṛ olc ḟṛiṫ iao.
Sochaiḋe ṛa cṛaiḋiuṛa ġa ṫṫinól; aġuṛ ceaḋaiġim-ṛi mo ċṛáḋ
ṛéin oom naimḋiḃ umṛu. Ro iméiġṛioṫ a ṁic uaḋ, aġuṛ ṛo ġaṛṛoṁ
aġ aiṫṛiġe oícṛa; ṫancuṫaṛ iaṛam clann Conla, aġuṛ ṛo ṁaṛb-
ṛao

ᵉory. Four Masters, A. D. 582, and Note.

ᵉ *Aedh, son of Ainmire.*—He was monarch of Ireland from A. D. 628 to 642.

ᶠ *The race of Connla.*—i. e. of Connla,
son of Breasal Breac, ancestor of all the
chiefs of Osraighe, except the seven here
mentioned.

ᵍ *Corca-Laighdhe.*—This was the name
of the inhabitants of the S. W. portion of
the present county of Cork. O'Driscoll was
chief of this race and territory after the es-
tablishment of surnames in Ireland. It was
co-extensive with the present diocese of
Ross. This interchange of the Kings of

went to heaven; and this was the reason, as Colum Cille had told to Aedh, son of Ainmire^e.

Feradhach was seized with great sickness; [and] the race of Connla^f came to take a house upon him, because Feradhach, son of Duach, was of the Corca-Laighdhe^g, for seven kings of the Corca-Laighdhe assumed the kingship of Ossory, and seven kings of the Osraighi took the kingship of Corca-Laighdhe.

He afterwards waged war with the race of Connla; and he was in his couch, having all his valuables^h there, as was the custom of kings to have couches of yew around them, in which they had a collection of their bars and ingots of silver, and their cups and vesselsⁱ, to give them for service by night, and their chess-men and chess-boards, and their hurlets of bronze for day service.

Many were the valuables in the possession of Feradhach, and great was his love of them; but in an evil way did he acquire them, for he had not heard of rich or poor in Osraighe, having little or much of gold or silver, that he did not seize, to take such property from him to ornament these valuables. His sons came to Feradhach, to his bed, to carry away the valuables with them. "What is your desire, O my sons?" said Feradhach. "To carry away the valuables with us," replied the sons. "Ye shall not carry them away," said Feradhach, "for they were ill-gotten. I have oppressed many in procuring them, and I consent to be oppressed myself by my enemies on account

Corca Laighdhe and Osraighe is not noticed in the "Tribes and Territories of the Corca Laighdhe," printed for the Celtic Society, "Miscell.," p. 1, *sq*.

^h *Valuables*, ꝼéꝺ.—Property of any kind; *gaza*, but particularly jewels. See the Will of Cathair Mor, in " Leabhar na gCeart,"

and O'Flaherty's "Ogygia," Part iii., c. 59.

ⁱ *Vessels*, eρcρaꝺa.—In the Life of St. Darerca the *escra* is described as a silver drinking vessel—" Quoddam argenteum vasculum unde potentibus personis haurire solent quod Hybernica lingua vocatur escra."—*Brussels MS*.

ṡaḋ Ḟeaṙaḋach, ⁊ ṗuccṙaḋ na ṙeoḋa ⁊ ḋo ċuaiḋ Ḟeaṙaḋaċ ḋo cum niṁe.

Ḳal. ⁊ a ṙí ṙo an ceaṫṙaṁaḋ Ḳal ṗṗ ḋon 32 Ḳal. ṫeṙṫa aṡ an ḋeeṙṫ.

Quieṡ Coloim Cille lṗṗui anno aeṫaṫiṡ ṙuae, unḋe Ḟeḋelm ceciniṫ:

  Uċ iaṗ ṗíṗ an ṫhe ṡabṫa iṡ in lín
  he bṙecc baoi i mḃóinn.

32 Ḳal. ṙeaċoṁ.

Ḳal. Ɑ° Ḋni. ḋċṗ. Ḟionṫan ua Eaċaċ Ɑb Cluana eiḋneċ, cſnn monaċ na hEoṙṙa quieuiṫ in quinṫa Ḟeṙia, unḋe Colman mac Ḟeaṙṡuṗa ceciniṫ:

  Ḋia Ḋaṙḋaoin ṙuccaḋ Ḟionṫan,
  Iṡ ṡo ṡineḋ aṗ ṫalmain,
  Ɑṡ ḋia Ḋaṙḋaoin aṫ baċ
  Ɑṗ mo ḟliaṙṫaiḋ coimṡela.

Ḳal. Iniṫium ṗeṡiminiṡ Ɑoḋa Uaiṗioḋnaiṡ.

Ḳal. Ɑoḋ Uaiṗioḋnaċ inciṗiṫ ṗeṡnaṙe uiii. anñ. .i. Ɑoḋ mac Ḋoṁnaill, mic Ṁuiṙċeaṙṫaiṡ, mic Ṁuiṙḟḋaiṡ, mic Eoġain.

Fſċṫ naon ḋa ṫṙainic ṙé na ṗiṡḋaṁna ḋaṙ laṗ Oṫna Ṁuṙa, ṗa inḋail a láṁa aṗ an aḃoinn aṫá ḋaṗ láṗ an ḃaile. Oṫain ainm

---

[j] *Valuables.*—Which were really their own; and therefore Feradhach, having voluntarily abandoned them, went to heaven.

[k] *The 24th.*—This correction of the observation, "I omit 32 years," is itself evidently an error; for, if the last entry relating to Feradhach, son of Duach, belongs to the year 582, the year 610 is the twenty-eighth year after it.

[l] *Boyne.*—A marginal note opposite these lines says: "Hæc erant in margine," i. e. in the margin of the original MS. The verses here quoted are not found elsewhere.

[m] *Fintann Ua Eachach.*—Who this Finntan was, is not yet cleared up. See Archdall's Monast. Hib., p. 591, and Colgan's

account of them." His sons departed from him, and he took to earnest penance. The race of Connla afterwards came and slew Feradhach, and carried away the valuables^j, and Feradhach went to heaven.

[594.] Kal. And this is the 24th^k [recte 28th] Kal. of the 32 Kals. omitted at the *Deest*.

The repose [*quies*, i. e. death] of Colum Cille, in the 76th year of his age. Unde Fedelm cecinit:

Alas! in truth he who was caught in the net;
The speckled salmon who was in the Boyne^l.

I omit 32 years.

Kal. A. D. 610, Fintan Ua Eachach^m, Abbot of Cluain-eidhnech, head of the monks of Europe, died on Thursday; hence Colman, son of Fergus, sung:

On Thursday Fintan was born,
And was conceived upon the earth,
And on Thursday he died
Upon my white sheets.

[605.] Kal. The beginning of the reign of Aedh Uairidhnachⁿ.

Kal. Aedh Uairidhnach began to reign [and reigned] 8 years; i. e. Aedh, son of Domhnall, son of Muirchertach, son of Muredach, son of Eoghan.

On one occasion he came, when a royal prince, to Othain-Mura^o; he washed his hands in the river which is in the middle of the town.

Othain

Acta SS., pp. 350, 355. The first of January, 610, was Thursday. This date is not found in any other Annals.

ⁿ *Aedh Uairidhnach.*—Monarch of Ireland from the year 605 till 612.

^o *Othain-Mura.*—Othain, or Fothain

Mura (Fothain of S. Mura), now Fahan, near Loughswilly, barony of Inishowen, county of Donegal. The river is now a very small stream. This singular story about Aedh Uairidhnach is not found elsewhere, so far as the Editor knows.

ainm na habann ap uaiṫe aimniġṫip an baile .i. Oṫain. Ra ġap ḋon uipce ḋa ċup má aiġiḋ, pa ġap pṡp ḋa muinṫip ppip, A pí, ap pé, na cuip an uipġe pin po ṫaġaiḋ. Céḋon? ap an pí. Ap nap lṡm a páḋ, ap pé. Cá náipe aṫa ḋuiṫ ap an p̓ipinḋe ḋo páḋ? ap an piġ. Ap eaḋ po, ap pé, ap paip an uipġe pin aṫa pialṫṡc na clépeċ. An ann, ap an pí, ṫéiḋ an clépeċ péin ap imṫelġuḋ? Ap ann ġo ḋeiṁin, ap an ṫócclaċ. Ni namá, ap an pí, cuippeaḋ pom aiġiḋ, aċṫ cuippeaḋ um bél ⁊ iḃaḋ, aġ ol ṫpí mbolġoma ḋe, uaip ap pacapḃaicc lṡm anṫ uipcce i ṫṫéiḋ a imṫelġun.

Ra hinnipioḋ pain ḋo Múpa, ⁊ po alṫaiġ buiḋc ḋo Ohia ap ipip map pin ḋo beiṫ aġ Aoḋ, ⁊ po ġaipmeḋ cuicce iapḋain Aoḋ Allain, ⁊ Aoḋ Uaipioḋnaċ ainm oile ḋo, ⁊ a pṡḃ po paiḋ Mupa pip: A ṁic ionṁain, ap pé, loġ na haipmiḋen pin ṫuġaipi ḋo'n Eġlaip, ġeallaim-pi ḋuiṫ i ppiaḋnaipe Dé pġe n-'Eipenn ḋo ġaḃail ġo ġaipiḋ, aġup ġo mbépa ḃuaiḋ ⁊ copġup ḋoḋ náimḋiḃ, ⁊ niḋ ḃépa ḃap anaḃaiḋ, ⁊ caiṫpe copp an ċoiṁḋṡḃ ap mo láiṁ-pi, ⁊ ġuiḋpeaḋ-pa an coimḋiḋ laṫ, ġo mba cpíne ḃépup ṫu ḋon ḃioṫ.

Níop buḋ cian ṫpa iapḋain co po ġap Aoḋ Allan piġe nEipenn, ⁊ ḋo pao pṡpanna puṫaċa ḋo Mupa Oṫna.

Rucc iapam Aoḋ Allan copġaip iomḋa ḋo Laiġniḃ, ⁊ ḋa naimḋiḃ ap ċeana.

Ro ḃuí ṫpa oċṫ mbliaḋna i piġe n-'Eipṡnn, ⁊ pa ġap ġalap baip

[p] *Jakes*, Pialṫċ.—i. e. veil-house, i. e. latrina, the Temple of Clausina.

[q] *Another name.*—This is a mistake; for Aedh Allan, monarch of Ireland, flourished from A.D. 734 to 743, whereas Aedh Uairidhnach came to the throne in the year 605, and died in 612. This mistake is continued throughout; and wherever, in this legend, our author has Aedh Allan, we must read Aedh Uairidhnach. For all that is known of the history of St. Mura Othna [or Mura of Fothain—*Othna* (for *Fothna*) is the *gen.* of Fothain], see Dr. Todd's Irish Nennius; Appendix, "Duan Eirennach." In the

Othain is the name of the river; and it is from it the town is named Othain. He took of the water to put it on his face, but one of his people checked him: "O King," said he, "do not put that water on thy face." "Why so?" said the King. "I am ashamed to tell it," replied he. "What shame is it for thee to tell the truth?" said the King. "This is it," said he: "It is upon this water the *jakes*[p] of the clergy is situated." "Is it into it," said the King, "the [chief] cleric himself goes to stool?" "It is verily," replied the young man. "Not only then," said the King, "will I put it [the water] upon my face, but I will put it into my mouth, and I will drink it" (drinking three sups of it), "for to me the water into which his fæces drop is a communion."

This was told to Mura, and he returned thanks to God for Aedh's having a faith like this; and he afterwards called unto him Aedh Allan; and Aedh Uairidhnach was another name[q] for him. And Mura said to him: "Beloved son," said he, "I promise to thee, in the presence of God, the reward of that veneration which thou hast shown to the church: [viz.] that thou shalt obtain the sovereignty of Erin soon, and that thou shalt gain victory, and triumph over thy enemies; and thou shalt not be taken off by a sudden death, but thou shalt take the body of the Lord from my hand; and I will pray to the Lord that thou mayest depart old from this world."

It was not long after this until Aedh Allan assumed the kingdom of Erin; and he granted fertile lands to Mura-Othna.

Aedh Allan afterwards gained many victories over the Leinstermen, and his enemies in general.

He was eight years in the sovereignty of Erin, and then his death sickness

margin of the MS. is this note: "*Vide infra*, p. 15, Aoḋ Allan et Aoḋ Uairioḋ- naċ sunt *diversi*:" i. e. Aodh Allan and Aodh Uairidhnach are different persons.

baiṗ anḋṗın Aoḋ Allan, ⁊ ṗa ċuaṗ uaḋ aṗ cṡnn Múṗa. Táınıġ Múṗa, ⁊ ṗo ṗáıḋ an ṗí ṗıṗ: A ċléıṗıġ, aṗ ṡé, ṗaṗ meallaıṗ, uaıṗ ḋo ṗaḋṗum ṗaıll aṗ áṗ n-aıṫṗıġe, uaıṗ ḋo ṡaoıleamaṗ ṫṗéḋ ḃṗéıṫıṗṗı beıṫ ġḋ mba cṗín mé ım ḃṡṫaıḋ : ⁊ an ḋaṗ lınn aċa ḃáṗ ı ṗṗacuṗ ḋaṁ. Aṗ ṡíṗ, aṗ an cléıṗeaċ, aċá ḃáṗ ı ṗṗoġuṗ ḋaıṫ, ⁊ ṗa ċımḃíḃeaḋ ḋo ṡaoġal ⁊ ṫuccaıṗ ṗeıṗcc an ċoıṁḋṡḋ, ⁊ ınnıṗ ġá ní ḋo ṗıġnıṗ ın ṗa ċṗáıḋıṗ an coımḋıḋ. Inḋıṗṡḋ, aṗ an ṗí, ḃuḋ ḋóıġ lṡm ḋo cṗáḋ an coıṁḋṡḋ. Ṙa ṗuaḋṗaṗ, aṗ ṡé, ṗıṗ 'Éıṗenn ḋo ṫınol ḋo ċum an ṫṗléıḃeṗı ṫaıṗ.¹. Caṗṗlaoıġ ḋa ċoṁaṗḋúccaḋ ṫuaṗ, ⁊ ṫṡaċ ḋíṁoṗ ḋo ḋṡnaṁ ann, ⁊ aṗṡḋ ṗoḃ aıl ġo ṗṗaıcıṫea ṫene an ṫıġı ṗın ġaċ ṫṗáṫnóna ı mḃṗṡṫnaıḃ, ⁊ ı n-Aıṗıuṗ Ġaoıḋıol², ⁊ ṗa ṗeaḋaṗ ṗo ba ḋıomaṗ moṗ ṗaın.

Ṙob olc ṗın, aṗ an cléıṗeaċ, ⁊ ní hṡḋ ṗınṗo ċımḋıḃṡḋ ḋo ṡaoġal.

Ṙa ṗuaıḃṗıuṗ ḋono, aṗ an ṗí, ḋṗoıċṡḋ ḋo ḋṡnaṁ ı cCluaın Iṗáıṗḋ³, ⁊ a ḋṡnam ġo mıoṗḃalċa ṗıum co ṗo maıṗṡḋ m'aınṁṗı ṗaıṗ ġo ḃṗáṫ.

Ṙa ınnıṗ neıċı ımḋa aṁlaıḋ ṗın.

Ní ní ḋıḃ ṗın, aṗ an cleıṗeaċ, ċımḋıḃıuṗ ḋo ṡaoġal.

Aċá ḋono aġum ní oıle, aṗ an ṗí.ı. an ṁıṗġaıṗ ṗuıl aġom ḋo Laıġnıḃ; uaıṗ aṗeaḋ ṗoḃ áıl ḋaṁ a ṗṗın uıle ḋo ċımaṗġaın ḋo ċum caṫa, ⁊ a maṗḃaḋ uıle ann, a mna ⁊ a moġaıḋ ḋo ċaḃaıṗṫ ṗṗı ṗoġnaṁ ḋo Uıḃ Néıll. Sınnı ṫuaıṗceaṗṫ n-'Éıṗṡnn ḋo ṫaṗaıṗṫ ṗo Mıḋe, ⁊ ṗıṗ Mıḋe ṗoṗ Laıġnıḃ. Uċ, uċ, ṫṗa, aṗ an cléıṗeaċ aṗṡḋ

---

¹ *Carrlaegh.*—Carrleagh, a mountain near Aileeh, in the barony of Inishowen, county of Donegal.

² *Airiur Gaeidhel.*—i. e. *regio Gadeliorum,* now Argyle, in Scotland.

³ *That was bad.*—Did the Irish erect palaces of great altitude, or great stone bridges, in the year 612, when King Aedh Uairidhnach died? It is very much to be suspected that this romantic story was written after the introduction of Norman towers and castles into Ireland.

⁴ *Cluain-Iraird.*—Now Clonard, in the county of Meath.

sickness seized on Aodh Allan, and he sent for Mura. Mura came, and the King said to him: "O cleric," said he, "thou hast deceived us, for we have neglected our penance, because we thought that through thy word it would come to pass that we should be aged in life, and now, methinks, death is near me." "It is true," said the cleric, "death is near thee! and thy life has been cut short, and thou hast incurred the anger of the Lord; and tell what thou hast done by which thou hast offended the Lord." "I will declare," replied the King, "what I think has offended the Lord: I desired," said he, "to collect the men of Erin to this mountain to the east; i. e. Carrlaegh^r, to raise it, and to erect a very great house upon it; and my wish was, that the fire of that house, every evening, might be seen in Britain, and in Airiur-Gaeidhel^s; and I know that that was a great pride."

"That was bad"^{t}, replied the cleric; "but that is not what has cut short thy life."

"I also desired," said the King, "to build a bridge at Cluain-Iraird^u, and to build miraculously, that my name might live upon it for ever."

He also told many things of a similar nature.

"It is not any thing of these," said the cleric, "that shortened thy life."

"I have another thing to tell," said the King : "the hatred which I have for the Leinstermen; for my wish would be, to collect all their men to battle, and to kill them all therein, and to bring their women and their slaves to serve the Ui-Neill^w; to bring our race in the north of Erin into Meath, and to settle the men of Meath in Leinster."

"Alas!

---

^{w} *The Ui-Neill.*—i. e. nepotes Neill, i. e. the race of Niall of the Nine Hostages, of whom Aedh Uairidhnach was at this time head and King. St. Mura was the patron of the Cinel-Eoghain, or Race of Owen, who formed a large section of this family.

arſō ſin ſo cimbibib bo ſaoġalſo, uaiſ an cineab ſin aſ mioſ-
caiſ lacſa .i. Laiġin, acaac naoiṁ oġ ſſnaiġċe leo ſſiabnaiſi an
coimbſō, ⁊ aſ moo aca bſiġib, ⁊ aſ cſeſe bá n-iſnaiġċe anbáſ
ḃom iſnaiġċi ſi. Aċc cſna aſ cſócaſ caonuſſaċ an coimbiu, ⁊
ḃſna hiobſaiſc ſéin no ḃaſ cſhn hainġibeaċca ſin ſo ḃaoi io
cſoibe bo Loiġnib ġo ſabaiſ a ſſlaiċiuſ* aſ buaine inaſ an ſlaiċiuſ
aimſioſba.
Ra honġab an ſain an ſi, ⁊ ſo caiċ coſſ ann coimbſō, ⁊ ſuaiſ
báſ ſo cſbuaiſ, ⁊ bo ċuaib bo ċum neime.
Sſċc Kal ſſchom.
Inicium ſeġiminiſ Maoilċoḃa.
Kal. Maolcoba mac Aoba, mic Ainmiſeċ ſeġnauic cſibuſ
anniſ. Scella uiſa hoſa ceſcia biei.
Kal.
Kal. Ġuin Maoilcoba mic Aoba la Suibne Menn mic Fiachna.
Quieſ Diaſmaba ceſcii abbaciſ Cluana Iſaiſb. Inicium ſeġiminiſ Suibne Minn.
Kal. Suibne mſhn ſo ġaſ ſíġe n-'Eiſenn i nbeaġaib Maoilċoba
ſiii. bliabna ġo cconchaiſ la Conġal caeċ mac Scanlain.
Laa aen b'Fiaċna b'aċaiſi an Suibne ſin aġ bul bſiuſa
aſaċaiſi, uaiſ níoſ ḃo ſí ſioṁ iciſ, bo ſab ba mſhmain aṁail ſo
ġab caċ a nbeaġaib a ċéle ſíġe na h-'Eiſenn. Caimcc miab
meanman ⁊ inbioċċbala móſa ſae, ⁊ ſainc ſíġe na h-Eiſenn bo
ġabáil bó, ⁊ cáiniġ ſeiṁe ba ċaiġ, ⁊ ſa inniſ bá ṁnaí, ⁊ a ſſō ſo
ſaib a bſn ſiſ: uaiſ naċ ſa ſuabſuiſ ġuſ anbiu ſin, aſ ſí, ní
ſaicim

* *Immolate.*—See Dr. Reeves's note on the signification of this word.—Adamnan, p. 435.
† *Seven years.*—In the margin: "Desunt hic 7 Kal."

* *Maelcobha.*—He began his reign in the year 612; "Ogygia," p. iii., c. 98, and was slain in 615.
² *A star.*—The appearance of this star is not mentioned in any other Annals.

" Alas ! alas !" said the cleric, "this is what has shortened thy life ; for this people, which is hateful to thee, i. e. the Leinstermen, have saints to pray for them before the Lord, and Brigit is greater than I, and her prayers are more powerful than my prayers. But, however, the Lord is merciful and forgiving, and do thou immolate[x] thyself to him for the cruelty which was in thy heart towards the Leinstermen, that thou mayest be in a kingdom more lasting than thy temporal kingdom.

The King was then anointed, and he took the body of the Lord, and, dying immediately, went to heaven.

I omit seven years[y].

[612.] The beginning of Maelcobha's[z] reign.

Kal. Maelcobha, son of Aedh, son of Ainmire, reigned three years. A star[a] was seen the third hour of the day.

Kal.

[615.] Kal. The killing of Maelcobha, son of Aedh, by Suibhne Menn, son of Fiachna. The repose of Diarmaid[b], third Abbot of Cluain-Iraird. The beginning of the reign of Suibhne Menn.

Kal. Suibhne Menn assumed the sovereignty of Erin after Maelcobha, for thirteen years, until he was slain[c] by Congal Caech, son of Scanlan.

One day, as Fiachna[d], the father of this Suibhne, was going to visit his ploughing—for he was not at all a king—he called to mind how persons succeeded to each other in the sovereignty of Erin; he was seized with great pride of mind and ambition, and a covetousness of

---

[b] *Diarmaid.*—The death of this third Abbot of Clonard is not recorded in the published Annals, nor noticed by Archdall.

[c] *Was slain.*—In the year 628.

[d] *Fiachna.*—This story of Fiachna, the father of the Irish monarch, Suibhne Menn, is not given by any of the other Annalists, nor even by Keating, who was very fond of giving stories of the same kind. It is clearly not very old.

ḟaicim a cuiḃḋe ṗe ṗíṗ ṫaoṗa aṡuṗ do ṗíṡcaṫṫaḋ ɪ ḟḟeaċṫṗa coṗnaṁ ṗiṡe, uaiṗ ní ——— ḃí ɪ ṫoṗṫ, aṗ ṗeiṗioṁ, na ṫaiṗmiṗṡ ɪmum ; aċṫ ṫuċṫuṗ lind aṡuṗ ḃiaḋ iṗṫiṡ, aṗ ṗé, aṡuṗ ṫinolṫuṗ maiṫe ɪnnaċ ċuċċainn, ⁊ ṫaḃaiṗ lóṗ dóiḃ; aṡuṗ ṡaiṗmiḋ a mnaoi ċuiċċe andṗain ⁊ ċomṗaiċiḋ ḟṗia, aṡuṗ ṡaċ imṗaḋhaḋ ṗa ḃui ṗeiṁe na miṡnmain ṗa ċuiṗ ṗa ċoimṗeṗṫ uaḋ, ⁊ aṗ aċ an mnaoi ṗa ḃaoi an ṫimṗaḋhaḋ ṗa ḃaoi aiċiṗiuṁ ɪaṗ ṗin, ⁊ aṗ and ṗin ṗa ċoimṗṗeḋ an Suiḃne Mṡnoṗa a mḃṗoinn a ṁáṫaṗ. In ṫan ṫṗa ṗa eiṗiṡṗiṁ ó mnaoi, ad ḃṡṗṫ an ḃṡn: an dṫinolṗaiḋeaṗ ċáċ iṗṫeaċ aṗ ṗí? Aċṫ, aṗṗ Ḟiachna, Ní dinṡnim aṗ ḟṗoċuiḃeḋ ṗéin .ɪ. ṗiṡe ṗṡṗṫa do ċoṗnaṁ. Ṫuiṡṫeaṗ aṗṗin ɪaṗam ċonid da aiṡniuḋ móṗ ṗemṫeċṫaċ na dṫuiṗṫiṡṫiḋ do ḃeṗaḋ na ċlanna aiṡenṫa móṗa.

Lá dono don ṫSuiḃne ṗi na ṡilla óṡ na ṫaiċċ ⁊ a ḃṡn, ṗa ṗaiḃ ṗia ṁnaoi; aṗ ionṡnaḋ liom, aṗ ṗé, a laiṡṡḃ ṗo ṡaḃ ó Cenel Eoṡain ṫiṡṡṗnuṗ ṗoṗ ċaċ ɪnoṗṗa : aṗeḋ ṗa ṗáiḃ an ḃṡn ṫṗe cenel ṗoċuindeḋ, ċiḋ duiḃṗi, aṗ ṗí, ṡan ċṗuaṗ do ḃṡnaṁ, ⁊ dul ṗomṗa do ċoċċaḋ ḟṗia ċáċ, ⁊ ċoṗṡuṗ do ḃṗeiṫ ṡo miniċ. Aṗ aṁlaiḋ ṗin ḃiaṗ, aṗ éiṗioṁ.

Ṫainiṡṗim ɪaṗ ṗin amaċ aṡuṗ ṗé aṗmṫa ṗa maiḃin aṗ na ḃáṗaċ, ⁊ do ṗála oċċlaoċ do luċṫ . . . . ⁊ eiṗiḋe aṗmṫa, ⁊ do ṗoine ċomṗaċ ḟṗiṗ ṡo ṗo ṡiall an ṫóṡlaċ do ṗind·ṡae ḋó, ⁊ ṗo ṡiall ṗluaṡ moṗ do aṁlaiḋ, ⁊ ṗo ṡaḃ ṗiṡe n-'Eiṗenn.

Kal. Moṗṗ Suiḃne Minn. [715.]

ᵉ The race of Eoghan.—i. e. the descendants of Eoghan, son of Niall of the Nine Hostages (ancestor of the O'Neills and other families of Ulster), father of Muiredhach, the great-grandfather of Suibhne Menn. See next note.

ᶠ The death of Suibhne Menn.—He was son of Fiachna, who was the son of Feradhach, son of Muirchertach, son of Muiredhach, son of Eoghan, son of Niall of the Nine Hostages, and was monarch of Ireland for thirteen years. He was slain by Congal Claen, King of Ulidia, according to the Four Masters, in 623, but, according to the Annals of Ulster, in 627; the true year was 628. See O'Flaherty's "Ogygia," Part

of assuming the sovereignty of Erin; and he came on to his house and told his wife so; and his wife said to him: "As thou hast not desired this till this day," said she, "I do not see its meetness in a man of thy age and antiquity now to contend for a kingdom, for not ———" "Hold thy peace," said he; "do not hinder me; but let ale and food be brought into the house, and let noble chieftains be invited to us, and let them have abundance." And he then called his wife to him, and cohabited with her, and all the aspirations which he had had previously in his mind he expelled from him by coition, after which the woman possessed the imaginations which he had had previously; and it was then this Suibhne Menn was conceived in his mother's womb. When he arose from the woman, the woman said: "Shall all be collected to the house," said she. "No," replied Fiachna, "we shall not mock ourselves by contesting for a kingdom." From this it is to be understood that it is from the previous aspiring notions of the parents that ambitious children are begotten.

One day, when this Suibhne was a young man, at his house with his wife: "It is a matter of wonder to me," said he, "how few of the race of Eoghan[e] have, up to this time, taken chieftainship over all." And the woman said, in a kind of derision, "Why dost not thou," said she, "exercise hardihood, and go in their van to fight with all, and to gain frequent triumphs?" "It is so it shall be," said he.

He afterwards came forth armed on the following day, and he met a young hero of the people of .... who was armed, and he fought with him, and the young hero submitted to him at the point of a spear, and a great host submitted to him likewise, and he assumed the sovereignty of Erin.

[628.] Kal. The death of Suibhne Menn[f].

[715.]

iii., c. 93. There is a chasm here of nearly a whole century—from 628 to 714; but the matter is nearly supplied by the second Fragment, to be presently given.

[715.] Foɣarcać hua Cfrnaiɣ do ṗiöiṗi na piɣe, unde dicerum:
Seṗṗa Poɣuṗcać an plaić
Cini fṗda oṗ bić bíṗ
Cin can aṗ mbeṗ ní bí ní
laṗ ṗin aṗ ṗi ṗia cinn míṗ.

[716.] Kal. Cumuṗcc aonaiɣ Caillcen la Poɣuṗcać i coṗćaiṗ mac Maoilṗuba ⁊ mac Duinnṗléibe.

[717.] Kal. Cinaṗcaṗiuṗ Ciuɣuṗcuṗ pellicuṗ. Fṗoṗ meala pluic ṗupeṗ ṗoṗṗam Laɣinoṗum: pluic eciam fṗoṗ aiṗɣid i n-Océain móiṗ, fṗoṗ cṗuićneaćca i n-Océain mbicc. Cunc nacuṗ eṗc Niall Condail, mac Feaṗɣail, unde Niall Fṗoṗać uocacuṗ eṗc.

Coṗonuccad Pfoaiṗ Aṗṗcol do ɣabáil do muincip lae foṗṗo; uaiṗ coṗónuccad Simóin Oṗuad ṗo baoi foṗṗo co nicce ṗin, amail aṗed ṗo baoi foṗ Colom cille féin.

[718.] Kal. Cheodoṗiuṗ imṗeṗac anno uno.
[719.] Kal. Leo imṗeṗac anniṗ iḋ.
[720.] Kal. Inṗfo Maiɣe bṗeaɣ la Cacal mac Fionnɣuine, ṗí Muṁan, ⁊ Muṗchad mac möṗain ṗi Laiɣfn. Inṗfo Laiɣfn la Feaṗɣal mac Maoilduín. In aṗailib leṗṗaib aiṗiṗfn foɣabam comad iṗin cṗfṗ bliadain peṁaind, .i. an deaćmhad bliadain plaićiuṗa

---

ᵍ *Fogartach Ua Cernaigh.*—See Four Masters, A. D. 712, 714, 719. The Annals of Ulster give the dates thus: 713. "Fogartach hua Cernaigh, de regno expulsus est, in Britanniam ivit." 715. Fogartach nepos Cernaigh, iterum regnat." He became undisputed monarch of Ireland in 719 [*O'Flah.*, 722], but was slain by Cinaeth, his successor, in 724.

ʰ *Tailltin,* now Teltown, on the River Blackwater, in Meath, midway between Navan and Kells. See Four Masters, 715, and Ulster, 716.

ⁱ *Anastasius.*—i. e. Anastasius II., resigned in January, 716.

ʲ *Othain-mor.*—Now Fahan, near Lough Swilly, in the barony of Inishowen. Othain-Beg is a subdivision of Othainmor. See p. 11, n. ᶜ, *supra.* These three showers are noticed by the Four Masters

[715.] Fogartach Ua Cernaigh[g], again in the sovereignty, unde dictum est :
> Fogartach the chieftain prevails.
> What is noble is above the world.
> When he says there is nothing,
> After that he is king before a month.

[716.] Kal. The confusion of the fair of Tailtinn[h] by Fogartach, in which fell the son of Maelrubha, and the son of Donnsleibhe.

[717.] Kal. Anastasius[i] Augustus pellitur. A shower of honey fell upon the foss of Leinster. It rained also a shower of silver at Othain Mor[j], and of wheat at Othain Beg. Then was born Niall Condail, son of Ferghal, whence he was called Niall Frosach [i. e. of the showers].

The tonsure of Peter the Apostle[k] was taken by the family of Ia, for it was the tonsure of Simon Magus they had till then, as had Colum Cille himself.

[718.] Kal. Theodosius[l] imperat anno uno.

[719.] Kal. Leo[m] imperat annis novem.

[720.] Kal. The plundering of Magh Breagh[n] by Cathal, son of Finguine, King of Munster, and Murchadh, son of Bran, King of Leinster. The plundering of Leinster by Ferghal, son of Maelduin. I find in other books that it was in the third year preceding ; i. e. the tenth

at A. D. 716, and by the Annals of Ulster at 717. The true year is 715. Niall Frosach, who received his cognomen from having been born in the year in which these remarkable showers fell, was monarch of Ireland from 763 to 770.

[k] *The tonsure of Peter the Apostle.*—" A.D. 718.—Tonsura coronæ super familia Iae."

—*Ann. Tighern.* See Bede's Eccles. Hist., lib. v., c. 21 ; Reeves's Adamn., xlvii., 350.

[l] *Theodosius.*—Meaning Theodosius III., A. D. 717.

[m] *Leo.*—A. D. 718.

[n] *Magh Breagh.*—A large plain in Meath. Four Masters, 717 ; Annals of Ulster, 720 [721].

plaiċiura Feaṙsail do ġniċea an cinnṙaḋṙa Laiṡln, ⁊ somaḋ na ḋiṡail ċáinic Muṙċaḋ mac Ḃṙain ṡo fṙṙaiḃ Muṁan d'inṫpṙḃ Maiṡe ḃṙeaġ. Ṡiḃé ḃliaḋain ḋiḃ ṙin cṙa do ṙiṡne Feaṙsal inṫpaḋa moṙa i Laiṡniḃ .i. aloṙṡaḋ ⁊ a nḋóḋ, ⁊ a maṙḃaḋ, ⁊ ṙa ṡeall naċ anṙaḋ ḋe ṙin, no so ccuṡċa ḋo an ḃoṙoṁa ṙo ṁaiċ Finnaċċa do Molinṡ, ⁊ so dcuṡċa ḃṙaiṡḋe ḋó ṙe ciṡeaṙnaṙ ⁊ ṙeṙ in ċiuṙ. Do ṙaoṙac laiṡin ḃṙaiṡḋe ḋó, ⁊ ṙa ṡeallṙac an cíṙ.

Iṙ ind aimṙiṙ ṙin do ṙiṡne Feaṙsal faiṙcini ḋá ṁacaiḃ .i. d'Aoḋ Allan, aṡuṙ do Niall Cunḋail, [ḋá nṡoiṙéí Niall Fṙa-ṙaċh] ⁊ aṙ aṙ ṙo ṙo áṙ ḋoṙoṁ on.

.l. Lá cancaccuṙ cuicce do h-Ailċë Fṙiṡṙṙnn, .i. Aoḋ an mac ba moo .i. óclaċ ṡlic, amnuṙ, ḃeoḋa, aḋacomṙaicṙiḋe, aṙ aṁlaiḃ ċainiṡ ṡo mḃuiḋniḃ móṙa daġaṙmċa ime do cum Aliġ. Aṙ aṁlaiḃ imuṙṙo cainiṡ an mac ba ṙóo, ṡo ciuin ⁊ ṡo mífṙaṙḋa, ṡo ṙíḋaṁail, ⁊ co n-uaiċiḃ, ⁊ aṙṙeḋ ṙo ṙáiḋ aṙ anaṙṙaiḋe féin, ⁊ aṙ onóiṙ ḋá aċaiṙ : aṙ cóṙa ḃaṁṙa, aṙ ṙé, dol aṙ aoiḋheċċ amaċ iná aiṙiṙiṁ ḋa aiṡiḋ aṡaḋṙa anoċċ. Cia dia ccaṁḋuiṙi, a ṁic, aṙ an caċaiṙ, ṙin do ṙáḋ? ⁊ an mac aṙ ṙiniu caoi, aṡaṙ acaṙaiḋe cṙí coimlíon fṙicṙa [ciḃ faḋeṙa] ṡan ḋánoċċ aṡaḋ im caiṙiṙim i n-Aileaċ inoċċ amhail acaṙuṁ aṡ caiṙiṙim co n-a ṁuincip ? Ra ṙaḋ maiċ líṁṙa, aṙ Niall, co nḋeaṙnaḋṙom inaile ċéḋna fṙicṙa. Ni ṙaṡa ioiṙ anoċċ, a ṁic, aṙ Feaṙsal, aṡuṙ ḃiaḋ i fṙaṙṙaḋ caċaṙ ⁊ do ṁáċaṙ.

Ruccaḋ

᷾ *Whichever year.*—The Four Masters state that Leinster was five times devastated by the Ui-Neill, in the ninth year of the reign of Ferghal.

ᵖ *Boromean tribute.*—See Annals of the Four Masters, A. D. 106, p. 100.

ᵍ *A prediction.*—i. e. a surmise, conjecture, or opinion concerning their future careers. This account of Ferghal and his sons is not in any other accessible Annals, and it evidently found its way into Mac Egan's vellum Book from some romantic

tenth year of the reign of Ferghal [721] this plundering of Leinster took place, and that it was in revenge for it that Murchadh, son of Bran, came with the men of Munster to plunder Magh Breagh. But whichever year° it was, Ferghal committed great depredations against the men of Leinster; i. e. he burned, consumed, and killed them, and he vowed that he would not desist until he was paid the Boromean tribute[p] which Finnachta had remitted to Moling, and until hostages were given him for [i. e. in acknowledgment of his] lordship and the tribute. The Leinster-men gave him hostages, and promised the rent.

At this time Ferghal gave out a prediction[q] to his sons: viz., Aedh Allan and Niall Condail, and the cause of his doing so originated thus:—

On a certain day they came to him to Ailech-Frigrinn[r]: viz. Aedh the elder son, who was a cunning, fierce, lively young hero, and he came to Ailech surrounded by numerous well-armed troops; but the younger son came silently, modestly, and peaceably, with few attendants; and he said, to humble himself and to honour his father: "It is fitter for me," said he, "to go and lodge out than to remain thy guest to night." "What induces thee to say this, my son," said the father, "while my elder son, who has thrice thy number [of attendants] is staying at Ailech to-night? Why hast thou not the same confidence to remain at Ailech to-night as he has, in remaining with his people?" "I should like," replied Niall, "that he would do the very same towards thee." "Thou shalt not depart hence to-night, O son," said Ferghal, "but thou shalt remain with thy father and thy mother."

After

story, probably no longer extant.

[r] *Ailech Frigrinn.*—So called from Frigrenn, the builder of the fort; now Greenan-Ely, an ancient cyclopean fort on Greenan Hill, near Lough Swilly, in the barony of Inishowen. For the history of this place, see the Ordnance Memoir of the Parish of Templemore, published in 1835.

Ruccaó iaρ ρin an mac bub ρine, .i. Aob, 'ρin ρig tſc móρ cona muinntiρ. Ruccaó ono an mac óg .i. Niall i tteac naoibinn noeρρio. Ra ρρicaigio iaρttain, ⁊ ρa b'áil oon atáiρ a noeaρbaò maille, ⁊ tanaice a noeiρeò oiòce do cum an taige i ρaibe an mac ba ρine, ⁊ ρa baoi acc cloiρtect ρρiρin tſc ρin : aρ òigaiρ tρa ρalac ρa báρ 'ρan taig ρin. Rá báttaρ ρuiρρeoiρi, ⁊ caintebba, ⁊ eaclaca, ⁊ obloiρi, ⁊ baclaig ag bſcſboig ⁊ acc buiρebaig ann; oρeam ag ól, ⁊ oρeam na ccoòlaó, ⁊ oρeam og ρgeatρaig, oρeam occ cuρlſnnaig ⁊ oc ρſccuiρig; timρanaig ⁊ cρuiciρi og ρſnmain; oρeam og imaρbagaò, ⁊ oc ρſρbagaib. Ao cuala Fſρgal amlaió ρin iaò, agaρ táinig iaρ ρin ò'innρoicéio an taige bεppio i ρaba an mac aρ ρóo, ⁊ ρa baoí ag cloiρtſčt ρiρ an tſc ρin, ⁊ ní cuala nac ní ann acht atluccao buiòe oo Dhia [ρa] gac ní ρuaρattuρi, ⁊ cρuiciρect ciúin bíno, ⁊ ouana molta an coimòeò gá ngabail, ⁊ ρa aiρig an ρí co móρ uamon ⁊ gρáò an coimoeò iρin taig ρin.

Táinig an ρí aρ a haitle ρin oá leabaiò ρéin, ⁊ tucc go móρ oa uiò ρuiòiuccaó an oá tſc ρin.

Táinic maoain mottρat ρan tſc móρ i ρaba an mac ba ρine, ⁊ aρ inbſctain ρa ρéo tabaill an taige ρa imaò ρgeatρaige ⁊ ρalcaiρ ⁊ bρſntataò, ⁊ imaò con oc ite ρgeatρaige. Cac imuρρo uile na ρρeanoρaòoig [no i otoiρchim ρuain] iρtaig amail beittíρ maρb, genmota mac an ρí ρéin; aρ amlaió imuρρo ρo baoiρibe ina coòlaò amail ρa beit ag iρnaiòe cata ⁊ ρé na ρiξleabaiò, ρgiat móρ òá leit clí, ⁊ oa lſcga lánmóρa oá leit veρ: claiveab moρ intlaiρi óρouiρn ρoρ a ρliaρaiò, analρaoac móρ imac ⁊ iρteac oá cuρ ò ó, amail nacaoa ouini oa cuρ aρ éρeiρi ⁊ aρ éρicce.

Níoρ

* *Snoring.*—There is probably here some defect of transcription; the words left out are probably no in-a b-coiρchim ρuain: the meaning doubtless is, that some were snoring, and others were lying senseless as if dead.

After this the eldest son, Aedh, was brought into the great regal house with his people; but the younger son, Niall, was conveyed into a beautiful private apartment. They were afterwards served [with food and drink], and the father wished to test them both; and he came, towards the end of the night, to the house where the eldest son was, and he remained to listen to [what was going on in] that house. They were indeed very dirty in that house. There were jesters, and lampooners, and horseboys, and clowns, and buffoons, roaring and vociferating there,—some drinking, some sleeping, and some vomiting; some piping, some whistling; tympanists and harpers playing; some disputing, some quarrelling! Ferghal heard them [getting on] so; and he afterwards came to the private house in which the younger son was [lodged], and he remained listening to [what was going on in] that house; but he heard nothing there but thanksgiving to God for all that they had received, and gentle, melodious harp-playing, and songs of praise to the Lord being sung; and the King perceived that the fear and love of God were in that house.

After this the King returned to his own bed, and he meditated deeply in his mind the condition of these two houses.

Early in the morning he came into the great house in which the elder son was, and it was with difficulty he could remain in the house, in consequence of the vomiting, filth, and stench, and the number of hounds that were eating the vomits. And all the persons in the house were snoring* [or sleeping] as if they were dead! except the King's son alone; but he was sleeping in his royal bed [in such a posture] as if he were awaiting a battle,—a large shield on his left side, and two great half darts on his right, a long polished golden-hilted sword on his thigh, and he inspiring and respiring as if another man were putting him to his strength and dexterity!

Níor ḟéḋ ṫno ruireḋ rair irtaig ná méḋ ṗob élneigte an t-aér irin tig rin, ⁊ táinig irin tṡé i ṗoiḃe an mac ba roo, ⁊ giṫ ṗoill táinice, ra airig an mac ó g é, uair níṗ bo coṫlaṫ ṫó, aḋt ag guiṫe an coimṫeṫ ra ḃaoi. Ra eirig ṗo ḋéṫóir i n-aigiṫ a aḋar ṫon ṫergṫṫ ríogḃa i ṗoiḃe, uair ar aṁlaiṫ na ḃaoí, ⁊ inar ṗróill ime go cciuṁraiṫ óir ⁊ airgiṫ, ⁊ no orlaig an tṡé ṗe na aḋair, ⁊ ó ḋainig an taḋair irtṡé ṫo raṫ ṫa láiṁ ṗo ḃragaiṫ a ṁic, ⁊ ṫo raṫ róg ṫo, ⁊ tancatur maille gur no ṗuiḃṡour ṗor an ṫergṫṫ ríogḃa; ra raig an mac coṁráṫ ar túr ar an aḋair, ⁊ arṡṫ no ṗáiṫ; a aḋair, ar ré, an ṫar linn ar impnímhaḋ nṡṁḋoṫoltaḋ rugair an aḃaig aréir ar, arṡṫ ar lṡt anora coṫlaṫ rin leaḃaiṫ rin go tráḋ eirge ṫo ló. Ṫo pigne an t-aḋair aṁlaiṫ, ⁊ mar táinig tráḋ eirge ṫo ló ra ergeṫor imaille, ⁊ ra ṗáiṫ an mac ṗria a aḋair: A aḋair inṁain, ar ré, arṡṫ ar ḋóir ṫuit rleḃuccaṫ ṫúinn male ṗria rérúnn, uair maraiṫ ogainn lṡt na ṫtugaṫ ṫo ḃiaṫ ⁊ ṫo lionn uaiṫri a ṗéir ṫúin, agar ní tarrnaig ṫo rain inuair tugraṫ timchinṫi an mac lṡṗoar mór lán ṫo ṁíoṫ ⁊ ḃiaṫ láiniomḃa, ⁊ ra rlegaiṫriot go taoi reiḋeaṁail i maille anorin.

'O no eirig caḋ, táinig an pi amaḋ na tṡé réin, ⁊ no innir i ṗriagnairi cáiḋ aṁail no biaṫ toigte na ṫá mac ún, ⁊ a ṫuḃairt go ngeḃaṫ an mac ra rine rige ⁊ go maṫ treaḃair, croṫa, beoṫa, creraḋ, rarḋolaḋ a rige. An mac ba luga imurro, co ngeḃaṫ rige go craiḃḃeaḋ conṫail, ⁊ go maṫ clúaḋ ríogḃa a clann, ⁊ go ngeḃṫair rige an ṫara real. Ireṫ ṫono rin no coṁailleṫ co nuigi rin.

Ingín ṫno Congail mic Ṗeargura Ṗánaṫ, mataip an mic ba rine ⁊ ṗo ḋliḋ rug rí an mac rin .i. Aoṫ Allan, agur no bé ro aḃḃar

¹ *Pure-minded.*—The word conḃail is glossed inṗraic (worthy, pure, honest), in H. 3, 18, p. 653.
ᵘ *Congal, son of Fergus of Fanaid.*—He was monarch of Ireland from the year 704 to 711. See Annals of the Fours Masters, A. D. 702, Annals of Ulster, A. D. 704, and O'Flaherty's "Ogygia," Part iii., c. 93.

He [the King] was not able to remain in the house in consequence of the great corruption of the air within it; and he came on to the house in which the younger son was, and, though he came stealthily, the young son perceived him, for he was not asleep, but praying to the Lord. He rose up at once, to meet his father, from the royal couch on which he was, for he was dressed in a satin tunic, with borders of gold and silver, and he opened the house for his father; and when the father entered the house, he folded his arms around the neck of his son, and kissed him, and they came together and sat upon the royal couch, and the son first began the conversation with the father, and said: "Father," said he, "thou hast, methinks, passed the last night pensively and sleeplessly, and thou oughtest now to sleep in this bed till the rise of day." The father did so; and as the day appeared, both arose up together, and the son said to the father: "Dear father," said he, "thou oughtest to entertain us in reason, for we have still remaining half what was given by thee last night to us of food and of drink;" and he had not finished [these words] when servants brought him a second great vessel full of mead and various viands, after which they feasted together silently and calmly!

When all had arisen, the King came forth into his own house, and told, in the presence of all, how the houses of his two sons were; and he said that the elder son would assume the sovereignty, and that he would be firm, brave, and vigorous, severe and self-willed, during his reign; also that the younger son would assume the sovereignty, and that he would be pious and pure-minded[t], and that his descendants would be illustrious and royal, and that they would assume the sovereignty alternately. And this was verily fulfilled so far.

Now the daughter of Congal, son of Fergus of Fanaid[u], was the mother of the elder son, and it was secretly she brought forth that son; i. e. Aedh Allan, and this is the reason why Ferghal had this

E 2   girl

aḃḃap beiṫe po cliṫ na hinġine oġ Feaṛġal : a haṫaiṛ, .i. Conġal ṅa hiḃḃaiṛṫ ṅon coimṁiḃ ⁊ a beiṫ a caillċeaċṫ, ⁊ ṅo ṛaḃ a haṫaiṛ iomaḃ óiṛ ⁊ aiṛġiḃ, aġuṡ cṛuiḃ ḃi a ċoiṁéḃ a ġṡnuṛa. Ġiḃeaḃ ṫṛa ṛa ṁeall náṁa coiṫċṡnn an ċinuḃa ḃaonḃa .i. Ḃiaḃal, í; ḃo ṛaḃ ġṛáḃ oFṡiṛġal mac Maoilḃúin, ⁊ ḃo ṛaḃ Fṡiṛġal ġṛaḃ ḃiṛi. Ro compaiġṛeaḃ ḃno maille Feaṛġal ⁊ inġṡn Conġail Cinṅmaġ-aiṛ. Rioġḃomna Eiṛṡnn an ṫan ṛin Fṡiṛġal. Rí Eiṛṡnn imoṛṛo Conġal. Ra iniṡ an ḟeaṛ ṛa ḃaí ṡṫuṛṛa ṛin ḃo Conġal. Ḃa ḃoiliḃ imuṛṛo co móṛ lá Conġal an ṛġel ṛin : .i. a inġṡn ḃo ṁeallaḃ, ⁊ a ḃuḃaiṛṫ ná maiṛṛṡḃ ḟeaṛ an ṛġeoil muna ḟṛáġḃaḃ ṡéin ḃeiṁin an ṛġeoil. Ro ḃaoi iaṛaṁ ḟeaṛ an ṛġeoil oġ iṛnaiḃe ġo mbeiṫṫíṡ a naoin ionaḃ, Feaṛġal ⁊ inġṡn Conġail, ⁊ maṛ ṛa báṫṫuṛ i n-aoin-ionaḃ, Feaṛġal ⁊ inġṡn Conġail, ṫainiġ ḟeaṛ an ṛġeoil ḃ'ionṅṛoiġhiḃ Conġail, ⁊ ṛa inniṡ ḃo a mbeiṫ i n-aoin-ionaḃ. Ṫainiġ Conġal ṛeiṁe ḃ'ioñṛoicchiḃ an ṫiġe i ṛaḃaṫṫuṛi, ⁊ maṛ ṛa aiṛiġ inġṡn Conġail éiṛion co na ṁuinṫiṛ ḃo ċum an ṫiġe, uaiṛ ṛo ba ġlic amnuṡ ainġiḃ iṛi, aṁail ṛo bṡḃ a h-aṫaiṛ, ṛa ṡoiliġ ḟon éḃaċ Fṡiṛġal, ⁊ ṛa ṡuiḃ ṡéin ḟoṛ an éḃaċ iaṛṫṫain. Ṫainiġ caṫ móṛ baoi iṡṫaiġ ḃ'ioñṛoiċċiḃ Fṡiṛġail co n-ḃuaiḃ a ċoṛa, ⁊ ġo ṛo ṡluiġ an caṫ ṛloiṫi moṛa ḃo ċoṛaiḃ Feaṛġail. Ḃo ṛaḃ Feaṛġal an laṁ ṛṡċa, ⁊ ṛa ġaḃ 'ma ṡlucaiṫ an caṫ, ⁊ ṛoṡ maṛḃ.

Ro ṡéġ ṫṛa Conġal an ṫṡċ ime, ⁊ ní ṡaca Fṡiṛġal ann. Ṫainiġ ṛoiṁe ḃ'innṛoiġhiḃ ṡiṛ an ṛġeoil, ⁊ ṛo báiḃ é i n-aḃainn. Ṫainiġ iaṛṫṫain ḃ'ioñṛoiġiḃ a inġine ṡéin, ⁊ ṛa ḃaoi aġ iaṛṛaiḃ loġṫa ṡuiṛṛe aṁail biḃ óġ iṛi ⁊ na beṫṫíṡ cioṛṫa ṡaiṛṛioṁ ṡṛia. San coṁṛac cliṫi ṛin ṫṛá ṛo coimṛṛiḃ Ꭺoḃ Ꭺllan.

Aṛ

* *Ceannmaghair.*—This place is still so called in Irish, and in the anglicised form Kinnaweer. It is situated at the head of Mulroy Lough, in the territory of Fánaid, barony of Kilmacrenan, and county of Donegal. See Four Masters, A.D. 702, note ᶜ, and A.D. 1392. In the old translation of the Annals of Ulster Cenn-Magair is referred to as if it were the same as Fanaid; but it is now considered as the

girl secretly: her father, Congal, had devoted her to God, and she was in a nunnery, and her father had given much gold and silver and cattle to her for preserving her virginity. But however, the general enemy of the human race, namely, the devil, deceived her; she fell in love with Ferghal, son of Maelduin, and Ferghal loved her. Ferghal and the daughter of Congal of Ceannmaghair' cohabited together. Ferghal, at this time, was a royal heir apparent of Erin, and Congal was King of Erin. The man who was [the messenger] between them told this to Congal, and Congal was much grieved at the news of the seduction of his daughter, and he said that the bearer of the story should not live unless he verified it to him. The bearer of the story was waiting until Ferghal and the daughter of Congal should be in one place; and when they were in one place, the bearer of the story came to Congal and told him of their being in one place. Congal came forward to the house in which they were, and as the daughter of Congal perceived him and his people approaching the house,—for she was cunning, sharp, and peevish, as was her father,— she covered Ferghal under the clothes, and afterwards sat upon the clothes herself. While Ferghal was in this position, a large cat which was in the house came to him, and biting at his legs, devoured large pieces of flesh off his legs. Ferghal put down his hand, and taking the cat by the throat, choked her.

Congal searched the house all round, but did not see Ferghal in it. He came forward to where the bearer of the story was, and drowned him in a river ! He afterwards came to his daughter, and asked forgiveness of her because she was [as he supposed] a virgin ! that his crime against her might not be upon him". By this secret connexion Aedh Allan was begotten !

Now,

north-west part of it.

" *Might not be upon him.*—i. e. that his sin in accusing his daughter, who was a consecrated virgin, might be forgiven him.

Ar na breit imurro, Aod Allain, ra ſib a mátair é do dib innáib (ra ba cairiri lé) dá bádab, ná rionnab a h-atair ruirre, ⁊ na fſrʒaibeb an catair fria. bſn do Cinél Conaill dibriden uno, ⁊ bſn do Cenel Eoʒain. An bſn Eoʒanać tra mar ra ʒair 'na láim an aoidin mbiʒ nálainn ra líonab ó ʒráb ⁊ ó ſeirc na naoidine ſ; irſb ro ráib ra mnaoi coméa, a ſiur iohmain, ar ſí, noća malairt na naoidineri ar cóir, aćt ar a coiméd ʒo mait. A rſb ro raibriöi, annra latra é ina re na mátair féin, ⁊ ir ſride ra ſrail roirne a bádub, ar iomoṁon feirʒi a hatair. Ra ʒaṗ feaſʒ hirioe, ⁊ ra ćuir an Leanaṁ for lár, ⁊ ro deabthaiʒriot maille .i. an dara dé ʒa anacal, ⁊ an di oile ʒa badub. Ʒibeab ro ropuairliʒ an bſn Eoʒanać an mnaoi oile, ⁊ ra ʒab a huball rluʒatan ʒo ra raoṁ cać ní ma rarattur ac deabaid .i. an lſnaṁ do lſruʒab. Ra lſraiʒeab leo mar aon iar rin an lſnaṁ.

Tárla trá fſćt aon matair an lſnaiṁ ir in tſć i raba an lenaṁ a ccinn ceithre mbliaban, ⁊ ʒan a riur di a beit a mbſtaib. Ar ann ro baoi an macaoṁ ʒá ćluići. Do rála mſnma a mátar fair, ⁊ ro fiarfuib cia aor an macaoiṁ ud ar ſi? Arſb ra ráib ćać ʒur bo mac ceithre mbliaban. Ro ʒairm ſí na mna cairiri úd ar a hamur ⁊ arſb ra ráib riu : ar mór an col do riʒmiura, ar ſi ar imʒabail feirʒe m'atar .i. mac na haoiri ud do malairt. Aćt ra ráibriot na mná friari : na déna toirri itir, ar riab, ar é rub an mac rin, ⁊ riñe ra coméd é. Do rab ſi airʒeba iomba do na mnáib iartain, ⁊ ruccab uaite an mac ʒo dicelta d'innroicćib a atar féin .i. Fſrʒal.

Inʒſn

* *Cinel-Conaill and Cinel-Eoghain.*— These were two kindred races in Ulster descended from Eoghan and Conall, two sons of the monarch Niall of the Nine Hostages, who died in 406. They gave names to the territories of Tir-Eoghain [Tyrone] and Tir-Chonaill [Tyrconnell]. O'Neill was, in later ages, the chief of the one, and O'Donnell of the other; but before the English invasion, Mac Laughlin was dominant in Tyrone, and O'Muldory, or O'Canannan, in Tyrconnell.

Now, when Aedh Allan was born, his mother gave him in charge to two women (who were dear to her) to be drowned, that her father might not discover her crime, or be angry with her. One of these women was of the Cinel-Conaill, and the other of the Cinel-Eoghain[1]. When the woman of the Cinel-Eoghain took into her hands the beautiful little infant, she was filled with love and affection for it, and she said to her female companion: "Dear sister," said she, "it is not right to destroy this infant, but to preserve it well." The other replied: "He is dearer to thee than to his own mother, who commanded us to drown him, from fear of the anger of her father." The other became angry, and laid the child on the ground, and they fought with each other, the one for preserving, and the other for drowning him. But the Cinel-Eoghain woman prevailed over the other, and held her by the apple of the throat until she consented to her wishes; namely, to rear the child. After this both conjointly reared the child.

On one occasion, at the end of four years, the mother of the child happened to come into the house in which the child was, not knowing that he was alive. The child was at his play, and the mother's mind was fixed upon him, and she asked: "What age is yon child?" said she. All replied that he was a child of the age of four years. She called these trusted women to her, and said to them: "I committed a great wickedness," said she, "in destroying a son [who would now be] of that age, to escape the anger of my father." But the women said to her: "Be not sad at all;" said they, "yon child is that son, and we were they who preserved him." She afterwards gave great rewards to the women, and the boy was conveyed away[7] from them privately to his own father, Ferghal.

Now,

[7] *Conveyed away.*—This is a better story than the account of his descendant Ferdoragh, Baron of Dungannon, who, according to Fynes Moryson, was fourteen years old before Con O'Neill, Earl of Tyrone, knew that he was his son.

Ingfn ımuppo pí Cıanacta mátaıp ın Néıll Conuaıl, ⁊ hıpıōe bfn ap caoını ⁊ ap pocpaıōe baoí a n-Eıpınn na haımpıp; act cfna bá huımbpıct í go poōa, go ttáınıg gup an ccaıllıg naoım, go Luatpınn o'ıappaıō puıppıpıōe epnaıgte oo ōénaım puıppe ppıp an coımoeō oá puptact, ⁊ oo pınne Luaıtpınn pın, ⁊ po coımppeō Nıall ıapttaın ı mbpoınn ıngıne pıg Cıanacta, ⁊ pugaō ıapttaın, ⁊ apí ba píogan 'Eıpenn an tan po ag Fípgal.

Cıō pıl ann tpa act ó po labaıp oo na macaıō amaıl a ouppa-map pa a plōıg, ⁊ pa pupaıl poppa ⁊ ap cac uıle léıptıonol oo ofnam pan bliaōaın buō nfpa o'ınnpoıgıō Laıgen oo tobac na bopuma poppa, uaıp níp comaıllpıt Laıgın amaıl po geallpat. Kal. Ab ınıtıo Munoı m. occcc.xxıııı. ab ıncapnatıone Domını occxxıı.

Cat Almaıne ıtıp Laıgnıu ⁊ huıb Neıll. In teptıo Decem- bpıp pa cuıpeō an cat pa. Cauıp an cata pa .ı. an bopoma po maıc Pınnacta oo Molıng a tobac bFfpgal ⁊ ırfō on na pa puıl- ngeauop Laıgın, nıp tuctat Laıgın oo Loıngpec mac Aongupa, ⁊ nı tuctat oo Congal Cınnmagaıp, cıa po puılngfttup oımnıō ó Congal, agup ní moo ono pob áıl uóıb a tabaıpt o'Fípgal, uaıp po taıpıpnıgpıōt ımbpıatpaıb Molıng pa geall na beptta uata tpé bíta an bopoma ó Laıgnıb. Ba tpom tpa la Fípgal pın .ı. Laıgın oo nmftomall angeallta pnıp, go po puacpaō pluaıgeō oıpeacpa

---

ᵃ *Cianachta.*—A territory in East Meath, of which Duleek was the capital, inhabited by a sept of the race of Tadhg, son of Cian, son of Oilioll Olum, King of Munster.

ᵇ *Luaithrinn.*—St. Luchrinna, a virgin, the patroness of the church of *Kill-Luaith-rinne*, in the territory of Corann, county of Sligo. Luchrinna was of the same race

as this Queen of Ireland; that is, of the race of Tadhg, grandson of Oilioll Olum.—See Colgan's "Acta Sanctorum," p. 756.

ᵇ *Almhain.*—Now Allen, a celebrated hill, situated about five miles to the north of the town of Kildare. This battle is entered in the Annals of the Four Masters at the year 718, in the Annals of Ulster at 721, and in the Annals of Tighernach

Now, the daughter of the King of Cianachtaᵃ was the mother of Niall Condail, and she was the fairest and the mildest woman that was in Erin in her time. She was, however, barren for a long time, until she came to the holy nun Luaithrinnᵃ to request of her to pray to God for her relief; and Luaithrinn did so, and Niall was afterwards conceived in the womb of the daughter of the King of Cianacta, and he was born [in due time] afterwards, and she was Queen of Erin, with Ferghal, at this time.

Howbeit when he spoke concerning his sons, as we have said, before his hosts, he commanded them and all in general to assemble all their forces in the following year to invade Leinster, to force the Borumean tribute from them, for the Leinster-men did not perform what they had promised.

[A. M. 5924.] Kal. *Ab initio Mundi* v.m. dcccc.xxiv. *ab incarnatione Domini* Dcc. xxii.

[722.] The battle of Almhainᵇ [was fought] between the Leinstermen and the Ui-Neill. *In tertio Decembris* this battle was fought. The cause of this battle was this: the Borumean tribute which Finnachta had remitted to Molingᶜ was demanded by Ferghal, and this the Leinstermen would not brook. The Leinstermen had not paid it to Loingsech, son of Aengusᵈ, nor to Congal of Cennmaghairᵉ, though they had suffered sore annoyances from the hands of Congal; neither were they willing to pay it to Fergal, for they insisted upon the

---

at 722, which last is the true year. It is stated in the Annals of Clonmacnoise that King Ferghal had 21,000 men in this battle, and the Leinster-men only 9000.

ᶜ *Moling.*—i. e. St. Moling, who was Bishop of Ferns, A.D. 691 to 697. See Lanigan, vol. iii., pp. 132-135.

ᵈ *Loingsech, son of Aengus.*—He was monarch of Ireland from A.D. 695 to 704.

ᵉ *Congal of Cennmaghair.*—He was monarch of Ireland from A.D. 704 to 711, when Fergal, son of Maelduin, succeeded. See "Ogygia," Part iii., c. 93.

ọireacra ḋíṁóṗ uaḋ ṗoṗ Lṫ Cuinn .i. ṗoṗ Eoġan ⁊ ṗoṗ Conall ⁊ ṗoṗ Aiṗġiallaiḃ ⁊ Miḋe, an cṡṗaṁaḋ ḃliaḋain a ḃlaiṫiuṗa ṗéin, no i cṗíṡṗ ḃliaḋain ḋéc, uc quiḃuṗḋam placec, ḋo ṫoḃaċ na boṗoṁa.

Ḃá ṗaḋa cṗa ṗo ḃáṗ oṡ an cinoḷṗain, uaiṗ aṗṗeḋ aḋ ḃeiṗeḋ ṡaċ ṗeaṗ ḋo Leiṫ Cuinn ṡuṗ a ṗoiċeaḋ an ṗuaccṗaḋ .i. "ḋá ccí Ḋonnḃó aṗ an ṗluaġaḋ, ṗaġaḋṗa." Ḋonnḃó imuṗṗo mac ḃain-cṗeaḃcaiġe eiṗiḋe oṗeaṗaiḃ Roṗṗ, aġaṗ ní ḋeaċhaiḋ lá na aiḋċi a caiġ a máṫaṗ imaċ ṗiaṁ, ⁊ ní ṗaiḃe i n-'Eiṗinn uile ḃuḋ caoiṁe, no ḃuḋ ṗíṡṗ cṗuṫ no ḋelḃ, no ḋíṡnam iṁáṗ. Ní ṗaḃa i n-Eiṗinn uile ḃuḋ ṡṗiaḃḋa, no ḃuḋ ṗíṡaine iṁáṗ, ⁊ aṗ uaḋ ḃuḋ ṗíṡṗ ṗann eṗṗa ⁊ ṗiṗṡela ṗoṗ ḋoṁon; aṗé ḃuḋ ṗíṡṗ ḋo ġléṗ eaċ, ⁊ ḋo inoṗma ṗlíṡ, ⁊ ḋ'ṗiġe ṗolc, ⁊ ḃuḋ ṗíṡṗ ṗiaiċni [.i. inġne inncḷecca] na einech; ḋe quo ḋiciṫuṗ:—

'Aille macaiḃ Ḋonnḃo báiḋ
Ḃinne a laíḃ luaiḋio ḃeoil
Aine óġaiḃ Innṗi Ṗail
Ra ṫóġaiḃ ṫáin cṗillṗi a cṗeoiṗ.

Niaṗ licc ḋno a ṁáṫaiṗ Ḋonnḃo la Ṗíṡṗṡal, ṡo ccuccaḋ Maol mic

ᶠ *During this world's existence.*—The writers of the Ui Neill, among whom Adamnan is set down, insisted that the great St. Moling obtained a remission of this tribute by an equivocation which was altogether unworthy of a saint, and therefore many subsequent monarchs of the Ui Neill attempted to compel the Leinstermen to pay it. See "Annals of the Four Masters," A. D. 106, p. 99, and A. D. 593, p. 216, *et seq.*

ᵍ *Leth-Chuinn.*—i. e. Conn's half, i. e. the north half of Ireland.

ʰ *Cinel Eoghain.*—i. e. the race of Eoghan, or the men of Tyrone [Tir-Eoghain] and their relatives.

ⁱ *Cinel-Conaill.*—i. e. the race of Conall, or the inhabitants of Tirconnell.

ʲ *Airghialla.*—i. e. the inhabitants of the present counties of Louth, Armagh, and Monahan.

ᵏ *Donnbo.*—No account of this personage is to be found in any other authority; and this legend must have found its way into

the words of Moling, to whom it was promised that the Borumean tribute should never, during this world's existence[f], be demanded from the Leinster-men. Now Fergal deemed this intolerable; namely, that the Leinster-men should not keep their promise to him, so that he ordered a very great and irresistible hosting upon Leth-Chuinn[g]; i. e. a hosting of the Cinel-Eoghain[h], Cinel-Conaill[i], and Airghialla[j], and of the men of Meath, in the fourth year of his reign, or in the thirteenth, as some will have it, to levy the Borumean tribute.

Long, indeed, was this muster of forces being carried on, for each man of Leth-Chuinn to whom the order came used to say: "If Donnbo[k] come on the hosting, I will." Now Donnbo was a widow's son of the Fera-Ross[l], and he never went away from his mother's house for one day or one night, and there was not in all Ireland one of fairer countenance, or of better figure, form, or symmetry, than he; there was not in all Erin one more pleasant or entertaining, or one in the world who could repeat more amusing and royal stories[m], than he; he was the best to harness horses, to set spears, to plait hair, and he was a man of royal intelligence in his countenance: of whom was said—

> Fairer than sons was Donnbo,
> Sweeter his poem than all that mouths rehearse,
> Pleasanter than the youths of Innis-Fail[n],
> The brilliancy of his example took the multitude.

His mother did not permit Donnbo to go with Fergal, until Mael-mic-Failbhe,

the old vellum Book of Nehemias Mac Egan from some romantic historical tale on the battle of Almhain, now unknown.

[l] *Fera-Ross.*—The name of a tribe inhabiting the district around the present town of Carrickmacross, county of Mo-

naghan, whose territory extended into the present county of Louth.

[m] *Royal stories.*—i. e. stories relating to kings.

[n] *Innis-Fail.*—This was one of the most ancient names of Ireland.

mic Failbe mic Erannain mic Criomtainn, comarba Colaim Cille, fria airic beo ⁊ go ttuccraibe Colam Cille ono oia cionn go riteb Donnbo plán oa caig péin a cric Laigrn.
Toconila ono Peargal for rév. Ra battur ona luct eolair reime, nír bó mait an t-eolur oo paorao oo .i. ⁊ ccumgaib gaca conaire ⁊ in-aimrébaib gaca conaire go rancuttur Cluain Oóbail i n-Almain. Ar ann buí Aoóan clam Cluana Oóbail ar a cinn. Do ronrat ono na rluaig a micortao .i. a aon bó oo marbao ⁊ a ruine ar brraib na riagnairi, ⁊ a tré oo breit oa cinn, ⁊ a lortcao; conripbrit an clam com ba oigal go brát for Uib Néill an oigal oo bereo an coimbib rairrin, ⁊ tainicc an clam reme go pubal Frrgail, ⁊ battur riogrraio Leite Cuinn uile ar a cinn i rin puball in tan rin. Ro baoi an clam ag acaoine a immio na ffiagnairi; ní tainig cribe neic oib fair, acc cribe Conbrtan mic Congura ri ffri Rorr, ⁊ a rev ón ná ba haitereé oo Coinbrtan, uair ni terna ri oo nrc ro baoi irin puball acc Cubrtan mac Congura a aonar ar in cat. Conav ann aubert Cubrtan :—

Ao agar cat for oearg flaino
A rir Frrgaile ao glionn;
bao bronaig muintir mic Maire
Ar mbreit an taig oar cionn,
bó an claim ro gaoo a norgaio a oaim,
Mairg laim ra toll a mbrao
Ar ní rimcomart mac brain, ⁊rl.
                                                              Ar

ᵒ *Mael-mic-Failbhe.*—This may be intended for *Conamhail mac Failbhe*, tenth Abbot of Hy, who was of the Airghialla. Tighernach calls him Conmael, and it is not impossible that our author, who is not very precise, may have called him Mael mc Failbe. His date comes very near this period, for he died 710.

ᵖ *Cluain-Dobhail.*—This name is now forgotten.

ᵠ *Cubretan.*—This name is not to be found in any of the published Irish An-

Mael-mic-Failbhe[o], son of Erannan, son of Criomhthann, successor of Colum Cille, was pledged for his return alive, and until he pledged Colum Cille for himself that Donnbo would return safe to his own house from the province of Leinster.

Fergal proceeded upon his way. Guides went before him, but the guidance they afforded him was not good; i. e. through the narrowness of each road, and the ruggedness of each pass, until they reached Cluain-Dobhail[p], at Almhain. And Aedhan the Leper of Cluain-Dobhail was there before them. The hosts ill-treated him: they killed his only cow, and roasted it on spits before his face, and they unroofed his house and burned it; and the Leper said that the vengeance which God would wreak on the Ui-Neill, on his account, would be an eternal vengeance; and the Leper came forward to the tent of Fergal, where the kings of Leth-Chuinn were before him. The Leper complained of the injuries done him, in their presence; but the heart of none of them was moved towards him, except the heart of Cubretan[q], son of Congus, King of Fera-Ross; and for this Cubretan had no reason to be sorry, for of all the kings who were in the tent, none escaped from the battle except Cubretan, son of Congus, alone. On which occasion Cubretan said:

A red bloody battle was waged,
O good Fergal, in thy valley;
The people of the son of Mary were sorrowful
After taking the roof off the house.
The cow of the Leper was killed, after its ox.
Woe to the hand that pierced their neck,
For the son of Bran did not defend, &c.

Then

nals. *Cubretan* signifies dog or hero of Britain. The ancient Irish had many names of men compounded with *cu*, a dog; as *Cu-mara*, dog of the sea; *Cu-Uladh*, Canis Ultoniæ, *Cu-Muman*, dog of Munster, *Cu-Caisil*, dog of Cashel, &c.

Ar anorin arrect Fsrsal fria Donnbó; oéna airrioeo oúin, a Doinnbó, fo bit ar tu ar oeac airrioe fuil i n-'Eirinn .i. i cúiris, asar i cuirlenooib, ┐ i cruiτib, ┐ ranoaib, ┐ raiorecoib, ┐ risrsé-laib 'Eirenn, ┐ ir in maoinri i mbárac oo béram-ne cac oo Laisnib. Ac, ar Donnbo, ní cumsaimri airrioe ouicri anocτ, ┐ nimτa aon sníom oib rin uile oo caiobrin anocτ, ┐ cirri airm i rabairi a márac, ┐ imbeora, oo bénra airrioe ouicri. Oénao imurro an riosoruc hua Maisléine airrioe ouic anocτ. Cusao hua Maisléni cuca iarctain. Ro sabraioe os inoirin cac ┐ comrama leice Cuinn ┐ Laisen ó τosail Cuama Crinbac, .i. Oeanoa ríz, in ra marbao Cobcac Caolbres, conisi an aimrir, rin, ┐ ní bá mór coualca oo rinneo leo in aiochi rin ra méo easla leo Laisin, ┐ la méio na oorninne, .i. uair aiòce féle Fhinniain saimrib rin.

Imtúr Laisin oo lotturraioe i cCruacán Claonca, oáis ní maio fon Laisniu oa noearnat a comairle ann, ┐ sur obar ciurao oo cum an cata. Lottur iarrain so Oinn Canainn, araioe oo cum an cata.

Conrancuttur tra ir in maioin ar na márac na cata cítarba, naoi míle oo Laisnib, mile ar ficit imurro oo Leit Cuinn. Ar cruaio ┐ ar feocair ra cuireo an catra leit fon lrt, ┐ ra sab cac na comraicib ann.

Ra

---

¹ *Maighleine.*—This personage is not mentioned in any other known Annals.

² *Tuaim Tenbath*, i.e. *Dinnrigh.*—O'Flaherty places this event so far back as A.M. 3682. This was the name of the ancient palace of the Kings of Leinster. The remains of its earthen works are situated on the west side of the River Barrow, in the townland of Ballyknockan, about a quarter of a mile south of Leighlin Bridge.

For a notice of the burning of this palace, see "Leabhar na g-Ceart," pp. 15, 16. The ancient Irish poets had a great many stories of this description which they used to recite to their kings and chieftains. See Campion's "Historie of Irelande," chap. vi.

³ *The eve of the festival of Finnian.*—i. e. the 11th of December. The Annals of Clonmacnoise make it the 3rd of the Ides

Then Fergal said to Donnbo: "Show amusement for us, O Donnbo, for thou art the best minstrel in Erin at pipes, and trumpets, and harps, at the poems and legends and royal tales of Erin, for on tomorrow morning we shall give battle to the Leinster-men." "No," said Donnbo, "I am not able to amuse thee to-night, and I am not about to exhibit any one of these feats to-night; but wherever thou shalt be to-morrow, if I be alive, I shall show amusement to thee. But let the royal clown, Ua Maighleine[r], amuse thee this night." Ua Maighleine was afterwards brought to them. He commenced narrating the battles and the valiant deeds of Leth-Chuinn and Leinster from the demolition of Tuaim Tenbath, i. e. Dinn-righ[s], in which Cobhthach Cael-mBreagh was killed, unto that time; and they slept not much that night, because of their great dread of the Leinster-men, and of the great storm, for it was the eve of the festival of Finnian[t], in the winter.

With respect to the Leinster-men, they repaired to Cruachan Claenta[u], for the Leinster-men would not be defeated if they should hold their council there, and proceed from thence to battle. They proceeded thence to Dinn-Canainn[v], and thence to the battle.

On the following morning the battalions of both sides met: nine thousand of the Leinstermen, and twenty-one thousand of Leth-Chuinn. Vigorously and fiercely was this battle fought on both sides, and all showed equal fight.

The

of December, which would be the 11th.

[u] *Cruachan Claenta.*—i. e. the round Hill of Clane, situated about five miles to the north-east of Allen, where this battle was fought. The Leinster-men believed that whenever they could hold their council of war here, they should not be defeated.

The origin of this belief is not yet discovered, nor is this superstition noticed in "Leabhar na gCeart," among the *Geasa* and *Urgarthæ* of the Kings of Leinster.

[v] *Dinn-Canainn.*— Now Duncannon, nearly midway between Clane and the Hill of Allen.

Ra ba oimóp pa innipi compama na Laoc Laiġen ⁊ Laoc Leice Cuinn. Arbept ʒo ppacap bpiġio op cionn Laiġen; avcfp ono Colum Cille op cionn hua Néill. Ra meaṁuio iapaṁ an cac pia Mupchao mac mbpain, ⁊ pe n-Cloo mac Oonncava, mic Colgan pí Laigen Oeapgaḃaip. Ra mapbao Peapʒal ann Cloo mb ⁊ Oonnchao mac Mupchava po mapbpac Ffpgal paveprin, ⁊ bile mac buain, pí Alban, ap uaiò aimnniʒcep Coppbile, i n-Clmaine. Ap é ono Cloo meno pa mapb Oonnbó. Ní copcaip imuppo Peapʒal ʒo ccopchaip Oonnbó. Ra mapbao ono pepca ap céo aṁup in ou pin. A coiṁlín péin po mapbaio Laiġin pan cac pin vo Leic Cuinn .i. naoi mile; ⁊ naoi nʒelci oib oo vol pop ʒelcacc, ⁊ cécpiġ oo piġaib. Aca Cnoc Ffpgail annpin; pa cuippioc Laiġin ilaiġ commaiomi ano ono, unoe oicicup:—

Oeoblaice Almaine,
Ap copnaṁ buaip bpfġmaine
Ro la baob bélveapʒ biopac,
Iolac im cfnn pFfpʒaile.

Scapapp

* *Valorous.*—The Irish word compama, deeds of valour or prowess. The substantive compuma is glossed copcup, victory, in H. 3, 18, p. 536.
* *Brigit.*—She was the patroness of all Ireland, but particularly of Leinster. See under A. D. 605, where St. Mura is represented as saying that St. Bridget was greater than he, and her prayers more powerful than his prayers.
ᶦ *Colum Cille.*—He was the principal patron of the Cinel Conaill. St. Mura was the patron of the Cinel-Eoghain, but Colum was the greater saint of the two, and is therefore introduced as contending with St. Bridget in protecting his kinsmen of the race of Niall.
ᶦ *Son of Bran.*—King of Leinster.
* *Fergal.*—King of Erin.
ᵇ *Bile, son of Buan of Albain.*—i. e. of Scotland. No account of this Scottish champion has been found in any of the authentic Irish Annals, and it is very probably that he is a mere fictitious character introduced here among the historical chiefs who really flourished at this time

The valorous[w] deeds of the heroes of Leinster and of Leth-Chuinn are very much spoken of. It is said that Brigit[x] was seen over the Leinster-men; Colum Cille[y] was seen over the Ui-Neill. The battle was gained by Murchadh, son of Bran[z], and Aedh, son of Donnchadh, son of Colgan, King of South Leinster. Fergal[a] himself was killed in it; and it was Aedh Menn, and Donnchadh, son of Murchadh, that slew Fergal himself, and Bile, son of Buan, of Albain[b], from whom Corrbile[c], at Almhain, is named. Aedh Menn was also the person who slew Donnbo. Fergal was not killed till Donnbo had first fallen. One hundred and sixty soldiers were killed on the occasion. The Leinster-men killed an equal number of Leth-Chuinn in this battle; i. e. nine thousand and nine of them ran mad[d], and one hundred kings. The hill of Ferghal[e] is at the place. The Leinster-men raised shouts of exultation there, *unde dicitur:*

At the end of the day at Almhain,
In defending the cows of Bregia,
The red-mouthed, sharp-beaked raven,
Croaked over Fergal's head.

Murchadh,

and fought in this battle.

[c] *Corrbile.*—i. e. Bile's Pit, would now be anglicized Corbilly; but there is no place of the name in the neighbourhood of the Hill of Allen.

[d] *Ran mad.*—Connell Mageoghan translates this—"There were nine persons that flyed in the ayre as if they were winged fowle." But this is hardly correct. For the Irish ideas about *gealtacht* and panic, the reader is referred to the "Buile Shuibhne," to the romantic tale called the "Battle of Finntraighe," or Ventry, and "Bat-

tle of Magh Rath," p. 231, and p. 234, note [c]. It is still believed in many parts of Ireland that all the lunatics of Ireland would make their way, if unrestrained, to a valley in the county of Kerry, called Gleann na nGealt, and remain there feeding on the herbs and water-cresses of the valley until they should recover their former sanity.

[e] *The hill of Ferghal.*—No hill of this name is now pointed out in this neighbourhood. The name would be now anglicized Knockfarrell.

Scaparr Murchaḋ ra mıḋlaıġ,
broġaır a rrıuna ı rralmuın,
Do roı raoḃar rrıa Feargal,
Ġo ffeın ḋearmaır oſr Almaın.
ḃaṫ ann ceḋ ruıreṫ raṫaṫ,
Cruaḋaṫ, corraḋaṫ, carnaṫ,
Im naoı ngelra gan míne,
Um naoı míle rear n-armaṫ.
Ceıṫrı ċeḋ caḃraıḋ a Cruaıṫ .ı. Cruaṫaın,
Lar an amraıġ gaoḋ ran ġlıaıḃ,
La rrí ceḋoıḃ Conaıll cruaıḃ,
A ré * * * * *

Ra gaḃaḋ annrain an ḋruth hua Maıġléine ┐ ḋo raḋaḋ
raır ġeım ḋruıṫ ḋo ḃenam, ┐ ḋo rıġne; ḃa mar ┐ ba bınn an
ġeım rın, go maırıḃ ġeım hUı Maıġléıne ó rın a le oc ḋruṫaıḃ
'Eırenn.

Ra gaḃaḋ a ċſnn ıarrraın ḋ'Feargal, ┐ ra gaḃaḋ a cſnn ḋon
ḋruṫ. Ro baoı macalla ġeımı an ḋrúıṫ rın aıeor go cſnn rrí la
┐ rrí noſḃċe. Ar ḋe ar mberan ġeım hUí Maıġléıne og rarann
na fſr 'ran mónaıḋ.

Do luıḋ ḋno Aoḋ Laıġen mac Fırċeallaıġ, ri hUa Maıne
Connaṫr ı raon maḋma ┐ reıċıḋ, go neḃerr rrıa macoıḃ: naċ
ma raċċḃaıḋ, a maċċa, ḃuḋ ferrḋe ḃur máṫaır rrıu mo ḃreıṫ rı
lıḃ. Nır ḃeraḋ, or Laıġın, conaḋ ann rın ro marḃaḋ Aoḋ Laıġen,
rı hUa Máıne. Ra rıaṫrarrur ımurro, a mıc [corr] Aoḋa Laıġın
ım Aoḋ Alláın mac Feargaıle, go Lılcaṫ, aırm a mḃuí Moḋıċu,

mac

_f *Aedh Laighean.*—i. e. Aedh, or Hugh of Leinster. He is not mentioned in the pedigrees of the Ui-Maine, printed for the Irish Archæological Society; but his brother Dluthach is set down as chief of Ui-Maine, and as dying in 738.

_g *Aedh Allan.*—He was afterwards monarch of Ireland from A. D. 734 to 743.

Murchadh, no companion of cowardice,
Brings his numerous heroes on the ground;
He turns his weapons against Fergal,
With great heroes, south of Almhain.
There perished there an hundred chieftains, prosperous,
Vigorous, contentious, victorious,
With nine gone mad without mildness,
With nine thousand men of arms.
Four hundred fell at Cruach, i. e. Cruachain,
By the soldiery, wounded in the conflict,
With three hundred of the hardy Cinel Conail;
And six   *   *   *   *   *   *

The clown, Ua Maighleine, was taken prisoner, and he was asked to give " a clown's shout," and he did so. Loud and melodious was that shout, so that the shout of Ua Maighleine has remained with the clowns of Erin from that forth.

Fergal's head was afterwards struck off, and the clown's head was struck off. The reverberation of the clown's shout remained in the air for three days and three nights. From which comes [the saying] " the shout of Ua Maighleine chasing the men in the bog."

Aedh Laighen[f], son of Fithcheallach, King of Ui-Mainè, in Connaught, was routed, and fled from this battle; and he said to his sons: " Do not leave me, O my sons; your mother will be the better of it, if you bring me with you." " They shall not bring thee," said the Leinster-men; so that then, Aedh Laighen, King of Ui-Mainè, was killed. But his sons carried the body of Aedh Laighen, with Aedh Allan[g], son of Fergal, to Lilcach[h], where Modichu, son of Amairgin, and the Gall Craibhthech[i] were; and it was on this occasion that the Ui-Neil

[h] *Lilcach*.—A place near Slane, in East Meath, not yet identified. See Annals of the Four Masters, A. D. 512, 723.
[i] *Gall Craibhtheach*.—i. e. the pious or

mac Amaiṗġin, ⁊ an Ġall Cṙaiḃḋeaċ, conaḋ ann ṗin claiḋiṗiṫ hUí Néill ⁊ Connaċta claḋ na cille, ⁊ iaḋ i ṗioċṫ na ġcléiṗeaċ, ⁊ aṗ amlaiḋ ṗin ṗa ṗaoṗaiḋ ṫṗi mioṗḃuile na naoṁ, ġo ffail coṫaċ hUa Néill ⁊ Connaċṫ ó ṗin ale 'ṗin cill ṗin: unḋe Aoḋ Allain ceċiniṫ:—

Ní ffuaṗamaṗ aṗ ṫalmain Almain baḋiḋ ṗéḋiṫiṗ;
Ní ṗanġamaṗ iaṗ ṗin caṫ Lilcaċ baḋiḋ neṁſṫaṗ.

ḃa buaḋaċ ṫṗa an lá ṗin ḋo Laiġniḃ. Ra hanaiceḋ imuṗṗo Cuḃṗeṫan mac Conġuṗa ṗi ffeaṗ Roṗṗ aṗ na ṗunna ḋo ṗiġne an aiḋhċe ṗeiṁe.

I Conḋail na ṗíoġ ḃáṫṫuṗ Laiġin an aiḋċi aġ ol fína ⁊ mſḃa aṗ ccuṗ an caṫa ġo ṗuḃaċ ṗoimſhmaċ, aġuṗ cáċ ḋíoḃ aġ inniṗin a coṁṗaṁa, iṗ iaḋ mſḃṗaiġ meaḋaṗċaoin. Aṗ anḋ ṗin ṗa ṗáiḋ Muṗchaḋ mac Ḃṗain: "Ḋo ḃéaṗainn caṗṗaṫ ceṫṗe cumala, ⁊ mo eaċ ⁊ m'ſṗṗaḋ ḋon laoċ ṅo ṗaġaḋ iṗin áṗṁaċ, ⁊ ḋo ḃéṗaḋ coṁaṗṫa cuġainn aṗ." Raġaḋ-ṗa, aṗ ḃaoṫġalaċ laoċ ḋim Muṁain. Ġeḃiḋ a ċaṫeṗṗaḋ caṫa ⁊ coṁlanna uime, ġo ṗáiniġ ġo haiṗm i mḃaoí coṗṗ Feaṗġaile, ġo ccuṗla ní i nſaġaiṗġaiṗe iṗin iṗin aeoṗ óṗ a cinn, conḋeṗeṗṫ. Aṗ cloṗṗ uile, ṫimaṗnaḋ ḋuiḃ ó ṗiġ ṗſċṫ niṁe. Ḋénaiḋ aiṗṗiḋe ḋá ḃuṗ ṫṫiġeaṗna anoċṫ .i. ḋ'Feaṗġal mac Maolḋúin, cia ḋo ṗoċṗaṗaiṗ ṗunn uile in ḃaṗ naoiṗ ḋana eiḋiṗ cuiṗleanḋċu, ⁊ coṗnaiṗe, ⁊ cṗuiṫiṗe, ná ṫaiṗmſṫċca eṗṗuaṫ no héġ comṗaṗṫ ṗiḃ ḋ'aiṗṗiḋeḋ anoċṫ ḋ'Feaṗġal.

ġ⁰

religious Gall, or foreigner, probably a Saxon or Englishman. This was the same Gall who gave name to Inis an Ghaill (Inchaguile) in Lough Corrib, county of Galway.

ʲ *The part he took.*—i. e. in sympathizing with the leper, whose hut the army of the Hy-Neill had pulled down.

ᵏ *Condail of the Kings.*—Now Old Connell, in the county of Kildare, about five miles to the east of the Hill of Allen.

Ui-Neil and the Connaught-men erected the wall of the church, they being in the disguise of the clergy, and they were thus saved through the miracles of the saints, so that the friendship of the Ui-Neill and the Connaught-men is in that church from that forward. Unde Aedh Allan *cecinit* :—

> We did not find on earth a smoother place than Almhain,
> We did not reach, after this, a place more sacred than Lilcach.

Now, the Leinster-men were victorious in this battle. Cubretan, son of Congus, King of Fera-Ross, was protected in consequence of the part he took[j] the night before.

It was at Condail of the Kings[k] the Leinster-men were that night drinking wine and mead, merrily, and in high spirits, after gaining the battle; and each of them was describing his prowess, and they were jolly and right merry. Then Murchadh, son of Bran, said: "I would give a chariot of [the value of] four cumhals, and my steed and battle-dress, to the hero who would go to the field of slaughter, and who would bring us a token from it." "I will go," said Baethgalach, a hero of Munster. He puts on his dress of battle and combat, and arrived at the spot where the body of [King] Fergal was, and he heard a noise in the air over his head, and he said, on hearing it: "All praise be to thee, O King of the seven heavens! ye are amusing your lord to-night; i. e. Fergal, son of Maelduin, though ye have all fallen here, both poets, pipers, trumpeters and harpers, let not hatred or ability prevent you to-night from playing for Fergal." The young warrior then heard the most delightful and entrancing piping and music in the bunch of rushes next him, a Fenian melody sweeter than any music. The young warrior went towards it. "Do not come near me," said a head to him. "I ask who art thou?" said the young warrior. "I am the head of Donnbo," said the head, "and I made

go ccualα ιαραṁ an τογlάċ an cuιρις ⁊ an ceol ρίρεαċταċ, go ccualα ϙαn 'ραn τum luαċρα ϙα nίρα ϙό αιι τόρϙ ριαnρα ϙα ϙιnne ceolαιϙ. Luιϙ an τογlάċ na ϙόċum; na ταιρ αρ m'αmuρ αρ αn cίnn ρριρ. Cίρτ, cια τu? αρ an τόγlάċ. Nιñ, mιρι cίñϙ Ϙuιnnϙό, αρ αn cίnn, ⁊ nαιϙm ρο nαιϙmίϙ ρριm α ρέιρ αιρριϙεϙ αn ρί αnοċτ, ⁊ nά ερċόιϙιϙ ϙαm. Cαιϙe coρρ Ρίργαιl ρunn, αρ an τ-όγlάċ? Αρ έ ϙο αιċτne ρμιτ αnαll. "Cειρτ αnϙαϙ ϙέρ lίm," αρ an τόγlάċ? "Αρ τύ αρ ϙεαċ lιm:" Nom ϙέρα, αρ an cίnn; αċτ ραċ Cρίρτ ϙοϙ ċιnn ϙα nom ρυγα, γο ϙτυγα mé αρ αmuρ mo collα ϙο ρίϙιρι. Ϙο ϙέρ έγιn, αρ an τόγlάċ, ⁊ ιmροι an τόγlάċ ⁊ an cίnn lαιρ conιγε Conϙαιl, ⁊ ρυαιρ Lαιγιn αγ όl αρ α cίnn 'ριn αίϙċι cέτnα. Αn ττυγαιρ comαρτα lατ? αρ Muρchαϙ. Τυγαρ αρ an τόγlάċ, cίnn Ϙuιnnϙο. Ροnαιm αρ an ρuαιċne ύϙ ċαll, αρ Muρchαϙ. Τυγραϙ an ρlυαγ uιle αιċne ραιρ γυρ ϙέ cίnn Ϙuιnnϙό, ⁊ αρεϙ ρο ράιϙριο uιle: ϙιρραn ϙυιτ α Ϙuιnnϙό, ϙά cαoṁ ϙο ϙεαlϙ, ϙέnα αιρριϙε ϙύιnn αnοċτ, ρεϙ ϙο ριγnιρ ϙοτ τιγεαρnα ιmϙυαραċ. Ιmροιγτερ α αιγιϙ ϙοno, ⁊ αττραċτ α ϙορϙ ριαnρα αττρυαγ αρ άιρϙ, γο mϙάττυρ uιle αγ cαoι ⁊ αγ τυιρρι. Ιϙnαιcιϙ an lαοċ cέοnα an cίnn ϙο ċum α collα αṁαιl ρο γεαll, ⁊ coιργιϙ έ αρ α ṁειϙε. Cιττραċτ ράιnιc Ϙοnnϙό γο τίċ α ṁάταρ, uαιρ αρριαϙ τρί ιοnγαnτα an cατα ρα .ι. Ϙοnnϙο ϙο ροċταιn nα ϙίταιϙ γο nιγε α τίċ ϙαρ cίnn ϙρειτρε Coluιm Cιlle, ⁊ γέιm an ϙρυιτ hUί Mαιγlέιne τρί lα ⁊ τρί hαιϙċε 'ραn αεορ, ⁊ nα nαοι mιle ϙο ρορυαιρlιγ an ρίcιτ, υnϙε ϙιcιτυρ:

   Caτ Αlmαιne, άρ γειn
   Μόρ an γníoṁ Ϙεcemϙειρ

Ρο

[1] *If thou bring me.*—i. e. if thou art minded to bring me at all, find my body, and bring my head and body together.

[m] *To its body.*—Stories of this kind are very common in Irish. See the Registry of Clonmacnoise, printed in the "Transactions of the Kilkenny Archæological Society," for the story of Coirpre Crom,

made a compact last night that I would amuse the King to-night, and do not annoy me." "Which is the body of Fergal here?" said the young warrior. "Thou mayest observe it yonder," said the head. "Shall I take thee away?" said the young warrior; "thou art the dearest to me." "Bring me," said the head; "but may the grace of God be on thy head if thou bring me¹ to my body again." "I will indeed," said the young warrior. And the young warrior returned with the head to Condail the same night, and he found the Leinster-men drinking there on his arrival. "Hast thou brought a token with thee?" said Murchadh. "I have," replied the young warrior, "the head of Donnbo." "Place it on yonder post," said Murchadh: and the whole host knew it to be the head of Donnbo, and they all said: "Pity that this [fate] awaited thee, O Donnbo! fair was thy countenance; amuse us to-night, as thou didst thy lord last night." His face was turned, and he raised a most piteous strain in their presence, so that they were all wailing and lamenting! The same warrior conveyed the head to its body^m, as he had promised, and he fixed it on the neck [to which it instantly adhered, and Donnbo started into life]. In a word, Donnbo reached the house of his mother. The three wonders^n of this battle were: the coming of Donnbo home to his house alive, in consequence of the pledged word of Colum Cille, and the shout of the clown Ua Maighleine, which remained [reverberating] three days and three nights in the air, and nine thousand prevailing over twenty-one thousand; *unde dicitur*:—

> The battle of Almhain, great the slaughter,
> Great the deed of December
>
> Which

whose head was put on by St. Ciaran of Clonmacnoise.

ⁿ *Three wonders.*—Three wonders are usually introduced into Irish romantic stories. Compare with the three wonders of the battle of Magh-Rath.

Ro bpir Mupchaṫ mopṫa cpeaċ
Mac bpain la laocpaiṫ laiġneaċ.
Meaṁaiṫ ap Peṅġal Pail
Ap mac Maoiliṫuin ṫipmaip
Ʒo melcír muille po leipġ
Ap lincib pola poipṫepcc,
Oċc pġ oċcmoġaṫ iap ppíop
Naoi míle, ġan imappíoṁ,
Ṫo Leiṫ Cuinn comal nġnaoi
Ṫo poċaip ann ap aon ċaoi.
Naoi nġeilce pop ġealcaċc ṫe
Loccup ṫíoḃ pop Piṫ nẒaiḃle,
Ra claoċloiṫpic ṫaċ iapccain,
Apa ġleċea caċ Almain.

haec punc nomina peġum qui incepṗecci punc in hoc bello, hi punc quiṫem ṫo píol ġCuinn.

Píṙġal mac Maoiliṫuin cum l.x. miliciḃup puip; Popḃapaċ, pi ḃoġaine; Píṙġal hUa Aiṫṙeṫa; Píṙġal Ua Caṁnaiġ; mac Eaċaċ Leaṁna; Conġalaċ mac Conaincc; Eicneaċ mac Conainġ; Coiḃṫenaċ mac Piaċaiṫ; Conall Cpau; Píṙġap Ġluc; Muipġṙ mac Conaill; Uṁcaiṫeaċ mac Conċapac; Anmċaiṫ macConcapac; Aeṫ- ġein hUa Maiċe; Nuaṫa Uipc pi Ġuill ⁊ Ipġuill, i-ġ-Cinel Conuill; .x. nepocep Maoilpicpiġ. Iċe pin pġ hUa Néill an cuaipcipc.

hi aucem qui pequuncup hUí Néill an ṫepġipc:—

Oilell mac Píṙaṫaiġ; Suiḃne mac Conġalaiġ; Aoṫ Laiġín hUa

° *Of Fail.*—i. e. of Ireland.
ᵖ *Fidh-Gaibhle.*—A celebrated wood of Leinster, situated in the parish of Cloonsast, about five miles north of Portarlington, in the King's County. It is now locally called Fee-Guile, or Fig-Isle!
ᵠ *Boghaine.*—Now the barony of Bannagh, in the west of the county of Donegal.

Which the majestic Murchadh of plunders gained,
Son of Bran, with the heroes of Leinster.
It was gained over Fergal of Fail[o],
The son of Maelduin the mighty;
So that mills in the plain did grind
[Turned] by ponds of red blood shed.
Eighty-eight kings, in truth,
Nine thousand [men], without exaggeration,
Of the men of Leth Chuinn, of fair faces,
Fell there in one battle-field.
Nine persons panic-stricken ran mad,
And went into the wood of Fidh-Gaibhle[p].
They changed colour afterwards,
For the Battle of Almhain blenched them.

These are the names of the kings who were slain in this battle. These were some of the race of Conn :—

Fergal, son of Maelduin, with sixty of his knights; Forbasach, King of Boghaine[q]; Fergal Ua Aithechta; Fergal Ua Tamhnaigh, the son of Eochaidh Leamhna; Congalach, son of Conaing; Eignech, son of Conaing; Coibhdenach, son of Fiacha; Conall Crau; Fergal Glut; Muirghes, son of Conall; Letaithech, son of Cucarat; Aedh-gen Ua Maithe; Nuada Uirc, King of Gull and Irgull[r] in Cinel-Conaill; ten grandsons of Maelfithrigh. These [foregoing] were the chiefs of the northern Ui-Neill.

The following were of the Ui-Neill of the south :—

Oilell, son of Feradhach; Suibhne, son of Conghalach; Aedh Laighen

[r] *Gull and Irgull.*—Two territories in the north of the barony of Kilmacrenan, county of Donegal, more usually called Ros-guill and Ros-Irguill. The name of the former is still remembered, but that of the latter has been long forgotten.

hUa Cfrnaıȝ; Nıa mac Coṗmaıc; Cloṫna mac Colȝan; Taḋȝ
mac Aıȝṫıḋe; Ḋuḃḋacṛíoċ mac Ḋuıḃḋaḃaıṛſnn; Mſncoṛṛaċ mac
Ȝammaıȝ; Eloḋaċ mac Ḟlaınn 'O'Sȝıȝı; Ḋunchaḋ Ua Ḟıaċ-
ṛaċ; mac Conloınȝṛı; mac Maoılemona; Ḋoıṛıaḋ mac Conla;
Ḟlann mac Aoḋa Oḋḃa; mac Concoınȝelṫ; mac Tuaṫaıl mıc
Ḟaolċon; Inḋṛſṫaċ mac Taıḋȝ; mac Ȝaṛḃáın; ḋa Ua Maoıl-
ċaıċ; ḋá mac Aıleni; Ḟocaṛṫa Ua Ḋomnaıll; Aılell mac
Conaıll Ȝṛaınṫ; Ḟıȯȝal mac Ḟıȯcheallaıȝ; Ḋuıḃoıl hUa
Ḋaımıne eṫ ḟṛaṫeṛ eıuṛ; ḋá mac Muıṛſḋaıȝ mıc Inḋṛſṫaıȝ;
Nuaḋa mac Ḋuıḃḋunċuıṛe; Rſṫaṛṛa hUa Cımuṛcuıȝ Ua
Maıne; Cſṛ Cſṛa; Ḟſṅȝaṛ Ua Eoȝaın no Leoȝaın; Ḟlaıṫeamaıl
mac Olúṫaıȝ; Ḋonȝalaċ hUa Aonȝaṛa; Conall Mſnn ṛí Ceneıl
Caıṛḃṛe; mac Eṛca mac Maoılıḋúın; Tṛí hUı Nuaḋaṫ; Ḟlann
mac Iṛȝalaıȝ; Aoḋ Laıȝen mac Ḟıṫċeallaıȝ; Nıall mac Muıṛȝſṛa.

Ḋolope auṫem eṫ ḟṛıȝoṛe moṛṫuı ṛunṫ clxxx. ṫaṛ éıṛ caṫa
Almaıne ı ṫṫoṛċuıṛ Ḟſṅȝal mac Maoılıḋúın, 7ca.

Inıṫıum ṛeȝnı Cıonaḋa, mıc Iṛȝalaıȝ, ṛecunḋum quoṛḋam.

Kal. Ro ȝaḃ ḋno Ḟoȝaṛṫaċ mac Néıll aınmnıuȝaḋ ṛıȝe
'Eıṛenn ṛo ċeḋóıṛ ı noſȝaıḋ Ḟſṅȝaıl, aoın ḃlıaḋaın, no a ḋó ıuxṫa
quoṛḋam, ȝo maṛḃaḋ la Cıonaoḋ Leıṫċaoċ mac Iṛȝalaıȝ. Aṛ
ṛaıṛ ṛo meaṁaıḋ an caṫ ı ṫTaılṫın ṛa Laıȝnıḃ.

Cıonaoḋ ımuṛṛo ıaṛṫṫaın ceıṫṛı ḃlıaḋna ı ṛıȝe nEıṛenn. Aṛ
ḋoṛaın ḋo ȝeall Aḋaṁnan 7 ṛé a mḃṛoınn a ṁáṫaṛ ȝo nȝeḃaḋ ṛıȝe
n-Eıṛenn. Ḃá maıṫ ḋno ṛıȝe an Cıonaoḋa. Inḋṛaḋ Laıȝen laıṛ an
céḋ

---

* *Odhbha.*—A place near Navan, in East Meath.

᷾ *Cinel-Cairbre.*—A sept of the south Ui-Neill, situated in the barony of Granard, and county of Longford, to which barony the name is still locally applied.

ᵃ *Aedh Laighen, son of Fithchellach.*— He was chief of Hy-Many, in Connaught.

' *Lethchaech.*—i. e. half-blind. The word caoċ, written also coċċ or caeċ, as now used, does not always mean blind, though

Laighen Ua Cearnaigh; Nia, son of Cormac; Clothna, son of Colgan; Tadhg, son of Aigthide; Dubhdachrioch, son of Dubhdabhairenn; Mencossach, son of Gammach; Elodhach, son of Flann O'Sgigi; Donnchadh Ua Fiachrach; the son of Culoingsi; the son of Maelmona; Doiriadh, son of Conla; Flann, son of Aedh Odhbha'; son of Cucoingelt, son of Tuathal, son of Faelchu; Indrechtach, son of Tadhg; son of Garbhan; the two Ua Maelcaichs; the two sons of Ailen; Focarta Ua Domhnaill; Ailell, son of Conall Grant; Fidhgal, son of Fithchellach; Duibhdil Ua Daimine, and his brother; the two sons of Muredhach, son of Indrechtach; Nuada, son of Dubhdunchuire; Rechtabhra, son of Cumascach Ua Maine; Cer of Cera; Ferghus Ua Eoghain (or Leoghain); Flaithcamhail, son of Dluthach; Donghalach Ua Aenghusa; Conall Menn, King of Cinel-Cairbre'; MacErca, son of Maelduin; the three grandsons of Nuadhat; Flann, son of Irghalach; Aedh Laighen, son of Fithchellach"; Niall, son of Muirghes.

One hundred and eighty died of sickness and cold after the Battle of Almhain, in which Fergal, son of Maelduine, was slain, &c.

[724.] The beginning of the reign of Cinaedh, son of Irgalach, according to some.

[722.] Kal. After Fergal, Fogartach, son of Niall, took the name of King of Erin at once, for one year, or two, according to some, when he was killed by Cinaeth Lethchaech', son of Irgalach. He had been defeated by the Leinster-men in the Battle of Tailtin.

[724.] After him Cinaedh was king of Erin for four years. It was to him, while he was in his mother's womb, Adamnan had promised" that he would attain to the sovereignty of Erin. The reign of this

it is certainly cognate with the Latin *cæcus*. It generally means purblind or one-eyed.

Adamnan had promised.—No notice of this promise has been found in any other Annals or historical tracts.

céo bliaöain 7 maiom pop Ouncháö mac Mupchaöa, ip pocháiöe oo paopclanoaiö po mapbaö cpep an éoȝaö po.
Inopíccaé mac Muippbaiȝ, pí Connacc, mopicup. Caé eioip Ounchaö mac Mupchaöa 7 Laioȝnéin pí hUa cCionnpiolaiȝ, 7 maioio an caé pop Laioȝnein.
Ϝal. Caé Cinnoelȝéen i ccopcup Poȝapcaé hUa Cípnaiȝ. Cionaoö mac Iopȝalaiȝ uiccop epac ; unoe Ruman cecinic :—

Meamaiö caé Cinn oelȝéín oo piȝ Lono buipp,
Luiö Ípȝall oap ípȝail, caé ceipopeé oepȝ Oomnaill.

Ȝo mbaö iap mapbaö Poȝupcaiȝ no ȝabaö Cionaoö piȝe iap ppaipino.
Cuinolíp ab. Cluana mic Noip, Paolchu ab. Iae.
Ϝal. Colman Uamaé, paoi Aipomaéa mopicup.
Colman banbáin, paoi Cille oapa mopicup.
Mac Ailepain Cille puaiö mopicup.
Ϝal. Cillene Poca ab. Iae.
Oachonna cpáiböeaé, Eppcop Conoeipe, quieuic.
Ȝuin Cpioméainn mic Ceallaiȝ, mic Ȝepciöe, piȝ Laiȝen, i ccaé bealaiȝ lice. Ȝuin Ailella mic boobéaöa Miöe. Caé eioip

---

ᵃ *Indrechtach, son of Muiredhach.*—His death is entered in the Annals of the Four Masters at the year 718, but it is an interpolation and a mistake.

ᵞ *Dunchadh, son of Murchadh.*—Annals of Four Masters, 722 ; Annals of Ulster, 727.

ᶻ *Cenndelgthen.*—Annals of Four Masters, 720, Annals of Ulster, 723. The chronology is confused here. Fogartach Ua Cearnaigh was slain in 724, and was succeeded by Cinaedh, who reigned till 727.

—*Ogygia*, Part iii., c. 93.

ᵃ *Rumann.*—He is usually styled the Virgil of Erin, and died, according to the Annals of Tighernach, in the year 747.—Four Masters, 742 ; Annals of Ulster, 746.

ᵇ *Cuindles, &c.*—The obits of these two Abbots are entered in the Annals of Ulster under A. D. 723, but the true year is 724.

ᶜ *Colman Uamach.*—The death of this Abbot, and also of Banbain of Cill-dara, are

this Cinaeth was good. He plundered Leinster the first year, and defeated Dunchadh, son of Murchadh, and many of the nobles were killed during that war.

Indrechtach, son of Muiredhach[x], King of Connaught, died. A battle [was fought] between Dunchadh, son of Murchadh[y], and Laidhgnen, King of Ui-Cinnselaigh; and Laedhgnen was defeated.

Kal. The Battle of Cenndelgthen[z], in which was slain Fogartach Ua Cernaigh. Cinaedh, son of Irgalach, was the conqueror; on which Rumann[a] sung:

The Battle of Cenn-delgthen was gained by the strong mighty king.
Battalion passed over battalion in the bloody battle of Domhnall.

[724.] It was after the killing of Fogartach that Cinaedh assumed the sovereignty, according to some.

Cuindles[b], Abbot of Cluain mic Nois, Faelchu, Abbot of Ia [died].

[725.] Kal. Colman Uamach[c], sage of Ard-macha, died.
Colman Banbain, sage of Cill-dara, died.
Mac Ailerain, of Cill-ruaidh[d], died.

[726.] Cillene[e] Fota, Abbot of Ia [died].
Dachonna[f], the Pious, Bishop of Coinneire, died.

The death of Crimhthann, son of Cellach, son of Geirtide, King of Leinster, in the Battle of Bealach-lice[g]; the death of Ailell, son of Bodhbhcha, of Meath. A battle [was fought] between Ederscel[h], King

---

entered in the Annals of the Four Masters at 720, but in the Annals of Ulster at 724. The true year, however, is 725.

[d] *Cill-ruaidh.*—Now Kilroot, in the barony of Upper Glenarm, county of Antrim. The obit of Mac Ailerain is not given in any of the published Annals.

[e] *Cillene.*—Four M., 725; Tigh. 726;

Reeves's "Adamnan," p. 382.

[f] *Dachonna.*—He was Bishop of Connor, and died, according to Four M., in 725.

[g] *Bealach-lice.*—i. e. road of the flagstone. See Ann. Four M., A. D. 721.

[h] *Ederscel*, King of Bregia: Compare Ann. Ult., 726.

eioip Eaoappséℓ, pig bpfg, ⁊ Paoℓán, pí Laigfn, ⁊ po meamaio ann pop Eacuppséℓ, pí bpeag.

Ip in bliaoain peo po mapbao Cionaoo Caoc mac Iopgaℓaig, ⁊ níop gab neac oa píoℓ pige n-'Eipenn. Plaicbfpcac mac Loinpig pop mapb.

Inicium pegni Plaicbfpcaig.

Kaℓ. 'San bliaoain pi po bpip Congap, pí Poippeann, cpí caca pop Opupc pig Aℓban. Cac Opoma Popnocca eioip Ceneℓ Conaiℓℓ ⁊ Eogain, i ccopcaip Pℓann mac Ioptuiℓe, ⁊ Sneogup Oeapg hUa bpacaioe.

Aoamnani peliquiae in hibepniam cpanppepuncup, ec ℓex eiup penouacup. bap Mupchaoa mic bpain, pig Laigfn. Cac Maircin ioip Laignib péin; meamaio imuppo pé n-Uib Ounlaing pop Uib cCionnpioℓaig, i ccopcaip Laiocfnn, ⁊ mac Conmeℓℓa, pí hUa g-Cinnpioℓaig, ⁊ Congap mac Paoℓcon mic Paoℓain, ⁊ Cfthepnach mac Naoi hUi Ceaℓℓaig. Ounchao uiccop epac.

Cac boipne, no Inpi bpeogain, eioip peapaib Lipe ⁊ peapaib Cuaℓann ⁊ Congaℓ mac bpain. Paoℓan uiccop puic.

Oopmicacio Céℓe Cpíopo.

Kaℓ. Pℓann ab. bfnnchaip quieuic. Leo Aug. popicup. Cac Opoma

---

ⁱ *Flaithbhertach.*—The true year of his accession was A.D. 727. The Four M. are wrong in placing it in 723.

ʲ *Fortrenn.*—i. e. Pictland, in Scotland. This entry is not in the published Annals. The Annals of Ulster have at 725—" Nechtain mac Deirile *constringitur* apud Druist Regem:" Reeves's "Adamnan," p. 382.

ᵏ *Druim-fornacht.*—A place near Newry, in the Co. Down. The Four M. place this battle under A. D. 721, but the Ann. Ult. under 726; the true year being 727.

ˡ *Relics of Adamnan.*—Ann. Ult. 726. The law of Adamnan, here referred to, prohibited women from going into battle, or on military expeditions.—Reeves's "Adamnan," p. 383, Pref. L-liii.

ᵐ *Murchadh, son of Bran.*—Ann. Four M., 721; Ann. Ult., 726.

ⁿ *Maistin.*—Now Mullaghmast, near Athy, in the county of Kildare.

King of Bregh, and Faelan, King of Leinster, in which Ederscel, King of Bregh, was defeated.

[727.] In this year Cinaedh Caech [the blind], son of Irgalach, was slain, and none of his descendants assumed the monarchy of Erin. Flaithbhertach, son of Loingsech, was he who killed him.

The beginning of the reign of Flaithbhertach[i].

Kal. In this year Aenghus, King of Fortrenn[j], gained three battles over Drust, King of Alba [Scotland]. The Battle of Druim-Fornacht[k] [was fought] between the Cinel Conaill and Cinel-Eoghain, in which were slain Flann, son of Irthuile, and Snedhgus Derg Ua Brachaidhe.

The relics of Adamnan[l] were translated to Erin, and his law was renewed. The death of Murchadh, son of Bran[m], King of Leinster; the Battle of Maistin[n] [was fought] between the Leinster-men themselves, in which the Ui-Dunlaing defeated the Ui-Ceinnsealaigh, in which Laidhcenn Mac Conmella, King of Ui-Ceinsellaigh, and Aenghus, son of Faelchu, son of Faelan, and Cethernach, son of Nae Ua Ceallaigh, were slain. Donnchadh was the victor.

The Battle of Boirinn, or of Inis-Breoghain[o], was fought between the men of Liffe and the men of Cualann, and Congal, son of Bran. Faelan was the victor.

The rest of Cele-Christ[p].

[728.] Kal. Flann, Abbot of Bennchair[q], died. Leo Augustus died[r]. The

[o] *Inis-Breoghain.*—i. e. Breogan's Island. This place has not been yet identified. This battle is entered in the Ann. Ult. at the year 726, but the true year is 727. The Four M. are wrong in placing it under 721.

[p] *Cele-Christ.*—i. e. the servant, or vassal of Christ. His death is entered in the Ann. Ult. at 726; Tighern. 727; Four M. 721.

[q] *Flann, Abbot of Benchair.*—He is called Flann Aentroibh, Four M. 722; Ann. Ult. 727; Tighern. 728.

[r] *Leo Augustus.*—This must be Leo. III., "the Isaurian." Died, June, 741, after a reign of 24 years.

Oroma Corcain eiḋir Flaiṫḃeartaċ mac Loinġriġ ⁊ mac Iorġa-
laiġ, ⁊ ttoṙċair Cionaot ⁊ Eoḋur mac Ailella, ⁊ Maolḋúin mac
Fearaḋaiġ, ⁊ Dunchaḋ mac Cormaic.

Caṫ Ailline eiḋir ḋá ṁac Murchaḋa mic Ḃrain .i. Faolán ⁊
Dunchaḋ. Faolan iunior uictor fuit, et reġnauit. Caṫal mac
Fionġuine ⁊ Ceallaċ mac Faolċair, rí Orraiġe euarerunt. Dunchaḋ mac Murchaḋa, ri Laiġſn interfectur ert. Aċt éſna
térna Dunchaḋ ar an ċaṫ, ⁊ ḃaoi reaċtmain 'na ḃſthaiḋ.
Ġabaiḋ Faolan riġe Laiġſn, ⁊ atnaiġ mnai an Dunchaḋa .i. Tua-
laiṫ, inġſn Caṫail mic Fionġaine, ri Muṁan.

Domnall, ri Connaċt, moritur.

In hoc anno comporuit Beda orur ruum magnum, hoc ert, in
nono anno Leonir.

Kal. Ecbertur ranctur Chrirti miler in hi-Coluim Cilli
quieuit. Beda in Cronicir cerrat.

Kal. Mac Onċon reriba Cille Dara ; Suiḃne ab Ard maċa
quieuit ; Ġall ó Lilcaiġ .i. pruḋenr quieuit ; Mac Concumbri
ruí Cluana mic Noir ; Aonġur mac becce ḃairce moritur ;
Cocall oḋar ruí Ḃſnċair moritur.

Caṫ Fearnmaiġe itir Cetamun * *

Kal. Colman hUa Liattain reliġionir ḋoctor [oḃiit].

Eochaiḋ mac Colġáin, ab Ard Macha, moritur.

Caṫ

---

¹ *Druim Corcain.*—Ann. Ult. 727; Tighern. 728.

² *Aillinn.*—Now Dun Aillinne, near Old Kilcullen, in the county of Kildare : Ann. Ult., 727. "*Bellum* Ailenne *inter duos germanos filios* Murchada, mic Brain, et Dunchu, *senior jugulatur; junior Foelanus regnat.* . . . . Domhnall mac Ceallaig, *rex* Connacht, *moritur.*"

ᵃ *Beda.*—Bede died in the year 734, according to the Saxon Chronicle and the Annals of Ulster, but the true year is 735. No account is given in any other work of the year in which he composed, or put out, his great work. The Emperor, Leo III., succeeded in March, 718, so that the tenth year of his reign was 727, when Bede is said to have composed [i. e. perhaps, pub-

The Battle of Druim Corcain[s] [was fought] between Flaithbhertach, son of Loingsech, and the son of Irgalach, in which were slain Cinaeth and Eodus, son of Ailell, and Maelduin, son of Feradhach, and Dunchadh, son of Cormac.

The Battle of Aillinn[t], between the two sons of Murchadh, son of Brann, i. e. Faelan and Dunchadh. Faelan, who was the junior, conquered and reigned; Cathal, son of Fingaine [King of Munster], and Cellach, son of Faelchair, King of Osraighe, escaped. Dunchadh, son of Murchadh, King of Leinster, was slain; but he survived the battle, and lived for a week after it. Faelan assumed the sovereignty of Leinster, and married the wife of Dunchadh; namely, Tualaith, daughter of Cathal, son of Fingaine, King of Munster.

Domhnall, King of Connaught, died.

In hoc anno composuit Beda[u] suum magnum opus, hoc est in nono anno Leonis.

[729.] Kal. Ecbertus[v] sanctus Christi miles in Hi-Coluim Cille quievit. Beda in Chronicis cessat.

[730.] Kal. Mac-Onchon[w], scribe of Cill-dara, and Suibhne, Abbot of Ard-Macha, quievit; Gall of Lilcach, i. e. the prudent, quievit; Mac-Concumbri, sage of Cluain-mic-nois; Aengus, son of Bec Boirche, died; Cochall Odhar, sage of Benchair, died.

The battle of Fernmhagh[x], between Cetamun * *

[731.] Kal. Colman Ua Altain[y], a religious doctor, died.

Colgu, son of Eochaidh, Abbot of Ard-macha, died.

[733]

lished] his work; for it is not to be supposed that Bede composed his work in one year.

[v] *Ecbertus.*—He died at Hy, according to Bede, and the Saxon Chronicle, on Easter Sunday, the 24th of April, A. D. 729.—Reeves's "Adamnan," p. 379, 383.

[w] *Mac-Onchon.*—Ann. Ult. 729; Tigh. 730.

[x] *Fernmhagh.*—Now Farney, a barony in the county of Monaghan. This entry is not in any of the published Annals. It is left unfinished in our MS.

[y] *Colman Ua Altain.*—A. D. 730. "Col-

Caṫ do ḃriġeḋ do Aoḋ Allan mac Firġail для Flaitḃeartach mac Loingriġ, rí 'Eirenn, go dtug Flaitḃeartac Loingiur a For- treannoiḃ ċuiġe a n-aiġiḋ Ciné́il Eoġain, aċt cṡna ra ḃáiḋeaḋ earṁór an ċoḃlaiġ rin. Morr Flaitḃeartaig féin 'rin bliaḋain rin, ⁊ rġartain rige n'Erenn ne Cenel ġConaill go раḋa iar- ttain.

Ir in bliaḋain ri ad ċṡr an ḃó ⁊ ré cora rúiṫe, ⁊ да corr aice, ⁊ aoin cṡnn; ro bliġeḋ ro trí hí caċ .ṡ. laoí .i. nDeilġinir Cualann. Kal. Aoḋ Allain mac Firġail do ġaḃáil riġe n-'Eirenn. Flann Sionna hUa Colla ab Cluana mic Nóir.
Princerr no pontirex Maiġe eo na Saxon ġarolt obit. Seḃdann inġen Chuirc, abbatirra Cille darа [d'écc].
Caṫ Connaċt ittir [. . . . in quo cecidit] Muireadaċ mac Indreaċtaiġ.

Caṫ do ḃririod d'Aoḋ Allan для Ultoiḃ, itir Aoḋ Róin rí Ulaḋ ⁊ Conċad ri Cruiṫne a Fochairḋ Muirṫeṁne, ttṡmpall Fochard ata ord Aoḋa Róin.
Caṫ do ríḃiri edir Aoḋ Allan ⁊ Cenel Conaill, itir Conaing mac

man *nepos* Littain, *religiosus doctor pausat. Mors Echdach mic Colggen Anachorete Ardmache."—Ann. Ult.*

ˣ *In that year.*—This battle was fought in 734, in which King Flaithbheartach died. The chronology of the Four Masters is incorrect. For Fortrenn the F. M. and Ann. Clonm. have Dal-Riada.

ᵃ *Deilginis-Cualann.*—Now Dalkey Island, near Dublin. F. M. 727; Ann. Clonm. 730; Ann. Ult. 732; but the true year would be 734, according to our text.

ᵇ *Aedh Allan.*—F. M. 730; Ann. Ult. 733; Tigh. 734.

ᶜ *Flann Sinna Ua Colla.*—This and the two obits succeeding are entered in the Ann. F. M. under 726, and in the Ann. Ult. under 731; but the true year is 732 (Tigh.), and they are clearly misplaced above.

ᵈ *Muiredhach, son of Indrechtach.*—The F. M. make him Bishop of *Magh-eo-na Saxon*, and enter his death under 726, but they are totally wrong. In the Ann. Ult. 731, and Tigh. 732, the true reading may be translated thus:—" The battle of Connacht, wherein fell Muiredhach, son of Indrechtach. *Pontifex Maighe heo Sax-*

[733, or 734.] Kal. A battle was gained by Aedh Allan, son of Fergal, over Flaithbhertach, son of Loingsech, King of Erin, so that Flaithbhertach brought a fleet out of Fortrenn [Pictland] to assist him against the Cinel-Eoghain. The greater part of that fleet was, however, drowned. The death of Flaithbhertach himself took place in that year[a], and the sovereignty of Erin was separated from the Cinel-Conaill for a long time afterwards. In this year was seen a cow with six legs under her, and two bodies, and one head. She was milked thrice each day; i. e. at Deilginis-Cualann[*].

[734.] Kal. Aedh Allan[b], son of Fergal, assumed the sovereignty of Erin.

Flann Sinna Ua Colla[c], Abbot of Cluain-mic-nois [died].

[732.] Gerald, pontifex of Maighco [Mayo] of the Saxons, died. Sebhdan, daughter of Corc, Abbess of Cill-dara [died].

A battle in Connaught between [. . . . . in which fell] Muiredhach, son of Indrechtach[d].

A battle was gained by Aedh Allan over the Ulta, at Fochard-Muirtheimhne[e]; i. e. over Aedh Roin, King of Uladh, and Conchadh, King of the Cruithnigh[f]. In the church of Fochard the Ord [thumb] of Aedh Roin is [preserved].

Another battle was fought between Aedh Allan and the Cinel-Conaill;

onum Garaalt obit."—See Ann. F. M., Ed. J. O'D., p. 324.

[e] *Fochard-Muirtheimhne.*— Now the church of Faughard, in the county of Louth, about two miles to the north of Dundalk. This battle is noticed in the Ann. F. M. at the year 732; Ult. 734; Tigh. 735.

[f] *Cruithnigh.*—i. e. of the Picts, i. e. of the Picts of Ulster. The Ann. Ult. and Tigh. call him "Conchad mac Cuanach rex Cobo (ꞃꞁ Cobha, *Tigh.*). The F. M. call him chief of East Ulster, Co. Down, and add, that the head of Aedh Roin was cut off on a stone called Clochan-commaigh, in the doorway of the church of Fochard, and that the cause of the battle was the profanation of the church of Cill-Conna [now Kilcoony, in Tyrone] by Ua Seghain, one of the people of Aedh Roin.

mac Congaile mic Feapgapa Fánav. Cat Catail do Domnall i cTailltin.

Ƙal. Oegſócap Eprcop nAonproma quieuit.
beva Sapienp lxxxiii anno aetatip puae quieuit.

[FRAGMENTUM II.]

aliud fragmentum ex eodem Codice extractum per eundum; incipienp ab anno cipcitep 661.

Ƙal. Cuimin Foda quieuit lxxii anno aetatip puae unde Colman Ua Cluapaiġ, aide Cuimin cecinit:

Marb frim anofr, marb antuaid,
Nibttup ionmuin aerluaiġ,
Do foip a rí nime glaip
An docaipte tatap laip.
Marbáin na bliadna pa,
Ní bo caointe ní occa,
Maoldúin becc mac Feapgupa,
Conainn, Cuimin Foda.

Má

ᵍ *Conaing, son of Congal.*—He was slain in the year 732 [733, *Tigh.*] in the battle of Magh-Itha, according to the Ann. Ult., F. M. 727. "*Congressio iterum inter* Aedh [Allan] mac Fergaile et *Genus* Conaill in Campo Itho, *ubi cecidit* Conaing mac Congaile mic Ferguso [Fanaid] et *ceteri multi.*"—*Ann. Ult.* 732. This battle is misplaced in our text. It was fought in the reign of Flaithbheartach.

ʰ *The battle of Cathal.*—This is a mistake. It is entered in the Ann. F. M. at 732, but in the Ann. Ult. at 736. Thus:—"*Congressio invicem inter Nepotes* Aedo Slaine *ubi* Conaing mac Amalgaid *moritur;* Cernach *vicit,* et Cathal mac Aedo *cecidit; juxta lapidem* Ailbe *ab orientali parte gesta est.*" See Tigh. 737.

ⁱ *Oeghedhchar.*—He was Bishop of Nendrum, an island in Lough Cuan, in the

Conaill; [i. e.] between Conaing, son of Congal[g], son of Fergus of Fanaid. .... The battle of Cathal[h], by Domhnall at Tailltin.

[734.] Kal. Oeghedhchar[i], Bishop of Oendruim, quievit.

[734, or 735.] Beda Sapiens[k] lxxxiii°., anno ætatis suæ quievit.

[FRAGMENT II.]

ANOTHER FRAGMENT extracted from the same Manuscript, by the same, beginning about the year 661.

[662.] Kal. Cuimin Foda[l] died in the seventy-second year of his age; hence Colman Ua Cluasaigh[m], tutor of Cuimin, sung:

Dead to me is the south, dead the north,
No second host is dear to me;
Relieve, O King of the blue heaven,
The sufferings that are with it.
The deaths of this year,—
Not one of them should be lamented[n],—
[Were] Maelduin Beg, son of Fergus
Conainn, Cuimin Foda.

If

county of Down.—*Ann. Ult.* 734; *Tigh.* 735.

[k] *Beda Sapiens.*—Ann. Ult. 734; Tigh. 735. Bede was born in the year 673, and died in the year 735, in the sixty-third year of his age. Therefore, either two of the x's should be struck out of our text, or all English authorities which treat of his age are incorrect, which is not likely.

[l] *Cuimin Foda.*—i. e. Cuimin, the Long or Tall. He was Bishop of Clonfert. See Four M. and Ann. Ult. 661; Book of Hymns, p. 84, *sq.*

[m] *Colman Ua Cluasaigh.*—He was the tutor of Cuimine Foda, and died in the same year.

[n] *Should be lamented.*—Because they all went straightways to heaven, and there was no need of sorrowing after them. See Colgan's "Acta SS.," p. 149, Note 7.

Má ꝛo ꝺligthe ꝼíꞃ ꝺaꞃ muiꞃ
Seiꞃꝼb iꞃꞃuiṫe nҮꞃioҕoiꞃ,
Maꝺ a h-Eiꞃinn ní baoí ní ꝺó
Inҕe Cuimine Foꝺo.
Seaċ ba heꝼꞃcoꝼꞃom ꞃom ba 'ꞃí,
ba mac tiҕeaꞃna mo Chuimin
Tꞅnꝺal 'Eiꞃenn aꞃ ꞃoaꞃ,
ba h-alainn maꞃ ꞃo choaꞃ.
Maiṫ a ċeinel, maiṫ a ċꞃuṫ,
bá líṫan a comꝥlonnaꝺ
Ua Coiꞃꝑꞃe ⁊ Ua Cuiꞃc,
ba ꞃaoi, ba hán, ba hoiꞃꝺeꞃc.

Caṫ Oҕamain, ꝺu i ttoꞃchaiꞃ Conaing mac Conҕaile, aҕuꞃ
Ultan mac Eꞃnine, ꞃi Ciannachta. Blaṫmac mac Aoꝺa Slaine
uictuꞃ eꞃt a ꞃociiꞃ Ꝺiaꞃmaꝺa. Maonac mac Finҕín ꞃi Muṁan
moꞃituꞃ.

Kal. Seiҕine .i. Mac hu Cuiniꝺ, ab Bꞅnchaiꞃ quieuit.

Moꞃꞃ Ҕuaiꞃe Aiꝺne, ꞃí Connaċt, unꝺe—

Caꞃn Conaill moꞃꞅluaҕ ꝼile na comaiꞃ
bi maꞃb uile ciata bi,
Duꞃꞃann ꝺo Ҕuaiꞃe Aiꝺni.

Ҕuin

* *A man over sea.*—i. e. a foreigner, viz. in reference to Italy. No Irishman ever yet was Pope of Rome. These lines are given differently by the Four Masters. The Irish, however, claimed Gregory the Great (whom they styled of the golden mouth) as one of their race, and they have engrafted his pedigree on the regal Irish stem of Conaire II., the ancestor of the O'Connells, the O'Falveys, and other families. The O'Clerys give his pedigree as follows in their work on the Genealogies of the Irish Saints :—" Gregory of Rome, son of Gormalta, son of Conla, son of Arda, son of Dathi, son of Corc, son of Conn, son of Cormac, son of Corc Duibhne, son of Cairbre Musc, son of Conaire." Baronius, however, shows from better evidence that he was born at Rome of a patrician family, being the son of Sylves and Gordian, the

If it were ordained that a man over sea°
Should sit [as Pope] more learned than Gregory,
If from Erin, no one for it
Except Cuimine Foda.
He was not more bishop than king ;
My Cuimin was the son of a lord[p],
The lamp of Erin for his knowledge,
He was beautiful, as all have heard.
Good was his race, good his form,
Extensive was his kindred,
.Descendant of Coirpre, descendant of Corc,
He was a sage, noble, illustrious.

[662.] The battle of Ogaman[q], in which fell Conaing, son of Congal, and Ultan, son of Ernin, King of Cianachta. Blathmac, son of Aedh Slaine, was conquered by the followers of Diarmaid. Macnach, son of Finghin, King of Munster, died.

[663.] Kal. Seigine[r], i. e. Mac hu Cuinn, Abbot of Benchar, died.
The death of Guaire Aidhne, King of Connaught, whence [the verses] :

.Carn-Conaill ; a great host is near it ;
They were all killed, though lively,
Sorrowful it was to Guaire Aidhne.

The noblest of the Senate, and the grandson of Felix, who had been Pope himself.

[p] *Son of a lord.*—He was an incestuous child, and his tutor, St. Colman O'Cluasaigh, might well have omitted this boastful allusion to his pedigree. This is quoted in Cormac's Glossary, *sub voce* Ꝼaṁ. Many illegitimate children became distinguished saints, as well as Cuimine Foda. See Dr. Todd's remarks on this subject, *Liber Hymnor.*, p. 92.

[q] *Ogaman.*—Not identified. See Ann. Clon. 658; Ann. F. M. 660; Ann. Ult. 661 ; Tigh. 662.

[r] *Seigene.*—A. D. 662. " *Quies* Segain micc U Chuinn abb benchoıp et. *Mors* Guaire Aidhne ; Jugulatio ii. filiorum Domnaill filii Aedo .ı. Conall et Colgu.

Ӡuin ѵa mac Ꭰomnaill .i. Conall aӡuр Colӡa. Ꮯuaṫal mac Ⅿoрӡainn moрiꞇuр.
Ꮯuenoc mac Ᵽionꞇain ab Ᵽeaрna móiрe quieuiꞇ. ѵaoѵan ab Cluana mic Nóiр.
Ral. Ⅿoрluiѵ mac Ⅽoѵa Sláine .i. ѵláṫmac [⁊ Ꭰiaрmaiѵ] i cCalaꞇрuim. ѵa maрѵ Ꭰiaрmaiѵ ѵono iрin ionaѵ céѵna, aӡuр ré ріnꞇe рe Cрoiр na ƒƒam̋ aӡ рaiӡрin рluaiӡ Ⅼaiӡen ċuiӡe ѵa maрѵaѵ; рa cuaiѵ a a   In quibuрѵam libрiр inѵeniꞇuр quoѵ hi ѵuo рeӡeр .i. ѵlaṫmac ⁊ Ꭰiaрmaiѵ ƒii. annip, in quibuрѵam —— annip quoр noр рequimuр. Ⅿaрѵ ꞇрa ѵon moрꞇlaiѵ ƒin .i. ѵo'n ѵuiѵe Conaill, na ѵá рiӡ рi Eiрenn .i. ѵlaṫmac ⁊ Ꭰiaрmaiѵ.
Ᵽeċin Ᵽoѵaiр; Ⅽilƒрan an ƒӡna; Colmán Caр, aӡuр Ⅽonӡuр Ulaiѵ. Ceiṫрe abaiѵ ѵƒnċaiр .i. ѵƒрaċ, Cuimine, Coluim, aӡuр Ⅽoѵán.
Cu ӡan máṫaiр, рi Ⅿum̋an, eꞇ cum ceꞇeрiр ꞇam pluрimiр. Eochaiѵ Iaрlaiṫe рi Ꭰail Ⅽрaiѵe ѵo maрѵaѵ ѵo com̋alꞇoiѵ Ⅿaoiƒoꞇhaрꞇaiӡ mic Ronáin. Uaiр inӡƒn ѵ'Eochaiѵ Iaрlaiṫe рo ѵaoi aӡ Ronán aӡ рi Ⅼaiӡƒn; óӡ an inӡƒn̋, ƒn̋ an Ronán, ӡo ꞇꞇuӡ рi ӡрáѵ ѵo m̋ac Ronáin .i. ѵo Ⅿaolƒoꞇhaрꞇaiӡ, ⁊ ӡo рaiѵ рi ӡá ӡuiѵe ӡo рaѵa, aӡuр ní ƒuaiр uaiѵ a рaom̋aѵ, ⁊ óр ná ƒuaiр aрeaѵ

Mors Gartnaid filii Domnaill, et Domnaill mic Totholain. Mors Tuathail mic Morgaind. Tueuog filius Finntin, abba Fernann, Indercach *episcopus*, Dima *episcopus quiescunt*."—*Ann. Ult.* See Tigh. 663.

' *Baedan.*—Ann. F. M. 663; Ann. Clonm. 660; Ann. Ult. 663; Tigh. 664.

' *The plague.*—i. e. the Buidhe Chonmailc. See Ann. F. M.; Ann. Clon. 661; Ann. Ult. 664; Tigh. 665.

" *Caltruim.*—Now Galtrim, in the county of Meath. This plague is also mentioned by Bede, who writes that in the year 664 a sudden pestilence depopulated the southern coasts of Britain, and afterwards, extending into the province of the Northumbrians, ravaged the country far and near, and destroyed a great multitude of men. He also states that it did no less harm in the island of Hibernia, where many of the nobility and of the lower ranks of the English nation were

The mortal wounding of the two sons of Domhnall, i. e. Conall and Colgu. Tuathal, son of Morgann, died.

Tuenoc, son of Fintan, abbot of Ferna-mor, died; Baedan, Abbot of Cluain-mic-Nois, died.

[664.] Kal. The death of the sons of Aedh Slaine by the plague'; namely, Blathmac and Diarmaid, at Caltruim". Diarmaid died at the same place, while he was standing up with his back against a cross viewing the hosts of Leinster approaching him to kill him. He went, &c. &c. It is found in certain books that these two kings, Blathmac and Diarmaid, reigned twelve years, but in others . . . . years", *quos nos sequimur*. Of this plague, i. e. of the Buidhe Chonaill, these two Kings of Erinn, Blathmac and Diarmaid, died.

Fechin of Fobhar", Aileran the wise, Colman Cas, and Aengus Uladh, died. Four abbots of Bennchair: viz. Berach, Cuimine, Colum, and Aedhan [died].

Cuganmathair, King of Munster, died, with many others. Eochaidh Iarlaithe*, King of Dal-Araidhe, was slain by the foster-brothers of Maelfothartaigh, son of Ronan; for the daughter of Eochaidh Iarlaithe was married to Ronan, King of Leinster; the daughter was young, Ronan was old, so that she loved Ronan's son, i. e. Maelfothartaigh, and she was courting him, but she obtained not his consent, and when she did not, what she did was to tear her head-dress⁷, to scratch and bleed her face, and to come into the presence of Ronan in this plight

at that time studying theology or leading monastic lives, the Scoti supplying them with food, and furnishing them with books and their teaching gratis. See also Colgan's "Acta SS.," p. 601.

* *Years.*—Here the number of years is left blank in the MS.

* *Fobhar.*—Now Fore, in the county of Westmeath. The Four Masters have these entries at the year 664, which is the true year.

* *Eochaidh Iarlaithe.* — He is called King of the Cruithnigh, or Picts of Ulster, in the Ann. F. M. 665.

⁷ *Her head-dress.* —This story is not found in the other Annals.

areaḃ do ṗigne, cuṁḃaċ a cinn do ṁionugaḋ ⁊ a haiẓiḃ do rgníobaḋ, ⁊ ruilreḃ 'ma haiẓiḃ, agur toiḃeaċt d'ionnroiẓ Ronain aṁlaiḃ rin. Crḟo rin? a inẓḟn, ar Ronán. Do ṁac rugaċ-ra, ar rí, Maolratharταiẓ, dom ṗárugħaḋ, ⁊ mo ḃririoḋ ḃó, ⁊ comrac rrium. Marḃtar Maolrotharταiẓ la Ronan iar rin. Τiagaiḋ dno tomaltaḃa Maolrotharταiẓ iar rin go nuig bail i raiḃe Eoċuiḃ Iarlaiċe, ⁊ gairmiḋ leo amaċ é o ċáċ, ⁊ marḃaiḋ i gcionta na ndírna a inẓḟn. Unde Plaittin cecinit :—

> Indiu ḋellioẓair liẓe
> Eochaḃa mic Ḟiachach Lurgan,
> I n-uir cille Coinḋeire
> Ro gaḃ roiτḟr a ẓulban.
> Ro gaḃ Eochaiḋ aon ċaimre
> Ina liẓe-leaḃaiḋ oirċṫe.
> Ḃrónan ril ror ceċ ḃuine
> Atá for Ḋun Soḃairce.

Initium regni Sċnaraiẓ mic Ḃlaṫmaic, u. annir. R. E.

Kal. Morr Oilella mic Doṁnaill, mic Aoḃa, mic Ainmirioc.

Kal. Maolcaiċ mac Scanḃail, ri Cruiṫne morirur. ḃaoiṫin ab Ḃḟnnċuir.

Kal. Críoτán ab Ḃḟnḋcuir quieuit. Cuimin Ḟionn, ab Iae, quieuit. Iomram Columbani cum reliquiir multorum ranctorum

---

ᵃ *Conneire.*—Now Connor, the head of an ancient episcopal see in the county of Antrim. The name is still locally pronounced *Connyer*, not *Connor*.

ᶜ *Dun-Sobhairce.*—Now Dunseverick, in the north of the county of Antrim.

ᵇ *Sechnasach.*—He succeeded in the year 665, and died in 671. See "Ogygia," p. 431.

ᵉ *Ailell, son of Dohmnall.*—His death is entered in the Ann. F. M. 665, but the true year was 666.

ᵈ *Maelcaich.*—F. M. 665 [*recte* 667].

ᵉ *Critan.*—Ann. Ult. 668 [*recte* 669].

plight. "What is this, my girl?" said Ronan. "Thy wanton son, Maelfothartaigh," said she, "has violated and forced me, and cohabited with me." After this Maelfothartaigh was killed by Ronan. But the foster-brothers of Maelfothartaigh afterwards came to where Eochaidh Iarlaithe was, and they called him out from all his people, and killed him, in revenge of what his daughter had done. Unde Flaithir cecinit :—

> This day distinguished the grave
> Of Eochaidh, son of Fiacha Lurgan,
> In the earth of the church of Conneire[z],
> Which has received the great heat of his mouth.
> Eochaidh has received one shirt
> In his grave-bed, slaughtered,
> Which has brought sorrow upon every person
> Who is at Dun-Sobhairce[a].

[665.] The beginning of the reign of Sechnasach[b], son of Blathmac, quinque annis, King of Erin.

[666.] Kal. The death of Ailell, son of Domhnall[c], son of Aedh, son of Ainmire.

[667.] Kal. Maelcaich[d], son of Scandal, King of the Cruithne, died. Baithin, abbot of Benchair, quievit.

[669.] Kal. Critan[e], abbot of Benchair, quievit. Cuimin Finn[f], abbot of Ia, quievit. The sailing of Colman[g], with the relics of many saints,

[f] *Cuimin Finn.*—i. e. "Comyn the Whyte," Ann. Clonn., Ann. Ult., 668 [recte 669]. This is the celebrated Cumineus Albus mentioned by Adamnan as author of a book on the virtues of St. Columbkille. He was also the author of a very curious letter on the Pascal Controversy, published by Ussher in his "Sylloge," No. 11.

[g] *Colman.*—The sailing of Colman to Inis-bo-finne, or *Insula vaccæ albæ* (now Bophin Island, situated off the west coast of the barony of Murcsk, in the south-west of the county of Mayo), is given in the

go hInip bó pinne, ubi punoauit ecclepiam. Cat peipcpi icip
Ulcuib ⁊ Cpuiéne, in quo cecioit Catupat mac Luippgne, pi Ulaö.
Mopp Ounchaöa hUi Ronáin. Paolan mac Colmain pi Laigen
mopicup. Mopp Maoilpochaptaig mic Suibne, pi hUu tTuiptpe.
Cat Oamoeipg, i ttopchuip Oíocuill mac Eachat, ⁊ Congal mac
Loicine. Guin bpain pinn mic Maoilóttpaig, pí na nOépi.
Kal. Mopp blatmaic mic Maoilcoba.
Kal. Guin Sfcnapaig, mic blatmaic R. E. Ouibbuin ⁊cā., oo
Chaipbpib po ṁapb i ppill Sfcnapat: oe quo oicitup:

ba ppianat, ba heatlapgat
An teat i mbíoö Sfcnapat,
ba hiomba puioeall pop plait
I ttig i mbíoö mac blatmaic.

Oppu, pi Saxon mopicup. Conptantinup Aug. mopicup.
Lopgaö bfnnéaip la bpeatnaib. Lopgaö Apomacha.
Mopp Cumapgaig mic Ronáin.
Cat Opoma Coepip. Cat Tolca ápo, ou i ttopcaip Oungaile
mac Maoiletuile, pi bogaine. Loingpioch uittop puit. Copmac
mac Maoilpochaptaig mopicup.

Initium

Ann. Ult. at A. D. 667. See also Bede's
"Eccl. Hist.," lib. iv., c. 4, and Ussher's
"Primordia," p. 825, 964, 1164, and
O'Flaherty's "West Connaught," pp. 115, 294.

[h] *Fersat.*—Ann. Tigh. 666; Ann. Ult. 667. This was probably the *Fersat*, or ford, which gave name to Bel-ferste, now Belfast.

[i] *Uí-Tuirtre.*—A tribe giving name to a territory comprising the present baronies of Upper and Lower Toome, in the county of Antrim.—*Four Masters*, A. D. 668, p. 280, note [k].

[k] *Damhderg.*—This was the name of a place in Bregia, but it has not been yet identified. See F. M., A. D. 738.

[l] *Deisi.*—i. e. Decies, in the present county of Waterford.

[m] *Sechnasach.*—Ann. Ult. 670. The true year was 671.

[n] *Ossa.*—i. e. Osney, King of the Northumbrian Saxons, who died, according to the Saxon Chronicle, 15th Feb., 670.

saints, to the island of Inis-bo-finne, where he founded a church. The battle of Fersat[h], between the Ulta [Ulstermen] and the Cruithni, in which was slain Cathasach, son of Luirgne, King of Uladh; the death of Dunchadh Ua Ronain; Faelan, son of Colman, King of Leinster, died. The death of Maelfothartaigh, son of Suibhne, King of the Ui-Tuirtre[i]. The battle of Damhderg[k], in which were slain Dicuill, son of Eochaidh, and Congal, son of Loichine. The mortal wounding of Bran, son of Maelochtraigh, King of the Deisi[l].

[670.] Kal. The death of Blathmac, son of Maelcobha.

[671.] Kal. The mortal wounding of Sechnasach[m], son of Blathmac, King of Erin. Duibhduin, and others of the Cairbri, slew Sechnasach by treachery, de quo dicitur:

> Full of bridles and whips,
> Was the house in which Sechnasach was,
> Many were the leavings of plunder
> In the house, in which was the son of Blathmac.

Ossa[n], King of the Saxons, died. Constantinus Augustus died[o].

[672.] The burning of Bennchair[p] in Britain. The burning of Ard-Macha.

The death of Cumascach, son of Ronan.

The battle of Druim Coepis[q]. The battle of Tulach-árd[r], in which fell Dungaile, son of Maeltuile, King of Boghaine[s]. Loingsech was the victor. Cormac, son of Maelfothartaigh, died.

The

---

[o] *Died.*—Wrong; for Constantine lived till 685. See note [n], *infra*, p. 70.

[p] *Bennchair.*—i. e. Bangor, in Wales, A. D. 671, "Combustio Bennchair Britonum."—*Ann. Ult.*

[q] *Druim Coepis.*—Not identified.

[r] *Boghaine.*—Now the barony of Bannagh, in the west of the county of Donegal.

[s] *Tulach-árd* (i. e. high hill), not identified.

Iniṫium ꞃeẓni Cinꝺꝼaolaið mic Cꞃuinnmail, mic blaiṫmic. in annıꞃ.

Ḳal. Conꞃꞇanꞇinuꞃ ꝼiliuꞃ Conꞃꞇanꞇini imꝑeꞃauiꞇ ꞅuii. anniꞃ.

Ḳal. Ẓuin Conẓaile Cꞅnꞃꝼoða mac Ꝺunchaða, ꞃi Ulað, beꞇꞇ boiꞃce ꞃoð nẓon. Ꝺoeꞃ mac Maolꞇuile, ꞃi Ciannaċꞇa ꝺo maꞃbað.

Ḳal. Caṫ in Ꝃiꞃcealꞇꞃa i ꞇꞇoꞃchaiꞃ Cꞅnꞃꝼolað mac Cꞃuinṁail ꞃí Eiꞃꞅnn; Ƒionnachꞇa mac Ꝺunchaða uicꞇoꞃ ꝼuiꞇ, unꝺe ꝺiciꞇuꞃ :—

Ra iaðꞃað um Ƒionnaċꞇa ꞃiana iaꞃṫaiꞃ ṫiꞃe,
Ro maolað móꞃ a ċoiꞃe um Cꞅnꞃꝼaolað a ꞃiẓe.

Ḳal. Colmán Inꞃi bó ꝼinne quieuiꞇ. Iniꞇium ꞃeẓiminiꞃ Ƒionnaċꞇa ṁeic Ꝺunchaða .ꞅꞅ. bliaðain.

Ḳal. Coꞃẓꞃað Ꝃiliẓ la Ƒionnaċꞇa. Caṫ eiðiꞃ Ƒionnaċꞇa ⁊ Laiẓniu aẓ loċ Ẓaðaiꞃ ꝼe ille ꝼe anonꝺ, ꞃeꝺ ꞇamen Ƒionnaċꞇa uicꞇoꞃ ꝼuiꞇ.

Ni ꝺo ꞃẓéluið Ƒionnaċꞇa ꞃo ꞃíoꞃ. Ꝃn Ƒionnaċꞇa ꞇꞃa ba ꝺaiððiꞃ ꝺoċonáiẓ é aꞃ ꞇúꞃ. Ro baoi ꞇꞅċ ⁊ bꞅn aiẓe : Ní ꞃaiðe imuꞃꞃo ꝺo ꞃeilb aiẓe aċꞇ aon ðaṁ ⁊ aon bó. Ƒꞅċꞇ aon ꝺo ꞃala ꞃí ꝼꝼꞅꞃ

---

¹ *Cennfaeladh, son of Crunnmhael.*— The Annals of Ulster call him son of Blathmac. "A. D. 671, Ceannfaeladh mac Blathmaic *regnare incipit.*" But our Annals may be right.

ᵘ *Constantinus.*—He was the son, not of Constantinus, but of Constans II., whom he succeeded in 668. He died in 685. This entry is therefore inserted in a wrong place.

ᵛ *Congal Cennfoda.*—"A. D. 673, *Jugulatio* Congaile Connfoti mic Duncho, *regis* Ult. Bccc Bairche *interfecit eum."—Ann. Ult.*

ᵡ *Doer, son of Maeltuile.*—This obit is not in any of the published Annals.

ˣ *Aircelltair.*—The situation, or present name of this place, which is somewhere in Meath, has not been yet identified. This entry is given in the Ann. Ult. at 674, more correctly, thus: "*Bellum* Cinnfaelad *filii* Blathmic filii Aedo Slaine *in quo* Cennfaelad *interfectus est.* Finnsneachta mac Duncha *victor erat.*"

The beginning of the reign of Cennfaeladhᵗ, son of Crunnmhael, son of Blathmac. [He reigned] three years.

Kal. Constantinusᵘ, son of Constantinus, governed seventeen years.

[674.] Kal. The mortal wounding of Congal Cennfodaᵛ, son of Dunchadh, King of Uladh; it was Beg Boirche that slew him. Doer, son of Maeltuileʷ, King of Cianachta, was killed.

[675.] Kal. The battle of Aircelltairˣ, in which fell Cennfaeladh, son of Crunnmael, King of Erin; Finnachta, son of Dunchadh, was the victor, *unde dicitur* :—

> There closed about Finnachta the soldiers of the western territory [i. e. Westmeath].
> They removed, though great his host, Cennfaeladh from his sovereignty.

[676.] Kal. Colman of Inis-bo-finneʸ quievit. The beginning of the reign of Finnachta, son of Dunchadh [R. E.]ᶻ [who reigned] twenty years.

[677.] Kal. The destruction of Ailech by Finnachta. A battle was fought between Finnachta and the Leinster-men on both sides of Loch Gabhairᵃ, but nevertheless Finnachta victor fuit.

Some of the stories about Finnachta are set down here. At first this Finnachta was poor and indigent. He had a house and a wife, but he had no property but one ox and one cow. On one occasion the

---

ʸ *Colman of Inis-bo-finne.*—See Ann. Ult., A.D. 675.

ᶻ *R. E.*—i. e. *Ri Erinn*, King of Ireland. These letters are in the margin.

ᵃ *Loch-Gabhair.*—Now Loughgawer, or Lagore, near Dunshaughlin, Co. Meath. This lake is now dried up, and many curious antiquities have been found where it was. See "Proceedings of the Royal Irish Academy," vol. i., p. 424. In the Ann. Ult. this entry is given under the year 676, thus: "A. D. 676, *Bellum inter* Finnsneachta et *Lagenios in loco proximo* Loch Gabar in quo Finnsneachta *victor erat.*"

ꝼꝼɼɼ Roɼ ꝼo ɼeaċɼan ⁊ mſjiuʓaḃ ı ʓcoṁꝼoċɼaıḃ boıċe Pınnaċta. Ní ɼaıḃe ɼempe ɼıaṁ aḃaıʓ bú mſɼa ınáɼ an aḃaıʓ ɼın, ꝺo ʓaıllım, ⁊ ꝺo ɼnſċta, aʓuɼ ꝺo ꝺoɼċaꝺaḃ, ⁊ an tſċ ḃáɼ bo aıl ꝺon ɼí ꝺul ⁊ ꝺ'á ṁnaoı ⁊ ꝺá ṁuıntıɼ níoɼ ɼo cumʓattaɼ ꝺola ɼa méıꝺ na ꝺoınınne ⁊ na ꝺoɼċaꝺaıḃ, ⁊ ba ıaꝺ a n-ıomɼáıte taıɼıɼıom ꝼo ḃonaıḃ na ccɼann. Aꝺ cuala ımuɼɼo Pıonnaċta ıaꝺ ꝼoɼɼ na hıomɼaıtıḃ ɼın, uaıɼ nıɼ bo ſḃ ꝼoꝺa ó ḃoıċ ɼıom ɼo báttuɼ an tan ɼın, ⁊ táınıc aɼ a ccıonn aɼ an tɼlıʓıḃ, ⁊ aɼeḃ ɼo ɼáıḃ ɼıu, ba ċóɼa ꝺóıḃ toıḃeaċt ꝺá ḃoıċɼıom; Cıbınnıɼ ɼa ḃaoı ɼí, ına ımċſċt na haıḃċe ꝺoıɼċe ꝺoınınne. Aɼſḃ a ꝺuḃaıɼt an ɼí ⁊ a ṁuıṅtıɼ, ıɼ ꝼíoɼ aɼ cóɼa aɼ ɼıaꝺ, ⁊ aɼ maıċ lınn eꝺıɼ a ɼaḃa ɼınn. Tanʓattuɼ ıaɼ ɼın ꝺá ċaıʓ ⁊ ɼo ba moo méıꝺ an taıʓı ıoná a ɼaıḃḃɼe. Ꝺo ɼaꝺ ımuɼɼo Pıonnaċta buılle a ccıonn a ꝺaım, ⁊ buılle oıle a ʓcſnn na bó. Ro ıoɼlaṁaıʓɼıt muınnteɼ an ɼí ꝼéın ʓo tɼıc ⁊ ʓo tınnſɼꝺaċ ꝺo ḃıoɼ ⁊ ꝺo ċoıɼe, ⁊ ɼo ċaıċɼıoꝺ ʓuɼ ba ɼáıċıʓ. Ra coꝺlattuɼ ʓo maıċ ıaɼttaın ʓo ttáınıʓ an ṁaıꝺın. Ro ɼáıḃ ɼı ꝼꝼɼɼ Roɼ ɼa ṁnaoı ꝼéın ıɼ ın maıꝺın. Naċ ꝼetaɼ, a ḃſn, ʓéɼ bo ꝺaıḃḃıɼ a nallana an tſċɼa, conıꝺ ꝺaıḃḃɼe anoɼɼa, aɼ nıaɼḃaꝺ a aon bó ⁊ a aon ꝺaṁ ḃúınne. Aɼ ꝼıoɼ tɼa ɼın, aɼ an ḃſn. Aɼeḃ aɼ cóıɼ anoɼ a ɼaıḃḃɼıuʓaḃ uaınne. Cıbé méıꝺ laıʓſḃ ꝺo ḃéɼaꝼae ꝺon ꝼıoɼ ꝺo beɼɼa a cuttɼuma ꝺá ṁnaoı. Aɼ maıċ na naḃɼae, aɼ an ɼí. Ꝺo ɼaꝺ tɼa an ɼí aıɼʓe lán móɼ bó ⁊ muca ıomḃa ⁊ caoıɼıʓ co na mbuaċaıllıḃ ꝺ'Pıonnaċta. Ꝺo ɼaꝺ ꝺno bſn an ɼıʓ ꝺo ṁnaoı Pıonnaċta an cuttɼuma ċéꝺna. Ꝺo ɼaꝺɼaꝺ ꝺno éꝺaıʓe ɼaıneaṁla, ⁊ eıch maıċe ꝺóıḃ, aʓuɼ ʓaċ ní ɼanʓattuɼ a lſɼ ꝺon tɼaoʓal.

Níoɼ bo cıan ıaɼttaın tɼa ʓo ttáınıc Pıonaċta maɼcſluaʓ móɼ ꝺo ċoıʓ ɼſtaɼ ḃó, aɼ na ċuıɼeꝺ ꝺon tɼıaɼɼ, ⁊ ꝼɼıċaıʓıꝺ aıce ꝼaıɼ.

[h] *Fera-Ross.*—A tribe and territory comprising the county around Carrickma- cross, in the county of Monaghan, and a part of the county of Louth.

the King of Fera-Ros[b] happened to wander and stray in the neighbourhood of Finnachta's hut. There never was before a worse night than this for storm, and snow, and darkness, and the King and his wife, with their numerous people, were not able to reach the house which they desired to reach, in consequence of the intensity of the cold and the darkness; and their intention was to remain under the shelter of the trees. But Finnachta heard them express these intentions—for they were not far from his hut at the time—and he came to meet them on the way, and said to them that they had better come to his hut—such as it was—than to travel on that dark, stormy, cold night. And the King and his people said: "It is true it were better," said they, "and we are glad, indeed, that thou hast told us so." They afterwards came to his house; and the size of the house was greater than its wealth. Finnachta, moreover, struck the ox on the head, and struck the cow on the head, and the King's own people actively and quickly prepared them on spit and in cauldron, and they ate thereof till they were satiated. They slept well afterwards till the morning came. The King of Fera-Ros said to his own wife, "Knowest thou not, O woman, that this house was at first poor, and that it is now poorer, the owner having killed his only cow and his only ox for us?" "This is indeed true," said the wife: "and it behoves us now to enrich it; whatever much or little thou wilt give to the man, I will give the same amount to his wife." "Good is what thou sayest," said the King. The King then gave a large herd of cows, and many pigs and sheep, with their herdsmen, to Finnachta; and the King's wife gave the same amount to the wife of Finnachta. They also gave them fine clothes, and good horses, and whatever they stood in need of in the world.

It was not long after this until Finnachta came with a great troop of horse to the house of a sister of his, who had invited him, to be invited

ꞅaiꞃ. Aṅ ꞇaiḃeċꞇ ḋóiḃ na n-impiṁ, aꞃ ann ꝺo ꞃala ꝺo Aḋaṁnán na ꞃṡolaiże óṅ beiꞇ aṅ imꞇeċꞇ na ꞃliṅḟo céꝺna, ⁊ ballán lan ꝺo lomom aꞃ a ṁuin, ⁊ oṅ ꞇeicḃ ꝺo ꞃéꞃ an maꞃcꞃluaṅ ꝺon ꞇꞃliṅiḃ ꝺo ꞃala a ċoꞃ ꞃꞃia cloiċ, ⁊ ꞇoꞃċaiꞃ ꞃéin, ⁊ ꝺno an ballán ṅo noꞅꞃ-naḋ bꞃioꞃṅ bꞃuaꞃ ꝺe, ⁊ ṅéꞃ bo luaċ ꝺo na ɦeoċaiḃ níoꞃ bó nꞅṁ, luaiċe ꝺo Aḋaṁnán ṅo na ballan bꞃiꞃꞇe ꞃoꞃ a ṁuin, ⁊ ꞃé ꝺuḃaċ ꝺobꞃónaċ. O ꞃo conꝺaic Fionnaċꞇá é ꞃo maiḋ a ꞃaiꞇbiuḋ ṅáiꞃe ꞅaiꞃ, ⁊ ꞃo baoi ṅá ꞃaḋ ꞃe ɦAḋaṁnán, ꝺo ṅéna ꞃin ꞃúḃaċ ꝺíoꞇ, uaiꞃ aꞃum compaꞇénꞅeꞃa ꞃꞃia ṅaċ n-imnꞅḃ ꝺo cumanṅ: ꞃoṅeḃꞃa a ꞃoṅlainꞇiḋ, aꞃ Fionnaċꞇa coimꝺꞅoḃnaḋ uaimꞃi, ⁊ na bí ṅo ꝺuḃaċ. Aꞃeḋ ꞃo ꞃaiḋ Aḋaṁnán, a ꝺꞅṅ ꝺuine, aꞃ ꞅé, aꞇá aḋḃaꞃ ꝺuḃ aṅam, uaiꞃ ꞇꞃí meic léiṅinn maiċe aꞇaiꝺ a naoinꞇiṅ, ⁊ aꞇaimne ꝺá ṅiolla aca ⁊ aꞃeḋ ḃíoꞃ ṅiolla aꞃ ꞇiméioll uainn aṅ iaꞃꞃaiḋ bꞅċamnaiꞃ ꝺon ċoiṅioꞃ, ⁊ ꝺamꞃa ꞃáiniṅ iaꞃꞃaiḋ neiċe ꝺáiḃ aniu : ꞃá ċuaiḋ an ꞇioꞃḃalꞇa ꞃá ḃaoi aṅamꞃa ꝺóiḃ ꞃo láꞃ, aṅuꞃ an ní aꞃ ꝺoilṅe ann .i. an ballán iaꞃaċꞇa ꝺo ḃꞃiꞃioḋ, ⁊ ṅan a ꞅoc aṅom. 'Icꞃaꝺꞃa an ballán, aꞃ Finnaċꞇa, ⁊ ꞇuṅꞃa laꞇ an cuiṅꞅꞃ ꞃuil aꞃ ꝺo ꞃṅáꞇꞃa anoċꞇ ṅan ḃiaḋ ṅo nuiṅe an ꞇꞅċ ꝺ'á ꞇꞇiaṅaimne; ꞃo ṅeḃaiḋ biaḋ ⁊ lionn aṅainne. Oo ꞃiṅnꞅḃ aṁlaiḋ ꞅin, ꞇuṅꞃaꞇ an coiṅioꞃ cléiꞃꞅċ, ⁊ ꞃo coiꞃṅꞅḃ an ꞇꞅċ leanna, lꞅꞇ an ꞇoiṅe ꝺo cléꞃciḃ ⁊ an leꞇ aile ꝺo laoċaiḃ. Aiꞇe Aḋamnáin ꞃo líonaḋ é ó ꞃaċ an ꞃꞃioꞃaꝺ naoiḃ, ⁊ ꞃꞃiꞃiꞇ ꞃaiꞃꞇine, ⁊ aꞃeḋ ꞃo ꞃáiḋ: buḋ aiꞃoꞃí Eiꞃeann, aꞃ ꞅé, an ꞅꞃꞃ ꝺá ꞇꞇuṅaꝺ an ꞃliṅꞃa: ⁊ buḋ cꞅno cꞃaḃaiḋ ⁊ eaṅna Eiꞃꞅn Aḋaṁnán, ⁊ buḋ e anmċaꞃa Fionnaċꞇa, ⁊ biaiḋ Finnaċꞇa i ꞃꞅcꞇnaiṅe móiꞃ, co ꞃo oilbeimniṅ ꝺo Aḋaṁnán.

Níoꞃ

ᶜ *Broken vessel on his back.*—It appears from a passage in Bede's "Eccl. History," lib. iii., c. 27, that the sons of the Saxon nobility who were studying in Ireland in 646 "went about from one master's cell to another, the Scoti willingly receiving them all, and taking care to supply them with food, and to furnish them with books to read, and their teaching gratis." It is curious how much this re-

vited by him in his turn. As they rode along they met Adamnan, who was then a young school-boy, travelling the same road, having a vessel full of milk on his back; and as he ran off out of the way before the horsemen, his foot struck against a stone, and he fell with the vessel, which was broken to pieces, and, though the horsemen rode swiftly, they were not swifter than Adamnan with his broken vessel on his back^e, and he being sad and melancholy. When Finnachta perceived him, he burst into a fit of laughter, and he said to Adamnan: " That shall make thee glad, for I am willing to repair every injury in my power: thou shalt receive, O school-boy," said Finnachta, " shelter from me, and be not sorrowful." What Adamnan said was :—" O good man," said he, " I have cause for being melancholy, for there are three good school-boys in one house, and they have us as two messengers, and there is always one messenger going about seeking food for the five; and it came to my turn to-day to seek for them. The gathering I had fell to the ground, and, what I grieve for more, the borrowed vessel has been broken, and I have not wherewithal to pay for it." " I will pay for the vessel," said Finnachta ; " and do thou bring with thee the five who are without food depending on thee, to the house to which we are going, and you shall receive food and drink from us." This was done accordingly: the four clerics were brought; and the ale-house was prepared, half the house for clerics, and the other half for laics. The tutor of Adamnan was filled with the grace of the Holy Spirit, and with the spirit of prophecy, and he said: —" The man by whom this banquet is given shall be supreme monarch of Erin, and Adamnan shall be the head of the piety and wisdom of Erin, and he shall be the spiritual adviser of Finnachta, and Finnachta shall be in great repute until he shall offend Adamnan."

Not sembles the modern " poor scholar of our own times," who went about on foot, and was everywhere entertained by the Irish peasantry on account of his learning.

Níor bo cian d'aimṛir iar ṛin co ttáinic Ḟionnaċta ⁊ ṗi ḟḟṡi Ror a ċara ḟéin leiṛ d'ionnraiġiḋ ḃráṫar a aṫar, .i. Cionnṛaolaḋ, do iarṛaiḋ ḟṡainn ṛair. Do ṛaḋ Cṡnoṛaolaḋ áṛḋmoeṛaiġeaċt na Miḋi uile ó Sionuinn go ṛairge ḋo, .i. ar ċeiṫri ṫuaṫaiḃ riċt. Ro ḃaoi Ḟinaċta ṛṗi ṛe n-aimṛiṛe amlaiḋ ṛin. Táinic d'á coṁairle ṛṗi a ċaṛuiḋ ṛén .i. ṗi Ḟer Rorr, cia do ġénaḋ, uaiṛ níṛ ḃó loṛ laiṛ mar ṛo ḃoí. Do ṛaḋraiḋe dna coṁairle cṛuaiḋ cṛóḋa ḋó, ⁊ areḋ ro ṛáiḋ ṛir: Naċ ṛoinnṡḃ Sliġe Arail Miḋe ror ḋó? Oṡnara an dara leiṫ do'n Miḋe coror taiṛiri duṫṛaċtaċ duic, ⁊ mar ḃúṛ taiṛiṛi ḋuit an leṫ rin, dṡna comḋal ḟṛiṛ in lṡṫ eile, ⁊ marḃ a nḋṡġḋaoine a ruinn caṫa raiḋe, ⁊ ní namá biar lainṛiġe na Miḋe aġat, aċt biaiḋ ciḋ ṛiġe Tṡmṛaċ beór, máḋ ail lṡt. Do ṛiġne iarraṁ Ḟionnaċta an comairle ṛin, ⁊ ṛa ṛuaġaiṛ caṫ iar rin ror ḃráṫaiṛ a aṫar .i. for Cṡnoṛaolaḋ. O do cuala ḃṡn Cinḋṛaolaḋ rin ro ḃoí aġ béim ror a ḟṡi 'man maoraiġeaċt do ṛaḋ d'Ḟinaċta; ar ann ro ċan an ḃṡn: Ra iaḋraḋ, ut ruṛra. Do ṛaḋaḋ caṫ go cṛuaiḋ cṛóḋa ṡtoṛṛa iar rin .i. eiḋir Cionnṛaolaḋ ⁊ Ḟionnaċta i n-Aircealltra, ⁊ ro marḃaḋ Cinḋṛaolaḋ ann ⁊ roċaiḋe maille ṛṛiṛ. Ro ġaḃ Ḟionnaċta iar rin ṛiġe n-Eirṡnn ṛa ṛicio bliaḋain.

Ar é an Ḟionnaċta rin ro ṁaiṫ an mborama do Moling, ar na toḃaċ la cṡtraċaiḋ ṛí ṛeṁi rin anall, .i. ó Thuaṫal Tṡċtmar

50

ᵃ *Sinainn.*—i. e. the River Shannon. Ancient Meath extended from the River Shannon to the sea.

ᵉ *Slighe-Asail.*—An ancient road extending from the Hill of Tara in the direction of Lough Owel and the Shannon. It divided ancient Meath into two equal parts, not east and west, as at present, but north and south. See Ann. Four M.,

A. D. 157, p. 104.
ᶠ *Ut supra.*—See above, under A. D. 675.
ᵍ *Twenty years.*—This is correct. He succeeded in 675, and was slain 14th Nov., 695.
ʰ *Borumha.*—This was an exorbitant tax, said to have been originally imposed on the Leinster-men by the monarch Tua-

Not long after this, Finnachta and his friend the King of Fera-Ros came to his father's brother, Cennfaeladh, to ask land of him, and Cennfaeladh gave him the head stewardship of all Meath from the Sinainn[d] to the sea, i. e. over twenty-four territories. Finnachta was thus situated for some time. He came to consult with his own friend, the King of Fera-Ros, as to what he should do, for he was not satisfied with his station. His friend gave him a hard and wicked advice, and he said to him : " Does not Slighe-Asail[e] divide Meath into two equal parts ? Make thou one half of Meath faithfully loyal to thee; and when this half is loyal to thee, appoint a meeting with the other half, and kill their chieftains who are their leaders in battle, and thou shalt not only have the full sovereignty of Meath, but also of Teamhair, if thou wilt." Finnachta followed this advice ; and he afterwards challenged his father's brother to battle, viz. Cennfaeladh. When Cennfacladh's wife heard this, she was reproaching her husband for having given the stewardship of Meath to Finnachta. It was then the woman sung : " There closed," &c., *ut supra*[f]. After this a battle was vigorously and bravely fought between them; viz. between Cennfaeladh and Finnachta, at Aircealtra, where Cennfacladh and numbers of others were slain along with him; after which Finnachta assumed the monarchy of Erin [and reigned] twenty years[g].

It was this Finnachta that remitted the Borumha[h] to Moling after it had been levied during the reigns of forty kings previously, viz. from

thal Techtmhar in the second century. It was the cause of many battles, but was at at length remitted by Finnachta at the request of St. Moling, who is represented in the text as having deceived him by a mental reservation. See Ann. F. M.,

696, p. 298. Acts of this kind attributed to the Irish saints, as if laudable, by their biographers, are a curious evidence of the rudeness of the times, and have been censured by the earlier Bollandists in the severest terms.

go Pionnacṫa, Ṫáiniġ iaraṁ Moling ó Laiġniḃ uile d'iarraiḋ maiṫme na boroṁa ror Pionnacṫa. Rá iarr ṫra Moling ar Pinnacṫa maiṫim na boroṁa rria lá ⁊ aiḋċe. Rá ṁaiṫ iaraṁ Pinacṫa an boroṁa rria la ⁊ aiḋċe. Rob ionann aġ Moling rin aġar a maiṫiṁ ṫre bíṫe : uair ní ffuil 'ran aimrir aċṫ lo ⁊ aiḋċe. bá ḋoiġ imurro la Pinnacṫa ar aon lo ⁊ aon aiḋċe namá. Ṫáiniġ Moling reiṁe amaċ, ⁊ arḃ ro ráiḋ; Ṫuġair cáirḋe imre ṫré bíṫe ⁊ ané; ro ġeall Moling nḟṁ ḋPionnacṫa. Ro ċuiġ ḋno Pinacṫa ġur ro ṁeall Moling é, ⁊ aḋrubairṫ rria a ṁuinṫir : eirġíḃ ar ré i norġaiḋ an ḋuine naoiṁ ḋo ċuaiḋ uaim, ⁊ abraiḋ rir naċ ṫṫuġura aċṫ cáirḋe aon laoi ⁊ aon aiḋċe ḃó; uair an ḋar lṁ, ro meall an ḋuine naoṁ mé, uair ní ffuil aċṫ la ⁊ aḋaiġ ir in mbioṫ uile. O ro rioir Moling imurro ġo ṫṫiocraiḋe na ḋġhaiḋ rá rioṫ ġo ṫric ṫinnearnaċ ġo ráiniġ a éṡ, ⁊ ní ruġraḋ ioir muinṫir an rí rair.

Aḋ beiraiḋ araile ġo ruġ Moling ḋuan lair ḋ'Pionnachta .i. Pionnacṫa ror Uiḃ Néill ⊤ċ (aṫá rin 'rin boroṁa 'rin lioburra rġriobṫa). Ro maiṫḃ ṫra an boroma ḋo Moling ó rin ġo bráṫ, ⁊ ciar bo haiṫreaċ la Pionnacṫa níor rḃ a ṫoḃaċ, uair ar ḋo ċionn niṁe ro ṁaiṫ. Eṫ hoc erṫ uerrur.

In ṙuº. anno ab hoc anno ro ṁaiṫ Pionnacṫa an boruṁa ṫainiġ Aḋaṁnán fó céḋóir ḋ'ionnraiġiḋ Pinacṫa ṫar éir Moling, ⁊ ro ċuir clépeaċ ḋ'á muinnṫir ar cionn Pionnacṫa ġo ṫṫíoraḋ ḋa aġ allaṁ. Ar ann ro boí Pinnacṫa aġ imirṫ riṫċille. Ṫair ḋ'aġallaṁ Aḋaṁnáin, ar an clépeaċ. Ní raċaḋ ġo ḋṫair an cluiċi ri, ar

---

[1] *The book called the Borumha.*—There is a copy of this historical tract preserved in the Book of Lecan, and another in Trinity College, Dublin, H. 2, 18. See Ann. F. M., A.D. 106, p. 100. It is much in the style of this story, but less modernized. It is interspersed with quotations from ancient Irish poems adduced in proof of the historical facts related by its author.

from Tuathal Techtmhar, to Finnachta. Moling came [as an ambassador] from all Leinster to request a remission of the Borumha from Finnachta. Moling asked of Finnachta to forgive the Borumha for a day and a night. Finnachta forgave the Borumha for a day and a night. This to Moling was the same as to forgive it for ever, for there is not in time but day and night. But Finnachta thought it was one [natural] day and night. Moling came forth before him, and said : " Thou hast given a respite respecting it for ever, and yesterday ;" Moling promised heaven to Finnachta. But Finnachta conceived that Moling had deceived him, and he said to his people : "Go," said he, " in pursuit of this holy man, who has gone away from me, and say unto him that I have not given respite for the Borumha, to him, but for one day and one night, for methinks the holy man has deceived me, for there is but one day and one night in the whole world." But when Moling knew that they were coming in pursuit of him, he ran actively and hastily till he reached his house, and the people of the King did not come up with him at all.

Others say that Moling brought a poem with him to Finnachta, beginning : " Finnachta over the Race of Niall," &c. (and this poem is written in the book called the Borumha)[i]. However, the Borumha was forgiven to Moling from that till judgment; and though Finnachta was sorry for it, he was not able to levy it, for it was for the sake of [obtaining] heaven he had remitted it. *Et hoc est verius.*

In the fifteenth year from the year in which Finnachta had forgiven the Borumha, Adamnan came to Finnachta after Moling, and he sent a cleric of his people to Finnachta that he might come to converse with him. Finnachta was then playing chess. " Come to converse with Adamnan," said the cleric. " I will not till this game is finished," said Finnachta. The cleric returned to Adamnan, and told him the answer of Finnachta. " Go thou to him, and say to him

ap Pionnacca. Táinig an clépeac o'ionnroigio Aoamnain, ⁊ po
innip ppígpa Pionnacta oó. Eipgio-pi oa ionnpoigio piom, ⁊ abaip
pip: gebao-pa caogao palm anaippo pin, ⁊ atá palm 'pan caogaio
pin, ⁊ guiopío-pa an coimoío pin tpalmpain conac geba mac na
ua ouitpi no pípi oo comanma go bpát pige n-'Eipenn. Ra cuaio
ono an clépeac, ⁊ po páio pe Pionnacta pin, ⁊ ní tapao Pionnacta
oa uioe, act po imbipi a pitcill go ttappaig an cluice. Taip
o'agallam Aoamnáin, a Pionnacta, ap an clépeac. Ni pag, ap
Pionnacta, go ttaip an cluicipi. Ro innip an clépeac pain oo
Aoamnán. Abaippi fpippiom, ap Aoamnán, gebaopa caogao
palm an aippo pin, ⁊ atá palm 'pan caogaio pin, ⁊ iappipaopa ipin
palm pin, ⁊ cuingpíopa ap an ccoimoío gaipoe paogail oopam.
Ra innip an clépeac pin o'Pinacoa, ⁊ ní tapao Pionnacta oa
paoioe, act pa imbip a pitcill go ttappaig an cluice. Taip
o'agallao Aoamnáin, ap an clépeac. Ní pag ap Pionnacta go
ttaip an cluicipi. Táinic an clépeac, ⁊ pa innip oo Aoamnán
fpeagpa Pionnacta. Eipgpi oá ionnpoigio, ap Aoamnán, ⁊ abaip
fpip, gebaopa an tpíp caogao, ⁊ ata palm 'pan caogaio pin, ⁊
guiopíopa an coimoío 'pan tpalm pain na puigipiom plaitiup nime.
Táinic an clépec peme go Pionnacta, ⁊ pa innip pin. Map po
cuala Pinnacta pain po cuip an pitcill go hobann uao, ⁊ táinic
o'ionnpoigio Aoamnáin. Ci oou tug annopa cugam, ap Aoamnán, ⁊ na ttángaip pip na tettaipeactaib eile? Apeo po oepa
oam, ap Pionnacta, an tomaoioío oo poinip peme po oipm .i. gan
mac na ua uaim oo gabáil pige, ⁊ gan peap mo comanma i pige
n-Eipínn, no gaipoe paogail oam; eopom popiom paio, an tan
imuppo po geallaipi ním oo gaio fopm, ap uime tánag go hobann
uo o'agallaopi; uaip ní ppuil a pulaingpaioe agam-pa.
An píop, ap Aoamnan an bhopama oo maiteann ouit lá ⁊
aioce oo Moling? Ap píop, ap Pionnacta. Ro meallao tu, ap
Aoamnan,

him that I shall sing fifty psalms during that time, and that there is a psalm among that fifty in which I shall pray the Lord that a son or grandson of his, or a man of his name, may never assume the sovereignty of Erin." The cleric accordingly went and told that to Finnachta, but Finnachta took no notice, but played at his chess till the game was finished. "Come to converse with Adamnan, O Finnachta!" said the cleric. "I will not go," said Finnachta, "till this [next] game is finished." The cleric told this to Adamnan. "Say unto him," said Adamnan, "that I will sing fifty psalms during that time, and that there is a psalm among that fifty in which I will ask and beseech the Lord to shorten his life for him." The cleric told this to Finnachta, but Finnachta took no notice of it, but played away at his chess till the game was finished. "Come to converse with Adamnan," said the cleric. "I will not," said Finnachta, "till this game is finished." The cleric told to Adamnan the answer of Finnachta. "Go to him," said Adamnan, "and tell him that I will sing the third fifty psalms, and that there is a psalm in that fifty in which I will beseech the Lord that he may not obtain the kingdom of heaven." The cleric came to Finnachta and told him this. When Finnachta heard this, he suddenly put away the chess from him, and he came to Adamnan. "What has brought thee to me now, and why didst thou not come at the other messages?" "What induced me to come," said Finnachta, "was the threats which thou didst hold forth to me, viz., that no son or grandson of mine should ever reign, and that no man of my name should ever assume the sovereignty of Erin, or that I should have shortness of life. I deemed these [threats] light; but when thou didst promise me to take away heaven from me, I then came suddenly, because I cannot endure this."

"Is it true," said Adamnan, "that the Borumha was remitted by thee for a day and a night to Moling?" "It is true," said Finnachta.
M "Thou

Aḋamnán, aṙ ionann ṙin ⁊ a maiṫṁ ṫṙé ḃiṫe, ⁊ aṙ aṁlaiḋ ṙo ḃoí
ɡa aṫṫoṙṙán, ⁊ ṙo ṙáiḋ an laoiḋ:—

Aniu ɡe cíṅɡlaiḋ cuaṫa an ṙí cṙinléiṫ ɡan ḋéḃa,
An buaṙ ḋo ṁaiṫ ḋo Moliṅɡ ḃeṫḃiṙ ḋon ciṅɡ niṙ ṙéḃa;
Ḃamaḋ miṙi Ṗionnaṫṫa, ṙɡo maḃ mé ṗlaiṫ Ṫeṁṙa,
Ɡo ḃṙáṫ noṫa aṫṫiḃeṙainn, ní ḋinɡenainn a noṫṙna.
Ɡaṫ ṙí naṫ maiṫṫṅn a ṫiuṙ aṙ ṙaḃa ḃíḋ a ṙɡéla.
Maiṙɡ ḋo ṙaḋ an ḃail, an ṫí aṙ laɡ aṙ ḋo aṙ méla.
Ḃo aṙnaṫṫaṙ ḋo ṙaoṙa, aṙ an baoṙa ɡo mbinne,
Maiṙɡ ṙiɡ ṙo ṁaiṫ a ṫiuṙa, a loṙa nímḃa niṁe.
Soṫla ɡaṫ nṫṫ o ṫṙeaḃuṙ, aṙ maiṙɡ lṁaṙ ḋo liaṫa,
Aṙ ṙaḃa an ḃalṙa macaiṫe, ba ṙaiṫe ɡomba ṙiaṫa.
Ḃáṁṙa ṙíṙi ṙuaḃuṙ cṙu, ṙo ṫaiṙnṙinn mo ḃíoḋḃaḋa
Ro ṫoiɡeḃainn mo ḋionɡna, ṙobṙaṫ iomḃa m'ioṙġala
Roboíṙ iomḃa m'ioṙġala, mo bṙiaṫṙa niḃoiṙ ɡuaṫa.
Roboíṙ ṙíoṙa mo ḋala, ṙoboíṙ lána mo ṫuaṫa.
Roboíṙ iomṙoiɡṙi m'aiṙḋe, mo ḋala ṙoboíṙ ḋninɡne.
An ḃál ṙa, cia ciam ba ṫecmaiṅɡ, ní léṫṙaiñ ṙe Laiġne.
Ɡuiḋimṙi iṫɡe ṙoṙi Ḃhia, naṫum ṫaiṙ báṙ no baoġal,
Ɡuṙ ṙo ṫeṙno aniu Moliṅɡ, ní ḋṫṫ ḋo ṙinn no ḋṙaoḃaṙ.
Mac Ṗaillen ṙíṙ ḋaṙ ṁ, ní claiṙiḋíṙ ḋaṙa maṙa.

Ro

ᵏ *Thou hast been deceived.*—This story is found in the tract called the "Borumha Laighen," but the antiquity of that tract, in its present form, cannot be very great. A writer in the "Dublin University Magazine" for Feb., 1848, p. 225, says "that it would have been better for the people of Leinster to have continued to pay the Borumean tribute to this day than that their St. Moling should have set an example of clerical special pleading and mental reservation, in the equivocation by which he is represented to have procured their release from that impost." The whole story is, however, a mere bardic fiction as regards Adamnan and Moling; but it must be confessed that it was universally read and received as true in ancient times by the people of Leinster and Ulster, and must have exercised a

"Thou hast been deceived"[k], said Adamnan, "for this is the same as to remit it for ever." And he went on scolding him, and sung the lay:—

> To-day, though they bind the locks of the white-haired toothless King,
> The cows which he forgave to Moling are due to a wiser head.
> If I were Finnachta[1], and that I were chief of Teamhair,
> Never would I forgive it; I would not do what he has done.
> Of every king who remits not his tribute, long shall the stories remain.
> Woe to him who gave this respite; to the weak it is sorrow!
> Thy wisdom has ended, and given way to folly.
> Alas for the King who forgave his tributes, O heavenly Jesus of heaven!
> Weak is every one who is anile; woe! who follow grey-beards!
> Long is this bargain to last; longer till the debts are due!
> Were I a king who sheds blood, I would humble my enemies,
> I would raise up my fortresses, many would be my conflicts.
> Many would be my conflicts: my words would not be false.
> Just would be my compacts, full would be my territories.
> Visible would be my qualities, firm would be my treaties.
> This treaty should it happen to me, I would not cede to Leinster-men.
> I ask a petition from God, that death or danger may not overtake me,
> That Moling may this day escape, may he not perish by point or edge [of weapon].
> Mac Faillen, from beyond the sea, will not be driven over sea.

He

---

demoralizing effect upon their minds.

[1] *If I were Finnachta.*—These lines were evidently fabricated by some warlike poet who wished to stimulate the race of Tuathal to renew this tribute. In one of the poems addressed to Turlough Luinech O'Neill, he is advised to renew the Borumha.

84

Ro ḟioip puna mic Dé, po ḟioip mac Dé apúna.
Cpí caoṡaiḋ palm ṡaċ Dia, apeḋ ṡeḃiup ap Dliia.
Cpí caoṡaiḋ boċt peolpoipċe, apeḋ biaċup ṡaċ noíḋċe.
An bile buaḋa bipiṡ, an pipiḋ ṡup na pḟppaiḃ
Long lḟpḋa po puaip ḟáilce, conn beapḋa baipce Ḃpeapail,
An lon óip ap an inne, an cláp óip op na clannaib,
'Eiṡne Duḃṡlaipi ḋuinne, puaim coinne conn pipia halla. Aniu.

Ro ċapinn cpa iap pin Pionnaċta a ċḟin a n-uċt Aḋaṁnáin,
⁊ ḋo piṡne aiċpiṡe 'na ḟiaḋnaipi, ⁊ po loṡ Aḋamnan ḋo maiċḟin na
ḃopaṁa.

Ral. Mopp Colṡan mic Pailḃe Plainn, pí Muman. Caċ eḋip
huiḃ Cinnpilaiṡ ⁊ Oppaiṡiḃ, in quo Cuaim pnáṁa .i. Cícaipe, pí
Oppaiṡe occipup epc. Paolán Sḟncupcul, pí hUa cCinnpiolaiṡ
uiccop puic. Unḋc—

An caċ la Cuaim pnáṁa níp éiḋip [.i. níp ba éiḋip]
Diambepc peaċċup naḋ ecail [.i. naḋpcoil leip a ċaḃaipc]
Paolan cáipḋe ap éiṡin

Dó

ᵐ *Berbha*.—i. e. the River Barrow, on the banks of which St. Moling erected his monastery. Breasal, here referred to, was Breasal Breac, one of the Pagan kings of Leinster, who is much celebrated by the Irish poets for his naval exploits. He is the ancestor of all the great families of Leinster and Ossory. See Reeves's "Eccl. Antiq. of Down, Connor, and Dromore," p. 200.

ⁿ *Dubhghlaise*.—Now Douglas, a stream in the east of the Queen's County, which falls into the River Barrow.

ᵒ *Forgave him*.—Finnachta had committed a great sin against the race of Tuathal by forgiving the Borumean tribute to gain heaven for himself, or by allowing himself to be outwitted by St. Moling. To remit the Borumha in order to gain heaven for himself was doubtless to deprive the race of Tuathal Techtmhar of a great revenue for a selfish purpose; but to allow himself to be outwitted by St. Moling was scarcely a sin on the part of the King, for it appears that Finnachta had no notion of remitting the Borumha at all. He merely promised to stay the levying of it for one natural day and night, which St. Moling, by a kind of logic not very intelligible, interpreted to mean *for ever*, and this interpretation Adamnan

He knows the secrets of the Son of God; the Son of God knows his secrets.
Thrice fifty psalms each day he sings to God;
Thrice fifty paupers, worthy deed, he feeds each night.
The virtuous, productive tree, the seer with the visions,
The foreign ship which has found welcome,
The wave of Berbha[m] of the ship of Breasal,
The golden treasure from the centre, the golden board over the tribes,
The salmon of the brown Dubhghlaise[n], the wave-sound, the wave against the cliff.

After this Finnachta placed his head in the bosom of Adamnan, and he did penance in his presence, and Adamnan forgave him[o] for the remission of the Borumha.

[678.] Kal. The death of Colgu[p], son of Failbhe Flann, King of Munster. A battle [was fought] between the Ui-Ceinnseallaigh and the Osraighi, in which Tuaim-snamha, i. e. Cicaire, King of Osraighe, was slain. Faelan Senchustal, King of Ui-Ceinnsealaigh, was the victor. On which was said :—

The battle by Tuaim-snamha could not be gained[q];
Which he fought against his will,
Faelan respite, with difficulty,

To

is represented as having approved of. In the historical tract called the "Borumean Tribute," St. Moling is represented as requesting the King to forgive the Borumha till *Luan*, i. e. Monday, in the ordinary sense of the word, but it appears that Luan also meant the Day of Judgment; and St. Moling insisted on this being the true meaning of the word as used in the compact between him and the head of the

race of Tuathal Techtmhar on this occasion, although the latter had no idea that the word was to be used in that sense. See Ann. F. M., A. D. 106, p. 99, and A. D. 593, p. 216, *et seq.*

[p] *Colgu.*—A. D. 677. "Toimsnama, *rex* Osraigi, *quievit. Mors* Colggen mic Failbei Flainn, *regis* Muman."—*Ann. Ult.*

[q] *Gained.*—The words within brackets in the Irish text are given as a gloss over

Dó dor nad ro cormaile ba bnaċ a bronnad
Ꙁo ccuꙅ ꙅialla Orraiꙅe o ċa buana ꙅo Cuman.
Caċ Dúin loċa. Caċ Liaꙅ Maoláin. Caċ i Calatror in quo uiccur erc Domnall breac. Faolan (.i. dalta Caoimꙅin) mac Colmain, rí Laiꙅean moricur.
Quier Failbe ab lae.
Kal. Caċ etir Fionnaċta ⁊ becc mboirċe. Incipit Fianamail reꙅnare ror Laiꙅnib.
Kal. Colman ab bfnnċair quieuit.
Lorꙅad na rioꙅ i nDun Ceitirn .i. Dunꙅal mac Sꙅanail, ri Cruitne, ⁊ Cfnnfaolad mac Suibne, ri Ciannaċta Ꙁlinne Ꙁaimin; la Maolduin mac Maolfitriꙅ ro lorꙅad.
Ciar inꙅfn Duibrea.
Kal. Ꙁuin Cinnfaolaid mic Colꙅain, rí Connaċt.
Caċ Raċa móire Maiꙅe line fri breaċnu, du i ttorċair Caċurać mac Maolduin, rí Cruitne, ⁊ Ulcán mac Diocolla.

Morr

nir eidir and na decail respectively.

' *From Buana to Cumor.*—This is probably a mistake for, "from Bladma to Cumar," i. e. from Slieve Bloom to the Cumar, or Meeting of the Three Waters, which was the extent of the ancient Ossory, and is still that of the diocese of Ossory.

* *Dun-locha.*—Probably Dunloe, in the county of Kerry. This entry, and the following, are not to be found in any of the other Annals.

' *Liag-Maelain.*—Not identified.

" *Calatros.*—A place in the west of Scotland. See Reeves' "Adamnan," p. 123, and Ann. Ult., A. D. 677. Domhnall Brec was King of Scotland.

' *Faelan.*—His death is entered in the Ann. Clonm. at the year 663, and in the F. M. at 665. St. Caoimhghin, the tutor of this king, died in the year 618.

* *Failbhe.*—Ann. Ult. 678, Tigh. 679. He was the immediate predecessor of Adamnan, who makes a distinct allusion to him in his "Vit. Columbæ," lib. i., c. 3 (Reeves, p. 26).

' *Bec Boirche.*—"A.D.678, Bellum contra Bec mBoirche."—*Ann. Ult. Tigh.* 679.

' *Colman.*—"A.D. 679[*Tigh.*680]. Colman, abbas Benchair, pausat."—*Ann. Ult.*

' *Dun Ceithirn.* — Now called the Giant's Sconce. It is an ancient cyclopean fort situate in the parish of Dunbo,

To him gave, in appearance, his grant was betrayal,
So that he took the hostages of Osraighe from Buana to Cumor[r].

The battle of Dun-locha[s]. The battle of Liag-Maelain[t]. A battle was fought in Calatros[u], in which Domhnall Breac was conquered. Faelan[v] (the alumnus of Caimhghin), son of Colman, King of Leinster, died.

[679.] The death of Failbhe[x], Abbot of Ia.

Kal. A battle between Finnachta and Bec Boirche[y]. Fianamhail began to reign over Leinster.

[680.] Kal. Colman[z], Abbot of Benchair, died.

[681.] The burning of the kings in Dun-Ccithirn[a], i. e. Dunghal, son of Sgannal, King of the Cruithni, Cennfaeladh, son of Suibhne, King of Cianacta-Glinne Gaimhin[b]; by Maelduin, son of Maelfithrigh, they were burnt.

Ciar[c], daughter of Duibhrea.

[682.] Kal. The killing of Cennfaeladh[d], son of Colgan, King of Connaught.

The battle of Rath-mor of Magh-line[e] against the Britons, in which were slain Cathasach, son of Maelduin, King of the Cruithni[f], and Ultan, son of Dicolla.

The

in the north of the county of Londonderry. "A. D. 680 [*Tigh.* 681.] Combustio Regum in Dun-Ccithirn," &c.—*Ann. Ult.*

[b] *Ciannachta-Glinne Gaimhin.* — Now the barony of Keenaght, in the present county of Londonderry.

[c] *Ciar.*—She is the patroness of the parish of Kilkeary, in the barony of Upper Ormond, county of Tipperary. See Colgan's Acta SS., p. 14–16, at 6th January, and Ann. F. M., A. D. 679; Tigh. 681.

[d] *Cennfaeladh.*—A. D. 681 [*Tigh.* 682]. Jugulatio Cinnfaela mic Colgen, regis Connacie."—*Ann. Ult.*

[e] *Rathmor of Magh-line.*—Now Rathmore, a townland containing the remains of a large earthen rath with a cave, situate in the parish of Donegore, near the town of Antrim. See Ann. F. M., A. D. 680.

[f] *Cruithni.*—i. e. the Picts of Dalaradia.

Mopp Suibne mic Maeluma ppincepip Copcaiġe [¹. ponτipicip Copcaġienpip].

Ƙal. Ðunchað Muipipġe mac Maoilðuib iuġulaτup epτ.

Aðamnan ðo ġabail abðaine lae.

Caτ Copainn i ττopchaip Colġa mac blaτmaic, ⁊ Ƒſpġup mac Maolðúin, pi Cineil Caippne.

Iniτium mopτaliτaτip puepopum in τenpe Oτδopιp, quae puiτ τpibup annip in hibepnia.

Quiep Aipmſðaiġ na Cpaibe.

Ƙal. Mopτaliτap piliopum in qua omnep ppincipep eτ pepe omnep nobilep iuuenum Sτoτopum pepiepunτ.

Ƙal. Saxonep campum bpeaġh ðeuapτanτ, eτ plupimap Ecclepia.

Ƙal. Ðomnall bpeac mac Eaċaċ buiðe mopτuup epτ.

Quiep banbáin pġpiba Cille ðapa.

Ƙal. Quiep Ðoċuma Chonoc, ab ġlinne ða loċa.

Quiep Roipene ab Copcaiġe.

Ip in bliaðain pi po puaplaiġ Aðamnán an bpaið puġpað Saxoin a hEipinn.

Caτ Ðuin Neaċτain iττip mac Oſſa, ⁊ bpuiτe mac bile uicτop puiτ [pic].

Sancτa

ᶠ *Suibhne.*— Ann. Ult. 681 ; Tigh. 682.

ʰ *Cork.*—The words in brackets in the Text are written as a gloss over the words "Princcpis [*sic*] Corcaighe."

ⁱ *Dunchadh Muirisge.*—Ann. Ult. 682 ; Tigh. 683 ; F. M. 681.

ᵏ *Adamnan.*—This entry is out of place here. It should have been inserted after the death of Failbhe, A. D. 679. See Reeves's "Adamnan," page xliv.

ˡ *The battle of Corann.*—Ann. F. M. 681 ; Ann. Ult. 682 ; Tigh. 683.

ᵐ *Mortality of children.*—Ann. Ult. 682 ; Tigh. 683 ; Brut y Tywysog. and Ann. Cambr. 683.

ⁿ *Airmeadhach of Craebh.*—i. e. Abbot of *Craebh Laisre*, a place near Clonmacnoise. Ann. Ult. 682 ; F. M. 681 ; Tigh. 683.

The death of Suibhne[e], son of Maelumha, prince [i.e. abbot] of Cork[h].
[683.] Kal. Dunchadh Muirisge[i], son of Maeldubh, was killed. Adamnan[k] assumed the abbacy of Ia.
The battle of Corann[l], in which were slain Colga, son of Blathmac, and Fergus, son of Maelduin, King of Cinel-Cairbre.
The beginning of the mortality of children[m] in the month of October, which continued for three years in Ireland.
The repose of Airmeadhach of Craebh[n].
[684.] Kal. The mortality of the children, in which all the princes and almost all the nobles of the youth of the Scoti perished.
[685.] Kal. The Saxons[o] devastated the plain of Breagh, and many churches.
[686.] Kal. Domhnall Breac, son of Eochaidh Buidhe [King of Scotland], died.
The repose of Banbhan[p], scribe of Cill-dara.
[687] Kal. The repose of Dochuma Chonoc[q], Abbot of Gleann-da-locha.
The repose of Roisene[r], Abbot of Corcach.
In this year Adamnan ransomed the captives[s] whom the Saxons had carried away from Erin.
The battle of Dun Neachtain[t], between the son of Ossa and Bruide[u], son of Bile, in which the latter was the victor.

The

[o] *The Saxons.*—Ann. Ult. 684; Tigh. 685; Ann. F. M. 683; Saxon Chron. 684.
[p] *Banbhan.*—Ann. Ult. 685; Tigh. 686.
[q] *Dochuma Chonoy.*—Ann. Ult. 686; Tigh. 687.
[r] *Roisene.* — " A. D. 686 [*Tigh.* 687]. Dormitatio Rosseni, abbatis Corcaidhe mare"[great Cork: *mare* for *móre*].—*Ann. Ult.*

[s] *Ransomed the captives.*—A. D. 686, or 687, Ann. Ult., and 689, Tigh. See Reeves's "Adamnan," pp. 186, 187, notes.
[t] *Dun Neachtain.*—Now Dunnichen, a parish in Forfarshire. The Ann. Ult. 685, and Tigh. 686, say that this battle was fought on Saturday, 20th May, which agrees with 685. See Sax. Chron. 685.
[u] *Bruide.*—He was King of the Picts;

Sancta Ederdrida, Chriſti regina, filia Annae regis Anglorum, et primo et alteri uiro permagnifico, et poſtea Ederfrido
regi, coniux data eſt; poſtquam xii anno thorum incorrupta
reruauit maritalem poſt reginam rumpto uelamine racro uirgo
ranctimonialiſ efficitur, quae poſt xui. repultuſae cum uerte
qua inoluta eſt incorrupta repericur.

A. D. 686. Kal. Cat Imbleacha Phích, ı ttorchaıſ Dubdáin-
bſr, rı Arda Cıannacta, ⁊ Uarcraıte hUa Oırrın: unde Jabor-
cſnn cecinit:—

Brónac Conaıllı moıu detbır dóıb ıar n-Uarcrıdıu,
Ní ba eallma bıar ſŋ, ı n-ard ıar n-Dubda ındſr.

In hoc bello alienam patienſ dominationem Cıannachtea
ſenſ rrıuata eſt reſno.

Seſıne Err ab Ardmacha.

Cutbertuſ Err quıeuit.

Cana mac Jartnaın moritur. Conrtantınuſ Imperator
moritur.

Kal.

"Rex Fortrenn;" Tigh. 686; Ult. 685.
Ecfrid, son of Ossa (i. e. Ecgfrith, son of
Oswin) is called King of the Saxons.
Reeves's "Adamnan," p. 186, note. Lap-
penberg (Hist. of Engl.). "Geneal. of the
Kings of Bernicia," vol. i., 289 (Thorpe's
Transl.).

ʸ *Etheldrida.*—Or Aedilthryd. Bede,
"Eccl. Hist.," lib. iv., c. 19. She is often
called St. Audry in England. She died A.D.
679, according to the Saxon Chronicle.

ᶻ *Ethelfrid.*—More correctly Ecgfrid, or
Ecgfrith. He was King of Northumbria.
This paragraph is extracted from Bede's

Chron. sive de sex ætatibus sæculi, A.D. 688
(Works, ed. Giles, vol. vi., p. 327), and is
very corruptly transcribed. Bede's words
are: "Sancta et perpetua virgo Christi
Ædilthryda, filia Annæ regis Anglorum,
et primo alteri viro permagnifico, et post
Ecfrido regi conjunx data, post quam xii.
annos thorum incorrupta servavit maritalem, post reginam sumpto velamine sacro
virgo sanctimonialis efficitur: nec mora
etiam virginum mater et nutrix pia sanc-
tarum, accepto in construendum monasto-
rium loco quem Elge vocant: cujus merita
vivacia testatur etiam mortua caro, quæ

The Queen of Christ, St. Etheldrida[y], daughter of Anna, King of the [East] Angles, who had been first given in marriage to another nobleman, and afterwards to King Ethelfrid[x]; after she had preserved her marriage-bed incorrupted for twelve years, the holy virgin, after she had become Queen, took the sacred veil, and became a nun; who sixteen years after her interment was found uncorrupted, as well as the shroud in which she had been wrapt.

[687.] A.D. 686. The battle of Imblech Phich[y], in which were slain Dubhdainbher, King of Ard-Cianachta[z], and Urchraithe Ua h-Ossin[a]; whence Gabhorchenn cecinit :—

Sorrowful are the Conailli this day; they have cause after Uarcraithe.
Not in readiness shall be the sword in Ard, after Dubhdainbher.

In this battle the race of the Cianachta passed under the dominion of another family, and was deprived of its power.

Segine[b], Bishop, Abbot of Ard-macha [died].
Cuthbertus, bishop, quievit.
Cana[c], son of Gartnan, died.   Constantine, the Emperor, died.
[689.]

post xvi. annos sepulturæ cum veste qua involuta est incorrupta reperitur."
  [y] *Imblech Phich.* — Now Emlagh, near Kells, county of Meath. Ann. F. M. 686; Ann. Ult. 687; Tigh. 688.
  [z] *Ard Cianachta.*—Now the barony of Ferrard, Co. Louth. The Cianachta were of the race of Cian, son of Oilioll Olum, King of Munster. Tadhg, son of Cian, obtained this territory in the third century from Cormac Mac Airt, King of Ireland; the district extended from the River Liffey

to near Drumiskin, Co. Louth.
  [a] *Urchraidhe Ua h-Ossin.*—"Huarcride nepos Osseni."—Ann. Ult. 687. "Uarcridhe hUa hOssine, righ Conaille."— Tigh. 688. See F. M. at A.D. 686.
  [b] *Segine.*—F. M. 686; Ann. Ult. 687; Tigh. 688. Cuthbert was Bishop of Lindisfarne. Ussher's "Primordia," pp. 944, 945; Bede, "Hist. Eccl.," iv. 27.
  [c] *Cana.*—See Tigh. 688; Ult. 687. The Emperor Constantine IV., surnamed *Pogonatus*, died in 685.

Kal. Ꮓuin Diapmaba Miḋe, mic Aipmḃaiġ Chaoic; de quo bancáinte i nAonaċ Tailltſin cecinit :—

Sia Diapmaid dop pop péin, pion ġabla po lenaid laoich,
ba hſd uball aḃla óip, pian mapa móip mac an Chaoic.

Kal. Quiep beccáin ab Cluana ipaipd.
Ꮓnatnat abbatippa Cille dapa.
Ꮓuin Congaile mic Maoileduin, mic Aoḋa bſnnáin, pí Muṁan. Iuptinianup minop impepat annip x.
Kal. Cpopán mac hUa Cualna ab bſnncaip quiéuit. Fic-ciollac mac Flainn pí hUa Máine mopitup. Ailill mac Dunġaile píCpuicne mopitup.

Kal. Aḋamnanup xiii anno popt obitum Failḃe ab. Iae aḋ hibepniam uenit. Fſpġap mac Aoḋáin, pí an cúigid mopitup. Ꮓuin Faolcaip pí Oppaige. Ꮓuin Cinnfaolaiḋ mic Maoilbpea- pail la Laiġniḃ.

Kal. Ḃpuide mac Bile pi Foiptpean mopitup.
Maicim na bopaina la Fionnacta do Moling, ap na bpeiċ la xl. pi, unde dicitup :—

Cſtpaca

ᵈ *Diarmaid Midhe.* — Or Diarmait of Meath, i. e. King of Meath. "Jugulatio Diarmata mᶜ. Airmethaigh, .i. r. Midhi, la h Aed mᶜ. nDluthaigh r. Fercul."—Tigh. 689; Ult. 688. The female poet here quoted is unknown.

ᵉ *Beccan.*—Ult. 689, where he is called "Dobccog of Cluain Aird," which is correct. Tigh. 690, and F. M. 687, have Cluain Iraird. The devotional name *Do- becog,* or *Dabeog,* instead of the diminutive *Beccan,* is used by Ult. and Tigh.

ᶠ *Congal, son of Maelduin.*—Ann. F. M. 687.

ᵍ *Justinianus minor.*—Began to reign 685, and reigned ten years, when he was deposed, and his nose cut off. This entry is out of its proper place.

ʰ *Cronan Mac Ua Cualna.*—Ann. F. M. 688; Ann. Ult. 690; Tigh. 691.

ⁱ *Fithchellach, son of Flann.*—Ann. F. M. 688; Ann. Ult. 690; Tigh. 691.

ᵏ *Ailell, son of Dunghal.*—Not in the published Annals.

[689.] Kal. The slaying of Diarmaid Midhc[d], son of Airmheadh-ach Caech [i. e. blind], of whom the female satirist said at the fair of Tailtin :—

Diarmaid placed a bush on himself; he of the fair arms who destroyed heroes.
He was the apple of the golden orchard; the King of the great sea was this son of the Caech [i. e. the blind].

[660.] Kal. The repose of Beccan[e], Abbot of Cluain-Iraird. Gnathnat, Abbess of Cill-dara, [died.]
The slaying of Congal, son of Maelduin[f], son of Aedh Bennan, King of Munster.
Justinianus minor[g] reigns ten years.

[691.] Kal. Cronan Mac Ua Cualna[h], Abbot of Benchair, died.
Fithchellach, son of Flann[i], King of Ui Maine, died. Ailell, son of Dunghal[k], King of the Cruithni, died.

[692.] Kal. Adamnan[l] came to Ireland in the thirteenth year after the death of Failbhe, Abbot of Ia. Fergus, son of Aedhan, King of the province[m], died. The slaying of Faelchar[n], King of Osraighe. The slaying of Cennfacladh, son of Maelbresail, by the Leinster-men.

[693.] Kal. Bruide, son of Bile[o], King of Foirtreann, died. ✗
The remission of the Borumha[p] by Finnachta to Moling, after it had been levied by forty kings, on which was said—
Forty

---

[l] *Adamnan.*—See Adamnan's "Vit. Co-lumbæ" (ed. Reeves), p. 378.

[m] *King of the province.*—i. e. of the territory of Uladh. "Fergus mac Aedain rex in Coicidh," [i. e. of the province] "obiit."—*Ann. Ult.*, A. D. 691.

[n] *Faelchar.*—"Faelchar hua Mailodrai." Tigh. 693. "Faelcar nepos Maele ordae."
Ult. 692. "Faolcar Ua Maolodra." F. M. 690; Clonm. 688.

[o] *Bruide, son of Bile.*—He was King of Fortrenn, or Pictland, and died in 693.—Reeves's "Adamnan," p. 378.

[p] *The remission of the Borumha.*—See note [o], p. 84, *supra*, and F. M., A. D. 106, p. 99, and A. D. 593, p. 216.

Cʄpaċa ꞅí vo ꞃala, laꞃa ꞃuᵹaṽ an ḃoꞃaṁa
'O aimꞃiꞃ Cuaċail Claċċᵹa ᵹo haimꞃiꞃ ꞃioꞃ Pionnaċta.
Ceteꞃa ꞅꞃeꞃcꞃiꞃꞃimuꞃ.
Moꞃꞃ Pianaṁla mic Maoiletuile, ꞃi Laiᵹꞅn. Poiċꞃꞅċan va
ṁuintiꞃ ꞅéin ꞃov maꞃḃ; unve Moliᵹ:—

An tan ċonᵹaiꞃ Pianaṁail ċuᵹéa a caoṁa uile,
A ꞃomꞅnav Poiċꞃꞅċán, bav beo mac Maoltuile.

Kal. Ḃꞃan mac Conaill incipit ꞃeᵹnaꞃe ꞃoꞃ Laiᵹniḃ.
Cꞃonán aḃacc ab Cluana mic Nóiꞃ.
Mochua ḃallna quieuit.
huioꞃine Maiᵹe bile quieuit.
ᵹuin Cꞅnḃaill mic Maoile oṽꞃa ꞃí hUa Néill.
Cat eivin Oꞃꞃaiᵹe ꞇ Laiᵹniu, in quo cecivit Paolċaiꞃ hUa
Maoile oṽꞃa.
Kal. Maꞃbav Pionnaċta mic Ounchava, ꞃí ꞌEꞃꞅin, vá ḃꞃáiċꞃiḃ
ꞅéin ꞇ ḃꞃeaꞃal a ṁac maile ꞅꞃiꞃ. Aꞃ aṁlaiv ꞃo ꞃo maꞃbav .i. in
tan ꞃo ꞃaoiṽ Pionnaċta a ṁac ḃꞃeaꞃal iꞃ in ꞃuball i n-Ᵹꞃeallaiᵹ
Dollaiṽ, taᵹataꞃ a ḃꞃaiċꞃe ꞃobttuꞃ auḃaꞃtnaiᵹċꞅċa vó .i. Aov
mac Oluċaiᵹ ꞇ Conᵹalaċ mac Conaiᵹ, ᵹan aiꞃꞃiᵹav vóiḃ iꞃin
puball

ᵠ *Fianamhail.*—This entry is out of place. It is given by the F. M. at 678, Ult. 679, the true year being 680, as in Tigh.

ʳ *Bran, son of Conall.*—Ann. Clonm. 685; F. M. 687.

ˢ *Cronan the Dwarf.*—See F. M. 692, and Ann. Ult. 693, where he is called Cronan Bec, i. e. the Little. Tigh. 694.

ᵗ *Mochua of Balla.* — This obit appears to be out of place here. It is entered in the Annals of Clonmacnoise, and in the Ann. F. M. at the year 637. St. *Cronan,* of Balla, died in 693, according to the Annals of Ulster. Tigh. 694; F. M. 692; so that there is probably confusion.

ᵘ *Huidhrine.*—F. M. 691; Ult. 693.
ᵛ *Cearbhall.*—Ann. Ult. 693.
ˣ *Faelchair.*—See above at A. D. 692.
ʸ *Finnachta.*—Ann. Clonm. 690; Ann. F. M. and Tigh. 693; Ann. Ult. 694.

Forty kings there were, by whom the Borumha was levied,
From the time of Tuathal of Tlachtgha, to the exact time of
Finachta.

Cætera præscripsimus.

The death of Finamhail[q], son of Maeltuile, King of Leinster. Foichsechan, one of his own people, killed him, of which Moling [said]—

When Fianamhail cried out, "At them, ye nobles all!"
Had Foichsechan withheld, the son of Maeltuile would have lived.

[694.] Kal. Bran, son of Conall[r], began to reign over the Leinster-men.

Cronan the Dwarf[s], Abbot of Cluain-mic-Nois, [died].

Mochua, of Balla[t], quievit.

Huidhrine[u], of Maghbile, quievit.

The slaying of Cearbhall[v], son of Maelodhra, King of the Ui-Neill [of Leinster(?)].

A battle [was fought] between the Osraighi and the Leinster-men, in which Faelchair[x], grandson of Maelodhra, fell.

[695.] Kal. The slaying of Finnachta[y], son of Dunchadh, King of Erin and of Breasal, his son along with him, by his own brethren. This is the manner in which he was killed: when Finnachta sent his son Breasal into the tent at Greallach-Dollaidh[z], his brethren, who were opposed to him, viz. Aedh, son of Dluthach, and Conghalach, son of Conaing, came, without being perceived by them, into the tent, and

The true year is 695. See O'Flaherty's "Ogygia," Part iii., c. 93, p. 432.

' *Greallach Dollaidh.*—This is probably the place now called Grellach, Anglice Girley, near Kells, in the county of Meath. See Ann. F. M., A. D. 693, note ᵠ, p. 297.

puball ⁊ na manbrac Fionnacca ⁊ a mac, ⁊ na bfirac a ccionna ofob; unoe oicicun :—

ba ounnan oFionnacca aniu laiṫe i ccnoiliṫe
Ron bé lá fsnaib nime oiolṫaò ionna bónaime.
Onṫain Caiòṫ mic Failbe i nṫlionn ṫaimin.
Quier Minobainfn, ab Ácaiò bó.
Ṫaimine Lúṫmaiṫ monicun.
Monn bnain, mic Conaill biṫ.
Ral. Loinṫrfc mac Aonṫana no ṫab niṫe n-Eneann i nofṫaiò Finnacca ne hocc mbliaònaib. Fionṫuine mac Con ṫan mácain monicun. Ffnṫal Aiòne, ⁊ Fianamail mac Maonaiṫ moniuncun.
Conṫalaċ mac Conainṫ mic Aoòa monicun.
Loicine Mfnò Sapienn, ab Cille oana, iuṫulacun ert.
Cummeni Muṫoonna quieuic.
Ral. Aoamnanun uenic in hibenniam, ec inoicic leṫem innocencium populir hibenniae .i. ṫan maca ṫan mná oo manbaò.
Carán rniba ó Lurca quieuic.
Moling Luacna, plenur oienum quieuic.
Maolfacunraiṫ niṫ na n-Ainṫiall quieuic.
Iomainfṫ Cnanoċa, i ccorċain Feanċain mac Maoil òuin.
bnfcnai ⁊ Ulaiò oo fánuccaò Maiṫe Muinċemne.

Ral.

^a *Tadhg, son of Failbhe.*—Ann. F. M. 693. Glenn Gaimin was the ancient name of the vale of the River Roe, near Dungiven, in the barony of Keenaght, county of Londonderry. It is called by Tighernach, A. D. 695, " Glen in Croccind ;" translated "vallis pellis," by the Ann. Ult. 694.

^b *Mennbairen.*—Ann. F. M. 693; Ult. 694. *Achadh-bo* is the present Aghabo, in the Queen's County. *Lughmhagh* is the present town of Louth.

^c *Bran.*—Ann. F. M. 687; Tigh. 690.

^d *Loingseech, son of Aenghus.*—Ann. Ult. and Tigh. 695, which seems the true year. But he reigned nine, not eight years. See O'Flaherty's " Ogyg.," p. 432.

^e *Finguine.*—Ann. Ult. 695; Tigh. 696.

^f *Law of the Innocents.*—There are two copies of this *Lex Innocentium*, called *Cain Adamnain*, still preserved, one in a

and killed Finnachta and his son, and cut off their heads, on which was said—

Pitiful for Finnachta this day, to lie in death.
He will be with the men of heaven for remitting the Borumha.

The slaying of Tadhg, son of Failbhe*, in Glenngaimhin.
The death of Mennbairen[b], Abbot of Achadh-bo.
Gaimide, of Lughmhagh, died.
The death of Bran[c], son of Conall Beg.

[695.] Kal. Loingsech, son of Aenghus[d], took the government of Erin, after Finnachta, for eight years. Finguine[e], son of Cu-gan-mathair, died. Ferghal Aidhne [King of Connaught], and Fian-amhail, son of Maenach, died. Conghalach, son of Conaing, son of Aedh[Slaine], died.

Loichine Menn the Wise, Abbot of Kildare, was killed.
Cummeni, of Mughdhorna, quievit.

[696.] Kal. Adamnan came to Erin, and promulgated the "Law of the Innocents"[f] to the people of Erin, i.e. not to kill children or women.

Casán[g], scribe of Lusca, quievit.
Moling Luchra plenus dierum quievit.
Maelfothartaigh[h], King of the Airghialls, quievit[i].

The battle of Crannach [was fought], in which was slain Fear-chair, son of Maelduin. The Britons and Ultonians devastated Magh Muirtheimhne[k].

[697.]

MS. in the Ambrosian Library at Brussels, and another in the Bodleian Library at Oxford, Rawl. 505.--See Ann. Ult. 696, and Reeves's "Adamnan," p. 179.

[g] *Casán.*—"Cassan scriba Luscan, quievit. Moling Luachra dormitavit."—*Ann. Ult.* 696. See F. M., 696; Tigh. 697.

[h] *Maelfothartaigh.*—See Ann. F.M. 695; Ann. Ult. 696.

[i] *Quievit.*—The word "moritur" is written over this word as a gloss, probably because *quievit* was properly applied only to the death of a saint.

[k] *Magh Muirtheimhne.*—This was the

Kal. Mopp Popanoain, ab Cille oapa.

Caċ Fġnmaiġe i ccopcaip Aoḃ mac Maoloúin, ⁊ Conċoḃap Aipṡo, pí Ðáil Apaiḃe, qui cecinic :—

Ap mé Concopup cpeaċaċ, pop Loċ Eaċaċ iomaḃḃal.
Mġclé pia ġail impeċiup, ip popceċiuc ron aoḃuc.

Kal. Cpep papmae in coelo quapi bellancep uipae punc ab opience in occiðencem in moðo unoapum, pluccuancium in cpanquilliġġima nocce Apcenpionip Ðomini. Ppima niuea, pecunoa iġnea, cepcia panġuinea. Quae, uc apbicpacup, cpia mala pequencia ppaepiġupaðanc. Nam in eoðem anno apmenca bouilia in coca hiðepnia pepe oeleca punc, [ec] non polum in hiðepnia, peo eciam pep cocam Eupopam. In alcepo anno pepcilencia humana cpiðup concinuip annip. Popcea maẋima pamep, in qua hominep ao inpamep epcap peoacci punc.

Caċ Piannamla mic Opene.

Mopp Muipġiupa mic Maoiloúin, pí Cineil Caippṡe. Iupcimianup Auġupcup pellicup.

Kal. Leo impepac annip iii.

Kal. Quiep Aoba Eppcoip Sleḃce. Piannamail

level part of the present county of Louth. "Britones et Ulaid vastaverunt Campum Muirthcimhne." Ann. Ult. 696; Tigh. 697.

ˡ *Forannan.*—Ann. F. M. 697; Tigh. 698.

ᵐ *Loch Eachach.*—Now Loch Neagh.

ⁿ *Three shields.*—This prodigy is not recorded in any of the published Irish Annals, nor in the Saxon Chronicle.

º *Herds of cows.*—"Accensa est bovina mortalitas in Hibernia in Kal. Februarii in Campo Trego i Tethbai."—*Ann. Ult.* 699; *Tigh.* 700.

ᵖ *Unmentionable foods.*—" Fames et pestilentia tribus annis in Hibernia facta est, ut homo hominem comederet."—*Ann. Ult.* 699; *Tigh.* 700.

ᑫ *Fiannamhail.*—He was probably the Fianamhail Ua Dunchadha, chief of Dal Riada, mentioned in the Ann. F. M. as slain in 698; vide *infra*, p. 100, note ⁿ.

ʳ *Muirghes.*—Ann. Ult. 697.

[697.] Kal. The death of Forannan¹, Abbot of Cill-dara.
The battle of Fearnmhagh, in which were slain Aedh, son of Maelduin, and Conchobhar Aired, King of Dal Araidhe, who said—

"I am the plundering Conchobhar, on Loch Eachach^m mighty.
Rapid they run before valour, they fly to the fortress."

[698.] Kal. Three shields^n were seen in the heavens, as it were warring from the east to the west, after the manner of undulating waves on a very calm night, being that of the Ascension of the Lord. The first was snowy, the second fiery, the third bloody; which prefigured, as is thought, three succeeding evils: for in the same year the herds of cows^o throughout Ireland were nearly destroyed, and not only in Ireland, but also throughout the whole of Europe. In the other year there was a human pestilence [which continued] for three successive years. Afterwards the greatest famine [set in], during which men were reduced to devour unmentionable foods^p.

The battle of Fiannamhail^q, son of Oisen.
The death of Muirghes^r, son of Maelduin, King of Cinel-Cairpre.
Justinianus^s Augustus is expelled.
Kal. Leo reigned three years.
[700.] Kal. The death of Aedh^t, Bishop of Sleibhte.

Fiannamhail

ˢ *Justinianus.*—This refers to the banishment of Justinian II., by the usurper Leontius, here (as well as by Bede, *Chron. in an.* 701) called Leo: who after having cut off his predecessor's nose, and banished him to the Chersonese, A. D. 694, occupied the throne until 697, when his own nose and ears having been cut off, he was imprisoned in a monastery by his successor Tiberius Absimarus; at length, in 704 or 705, Justinian recovered the throne, and put both Leontius and Absimarus to death.

ᵗ *Aedh.*—He is called "Anchorita," not *Bishop*, of Slebhte: Tigh. 700; Ult. 699; F. M. 628. Sleibhte, now called Slatey, is situated in the Queen's County, near Carlow.

Fiannamail hUa Dunchada, ri Dail Riada moriṫur.[u]

Irin bliadain ri do rala eidir lorgalaċ mac Conaing ⁊ Adaṁ-
nan ar rarugad Adaṁnain do lorgalaċ im marbad Néill a braṫar
dó ar comairge Adamnáin. Aread do ġníod Adamnan trorgad
gaċ n-oidċe, ⁊ gan codla, ⁊ beiṫ i n-uirgib uarib, do ṫimdibe rao-
gail lorgalaig. Ar ead imurro do ġníod an córaid rain.[v] lorgalaċ
a riarraigid do Adaṁnán, "Créd do ġénara anoċṫ a cleirig?"
Ní ba hail do Adamnán brég do rada frir. Ro innired dó go
mbiad a ttrorgad gan ċodlad i n-uirge uar go maidin. Do ġníod
an t-lorgalaċ an ċédna.[v] da raorad ar frguine Adamnáin. Aċṫ
ċena ro meall Adamnan érioṁ.[v] ro boí Adamnan 'ga rad ra
clereaċ dá ṁuintir, "bíri runna anoċt um rioċt-ra ⁊ ṁédaċ-ra
iomad, ⁊ da ttí lorgalaċ dá iarraighid díot, créd ra ġena anoċt,
abairre bud flṫugad, ⁊ codlad do ġéna, ar daig go ndearnaroṁ
na ċédna, uair arru ra Adamnán brḟ da rior muintire quam do
fén. Táinig iaram lorgalach diorroigid an cleirig rin, ⁊ an dar
leir, ba é Adamnán baoi ann, Ro iarraig lorgalaċ de, créd do
ġénara anoċt, a cleirig? Flṫugad ⁊ codlad, ar an cléreaċ.
Do roine dno lorgalaċ flṫugad ⁊ codlad an aidċe rin. Do rine
imurro Adamnan aoine, ⁊ friotaire, ⁊ beiṫ 'r an bhóinn go maidin. An tan dno ro baoi lorgalaċ 'na ċodlad a readh ad connairc
Adamnán do beiṫ go nuige a bragaid ir in uirge, ⁊ ro biog go mór
tríd rin ar a ċodlad; ⁊ ra innir dá mnaoí. An bfn imurro, ba
huṁal

---

[u] *Fiannamhail Ua Dunchadha.*—Ann. F. M. 698; Ann. Ult. 699.

[v] *Irgalach, son of Conaing.*—The cursing of this chieftain by Adamnan at Rath-na Seanadh, at Tara, is mentioned in an ancient poem published in Petrie's "Antiquities of Tara Hill," p. 122-148. See Reeves's "Adamn.," liii., liv., 179.

[a] *Should tell a lie.*—Adamnan (according to this story) did not wish to tell a lie himself, but he had no objection that one of his clergy should tell a lie to screen him. This is a mere legend, and much more modern than the Age of Adamnan. It

Fiannamhail Ua Dunchadha", King of Dal-Riada.
In this year a dissension arose between Irgalach, son of Conaing', and Adamnan, after Adamnan had been sacrilegiously violated by Irgalach, by killing his brother Niall, who was under the protection of Adamnan. What Adamnan used to do was to fast every night, and remain awake, and stay [immersed] in cold water to cut short the life of Irgalach. And what this champion, i. e. Irgalach, used to do was to ask Adamnan, "What wilt thou do to-night, O clerk?" Adamnan did not like to tell him a lie. He used to tell him that he would be fasting without sleep in cold water till morning. Irgalach used to do the same to free himself from the curse of Adamnan. But, however, Adamnan deceived him. He said to a clerk of his people : " Be thou here to-night in my stead, with my clothes upon thee, and if Irgalach should come to ask thee what thou wilt do to-night, say thou unto him that thou wilt feast and sleep, in order that he may do the same, for Adamnan had rather that one of his people should tell a lie* than himself. Irgalach afterwards came to that clerk, and thinking that it was Adamnan who was there, he asked him, " What wilt thou do to-night, O clerk?" "Feast and sleep," replied the clerk. Irgalach, therefore, feasted and slept that night. But Adamnan fasted, and watched, and remained in the Bóinn' till morning. Now when Irgalach was asleep, he saw [in a dream] that Adamnan was immersed to the neck in the water, and he started violently from his sleep in consequence of it, and told it to his wife. The wife, however, was humble and submissive to the Lord and to
Adamnan,

occurs in the Irish Life of Adamnan. See Reeves, p. liv., and note *. Stories of this nature in the lives of Irish saints are severely censured as *fabulæ futiles* by the early Bollandists. They are evidence, not of lax morality in the saints, but of the rude ignorance of the times in which such tales were invented and told as not inconsistent with a saintly character.

' *The Bóinn.*—i. e. the River Boyne.

humal inípil í don coimdrd, ⁊ do Adamnán, uaip ba toppać í, ⁊ ba hígail lé a clann do lot tpé fpguine Adamnáin, ⁊ pa guideađ go meinic Adamnán gan a clann do lot no d'epguine. Ra eipig iapam Iopgalać moćtpáć ap na bápać, ⁊ do pala Adamnán na aigid. Apeađ pa páid Adamnán pip; "a mic malluigte (ap pé), ⁊ a đuine ap cpóđa, ⁊ ap mífpa do pigne Dia, bioć a fiop agat gup ob gaipid gup poopgeptup pic plaitiup, ⁊ paga do ćum n-Ifpinn." O đo ćuala bfh Iopgalaig pin, tainig ap amup Adamnáin, ⁊ po luig po coppaid Adamnáin, pa attaig Dia pipp gan a clann d'eap-guine, ⁊ gan an gein po baoi'na bpoinn do lot. Apeađ po páid Adamnán, bud pi go deimin, ap pé," an gen pail io bpoinn, ⁊ ap bpipte a lífpúil anoppa tpe eapguine a atap. Agap ap amlaid pin do pála. Rugađ po ćéđoip iappain an mac, ⁊ ap amluid po baoi ⁊ pé leattaoć.
Féiđlimiđ mac Maoile cataig. Ailell mac Con-gan mátaip, pí Muman (déc.).
Opgain Néill mic Cfpnaig, ut Adamnanup pprophetauit.

  Opgain Néill oc Dpfip Eappnaig,
  Dia láipp dáig do Mullać pi,
  Dia ffpi áp pop fopbap cuan
  Dia luain i n-Imliơć Fich.

Ipgalać mac Conaing [occidit illum].
Kal. Faoldobap Chlocaip obiit.
                 Tibepiup

ª *Shall verily be a king.*—He was Cinaedh, son of Irgalach, who reigned as monarch of Ireland from 724 to 727. It does not appear from any other authority that he was a one-eyed king.

ª *Feidhlimidh, son of Maeloothaigh.*—Not in the published Annals.

ᵇ *Ailell, son of Cu-gan-mathair.*—Ann. F. M. 699; Ann. Ult. 700; Tigh. 701.

ᶜ *Niall.*—" *Occisio* Neill mic Cearnaig. Irgalach nepos Conaing *occidit illum.*" Ann. Ult. 700; Tigh. 701. Reeves's "Adamnan," p. liii., liv. Here the compiler of these Annals mixes up two entries,

Adamnan, for she was pregnant, and she was afraid that her child might be destroyed through Adamnan's curse, and she often besought Adamnan not to injure or curse her child. Irgalach rose early the next morning, and Adamnan came to meet him. What Adamnan said was: "O cursed man" (said he), "and thou bloodiest and worst man that God hath made, be it known unto thee that in a short time thou shalt be separated from thy kingdom, and shalt go to hell." When the wife of Irgalach heard this she came to Adamnan, and, prostrating herself at his feet, she besought him, for God's sake, not to curse her children, and not to destroy the infant she had in her womb. Adamnan said: "The child that is in thy womb," said he, "shall verily be a king"; but one of his eyes is now broken in consequence of the cursing of his father." And thus it came to pass. The son was born immediately afterwards, and it was found that he was half blind.

Feidhlimidh^a, son of Maelcothaigh, Ailell, son of Cu-gan-mathair^b, King of Munster, [died].

The killing of Niall^c, son of Cearnach, as Adamnan had prophesied.

<blockquote>
The plundering by Niall at Dris-Easfraigh,
As he burned to Mullach-ri,
As he inflicted slaughter on numerous troops
On Monday at Imleach-Fich.
</blockquote>

Irgalach, son of Conaing [killed him].

[702.] Kal. Faelcobhar^d of Clochar died.

Tiberius

—one relating to the triumph of Niall, the son of Cearnach Sotal, over his enemies at Imlech Phich, which actually took place in the year 687, and which our compiler has noticed at the proper place—and the other, his death, which occurred in 701. The verses here quoted belong properly to the year 687. See p. 91.

^d *Faelcobhar.* — Faoldobhair. Ann. F. M. and Ann. Ult. 701; Tigh. 702.

Tiberiur impepac annir uii.
Ir in mbliaḋainri ro marḃaḋ Iorgalaċ mac Conaing .i. i rġcṫmaḋ bliaḋain flaṫa Loingrıġ, ṫre Frguine Aḃamnáin, ⁊ ro connairc ḟén i n-airlinge a naḋoiġ ré na marḃaḋ amail ro marbaḋ. Tainig iaram Iorgalaċ an la iar ffaigrıṁ a airlinge ar carraig amaċ, ⁊ aḋ ċuala an guṫ áṗḋ .i. ṗá na ffrannaiḃ comffoigri ḋuiḃ (ar ré) ⁊ ḋoofḋ ⁊ loirgfḋ ⁊ airgfḋ iaḋ: ⁊ ra connaic ar a haiṫle rin na flaaiġ ⁊ na roċuiḃe og innreaḋ an ffrainn; ⁊ táinigriom reṁe go hairḋ ra inir mac Nefáin amar, ⁊ ir in uair rin ḋo rála coblaċ Lrfṫnaċ ḋo ċor i rorṫ ann, ⁊ anfaḋ lán mór ḋoiḃ; Ro ċonnaic miliḋ ḋibriḋe airlinge an aḋaig reime, .i. tréḋ ḋo ṫorcuiḃ ḋo criotuġaḋ uime, ⁊ an tor ba móḋ ann ḋo marḃaḋ ḋo ḋ'aonḃuille raiġḋe; agar areaḋ ón rá fioraḋ, uair ba hé Iorgalaċ an tor mór rain, ⁊ ba hé a fluaġ frcaċ mallaċṫnaċrom an tréḋ úḋ. 'On miliḋ rin tra aḋ ċonnairc an airlinge ro marḃaḋ Iorgalaċ.

Kal. Colman mac Fionnḃain ab lir mór moriṫur.

Mórffluaġ la Loingrioċ, mac Aongura, i g Connaċṫaiḃ, ḋ'argain agar ḋ'innrḋ Connaċṫ. Ro ḃaṫṫur filiḋ loingriġ ag aoraḋ ri Connaċṫ .i. Ceallaċ, mac Ragallaig, ⁊ ḋo ḃíḋír ga ráḋa, nár bo cuḃuiḋ ḋo frnrig criotánaċ mar Ceallaċ comṫógḃail no comḃuartur re riġ n-Eirfnn, ⁊ gé ḋo nfṫ, ro ba fair buḋ maiḋm. Aṫṫ ċna, ni haṁlaiḋ rin ḋo rála, aṫṫ a coḋarrna, uair ó ḋo connairc an Ceallaċ ri Connaċṫ a ṫír ⁊ a ṫalaṁ ga loṫṫ ⁊ ḋa hinnrḋ, ro ġairim ċuige na ḋá Ḋúnċaḋ .i. Ḋúnċaḋ Muirirge, ⁊ an Ḋúnċaḋ
eile

---

* *Tiberius.*—This was Tiberius Apsimarus. See note ᵉ, p. 98, *supra*.

ᶠ *Irgalach.*—" *Irgalach Nepos* Conaing *a Britonibus jugulatus* in Insi mic Nesan."
—*Ann. Ult.* 701; *Tigh.* 702.

ᵍ *Loingsech.*—Loingsech began his reign in the year 795, and the true year of Irgalach's death was 702.

ʰ *Inis-mac Nesain.*—i. e. the island of the sons of Nesan, now Ireland's Eye, [i. e. Ireland's Island], near the Hill of Howth, in the county of Dublin.

Tiberius[e] reigned seven years.

[702.] In this year Irgalach[f], son of Conaing, was slain, i. e. in the seventh year of the reign of Loingsech[g], in consequence of the curse of Adamnan. And he himself had seen in a dream, the night before his death, how he was [to be] killed. Irgalach came the day after he had seen this vision out upon a rock, and he heard a loud voice, saying, "Into the nearest lands go ye, and burn, consume, and plunder them;" and he saw, after this, hosts and troops plundering the land; and he came forward to a hill to the west of Inis-mac Nesain[h]; and at that time there came a British fleet into port there, being overtaken by a very great storm. A hero of these had seen a vision on the night before, viz., that a herd of swine made an attack upon him, and that the largest boar of them was killed by him with one blow of a dart; and this was indeed verified, for Irgalach was that great boar, and his sinful and cursed host was that herd. By that very champion who had seen this vision was Irgalach slain.

[703.] Kal. Colman[i], son of Finnbhar, abbot of Lis-mor, died.

A great host was led by Loingsech, son of Aenghus, into Connacht, to plunder and waste that province. The poets of Loingsech were satirizing the King of Connacht, i. e. Ceallach, son of Raghallach, and they used to say that it was not proper for a palsied old king like Ceallach to vie or contend with the King of Erin, and that, if he did, he would be defeated. But, however, this did not happen to be the case, but the very opposite: for when Ceallach, King of Connacht, had perceived that his territory and land were being injured and plundered, he called unto him the two Dunchadhs, i. e. Dunchadh Muirsa, and the other Dunchadh, and he determined beforehand that they should succeed to the kingdom of Connacht after

---

[i] *Colman.*—Ann. Ult. 702; Tigh. 703; F. M. 702. See Colgan, Acta SS., pp. 154, 155. He was commonly called *Mocholmoc*, i. e. "my little Coluin," accord-

eile, ⁊ ꞃa cinbaiġe ꞃeime ꞅo mað iað ꞃa ꞅeḃað ꞃiġe Connachꞇ na ðꞅġaið ꝼéin. Ro ḃaoi ꝼén imuꞃꞃo aꞃ na ꝼoꞇꞃuccað, ⁊ aꞃ ccuꞃ ola ⁊ luiḃe iomða ꞃioġða ꝼaoi. Oo ꞃað ꝼꞅꞃ ðon ðíꞃ ꞅꞅmꞃáiꞇe (.i. ðo na ðá Ouncað) ðá lꞅiꞇ ðeiꞃ ⁊ ꞃꞅꞃ ḃa leiꞇ clí, ⁊ ꞃa coꞃaiġ Connaċꞇa uime ðo ċum an ċaꞇa. Rá linġ ꝼén .i. Ceallaċ aꞃ a caꞃḃað amaċ ġo ꞇꞃic, ⁊ ġo ꝼaða ón caꞃꞃað, ⁊ að cualað ḃꞃiꞃġleaċ cnáma an ꞇꞃꞅnóꞃaċ oġ léim aꞃ an ċaꞃḃað, ⁊ ꞃo ꞃaið iaꞃ ꞃin ó ġuꞇ móꞃ, oġ léim ðo ċum an ċaꞇa comaiꞇiġ: a Chonnaċꞇa, aꞃ ꞃé, ðíðnið ⁊ coiméðoiġ ꝼén buꞃ ꞃaoiꞃe, uaiꞃ ní huaiꞃli ⁊ ní ḃeoða an cinꞅð ꝼail in buꞃ n-aiġið ionðáꞇíꞃi, ⁊ ní mó ðo ꞃonꞃað ðo maiꞇ ġuꞃ aniu; ⁊ amlaið ꞃa ḃaoi ġá ꞃáð, ⁊ a ġuꞇ ꝼo cꞃioꞇ ⁊ a ꞃúile ꝼoꞃ laꞃað. Oo ꞃaðꞃað iaꞃam Connaċꞇa ðá nuið ꞃin, ⁊ ꞃa ġaḃ an ní cꞃioꞇánaċ ꞃin ꞃeamꞃa a ġcꞅon caꞇa ní Eiꞃꞅnn, ⁊ ꞃa maið ꞃeime ꝼoꞃ ní Eiꞃꞅnn, ⁊ ꞃo maꞃḃað Loinġꞃioċ ꞃi Eiꞃꞅnn ann, ⁊ ðꞅꞃġáꞃ a muinꞇiꞃe, ⁊ a ꞇꞃí mac, ⁊ ðá mac Colġán, ⁊ Ouḃðiḃeꞃġ mac Ounġaile, ⁊ Eochaið lꞅmna, ⁊ Fꞅꞅġuꞃ Foꞃcꞃaið ⁊ Conall Ġhaḃꞃa. l quaꞃꞇ luil ꞃo cuiꞃꞅð an caꞇ ꞃo .i. caꞇ Coꞃainn. Aꞃ ꞇꞃiaꞃ na ꞃannaiḃ ꞃi imuꞃꞃo ꞃa cuiꞃeð an caꞇ. Conall menð ceciniꞇ:

ḃáꞃa aðaiġ i ccoꞃann, baꞃa uaċꞇ, baꞃa omunn,
Manaḃa ðaġocu laꞃ mḃa i Coꞃann mac nOunchaða,

Oa

ing to the Irish mode of expressing personal devotion to a saint. See Colgan's Acta SS., p. 71, notes 2 and 3.

ᵏ *King of Erin.*—"*Bellum* Corain, *in quo cecidit* Loingsech mac Oengusa *rex Hiberniæ,*" &c. Ann. Ult. 702; Tigh. 703; F. M., A. D. 701, p. 302.

ˡ *Fourth of July.*—Tigh. and the Ann. Ult. say: "4° id. Julii, 6° hora diei Sabbati hoc bellum confectum est." Therefore the year must have been 704, as

O'Flaherty remarks (Ogyg., p. 432), not 703, as in Dr. O'Conor's edition of Tighernach. The Chron. Scotor. has "Id. Julii," or July 15, which corresponds to 703.

ᵐ *Corann.*—"Coranna regio olim Galengam in agro Mayonensi, Lugniam, et hodiernam Corannam in agro Sligoensi complexa est."—O'Flaherty's *Ogyg.*, p. 334.

ⁿ *Conall Menn.*—In the Leubhar Gabhala of the O'Clerys (p. 194), and in the F. M. (p. 305), the last two lines of this

after himself. He himself was after bathing, and after applying oil, and many precious herbs. He placed one of the two aforesaid, i. e. of the two Dunchadhs, on his right, and the other on his left, and he arrayed the Connacht-men about him for the battle. Ceallach himself rushed from his chariot actively, and he went a far distance from it, and the crackling of the bones of the old man was heard as he leaped from the chariot; and he after this said in a loud voice, in springing to the battle: "O men of Connacht," said he, "do you yourselves preserve and defend your liberty, for the people who are against you are not nobler or braver than you, and they have not done more good to this day." And he said these words with a trembling voice, and with eyes on fire. The men of Connacht took heed of this, and this palsied king proceeded at their head to meet the army of the King of Erin, and he drove the King of Erin[k] before him; and Loingsech, King of Erin, was killed there, and his people were dreadfully slaughtered, and his three sons were killed; as were the two sons of Colgan; and Dubhdibherg, son of Dunghal; and Eochaidh Leamhna, and Fergus Forcraidh, and Conall Gabhra. On the fourth of July[l] this battle was fought, i. e. the Battle of Corann[m]. It was in consequence of these verses this battle was fought. It was Conall Menn[n] that composed them:

I was a night in Corann; I was cold, I was timid,
Were it not for the goodly youths who were with him in Corann of
    the sons of Dunchadh.

If

poem are attributed to Cellach himself. The F. M. quote also the 3rd, 4th, 5th, and 6th lines, and attribute them to Conall Menn, chief of the Cinel Cairbre. The Dublin copy of the Ann. Ult. has in the margin the following second account of the battle:—Cat Copainꝺ in quo occidit Loinꝼꝛeꝺ mac Oenꝼuꞃa ꞃi Eꞃenꝺ cum tribus filiis suis, ⁊ ꞃi Caiꞃꝑꞃi Oꞃoma cliaƀ [Drumcliff] ⁊ ꞃi hUa Conail Ꝼaƀꞃa, ⁊ .x. ꞃiꝼ ꝺo ꞃiꝼaiƀ Eꞃonn imaille ꞃiu ꞃein hi cloinꝑinꝺ hi cinn oenaiꝼ

Da ttí Loingpioć do bannai, co na tpi céduib céd ime,
ṡiallpaid cid leadop a bhiać, Ceallać liat Loća Cime.
Teacpaiṡ Ceallać ceiptli ćpuinni cpo tpi pinne
boöb mopLingi, la piṡ láimbfapṡ Loća Cime,
ba huilṡ ćuilṡ maidfn pa baoi aṡ ṡlaipp Chuilṡ
beopa Loingpioć an do ćailṡ aipupiṡ 'Eippnn ime cuipd.

Ra ćuaid iapttain Ceallać mac Raṡallaiṡ d'fcclaip, ⁊ po pá-
ṡaib an dá Dunćad 'na piṡe, ⁊ ba mapb an Ceallać i ṡcionn da
bliadain iapttain.
Cat Maiṡe Cuillinn eidip Ultuib ⁊ bpeatnuib i n-Apd hua
n-Eaćdać, i ttopćaip mac Radṡund, aduepfapiup eccleriapum
Dei. Uladh uictopep epant.
bpan mac Conaill, pí Laiṡfn, mopitup.

INITIUM REGNI FOGARTAIG.

Kal. Ceallać mac Ṡeiptide i piṡe Laiṡfn.
Foṡaptać apíp do ṡabáil piṡe aoin bliadain ṡo ttopćaip i ccat
Cinndelṡtin la Cinaot mac Ionṡalaiṡ.
Sluaṡ la Foṡaptać i Laiṡnib, ṡo ttuṡpad Laiṡin cat dó .i. cat
Claonta, ⁊ po maid pe Laiṡnib an cat, ⁊ po mapbad deapṡáp
muintipe

Loṡa icep Conaill ⁊ Connaćta.
° *If Loingsech.*—O'Reilly quotes this line and the next from O'Clery, but reads *Cellach* instead of Loingsech.—*Dict., voce* biać. See note ᴾ, F. M., p. 303.
ᵖ *Loch Cime.*—Now Lough Hacket, in the parish of Donaghpatrick, barony of Clare, and county of Galway.
ᑫ *Glais-chuilg.*—Situation unknown. It was probably the name of a stream in this barony.
ʳ *Into the Church.*—i. e. took the monastic habit.
ˢ *Two years.*—"Ceallach mac Ragallaigh, rex Connacht, *post clericatum*, obiit."—*Tigh.* 705; *Ult.* 704.
ᵗ *The Battle of Magh Cuillinn.*—Tigh. 703: Ult. 702.

If Loingsech° should come to the Banna, with his three hundred
hundreds about him,
He will make submit, though large his parts, Ceallach the Gray of
Loch Cime;
Ceallach of the round balls was active, a circle of spears,
Terrible, was leaped over by the red-handed King of Loch Cime^p.
Ambitious were his deeds, the morning he was at Glais Chuilg^q.
I slew Loingsech there with a sword, the arch King of Erin all round.

Ceallach, son of Raghallach, afterwards went into the Church^r,
and left the two Dunchadhs in his kingdom, and this Cellach died at
the end of two years' afterwards.

The Battle of Magh Cuillinn^t [was fought] between the Ultonians
and the Britons in Ard Ua n-Eachdhach, in which Mac Radgund, the
adversary of the Churches of God, was slain. The Ultonians were
the victors.

Bran, son of Conall^u, King of Leinster, died.

THE BEGINNING OF THE REIGN OF FOGARTACH^v.

[722.] Kal. Ceallach, son of Geirtide, in the kingdom of Leinster.
Fogartach again assumed the sovereignty for one year, when he
fell in the Battle of Cenndeilgtin^x by Cinaeth, son of Irgalach.

A hosting by Fogartach into Leinster; and the Leinster-men
gave him battle, i. e. the Battle of Claenadh^y. The battle was gained
by

^{u} *Brann, son of Conall.*—Ann. F. M.
787; Tigh. 690. This entry is out of
place here.

^{v} *Fogartach.*—He began his reign in
722, and was slain in 724 by Cinaedh,
son of Irgalach, his successor.

^{x} *Cenndeilgtinn.*—Ann. Ult. 723; Tigh.
724. The place is now unknown. See F.M.
719, 720. Tigh. says that this battle was
fought on Saturday, the Nones of Oct. (or
Oct. 7), which agrees with A. D. 724.

^{y} *Claenadh.*—Now Clane, county Kil-

muincipe Pozapcaiʒ im boobcap mac Diapmaba Ruanaib unbe Opcanac :

Uince [.i. cac] copʒap cpuaib, paon poclaoncaip caca ʒpáin ʒo ccopcaip lap an pluaʒ boobcap bile buibfn báin.

Moρρ Plainn Píona mic Ορρa ρι Saxan, in cfʒnaib ampa, balca Abamnáin, be quo Riaʒuil bfnncuip cecinic:

Iniu pfpap bpuibe [.i. m° bepil] cac, im popba a pfnacap,
Manab alʒap la mac Dé, conibé ab ʒfnacap
Iniu po bic mac Oρρa a ccac ppia claibme ʒlapa
Cia bo paba aicpiʒe, ip hí inb hí iap nappa.
Iniu po bic mac Ορρa, lap ambibíp buba beoʒa
Ro cuala Cpípc áp nʒuíbe poipaopbuc bpuibe bpfʒa.

Ip in bliabainpi po paompab pip 'Eipfnn aon pmacc ⁊ aoinpiaʒail bo ʒabail ó Abamnán um ceile abpab na Cápʒ ap Domnach an cfcpamab béc epʒa Appil, ⁊ im copónuʒ Pfbaip bo beic pop cléipcib Eipfnn uile. Uaip bá móp an buaibpfb pá baoi i n-Eipinn ʒo niʒe pin .i. buibfn bo cléipcib 'Epfnn aʒ celeabpab na Cápcc ap Dhomnac an cfpamab oʒ Epʒa Appil, ⁊ coponuʒab Pfbaip appcoil, ap pliocc Phábpicc ; buibfn eile bno óc pechim Choloim Cille, .i. Caipcc bo ceileabpab ap cfpamab bécc epʒa Appil ʒibé láice pfpmuine ap a mbeic an cfpamab bécc, ⁊ copónuʒab Simoin Opuab popna. An cpfp buibfn, níop b'ionann uile iab pe peiccibib Pacpaicc, no pe peiccibib Choloim Cille, ʒo mbibíp peanaba iombba oʒ cléipcib Eipfnn, ⁊ ap amlaib ciʒbíp na cléipiʒ pin na pfnabaib,

⁊ a

dare.—F. M. 702 ; Ult. 703 ; Tigh. 704.
' *Flann Fiona.*—See Tigh. 704, and Reeves's "Adamnan," p. 185. His real Anglo-Saxon name was Aldfrith. He was King of Northumbria.—Lappenberg. Hist. of Engl., vol. i., p. 187 n.

* *Bruide.*—The words .i. Mc Depil are in the margin of the MS. See Tigh. 706,

by the Leinster-men, who cut off the people of Fogartach with great slaughter, with Bodhbhchar, son of Diarmaid Ruanaidh. Unde Orthanach [said]:

A battle, a hard victory; lowly they prostrated the battalions of triumph,
And there fell by the host Bodhbhchar, the scion of the white troop.

[704.] The death of Flann Fiona[a], son of Ossa, King of Saxonland, the famous wise man, the pupil of Adamnan, of whom Riagail of Bennchair sung:

This day Bruide[a] fights a battle for the land of his grandfather,
Unless the Son of God wish it otherwise, he will die in it.
To-day the son of Oswy was killed in a battle with green swords,
Although he did penance, he shall lie in Hi after his death;
This day the son of Oswy was killed, who had the black drinks;
Christ heard our supplications, they spared Bruide the brave.

In this year the men of Erin consented to receive one jurisdiction and one rule from Adamnan, respecting the celebration of Easter[b], on Sunday, the fourteenth of the moon of April, and respecting the tonsuring of all the clerks of Erin after the manner of St. Peter, for there had been great dissension in Erin up to that time; i. e. some of the clergy of Erin celebrated Easter on the Sunday [next after], the fourteenth of the moon of April, and had the tonsure of Peter the Apostle, after the example of Patrick; but others, following the example of Columbkille, celebrated Easter on the fourteenth

---

where we have his death—"Bruide m^c Derile mortuus est."—*Ult.* 705.

[b] *Easter.*—The scribe has written in the margin—Ceileabṗaḋ na Carġ ro. "The celebration of Easter, here." See Reeves's "Adamnan," p. 26 n., and Introd., p. liii.

⁊ a ttuata leo go mbíoír compaicte cata, ⁊ mapbta iomba eatorpia; go ttangattap uile iomba i n-Eipinn tpío pin .i. an bó áp móp, ⁊ an gopta pó móp ⁊ tfomanna iomba, ⁊ eattupcinfbuig bo loc na h-'Eipfnn. battup amlaib pin go paba .i. go haimpip Abamnáin. 'Eipibe an nomab abb po gab la tap éip Coluim Cille. bpab móp bo bpeit bo Saxoncaib a hEipinn: Abamnán bo bul bo hattuingib na bpaice, ⁊ amail innipip béib 'pan pcaip bhéib pá cionoilpit fpmóp eppcop Eoppa uile bo bamnab Abamnáin ap an caipg bo celeabpab ap pliott Coluim Cille, ⁊ ap copónugab Símoin Opuab bo beit paip .i. ab aupe ab aupem. Abbeip béib gép ba hiomba fgnaibe pan tp.'nab pain po popuaiplig Abamnan iab uile a hfgna, ⁊ a hfplabpa, ⁊ apeb po páib Abamnán, ní ap aitipip [Simoin Opuab] po baoi an copónugab ub paip, att ap aitipip Iohannip bpuinne, balta an tSláinicíoba, ⁊ ap é pub copónugub po baoi paippibe, ⁊ ciap bo annpa pe Pfoap a Sláinicib piob annpa pip Slainicib Iohan; ⁊ ono ap ap cftpamab bétt ergo Appil, gibé lá pfttmaine ap a mbeit, po celeabpattup na happtail an cáipg. Ap ann pin po eipig pfnóip ann, ⁊ po páib : cia é Colom Cille péin? bia po beit ap áipb punna, ní gebmaoipne uab go mbeit po aoinpiagail pinne. Sibpe imuppo, ní gebtua uaib go mbeití po aoinpiagail
fpinn.

^c *Simon Magus.*—The scribe writes the Latin word "calumnia" in the margin. On this subject see note to the first Fragment of these Annals, under A. D. 718.

^d *Rattles.*—Here again the scribe has written "calumnia" in the margin.

^e *Bede.*—The scribe writes in the margin—"Non legit Scaip béib" [Historium Bedæ] "et si legerit non intellexit." See Bede, H.E., v., c. 15.

^f *Europe.*—Bede does not say a word about this. The compiler of these Annals here confounds the dispute which Colman, Bishop of Lindisfarne, had with the English clergy about the tonsure (Bede, iv., c. 25), with the dispute about Easter.

^g *Excelled them all.*—Bede says the very contrary; viz., that Adamnan, being admonished by many who were *more learned* than himself, not to presume to live contrary to the universal custom of the Church, &c., he changed his mind, and readily

teenth of the moon of April, on whatever day of the week the fourteenth should happen to fall, and had the tonsure of Simon Magus[e]. A third party did not agree with the followers of Patrick, or with the followers of Columbkille; so that the clergy of Erin used to hold many synods, and these clergy used to come to the synods accompanied by the laity, so that battles[d] and deaths occurred between them; and many evils resulted in Erin in consequence of this, viz., a great murrain of cows, and a very great famine, and many diseases, and the devastation of Erin by foreign hordes. They were thus for a long time, i. e. to the time of Adamnan, who was the ninth abbot that took [the government of] Ia after Columbkille.

A great booty was carried off by the Saxons from Erin, [and] Adamnan went to demand the booty, and, as Bede[e] relates in his History, the greater part of the bishops of all Europe[f] assembled to condemn Adamnan for celebrating Easter after the manner of Columbkille, and for having the tonsure of Simon Magus upon him, i. e. from ear to ear. Bede says that though many were the wise men [assembled] at that synod, Adamnan excelled them all[g] in wisdom and eloquence; and Adamnan said that it was not in imitation of Simon Magus that he had this tonsure, but in imitation of John the Beloved, the alumnus of the Saviour; and that this was the tonsure which he had upon him; and though Peter loved the Saviour, the Saviour loved John; and [he urged] that it was on the fourteenth of the moon of April, whatever day of the week it should fall upon, the Apostles celebrated Easter. It was then a certain senior rose up there, and said, " Who was Columbkille himself? If he were here present, we would not part from him until he should be of the same rule with us; but we shall not part from you until you are of the same

preferred those things which he had seen and heard in the English churches to the customs which he and his people had hitherto followed.

ꝼꞃinn. Tuᵹ Aḋaṁnán ꝼꞃíᵹꞃa ꝼaiꞃ, ⁊ a ꞃé ꞃo ꞃáiḋ; ḃiaḋꞃa, ꝼo aoinꞃiaᵹuil ꝼꞃiḃ. Cóiꞃniᵹéꞃ́i ėu ḃeꞃiḋe, aꞃ na heꝼꞃcoiꞃ. Aꞃ lóꞃ, aꞃ Aḋaṁnan acom mainiꞃciꞃ ꝼén: acc, aꞃ iaḋꞃoṁ, acė a céḋóiꞃ. Ḋo níėꞃi cꞃa cóiꞃniuᵹaḋ Aḋamnain ann ꞃin, ⁊ ní cuᵹaḋ ḋo ḃuine ónoiꞃ aꞃ moo ina an ccuᵹaḋ ḋo Aḋamnan annꞃin, aᵹuꞃ aḋ naᵹuꞃ an ḃꞃaiḋ móꞃ ꞃain ḃó, ⁊ ciᵹ ꞃeiṁe ᵹo nuiᵹe a mainiꞃciꞃ ꝼén ᵹo hia. Ro ḃá maccnuᵹaḋ moꞃ ꞃa coiṁéionol a ꝼaiᵹꞃin ꝼon coꞃonuᵹaḋ ꞃain. Rá ḃaoiꞃioṁ ᵹá ioꞃail aꞃ an coiṁéionol an coꞃonuᵹaḋ ḋo ᵹaḃáil, ⁊ níꞃ ꝼéḋ uaėa. Seḋ Ḋeuꞃ ꞃeꞃmiꞃic conuencui ꞃeccaꞃe .i. iꞃꞃum Aḋamnanum eꞃꞃellꞃe qui miꞃeꞃcuꞃ eꞃc hiḃeꞃniae. Sic ḃeḋa ḋiꞃic. Uaiꞃ ꞃa ḃaoi ḃéiḋ maille ꞃe hAḋaṁnán céin ꞃo ḃaoí iꞃ Saꞃain.

Táiniᵹ cꞃa Aḋamnán i n-'Eiꞃinn iaꞃccain ⁊ ꞃo loꞃḋaꞃcaiᵹ ꞃain ꝼoꞃ 'Eiꞃinn, ⁊ ní ꞃo ᵹaḃaḋ uaḋ an caonꞃmacė ꞃain na Caꞃcc ⁊ an coꞃónaiᵹée ᵹo nuiᵹe am ḃliaḋainꞃi.

Ḃa maꞃḃ ḋno Aḋaṁnán ꞃin ḃliaᵹainꞃi, lꞃꞃꞃiii°. aecaciꞃ ꞃuae.

[FRAGMENTUM III.]

Teꞃciuṁ ꝼꞃaᵹmencum eꞃ eoḋem Coḋice ꞃeꞃ eunḋem Ꝑeꞃḃiꞃium eꞃcꞃaccum, inciꞃienꞃ ab anno 5°, ꞃeᵹni Maoilꞃeachloinn mic Mailꞃuanaiᵹ, ꞃeu (uc habenc A. Ḋunᵹ.), 849.

Ꝑoꞃcoiṁeḋaiᵹe imuꞃꞃo na Loėlann maꞃ ꞃo ḃáccaꞃ ᵹo ꝼꞃié ᵹnaṁaė

---

[h] *Compassion.*—"Misertus est Hiberniæ," i. e. honoured Ireland with his presence.

Thus Bede says.—One would think from this that the Irish writer was telling the story exactly as Bede has it, but this is not so. He tells the story after his own bardic manner, exaggerates the whole affair, and confounds what Bede says of Colman with what he says of Adamnan. Comp. Bede, H. E., v., c. 15.

[k] *Eighty-third.*—See Reeves's "Adam-

same rule with us." Adamnan made answer to him, and said, "I will be of the same rule with you." "Be thou, therefore, tonsured," said the bishops. "It will be sufficient," said Adamnan, "at my own monastery." "Not so," said they, "but at once." Adamnan was, therefore, tonsured there; and no greater honour was ever given to a man than was given to Adamnan there. And the great booty was restored to him; and he came forward to his own monastery to Hi, and his congregation marvelled much to see him with this tonsure. He was requesting of the congregation to take the [same] tonsure, but God permitted the convent to sin, and to expel Adamnan, who had compassion[h] upon Ireland. Thus Bede says[i]; for Bede was along with Adamnan while he was in England.

Adamnan afterwards came to Erin, and he excelled all Erin; and that one regulation of Easter was not received from him, nor the tonsure, until this year.

[704.] Adamnan died in the eighty-third[k] year of his age.

[FRAGMENT III.]

A third fragment, extracted from the same manuscript by the same Firbissius, beginning at the fifth year of the reign of Maelsechlainn, son of Maelruanaigh, or (as the Annals of Donegal have it) 849.

[A. D. 851.] As now the sentinels of the Lochlanns[l] were vigilantly

nan," p. xl., note [g]. Tigh. records his death at A. 704, and says his age was 77.

[l] *Lochlanns.*—These were the Norwegians, who were settled in Ireland for about half a century previously. This extract, which is evidently a continuation of a long story, seems to have been taken from some history of the Danish invasions now lost.

ᵹnaṁaċ aᵹ ṗſᵹaḃ an mapa uaċa aḃ ċonncaccap an mupċoḃlaċ móp muipiḃe ḃ'ǎ n-ionnpoíᵹhiḃ. Ro ᵹaḃ uaṁan móp ꞇ ſᵹla iaḃ: aċc ḃpſm ḃíḃ apſḃ aḃbepḃíp, coniḃ Loċlannaiᵹ ḃa ḟpupcaċcpam ꞇ ḃa ṗpoipiᵹin. Ḋpeam oile, ꞇ ap ṗſpp pa cuiᵹpioccpaiḃe; coniḃ Ḋauniċep.ⁿ. Ḋanaip pa bácꞇup ann ḃǎ n-apᵹainpiom ꞇ ḃa n-inḃpſḃ; ꞇ apeaḃ ón bǎ ṗſpe ann. Ra ċuippioc na Loċlonnaiᵹ lonᵹ lǎnluaċ na n-aiᵹiḃ ḃǎ ṗpiup. Ꞇainiᵹ ḃna lonᵹ lǎnluaċ an ᵹiolla óiᵹ peim-paiḃce, aenap pép na lonᵹoi ḃoile, ᵹo cꞇǎplaccup na ḃǎ loinᵹ ḃ'aiᵹiḃ iꞇ'aiᵹiḃ, ᵹo nebepc Sꞇiupupman na loinᵹe Loċlannaiᵹe; pibpi, a ṗiupa, ap pé, ᵹa cíp ap a ccanᵹaḃaip ap an muippi? an pa píḃ canᵹaḃaip, no an pa coᵹaḃ? Qpé ṗpeaᵹpa cuᵹaccup na Ḋanaip ṗaippin, ṗpopp póṁóp ḃo paiᵹḃiḃ poca. Cuipiḃ a ċċéḃóip cſnn i ccſnn luċċ na ḃa lonᵹ pin; po ṗopuaiplᵹ lonᵹ na nḊanap lonᵹ na Loċlannaċ, ꞇ mapḃaiḃ na Ḋanaip luċċ loinᵹe na Loċlannaċ. Lſn-ᵹaiċ a n-aoinṗeaċċ uile na Ḋanaip i ccſnn na Loċlannaċ, ᵹup po bácup pin cpǎiᵹ. Cuipiḃ caċ ᵹo cpuaiḃ, ꞇ mapḃaiḃ na Ḋanaip a ccpí coimlíon ṗén ḃíoḃ, ꞇ pa ḃíċſnpac ᵹaċ aon po mapḃpaċ: Ꞇuᵹpac na Ḋanaip lonᵹa na Loċlannaċ leo ᵹo popc. Raᵹaḃpac cpa na Ḋanaip ap pain mnǎ ꞇ óp ꞇ uile maiċiup na Loċlannaċ; ᵹo puᵹ an coimḃe uaċa amlaiḃ pin ᵹaċ maiċ puᵹpac a ceallaiḃ, ꞇ neiṁḃaiḃ ꞇ pᵹpíniḃ naoṁ 'Eipeann.

Iſ in aimpip ḃno pa ċuip Maoilpeaċloinn ceaċca ap cſnn Cionaoiċ inic Conainᵹ, pí Cianaċca, ꞇ ap éipiḃe po loipᵹ Cealla ꞇ ḃipċiᵹe na naoṁ (aṁail po innipiomap pſṁaiñ) aṁail biḃ ḃo comaiple

ᵐ *Young man.--* i. e. who was in the command of the Lochland ship, and mentioned, perhaps, in the former part of the narrative.
ⁿ *Steersman.*—Sꞇiupapmann. This is a Teutonic word, and is probably derived from the Danish, *To steer*.

º *Maelsechlainn.* — Maelsechlainn, or Malachy I., began his reign in 846, und died on the 13th of November, 863.
ᵖ *Cianachta.*—A territory in the east of ancient Meath, in which a sept of Munster-men of the race of Cian, son of Oilioll

lantly observing the sea, they saw a great marine fleet coming towards them. They were seized with great fear and terror. Some of them said that they were Lochlanns who were coming to aid and assist them; but others, who understood better, said that they were Daunites, i. e. Danes, who came to plunder and rob them; and this was indeed the truth. The Lochlanns sent a very swift ship towards them to know who they were, and the swift ship of the young man[m] aforesaid came alone to one of the other ships, and the two ships met face to face; and the steersman[n] of the Lochlann ship asked, " Ye, O men," said he, " from what country have ye come upon this sea ? Have ye come with peace, or with war ?" The answer which the Danes gave him was to discharge a large shower of arrows at him ! The crew of the two ships set to at once: and the ship of the Danes overcame the ship of the Lochlanns, and the Danes killed the crew of the ship of the Lochlanns. The Danes then altogether made for the place where the Lochlanns were, and arrived at the shore. They fought a battle fiercely, and the Danes killed thrice their own number of them, and they beheaded every one they killed. The Danes brought the ships of the Lochlanns with them to a port, and they also took the women, the gold, and all the property of the Lochlanns with them; and thus the Lord took away from them all the wealth which they had taken from the churches, and sanctuaries, and shrines of the saints of Erin.

Now at this time Maelsechlainn[o] sent messengers for Cinaeth, son of Conaing, King of Cianachta[p], and it was he who had burned the churches and oratories of the saints (as we have narrated before[q]), as if to consult with him how they should act with respect to the cause

Olum, were seated at this period. Dulcek was its principal church. They were soon after overwhelmed by the southern Ui-

Neill, who detested them.
[q] *Narrated before.*—Not narrated in this Fragment, although it was, no doubt,

aiple pir cionnar do ġéndaoir im caingin na nDanar, uair rá baoi amail bíd ríd eidir Maoilreaċloiṁ ⁊ Cionaod, ⁊ cia ra baoi Cionaoḋ i ngalar rúla, aċt do piġne tuideaċt d'ionnroiġ Maoilreachloinn, ⁊ rluaġ uime mar bad da ċoiṁfd.

Ra coṁraigrioc iaraṁ Maoilrċlainn ⁊ Cionaod a n-aoinionad ⁊ Tigſrnaċ, ni brſġ; areaḋ rob áil do Maoilreaċloinn é pén ⁊ rí brſġ do marbad rí Cianaċta. Ní óſrna ono Maoilreaċloinn a ccédóir rin, uair ba róċaide do Chionaod, ⁊ rab ſgail leir coṁmarbad do ofnaṁ ann. Areaḋ do poine a puireaċ go maidfn ar na bárac. Ro deilb ono Maoirlrċloinn cúiri bréaġaċa go tciordaoir go nige a n-ionad cédna ar na bárac, ⁊ ra puaġair do na rluaġaid imteaċt. O ra imtiġ a rluaġ ón Chionaod, táinig Maoilrċloinn go rluaġ mór lair d'ionnroiġ an Chionaod, ⁊ níor bo lá go mait ann, ⁊ areaḋ ro ráid Maoilreaċloinn ó ġut mór cródha náiṁdiġe fria Chionaod. Cid, ar ré, 'mara loirgir dirtiġe na naoṁ, ⁊ cid ma ra ra ṁillir a neṁaḋa, ⁊ rgrearcra na naoṁ ⁊ Loċlannaiġ lat? Ra fidir imurro an Cionaod na tarmnaiġreaḋ ní do earlarra caoin do ófnaṁ, areaḋ do riġne beit na tocċ. Ra tairnġfd iar rin an mac raorclannaċ, roiċinelaċ, ronairt rin amaċ, ⁊ ro báidheḋ é tré ċoṁairle Maoilreaċloinn i rrután ralaċ, ⁊ fuair bár aṁlaid rin.

Ir in bliadain-ri, .i. an coigfd bliaġain flaċa Mhaoilreaċlainn, ra tionolrat dá toirfċ loingri na Loċlonn .i. Ẓain ⁊ larġna ríóiġ móra ar ġaċ áird a n-aiġid na n-Danar. Tionolaid iaraṁ go rabadar

narrated in the original work from which this extract was taken.

' *Breagh.*—A large territory comprising the greater portion of East Meath, and of which Cianachta was a subdivision.

' *Dirty streamlet.*—The Ann. Ult. 850,

say that he was "demersus in lacu crudeli morte." According to the Four Masters (A. D. 849), he was drowned in the River Ainge, now the Nanny Water, a river flowing through the very middle of Cianachta, and dividing the barony of

cause of the Danes, for there was a kind of peace between Maelsechlainn and Cinaeth, and though Cinaeth was labouring under a disease of his eye, he nevertheless came to meet Maelsechlainn with a host about him, as if it were to guard him.

After this, Maelsechlainn, and Cinaeth, and Tighernach, King of Breagh[r], met together: and Maelsechlainn's desire was that he and the King of Breagh should kill the King of Cianachta. Maelsechlainn, however, did not do this at once, for Cinaeth had more forces, and he was afraid that mutual slaughter might take place. What he did was to wait till the next morning. Maelsechlainn feigned false reasons, for which they should come to the same place the next morning, and he ordered the forces [of Cinaeth] to go away. When his army went away from Cinaeth, Maelsechlainn came with a great host to meet Cinaeth before it was clear daylight, and Maelsechlainn said with a loud, fierce, and hostile voice to Cinaeth: "Why," said he, "hast thou burned the oratories of the saints, and why hast thou destroyed their sanctuaries and their writings, the Lochlanns assisting thee?" Cinaeth knew that it would be of no avail to him to make use of fair speeches; what he did was to remain silent. That noble, goodly born, brave youth was afterwards dragged out, and drowned in a dirty streamlet[s], by advice of Maelsechlainn, and thus he perished!

[851.] In this year, i. e. in the fifth year of the reign of Maelsechlainn[t], the two chiefs of the fleet of the Lochlanns, i. e. Zain and Iargna, collected great hosts from every quarter against the Danes. They afterwards assembled to the number of threescore and ten ships, and proceeded

Upper Duleek from that of Lower Duleek, in the county of Meath. See the "Tripartite Life of St. Patrick," Part I., c. 54. —Colgan, *Triad. Thaum.*, p. 125.

[t] *The fifth year of the reign of Maelsechlainn.*—This king succeeded in 846, so that this battle between the Norwegians and Danes took place in the year 851.

rabaoan oec longa ⁊ trí ríciö, ⁊ tfgaio go Snám aignfc ⁊ ar annraioe baccur na Oanair an can rin. Comraicic ann rin leic for leac, ⁊ cuirio cac cruaiö ouaibrioc lfc for lfc : uair ní cualaman reimi rin a n-ionaö oile riam ar muir an ár ro cuirrioc fcurra annro .i. eioir Oanara ⁊ Loclannaig. Acc cfna ar forr na Oanaroib ro maiö. Ra cionóilrioc na Oanair iar rin, ar mbrireaö maöma forra, ⁊ an gorca ga marbaö, ⁊ areö ro ráiö a cciagarna .i. Iorm friu, ⁊ conige ro ba rfi cruaiö corgrac eiríöe : Rugrabair-ri conige ro (ar ré) corgair imöa cia ra ronuairligeaö riö ronn tré iomarca rluaig. 'Ercíö rir na briacraiö aböérra riö : "gac buaiö ⁊ gac corgur ⁊ gac blaö ruarabair crio rin, ra malarcfö ra bloig mbig aon laoi rin. Fegwio lib iaram an cacugaö do rioiri do gfncaoi rir na Loclannaiö, uair acáö bur mná, bur n-uile maiciur aca, ⁊ bur longa; ⁊ ar rubac iaorum do breic Luaöa ⁊ corgair uaibri areaö ar cóir oiö anora oul go haonmfnmnac na gcfnn amail na raoileaö riö far in bfchaiö, acc na beic riö og iornaiöe báir : ⁊ far noiogail fén forra, ⁊ gen go raiö corgur raimeac ouibri derin, ⁊ biaiö a m-bérao ar noec ⁊ ár ccóicce oún; muna raibe maic öúin ann, biaiö commarbaö coiccfnn leic for lfc ann.

Ag ro comairle oile leam öuib : an Rádraicc naom ra ar airo ercor ⁊ ar cfnn naom na h'Eirfnn, rir a noearnrac na namuioraifc ogainne uilc imöa, guiömiöne go ofocra, ⁊ cabram almrana onóraca öó, ar buaiö ⁊ corgur do breic do na náimöiö rin.

Ro freagraccur uile é, ⁊ areaö ro ráiörio : "ar comairce," ar rian, an tí naom Rádraicc ⁊ an coimöe ar tígearna do rin fén,

---

" *Snámh Aighneeh.*—Now Carlingford Lough, near which, at a place called Linn-Duachaill, the Norwegians had a fleet and strong fortress. Ann. Ult. 851 ; F. M. 850.

proceeded to Snámh Aighnechª where the Danes were [stationed] at that time. There they fought on either side, and engaged in a hard and stubborn battle on either side, for we have never heard before this time of so great a slaughter at sea as was caused between them, i.e. between the Danes and the Lochlanns. But, however, it was against the Danes the defeat was. The Danes, after being defeated in this battle, being sore oppressed by famine, assembled their people, and what their Lord, Horm, who hitherto had been a firm, victorious man, said to them was,—" Hitherto," said he, " ye have gained many victories, although ye have been defeated here by superior forces. Listen to the words which I shall say unto you: 'Every victory, every triumph, and every fame which ye had gained was obscured by the little fame of that day.' Look ye sharp to the battle which ye shall next make with the Lochlanns, for your women and all your property are in their hands as well as your ships; and they are rejoicing for having gained victory and triumph over you! What is proper for you now to do is to go unanimously against them, as if ye did not think of life, but not to be waiting for death, and to revenge yourselves upon them, and though ye may not gain a prosperous victory thereby, ye shall have whatever our gods and our fate will give us; if it be of no advantage to us, there shall be at least equal slaughter on either side.

"This is another advice of mine to you: 'This Saint Patrick, against whom these enemies of ours have committed many evils, is archbishop, and head of the saints of Erin. Let us pray to him fervently, and let us give honourable alms to him for our gaining victory and triumph over these enemies."

They all answered him, and what they said was: " Let our protector," said they, " be the holy Patrick, and the God who is Lord over him also, and let our spoils and our wealth be [given] to his church."

R   They

féin, ⁊ ar ccorgur d'á fglair, ⁊ ar n-ionoṁnur. Tfgaid iar rin go haonmfinmnaċ, rfhöa, feararṁail i n-aoinfiċt i gcionn na Loċlannaċ, ⁊ cuiric caċ.

Ir in uair rin táinig Ƶain leiṫrí na Loċlann, ⁊ Macovan rí Ulaḋ d'ingrim na nDanar do ṁuir ⁊ tír, gion go raba a fior rin reṁe ag Ƶain Loċlannaċ, táinig ⁊ an t-uaitfö ro baoi na farraḋ d'ionroigh na nDanar don dara leiṫ agar largna leiṫrí oile na Loċlann don leiṫ eile do na Danaroib. Ar cruaid tra ra cuirfö an caṫra. Ra ċlor ar leiṫ rgfingail na rlſg, agur gloinn- beimnſċ na ccloiöfṁ, ⁊ tuairgnſċ na rgiaṫ gá mbualaḋ, ⁊ béicfoaċ na mileḋ ag imirt éccoṁloinn orra. Aċt trá ċíò fada ſá bár imi rin, ar forr na Loċlannaib ro maiö, ⁊ ir iaḋ na Danair rug huaiḋ ⁊ corgar tria raṫ Páoraicc gé ro báoar na Loċlannaig trí ċuttroma rir na Danuroib, no ceiṫre cudruma. Tiagaid na Danair iarrin for longrort na Loċlann, ⁊ marbaid dream ann, gabaid dream eile, ⁊ cuirid dream eile i tteiṫfö, ⁊ gabaid gaċ maiṫiur óir ⁊ airgid, ⁊ gaċ maiṫiur ar ċfna, ⁊ amná ⁊ a longa. Aċt ċfna ní raib Ƶain fén ag cur an ċaṫa, uair ní táinig maille ra ṁuintir ar ammur an longruirt, uair ro baoi aige coṁairle a n-ionaḋ oile. An uair táinig do ċum an longruirt arriaḋ na námuid aḋ ċonnairc ann, ⁊ ní hiaḋ a ṁuintir féin. A n-égmair anneoċ ro marbaḋ do na Danuraib féin, areaḋ ra marbaḋ do na Loċlannaib cúig mile fear roiċinelaċ : foċuiḋe imurro do míleaḋaib ar ċfna, ⁊ do baoinib in gaċ áird ra marbaḋ a n-égmair na nuimre rin.

Ar in tan rin ra ċuir Maoilreaċloinn, rí Tfṁra teaċta d'ionnroige na nDanar. Ar aṁlaiḋ ro báttur na Danair ag
luċtairfċt

¹ *Five thousand.*—This is perfectly incredible.

² *Heaps of the bodies.*—This presents a curious picture of the ferocity of the Scan-

They afterwards came unanimously, bravely, and manfully together against the Lochlanns, and joined battle.

At this time Zain, half king of the Lochlanns, and Matodan, King of Uladh, came to attack the Danes by sea and land; although Zain, the Lochlann, had not known of this before, he came with the party who were with him to harass the Danes on the one side, and Iargno, the other half king of the Lochlanns, came to attack them on the other side. This battle was a hard fought one. The whizzing of lances, the clashing of swords, the clattering of shields when struck, and the shrieks of soldiers when subdued, were heard! But, however, though long they were *at it*, the Lochlanns were defeated, and the Danes gained victory and triumph, on account of the tutelage of Patrick, though the Lochlanns were three or four times their number! The Danes, after this, entered the camp of the Lochlanns, killed some of them, made prisoners of others, and put others to flight; and they possessed themselves of all their treasures of gold and silver, and other property, as well as of their women and ships. Zain himself, however, was not present at this engagement, for he did not come towards the camp along with his people, for he was holding a council elsewhere. When he had arrived at the camp, it was his enemies he saw there, and not his own people! Independently of those killed by the Danes, there were slain of the Lochlanns five thousand[x] goodly-born men; also many soldiers and people of every grade were slain in addition to this number.

Now, at this time Maelsechlainn, King of Teamhair, sent ambassadors to the Danes. And at their arrival the Danes were cooking, and the supports of their cauldrons were heaps of the bodies[y] of the Lochlanns,

dinavian nations, who were Pagans at this period. The favourites of their god Odin were all those who died in battle, or, what was considered equally meritorious, by their own hand. The timid wretch, who allowed himself to perish by disease or age, was considered unworthy of the joys of their paradise. These joys were fight-

Luċtairſċt ar a ġcionn, ⁊ ar iad ba ġabla dá ccoireḋaiḃ cáirn do
ċorpaiḃ na Loċlann ⁊ cid na bſṗa ar a mḃíoḋ an ḟeoil, ar ḟor
corpaiḃ Loċlann no ḃíoſr a leiṫcinn, ⁊ an tine aġ lorġaḋ na corp,
ġo mḃíoḋ an ḟeoil ⁊ an méaṫraḋ ra ċaiṫrioc an aḋaiġ reṁe aġ
maiḋm ar a nġailiḃ amaċ.

Ra battur dna tſċta Maoilreaċloinn ġá ḟḟéġaḋ aṁlaiḋ rin,
⁊ ra báttur ġa ttataoir um na Ḋanaraiḃ rin. Areaḋ ra ráid-
rioc na Ḋanair; ar aṁlaiḋ buḋ maiṫ leorum ár mbeiṫne. Clar
mór lan aca do ór, ⁊ da airġeaḋ dá ṫaḃairṫ do Ráḋraicc, uair
aṁlaiḋ ra báttur na Ḋanair ⁊ cinéle craḃaiḋ aca .i. ġaḃaid
realaḋ ḟri ḟeoil, ⁊ ḟri mnáiḃ ar craḃuḋ. Tuġ tra an caṫ ro
mínma maiṫ do Ġaoiḋealaiḃ uile ar an rġrior ro do ṫaḃairṫ ar
na Loċlannaiḃ.

'S in bliaḋain reo dna ro ḃrir Mooilreaċlainn caṫ forr na
raġánaiḃ, ⁊ dna ro ḃririrṫ Ciannaċta caṫ ḟá ḋó forr na
ġertiḃ.

Kal. Forḃairi Maoilreaċlainn i cCrurait unde Maoilreċini
cecinit :—

Miṫhiḋ dul tar ḃóinn mḃáin, i ndail moiġe Miḋe mín,
Ar andra beiṫ ḟri ġaoiṫ nġluair irind uair i cCrurait crín.

Inorſċtaċ, ab Ia, do ṫiaċtain i n-Eirinn ġo mionnaiḃ Coloim
Cille Lair. Iſ in mḃliaḋain ri ḃeor .i. in rexto anno reġni Maoilreaċlainn,

ing, ceaseless slaughter, and drinking beer
out of the skulls of their enemies, with a
renovation of life to furnish a perpetuity
of the same pleasures. The Scandinavians
placed their whole delight in war, and
entertained an absolute contempt of danger
and of death; and their glory was esti-
mated by the number they had slain in
battle. Of this we have a faithful picture
in the death-song of Regner Lodbrok (who
was probably the Turgesius of Irish history). This great conqueror comforts himself in his last agonies by recounting all
the acts of carnage he had committed in
his lifetime. See Mallet's "Northern Antiquities," Bohn's edition, pp. 105, 383;

Lochlanns, and one end of the spits on which the meat was hung was stuck into the bodies of the Lochlanns, and the fire was burning the bodies, so that they belched forth from their stomachs the flesh and the fat which they had eaten the night before.

The ambassadors of Maelsechlainn beheld them in this condition, and they reproached the Danes with this [savage conduct]. The Danes replied: " This is the way they would like to have us !" They had a great wide trench [filled] with gold and silver to give to Patrick, for the Danes were a people who had a kind of piety, i. e. they gave up meat and women awhile for piety ! Now this battle gave good courage to all the Gaeidhil[a] on account of this destruction brought upon the Lochlanns.

In this year Maelsechlainn gained a battle over the pagans, and the Cianachta[a] defeated the Gentiles a second time in battle.

[852.] Kal. The encampment of Maelsechlainn was at Crufait[b], unde Maelfeichine cecinit:—

Time to cross the fair Boinn to the plain of smooth Meath ;
It is difficult to be in the pure wind at this hour in withered Crufait.

Indrechtach, Abbot of Ia, came to Erin with the relics of Colum Cille. In this year also, the sixth year[c] of the reign of Maelsechlainn, Amhlaeibh

and Tytler's "Elements of General History," p. 136.

[a] *The Gaeidhil.*—i. e. the Scoti, or native Irish, in contradistinction to Gaill, i. e. Galli, or foreigners.

[a] *Cianachta.*—Ann. Ult. 851 ; F. M. 850.

[b] *Crufait.*—Ann. F. M. 847. The present name is unknown unless it be Cro-

boy, in Meath.

[c] *The sixth year.*—This was the year 852.—O'Flah. Ogyg., p. 434. Indrechtach, Abbot of Hy, appears to have come to Ireland with the relics of St. Columbkille so early as the year 849 or 850 ; he was killed in 854 by the Saxons. See Reeves's "Adamnan," p. 390, and Ann. Ult., A. D. 853.

reaclainn, táinig Amlaoiḃ Conung, .i. mac ṗiġ Loclann, ı n-'Eiṗinn, ⁊ tug leiṗ eṗṗuagṗa cíoṗa ⁊ cánaḋ n-imḋa ó a ataiṗ, ⁊ a ṗáġḃail-ṗiḋe go hobann. Táinig ono lomáṗ an bṗátaiṗ ba ṗoo 'na ḋíġaiḋ-ṗiḋe ḋo toḃac na ccíoṗ cḋna.

Kal. Loc Laoiġ ı cṗíc Umaill ḋo élóḋ.

Kal. Ṙíoġḋal ffṗi n-'Eiṗfnn in Aṗḋmaca eiḋiṗ Maoilṗeaclainn ⁊ Matoḋan ṗí Ulaḋ, ⁊ Ḋiaṗmaiḋ ⁊ ḟeṫġna go ṗamaḋ Ṗaḋṗaicc, ⁊ Suaiṗleac go ccléiṗciḃ Míḋe.

Inḋṗeactac Ua ḟinnacta Comaṗba Coluim Cille, ⁊ Ḋiaṗmaḋa ṗaṗiencirrimi, ḋo maṗḃaḋ ḋo ṗlaḋaiġiḃ Saẋanaca oġ ḋol ḋo Ṙoim, ⁊ maiṗiḃ a ṗuil eannag ṗain ḃeoṗ iṗ in ionaḋ in ṗo maṗḃaḋ ı gcomuṗca a ḋioġalta ḋo Ḋhia ṗoṗ an Luct ṗoṗ maṗḃ.

Iṗ in ḃliaḋainṗi ṗa tocuiṗeaḋ ṗiġ Loclann ḋo cum Maoilṗeaclainn ḋ'ól, ⁊ ṗo ḃoí ṗleaḋ lánmóṗ aṗ a cionn, aġaṗ ġac ní ṗa ġeall ṗu Loclann ḋo comall co na luige ; act cfna ní ṗa comaill a ḃfg aṗ noul a tiġ Maoilṗeaclainn amac, act ṗa ġaḃ a gcéḋóiṗ aġ ionnṗaḋ ṗeaṗainn Maoilṗeaclainn. Act cfna ní ṗfctnac ṗáinig leiṗ an coġaḋ ṗin.

Iṗ in ḃliaḋainṗi ono ṗo tṗéigṗiot ṗochaiḋe a mbaitiṗ Cṗíoṗ-taíḋacta ⁊ tangattaṗ malle ṗiṗ na Loclannaiḃ, ġuṗ aiṗgṗiot Aṗḋmaca, ⁊ go ṗuġṗat a maitiuṗ aṗ. Seḋ quiḋem ex iṗṗiṗ poenitenciam exeṗe, et ueneṗunt aḋ ṗatiṗfaccionem.

Kal. Ḋo abb Aṗḋmaca Foṗannán Eṗṗcop ⁊ ṗgṗíḃai ⁊ anchoiṗe ⁊ Ḋiaṗmaiḋ ṗaṗiencirrimuṗ Scotoṗum quieueṗunt.

Cṡṗḃall

---

[d] *Amhlaeibh Conung.*—Ann. Ult. 852, where he is called Amlaimh, or Amlaiṗ, son of the King of Lochlinn. *Quære*, is *Conung* an Hibernicized form of the Teutonic *koenig* or *koenung*, king ?

[e] *In Umhaill.*—i. e. in Burrishoole, county of Mayo. Todd's "Irish Nennius," p. 207, and Ann. F. M. 848.

[f] *A royal meeting.*—This is noted in the Ann. Ult., A. D. 850; F. M. 849.

[g] *Indrechtach Ua Finnachta.*—Ann. Ult. 853, "iv. Id. Martii ;" F. M. 852.—

Amhlaeibh Conung[d], i. e. the son of the King of Lochlann, came to Erin, and he brought with him commands from his father for many rents and tributes, but he left suddenly. Imhar, his younger brother, came after him to levy the same rents.

Kal. Loch Laeigh, in Umhaill[e], migrated.

Kal. A royal meeting[f] of the men of Erin at Ard-Macha, between Maelsechlainn and Matodan, King of Uladh, and Diarmaid and Fethghna with the congregation of Patrick, and Suairlech with the clergy of Meath.

[854.] Indrechtach Ua Finnachta[g], successor of Colum Cille, and Diarmaid, very wise men, were killed by Saxon plunderers on their way to Rome, and their pure blood still remains at the place where they were killed as a sign of the vengeance of God against those who killed them.

In this year the King of Lochlann was invited to [the house of] Maelsechlainn to drink, and there was a great feast prepared for him; and the King of Lochlann [made many promises], and promised on his oath to observe them; but, however, he did not observe the smallest of them after leaving the house of Maelsechlainn, but he proceeded at once to plunder the land of Maelsechlainn. But, however, this war did not turn out lucky for him.

In this year many forsook their Christian baptism[h] and joined the Lochlanns, and they plundered Ard-Macha, and carried away all its riches; but some of them did penance, and came to make satisfaction.

[852.] Two abbots of Ard-Macha[i], Forannan, bishop and scribe, and Diarmaid, the wisest of the Scoti, died.

Cearbhall,

Reeves's Adamnan, p. 390.

[h] *Many forsook their baptism.*—i. e. many of the Irish joined the Danes, and lapsed into Paganism. This extraordinary fact

is not noticed by the Ann. Ult. or by the F. M.

[i] *Two abbots of Ard-Macha.*—" Duo heredes Patricii, viz. Forinnan, Scriba et

Cṙḃall mac Ḋunlainʒ ṙí Oṙṙaiʒe (cliaṁuin Maoilṙeaclainn .i. ḋeaṙḃṙiuṙ Cṙḃaill oʒ Maoilṙeaclainn .i. lanḋ inʒ́ṅ Ḋunlainʒ, ⁊ ḋna inʒ́ṅ Maoilṙeaclainn oʒ Cṙḃall) ḋo cuṙ ḃo Maoilṙeaclionn i Muṁain ḋo cuinnʒ́iḃ ʒiall, aṙ néʒ a ṙiʒ́ .i. Ailʒṅán. Cac no caḃaiṙc ḋ'Aoḃ ḋo ṙiʒ́ Ailiʒ́ .i. ḋon ṙiʒ́ aṙ ḟeṙṙ ṡʒnaṁ 'na aimṙiṙ, ḋo loinʒiuṙ na nʒall nʒaoiḃeal .i. Scuic iaḋ ⁊ ḋalcai ḋo Noṙmannoiḃ iaḋ, ⁊ can ann aḋ ḃṙṙaṙ ciḋ Noṙmainniʒ́ ṙṙiu. Maiḃiḋ ṙoṙṙa ṙe nAoḃ, aʒuṙ cuiṙceaṙ a nḋeaṙʒáṙ na nʒall nʒaoiḃeal, ⁊ cinn imḃa ḋo ḃṙeic ḋo [Aeḋ mac] Niall leiṙ, ⁊ ṙa ḃliʒ́ṙioc na h-Eiṙṡnnaiʒ́ an maṙḃaḋ ṙoin, uaiṙ aṁail ḋo níḋíṙ na Loclannaiʒ́ ḋo níḋiṙṙioṁ.

Sloiʒ́ṡḃ la hAoḃ mac Néill ḋo innṙaḋ Ulaḃ. Acc cṡna ní ṙéiḃ ṙáiniʒ ḋo, uaiṙ cuʒṙac Ulaiḃ maiḋm ṙoṙ Cinél n-Eoʒ́ain, ⁊ ṙo maṙḃṙac Ṗlaiṫḃeaṙcac mac Néill, ⁊ Conacán mac Colmáin ann cum mulciṙ aliṙ.

Iṙ in aimṙiṙ ṙi acc ḃṡʒ cáiniʒ Roḃolḃ co na ṙloʒ́aiḃ ḋ'innṙaḋ Oṙṙaiʒ́e. Ra cionoil ḋno Cṙḃall mac Ḋunlainʒ ṙloʒ́ na n-aʒ́aiḃ, ⁊ cuʒ cac ḃóiḃ, ⁊ ṙo ṁaiḃ ṙoṙṙ na Loclannaiḃ. Ra cuaḋaṙ imuṙṙo buiḋṡn ṁóṙ ḋo lucc na maḋma ṙoṙ a n-ṡcoiḃ i cciolaiʒ́ n-áiṙḋ, ⁊ ṙo ḃáccuṙ aʒ ṙéʒ́aḋ an ṁaṙḃca imṙṙu, ⁊ aḋ conncaccuṙ a muinceṙ ṙéin ʒ́á maṙḃaḋ aṁail na maṙḃḋaiṙ caoiṙiʒ́. Ra ʒ́aḃ aiṙéḋ moṙ iaḋ, ⁊ aṙeḋ ḋo ṙoṙṙac a cclaiḃiḃ ḋo nocéaḃ, ⁊ a n-aiṙm ḋo

---

Episcopus et anchorita, et Dermaid, sapientissimus omnium doctorum Europæ qui-everunt."—*Ann. Ult.* 851; *F. M.* 851. Dermaid is said above to have suffered martyrdom with Innrechtach on their way to Rome; but the F. M. record his death the year before, the Ann. Ult. two years before, the martyrdom of Innrechtaeh.

ᵏ *Daughter.*—His daughter by a different marriage.

¹ *Ailghenan*, King of Munster, died, according to the Four Masters, in 851, but the true year is 853.—Ann. Ult. 852.

ᵐ *Gall-Gaeidhil.*—i. e. the Dano-Irish, or rather the Norwegian Irish who had lapsed into paganism, and plundered the churches in as profane a manner as the Norwegians themselves. The Four Mas-

Cearbhall, son of Dunlaing, King of Osraighe (the brother-in-law of Maelsechlainn, for the sister of Cearbhall, *was married* to Maelsechlainn, i. e. Lann, daughter of Dunlaing, and besides the daughter[k] of Maelsechlainn, was married to Cearbhall), was sent by Maelsechlainn into Munster, to demand hostages, on the death of their King Ailghenan[l].

A battle was given by Aedh, King of Ailech, the most valiant king of his time, to the fleet of the Gall-Gaeidhil[m], i. e. they were Scoti and foster-children to the Northmen, and at one time they used to be called Northmen. They were defeated and slaughtered by Aedh, and many *of their* heads were carried off by [Aedh, son[n] of] Niall with him, and the Irish were justified in committing this havoc, for these were accustomed to act like the Lochlanns.

A hosting was made by Aedh, son of Niall, to plunder Uladh[o], but he did not find this easy, for the Ulidians defeated the Cinel-Eoghain, and slew Flaithbhertach, son of Niall, and Conacan, son of Colman, with many others.

Nearly at this time Rodolph[p] came with his forces to plunder Osraighe. But Cearbhall, son of Dunlaing, assembled a host to oppose them, and gave them battle, and defeated the Lochlanns. A large party of the defeated, however, went on horseback to the top of a high hill, from which they viewed the slaughter around them, and saw their own people slaughtered like sheep. They were seized with a great desire of revenge, and what they did was to draw their swords

ters state that this victory was gained by Aedh, son of Niall, at Glennfhoichle (now Glenelly, near Strabane, in the county of Tyrone), in the year 854. The Annals of Ulster place it in 855.

[n] *Son of.*—The text has "by Niall,"

but in the margin are the words "Cob potius." We ought, therefore, certainly to read Cob mac Niall.

[o] *Uladh.*—Ann. F. M. 853; Ult. 854.

[p] *Rodolph.*—There is no notice of this chieftain in the published Annals.

do ġabail, ⁊ tuiḃſét cum na n-Oṛṛuiġeaċ, ġuṛ ṛo maṛḃṛat oṛeam ḋíoḃ; ġiḃeaḋ aṛ aba ṛa cuiṛſḃ iaḋṛaiḋe aṛ ccúla na maiḋm .i. aġ Áṫ muiceaḋa tuġaḋ an maiḋm ṛi. Do ṛala imuṛṛo Ġliṛit ṛonn do Chſṛḃall ṛén .i. anuaiṛ taḃaṛta an ṁaoma, ⁊ ṛġaoileaḋ da ṁuinntiṛ uaḋ; oṛeam do na Loċlannaiḃ do toiḃſét ċuiġe ⁊ a eaṛ-ġaḃail ḋóiḃ. Áċt tṛe ṛuṛtaċt an coimḋeaḋ ṛuaiṛ a ṛóiṛiéin: ṛa bṛiṛ ṛén a eḋaċ, ⁊ na cſhġail ṛa ḃáttuṛ ṛaiṛ, ⁊ ṛa ċuaiḋ ṛlán uaiḋiḃ. Aṛ móṛ tṛá an t-áṛ tuġaḋ ann ṛoṛṛ na Loċlannaiḃ.

Caṫ no ḃṛiṛeḋ do Saxonoiḃ ṛoṛṛ na Noṛmainnaiḃ.

Iſ in aimṛiṛ ṛi tanġattuṛ Danaiṛ .i. hoṛm co na muiñtiṛ d'iannṛoiġiḋ Cſṛḃaill mic Dunlainġ, ġo ṛo conġnaiḋ Cſṛḃall leo i ccſhn na Loċlann, uaiṛ bá heaġail leo a ffoṛuaiṛluġaḋ tṛe ċeal-ġaiḃ na Loċlann. Ra ġaḃ ḋno Cſṛḃall ġo honóṛaċ ċuiġe iaḋ, ⁊ ṛo ḃáttuṛ maille ṛiſ ġo minic oġ bṛeiṫ ċoṛġaiṛ do Ġhallaiḃ ⁊ do Ġhaoiḋealaiḃ.

Aṛ móṛ la Ciaṛṛaiġiḃ oġ bealaċ Conġlaiṛ ṛoṛ Loċlannaiḃ, uḃi ṛluṛimi tṛuciḋati ṛunt ṛeṛmiṛṛionne Dei.

'Aṛ ono la h-'Aṛaḋa Cliaċ ṛoṛṛ na ġentiḃ céona.

Iſ in bliaḋain céona ṛa ċuiṛṛiot ṛiṛ Muṁan teachta d'ionn-ṛoiġiḋ Chſṛḃaill mic Dunlainġ, ġo d-tſoṛaḋ na Danaiṛ leiſ, ⁊ tionol Oṛṛaiġe da ffuṛtaċt, ⁊ da ffóiṛiḋin an aġaiḋ na Noṛ-mainneċ ṛa baḋaṛ ġá n-ionnṛaḋ ⁊ ġa n-aṛġain an tan ṛoin. Ra fṛſġaiṛ ḋno Cſṛḃall ṛin, ⁊ ṛa ṛuaġaiṛ do na Danaṛaiḃ ⁊ d'Oṛ-ṛaiġiḃ toiḃeaċt ġo léiṛ [tinóilte] oṛuṛtaċt ṛſṛ Muṁan, ⁊ aṛ eaḋ on do ṛonoḋ ṛaiṛ. Tainic iaṛam Cſṛḃall ṛeiṁe d'ionnṛoiġhiḋ na Loċlann

---

ⁿ *Ath muiceadha.*—i.e. ford of the swine-herd. This narrative does not occur in any other Annals known to the Editor.

ᵣ *The Saxons.*—This is probably the victory recorded in the Anglo-Saxon Chronicle at the year 851, when King Ethelwulf and his son Æthelbald fought against the Northmen at Ockley, "and there made the greatest slaughter among the heathen army that we have heard tell of unto the

swords and take their arms and come [down] to the Osraighi, a party of whom they slew. They were nevertheless driven back in defeated rout. This defeat was given them at Ath muiceadha^q. Here Glifit met Cearbhall himself at the time of the defeat, his people having separated from him. A party of the Lochlanns came up with him and took him prisoner; but by the Lord's assistance he was relieved. He himself tore his clothes and the bonds that were upon him, and escaped in safety from them. Great, indeed, was the slaughter that was made of the Lochlanns there.

A battle was gained by the Saxons^r over the Northmen. At this time came the Danes, i. e. Horm and his people, to Cearbhall, son of Dunlaing, and Cearbhall assisted them against the Lochlanns [Norwegians], for they were afraid of being overpowered by the stratagems of the Lochlanns. Cearbhall therefore took them to him honourably, and they frequently accompanied him in gaining victories over the foreigners and the Gaeidhil [Irish].

A great slaughter of the Lochlanns was made by the Ciarraighi at Bealach Chonglais^s, where many were killed by the permission of God.

A slaughter, too, was made by the Aradians of Cliach^t, of the same Gentiles.

In the same year^u the men of Munster sent messengers to Cearbhall, son of Dunlaing [to request] that he would come, bringing the Danes with him, and the rising out of Osraighe, to assist and relieve them against the Northmen [Norwegians] who were harassing and plundering them at that time. Now, Cearbhall responded to this [call]

present day."

^s *Bealach Chonglais.*—A place near the city of Cork. There is no notice of this battle in the published Annals.

^t *Aradians of Cliach.*—This entry is not in the published Annals.

^u *In the same year.*—Not in the published Annals.

Loclann go slóg mor Danar ⁊ Gaoideal. Od concattur na Loclannaig Csiball co na fluag, no muinntir, ro gad aduat ⁊ uaṁan mor iad. Ra cuaid Cearball i n-ionad áro ⁊ ro baoi ag agallad a muinntire féin ar tús; areað ro ráid, ⁊ sé og fégad na ffsrann ffaraige imme: Nac ffraictí lid, ar sé, mar ra fáruigriot na Loclannaig na feararna-ra ar mbreit a cruid ⁊ ar marbad a daoine; mad treiri dáib iniu iná duinne, do génad na cétna 'nar ttís-ne, uair imurro atáimne rocraide mór aniu, caiéigsm go cruaid na n-aigid. Fat oile ar nod cóir dúin catugad cruaid do dénoṁ, nar rionnat na Danair failet maille fsinn mstatt ná miodlaecur foirn, uair ra teigéṁad, gid maille rinn atáo aniu, go mbedís 'nár n-agaid dorióirsi. Fat oile, gur ro tugad fir Muṁan i ttangamar róiridin ár cruar forainn, uair is minic ar naṁaid iad.

Ra agaill iarttain na Danair, ⁊ areað ro ráid riuraide: déníórs calma aniu, uair ar naṁuid dunaid duid na Loclannaig, ⁊ ra cuirsit cata eattruib, ⁊ áir móra anallána. Ar mait duid rinne maille rib aniu na n-agaid, ⁊ dna ní eile ann, ní fiu duid tréite no laige do tuigrin duinne foraid. Ra ffeagratur uile edir Dhanaru ⁊ Ghaoidealu, ná rionnfaite tréite no mstatt forra. Ro eirgsdur iarttain eirge naoinsin isin uair rin d'ionnroigid na Loclann. Na Loclannaig immurro ó do concattur rin, ní cat ro iomsuidrios do tadairt, act ar teitíd fo na cailltib, ar ffágbail a maitiura, do ronrat. Ra gabaid na caillte dá gac leit forra, ⁊ ra marbad a ndeargán na Loclann. Act cṁa conige ro ní ra fuilngiottur na Loclannaig do'n coiṁlíon

¹ *As he looked upon.*—Ag sé og fégad. In modern Irish this would be, agur é ag féacain na bfearann b-far uime.
² *They were killed with great slaughter.*

—Ro marbad a ndearg-ár na Loclann. The modern construction would be, Ro marbadar dearg-ár na Loclannach, which is better.

[call], and he commanded the Danes and the Osraighi to proceed fully [assembled] to relieve the men of Munster, and this was accordingly done at this summons. Cearbhall afterwards came forward to attack the Lochlanns with a great host of Danes and Gaeidhils. When the Lochlanns saw Cearbhall with his host, or people, they were seized with great fear and dread. Cearbhall went to a high place, and he began to address his own people first, and he said, as he looked upon the deserted lands around him : " Do ye not perceive," said he, " how the Lochlanns have desolated these lands, having carried off their cattle and killed their inhabitants? If they be more powerful this day than we, they will do the same in our territory. But as we are very numerous this day, let us fight bravely against them. Another reason for which it is right for us to fight bravely is, that the Danes, who are along with us, may not perceive cowardice or want of heroism in us, for it may happen that, though they are on our side this day, they may hereafter be against us. Another reason is, that the men of Munster, whom we have come to relieve, may understand our hardihood, for they too are often our enemies." He afterwards addressed the Danes, and what he had said to them was : " Exhibit your bravery this day, for the Lochlanns are your radical enemies, for ye fought battles, and slaughtered one another formerly. It is well for you to have us with you against them this day, and, moreover, it is not worth your while to let us observe dastardliness or cowardice among you." They all made answer, both Gaeidhil and Danes, that neither weakness nor cowardice should be observed in them. They afterwards rose out as one man at that time to attack the Lochlanns. However, when the Lochlanns observed this, they did not close to give battle, but fled to the woods, leaving their property behind. The woods were surrounded on every side upon the Lochlanns, and they were killed with great slaughter. Up to this time

the

líon ꝛo a n-Eiꝛinn uile. A cCꞃuacain i n-Eoganacc cugaꝺ an maiómꝛi.

Táinic Cꞃꝛball go mbuaiꝺ ⁊ coꞃgaꞃ amlaiꝺ ꞃin ꝺ'á ċiġ. Ro hioꝺnaiceꝺ hoꞃm iaꞃccain co na muinnciꞃ ó Cꞃꝛball go ꞃí Cꞃmꞃaċ. Rá ꝼꞃꞃ ꞃí Cꞃmꞃaċ ꝼáilce ꞃiꞃ, ⁊ cug onóiꞃ móꞃ ꝺó: Rá ċuaiꝺ aꞃꞃin ꝺo ċum maꞃa. Ra maꞃbaꝺ iaꞃccain an choꞃm ꞃin la Roꝺꞃi, ꞃí bꞃꞃcan.

hoc anno quieuic Mac Giallain aꞃ mbeiċ xxx. bliaꝺain i n-aíne.

Niall mac Gilláin iaꞃ mbeiċ cꞃioċa bliaġain gan ꝺig gan biaꝺ, ꝺécc A. D. 854.

Kal. Ainꝺli ꞃaꞃienꞃ Cíꞃe ꝺa glaꞃ moꞃicuꞃ.

Cáꞃċaċ ab Cíꞃe ꝺa glaꞃ, quieuic.

Ailgꞃnan maċ Donngaile ꞃí Caiꞃil, moꞃicuꞃ. Amlaoiꝺ mac ꞃí Loċlann ꝺo ċoiꝺeaċc i n-Eiꞃinn, ⁊ ꞃa giallꞃac gaill 'Eiꞃeann ꝺó.

Kal. Iꞃ in bliaꝺain ꞃi, an ꝺaꞃa bliaꝺainn ꝺécc ꝼlaċa Maoilꞃechloinn ꝺo ꞃonaꝺ móꞃꝼluaġ la Maoilꞃeaċloinn i n-Oꞃꞃaigiꝺ ⁊ im Mumain, aꞃ na ꝼáꝺ ꝺ'ꝼeaꞃaib Mumon na ciꞃꝺióꞃ bꞃaiġꝺe ꝺó, gonaꝺ aiꞃe ꞃin ꞃa ꝼuagaiꞃ Maoilꞃeaċloinn caċ ꞃoꞃꞃa; ⁊ ꝼáċ moꞃ oile ag Maoilꞃeaċloinn .i. Cꞃꝛball mac Dunlaing, ꞃi Oꞃꞃaige, ꝺuine ón gaꞃ bo ꝺingbála Eiꞃe, uile Do ꝺeiċ, aꞃ ꝼeaꝺuꞃ a ꝺealba ⁊ a eniġ ⁊ a ꞃngnama, cíꞃa móꞃabliaꝺ naiꝺe ꝺo bꞃeiċ ꝺó .i. o na cuaċoib ꝺo Laiġniꝺ ꞃa ꝺáccuꞃ aiġe. In luċċ imuꞃꞃo ꞃa ċuaiꝺ ꝺo ċoꝺaċ

---

[1] *Cruachain Eoghanacht.*—This place is otherwise called *Cruachan Maighe Eamhna*, now Crohane, in the barony of Slievardagh, in the county of Tipperary. It is mentioned in the " Feilire Aenghuis" at 5th October, as in the territory of Eoghanacht-Chaisil.

[2] *Horm.*—" A.D. 855, Horm, chief of the Black Gentiles, was killed by Ruarai mac Merminn, King of Britain."—*Ann. Ult.* The true year was 856, so that the preceding events must have taken place in the years 854 and 855.

[3] *Mac Giallain.*—His death is entered

the Lochlanns had not suffered so great a loss in all Erin. At Cruachain in the Eoghanacht⁷ this victory was gained.

Cearbhall thus returned to his house with victory and triumph. Horm and his people were afterwards escorted by Cearbhall to the King of Teamhair. The King of Teamhair welcomed him, and gave him great honour. He afterwards went to sea. This Horm[a] was afterwards killed by Roderic, King of the Britons.

In this year died Mac Giallain[a], after having fasted for thirty years.

Niall Mac Giallain died in the year 854, after having been thirty years without drink, without food.

[853.] Kal. Aindli, wise man of Tir-da-ghlas, died.

Carthach[b], Abbot of Tir-da-ghlas, died.

Ailgenan, son of Dunghal, King of Cashel, died.

[856.] Amhlaeibh, son of the King of Lochlann, came to Erin, and the Galls of Erin submitted to him.

[858.] Kal. In this year, the twelfth[c] of the reign of Maelsechlainn, Maelsechlainn marched with a great army into Osraighe and into Munster, the Munster-men having said that they would not give him hostages, wherefore Maelsechlainn proclaimed battle upon them; and Maelsechlainn had another great cause, which was this: Cearbhall, son of Dunlaing, King of Osraighe, a person who was indeed worthy of possessing all Erin for the goodness of his countenance, hospitality,

in the Ann. F. M. at the year 854, and again at 858; Ann. Ult. 859. "Niall Mac Fiallain [Mac Giallain, F. M.] *qui passus est paralisi 34 annis, et qui versatus est visionibus frequentibus, tam falsis, quam veris, in Christo quievit.*" The double entry of his death here (and by the F. M.

854, 858), shows that these Annals were compiled from different sources.

[b] *Carthach.*—This and the following entry are given the by F. M. at 851, and are evidently out of place here.

[c] *The twelfth of the reign of Maelsechlainn.*—i. e. 858 ; Ann. Ult. 857.

tobac an cíora rin .i. maoir Crnbaill mic Dunlaing, imcornam mór do dénam dóib ag tobac an cíora, ⁊ tarcorral mór do tabairt doib for Laignib. Laigin do dola ar roin go gearánac d'ionnroighid Maoilreacloinn, ⁊ a mbrin do Maoilreacloinn. Fsrg mór do gabail Maoilreacloinn, ⁊ an cionol mórra do breit d'ionnroighid Crnbaill ⁊ fear Muman battur ag congnam la Crnball. Tangattur iarroin Maoilreacloinn cona plóig go Gabrán, ⁊ ar na bruinne Gabrain ra battur na rlóig oile. Gér bo líonmaire imurro do Maoilreacloinn, ní hcb ra cuaid na ccfnn act ar conair oile ná ro raoileab a ndola ra cuattur, go rángattur Cárn Lugaba, ⁊ ro baoi Maoilreacloinn armta éidigte annrain ar cfnn cáic. 'Od concadar fir Muman rin, rá fagrat a longront ⁊ ra rainnrit a rluag ar dó, ⁊ táinig rí Muman .i. Maolguala co marcrluagaib moraib ime in n-aigid Maoilreacloinn. Crnball imurro ⁊ a Dhanair, doneoc ra taipir do muintir horm ra taipir i frarad Crnbaill, arfb ba longront dóib caill drirod dlút aimréid, ⁊ rá baoi cionol mór ann rin um Crnball. Arsb rá innirit na heolaig go raba buaidreab mór annrin for Crnball ar n-imirt driageacta do Chaircealtac mac na Cearta fair, go mbab lugaide no digrid do cum an cata, go nerbeart Crnball ar coulab do génad ann rin, ⁊ ní do cum an cata do ragad. In cat tra i raba rí Muman tugrat maibm ar tur ar muintir Maoilreacloinn. Tangadar dna a coirigeba ba fóirieinribe .i. Maoilreacloinn co na muintir, go ttugab maibm for fearaib Muman ⁊ rá cuiread an deary ár. Ro marbaid rocaide do

raorclannoib

---

[d] *Gabhran.*—Now Gowran, in the county of Kilkenny.

[e] *Carn Laghdhach.* — i. e. Lughaidh's carn. This place is somewhere near Gowran, but its exact situation or modern name has not been yet determined.

[f] *Fircheartach mac na Cearta.*—A famous necromancer often referred to in old Irish romances. He is sometimes called Mac Aenchearda. He seems to have been

lity, and valour, levied great yearly rents from the territories in Leinster, which he possessed; but the people who went to levy the rent, i. e. the stewards of Cearbhall, son of Dunlang, used great violence in levying the rent, and offered great insult to the Leinster-men. The Leinster-men consequently went querulously to Maelsechlainn and told it to him. Maelsechlainn was seized with great anger and led this great muster against Cearbhall and the men of Munster who were aiding him. Maelsechlainn, after this, proceeded with his host to Gabhrán[d], at the confines of which the other hosts were. However, though Maelsechlainn had more numerous forces, he did not go against them, but proceeded by another road where he did not think they would go, until he reached Carn Lughdhach[e], and here Maelsechlainn was armed and accoutred to meet all. When the men of Munster perceived this, they left their camp, and divided their host into two parts, and the King of Munster, Maelguala, came with large squadrons of horse to oppose Maelsechlainn; but Cearbhall and his Danes (such of the people of Horm as remained with him), encamped in a briery, thick entangled wood, and there was a great muster there about Cearbhall. And the learned relate that there was a great trouble on Cearbhall here, Tairchealtach Mac na Cearta[f] having exercised magic upon him, so that he was less inclined to go to battle, and so that Cearbhall said that he would retire to rest and not go to battle! Now, the battalion in which the King of Munster was [the commander] at first defeated the people of Maelsechlainn, but foot soldiers came to their relief (i. e. to the relief of Maelsechlainn and his people), so that the men of Munster were [in their turn] defeated and cut off with dreadful slaughter. Many nobles were killed

the presiding spirit of Carn Lughdhach, where this battle was fought, but the modern name or situation of the place still remains to be determined.

ṗaoṗċlannoiḃ annṗin. Inoiṗic eolaiġ conaḋ hí numiṗ an cṗlóiġ aṗ a ḋcuġaḋ an maiḃm ⁊c. milium.

Aṗi comaiṗle ḋo ṗinne Cṗḃall, maṗ ṗa ċuala ṗin, ḃṗaiġḋe ḋo ċaḃaiṗc ḋo Maoilṗeaċlainn, ⁊ ġan a ṫiṗ ḋo loc, ⁊ ṗo ġaḃ Maoilṗeaċlainn ḃṗaiġḋe uaḋ, uaiṗ lanḋ inġṡn Ḋunlainġ, ḋeṗḃṗiuṗ Chṡṗḃaill, ḃṡn Maoilṗeaċlainn.

Ra ċuaiḋ Maoilṗeaċlainn ḋon Muṁain, ġo ṗaḃa ṗe ṗé míṗ oġ ionnṗaḋ Muṁan ann Eimliġ, ġo ccuġ ḃṗaiġḋe Muṁan ó Comuṗ cṗí n-uiṗġe ġo hinnṗi Caṗḃna iaṗ n-'Eiṗinn. Caċ Caiṗn Luġḃaċ ṗain. Iṗ in caċ ṗoin ṗo maṗḃaḋ Maolcṗóin mac Muiṗṡḃaiġ leiċṗiġ na nḊéiṗi.

Ġen ġo ccioṗaḋ Maoilṗeaċlainn an cuṗuṗ ṗo ḋo ġaḃáil ṗiġe Muṁan ḋo ṗéin, ṗo ḃo ċuiḋeaċca ḋo maṗḃaḋ an ṗo ṁaṗḃaḋ ḋo Ġhallġaoiḃealaiḃ ann, uaiṗ ḋaoine iaṗ ccṗéġaḋ a mḃaiṗce iaḋṗaiḋe, ⁊ aoḋeṗcaiṗ Noṗmannaiġ ḟṗiu, uaiṗ ḃéṗ Noṗmannaċ aca, ⁊ a n-alcṗum ṗoṗṗa, ⁊ ġéṗ ḃo olc na Noṗmannaiġ ḃuṗaiḋ ḋo na hṡġlaiṗiḃ ḃá míṡa ġo móṗ iaḋṗaiḋe .i. an luċc ṗa, ġaċ coṗaiṗ ṗo 'Eiṗinn a mḃṡiṗ.

Poġmuṗ ġoṗcaċ iṡ in mḃliaḋain ṗi.

Inṗiuḋ Laiġṡn uile la Ceṗḃall mac Ḋunlainġ, ⁊ níoṗ ḟṗeṗṗḋe ḃṗaiġḋe uaḋ a laiṁ Maoilṗeaċlainn, ġuṗ ġaḃ Cṗḃall mac Ḋunlainġ ḃṗaiġḋe Laiġṡn um Coṗpmac mac Ḋunlainġ, ⁊ im Suiċṡman mac

---

ᵍ *Lann.*—The meaning is, that this connexion rendered Maelsechlainn more placable, or that Lann had employed her intercession with her husband.

ʰ *Imleach.*—Now Emly, in the county Tipperary.

ⁱ *Cumar-na-tri-n-uisce.*—i.e. the meeting of the Three Waters, near Waterford.

ᵏ *Inis Tarbhna.*—Now the Bull, a small island in the barony of Beare, and county of Cork.

ˡ *Gall-Gaidhil.*—The published Annals give us no idea of this class of Iberno-Norwegian or Norwegian-Irish heathens who infested Ireland at this period. O'Flaherty thought that the name was confined

killed there. The learned relate that the number of the army which was there routed was twenty thousand.

When Cearbhall heard of this [defeat], the resolution he adopted was to give hostages to Maelsechlainn, to prevent him from destroying his country; and Maelsechlainn accepted of hostages from him, for Lann[g], daughter of Dunlang and sister of Cearbhall, was the wife of Maelsechlainn.

Maelsechlann then proceeded into Munster, and remained for the space of a month at Imleach[h], plundering Munster, and he obtained the hostages of Munster from Cumar-na-tri-nu-isce[i] to Inis Tarbhna[k], in the west of Erin. This was the battle of Carn Lughdhach. In this battle was slain Maelcron, son of Muircadhach, half King of the Deisi.

Though Maelsechlainn had not come on this expedition to take the kingdom of Munster for himself, he ought to have come to kill all the Gall-Gaidhil[l] who were killed there, for they were a people who had renounced their baptism, and they were usually called Northmen, for they had the customs of the Northmen, and had been fostered by them, and though the original Northmen were bad to the churches, these were by far worse, in whatever part of Erin they used to be.

There was a dearth in the autumn of this year.

[858.] All Leinster[m] was plundered by Cearbhall, son of Dunlang, and his hostages in the hands of Maelsechlainn did not render him the better subject, so that Cearbhall, son of Dunlang, took the hostages of Leinster, together with Cormac[n], son of Dunlang, and Suitheman,

to the inhabitants of the western islands of Scotland, and it is very certain that the mixed race of these islands were so called. See Ann. F. M., A. D. 1154, p. 1113; where they speak of the Gal-Gaidhil of

Aran, of Cantire, of the Isle of Man, and of the coasts of Scotland (Alban).
[m] *All Leinster.*—Ann. F. M. 856.
[n] *Cormac.*—The F. M. 856, call him Coirpre, son of Dunlang.

mac Aptúip. Maiom pe Cpball mac Ounlaing, ⁊ pe Niap po Ghallgaoibealaib i n-Apabaib tipe.

Kal. Anno Domini, ucccłu. Maolguala, pi Caipil do gabáil do Nopmannoib, ⁊ a écc allaiṁ acca.

Sluag mór la Cpball mac Ounlaing ⁊ pluag Loclañ laip i Miöe ⁊ ní pa oeig . . . . . a bpaigoe báttup ag Maoilpeaclainn, go paba na tpí míopaib ag innpaö pppainn Maoilpeaclainn ⁊ ní po an gup po polṁuig an típ uile 'ma maiéiup. Ip pocaibe tpa o'ppaib bána Eipeann do ponpat ouana molta do Cpball, ⁊ taitmpo gac copgup pug inncib; ⁊ ap mó do pine Aongap an t-áip-ofgnaib, comapba Molua.

Ut tpa an ní ad bppam go minic : Ap tpuag do na h-Eipfnncaib an mí-bép doib tacup ftuppa péin, ⁊ nac anaoineact uile éipgit a ccfnn na Loclann. Ra eipge ona Aoö mac Néill, ap na apłac do pí Ciannacta paip eipge i ccfnn Maoilpeaclainn, uaip Maoilpeac-lainn pa báib deapbpataip píg Ciannacta, .i. Cionaoð ut ppae-pcpippimup.

Rigbáil maite 'Eipeann og Rat Aoba um Maoilpeaclainn, pí Eipeann, ⁊ um ppfgna comapba Pápaicc, ⁊ um Suaipliot, com-apba

* *Aradh Tire.*—Now the barony of Arra, or Duharra, in the county of Tipperary, Ann. F. M. 857.

p *Anno Domini*, 855.—This date is incorrect, and the scribe writes in the margin : Ap aṁlaiö an nuimippi Annopum Do-mini ⁊ ceiépi bliaöna do bénam don aoin bliaöain pfṁuinn, in po innapb Popannán ab cubaið Apðmacha. "The way that this number Annorum Domini [happened to come here] is, that four years are made of the one year [recte, one year is made of four years] before us, viz. that in which Forannan, legitimate abbot of Ard Macha, was expelled." This remark seems to be out of its proper place, for Forannan was carried off in the year 843.

q *Maelguala, King of Cashel.*—Ann. F. M. 857; Ult. 858. The Four Masters tell us that this year coincided with the thirteenth of Maelsechlainn, which would make the true date 859, according to O'Flaherty's Chronology, *Ogyg.*, p. 434.

r *In Meath.*—Ann. Ult. 858 (= 859).

Suitheman, son of Arthur. A victory was gained by Cearbhall, son of Dunlang, and by Niar over the Gall-Gaidhil in Aradh Tire°.
[859.] Kal. Anno Domini, 855[p]. Maelguala, King of Cashel[q], was taken prisoner by the Northmen, and he died in their hands.

A great hosting [of his own people, and] a hosting of Lochlanns by Cearbhall, son of Dunlaing, into Meath[r], his hostages[s] . . . . . . who were in the hands of Maelsechlainn not preventing him, and he continued for three months to plunder the land of Maelsechlainn, and he did not desist until he had stripped all the territory of its property. Many of the literati of Erin composed laudatory poems for Cearbhall, in which they commemorated every victory which he gained, and Aenghus, the high wise man, successor of Molua[t], did so most [of all].

Alas! for the fact which I shall often mention : It is pitiful for the Irish to continue the evil habit of fighting among themselves, and that they do not rise together against the Lochlanns! Aedh, son of Niall[u], at the solicitation of the King of Cianachta[x], rose up against Maelsechlainn, for it was Maelsechlainn that had drowned the brother of the King of Cianachta, as we have written before.

[858 or 859.] A royal meeting of the chieftains of Erin at Ráth-Aedha[y] with Maelsechlainn, King of Erin, Fethghna, Comharba of Patrick,

[s] *His hostages.*—In the margin of the MS. is this note : ɔeopꞇ beʒán, " a small portion is wanting."

[t] *Successor of Molua.*—i. e. Abbot of Clonfertmulloe, at the foot of Slieve Bloom, in Upper Ossory. It is highly probable that these Annals, so laudatory of the kings of Ossory, were preserved in this monastery, and drawn from the poems here referred to.

[u] *Aedh, son of Niall.*—i. e. Aedh Finnliath, who succeeded Maelsechlainn, or Malachy I. in the throne of Ireland. Ann. Ult. 858 ; F. M. 859.

[x] *King of Cianachta.*—i. e. Flann, son of Conang, the nephew of Aedh Finnliath, whose brother Cinaedh had been taken in 851, and drowned in the Nanny Water. See note ', p. 118, *supra.*

[y] *Ráth-Aedha.*—Now Rahugh, in the

αρδα Ριnnιαιn do ófnam ríoda ┐ caon comραιc na h-Єιρeann uιle, ʒonαδ ιr ιn dáιlrιn cuʒ Crρball mac Ɒunlαιnʒ a οιʒρéιr do Maoιl-ρeaclαιnn do ρéιρ comaρba Ρhadραιcc, αρ mbeιξ do Crρball ρoιmιrιn ι n-Ιραρuρ ┐ mac ρι Loclann maιlle ρριr ρa cftραcαιc αíδce oʒ mιlleαδ ffραιnn Maιlρeaclαιnn.

Aoδ Ριnnlιαξ mac Néιll do ιnnραδ Míδe, ┐ Ρlann mac Co-nαιnʒ ρí Cιannaέτα maιlle ρριr, ┐ ιρ eιρíδe ρa αρ lαιʒ αρ Aoδ an cιnnριuδ δénam. Ράξ oιle dno, uαιρ ρa ιnρfrτuρ Maoιlρeaclαιnn ρeaρann Aoδa ρe τρí blιαδnαιδ dιαιδ ιndιαιδ. Mac ιnʒeιne dno Neιll an Ρlann. Ɒo ρóna dna Aoδ αρ an ρΡlann an coʒαδρα, uαιρ ní ραδα α ροιρ aca an ní ρa δaoí δe; ┐ αρ eaʒla na coιmeιρʒe ριn do ριʒne Maoιlρeaclαιnn ρíδ ρe Crρball, αmαιl a δuδραmαρ ρomαιnn.

Oρʒoιn Loca Crnd ιαρ nαιʒρeαδ ρommor ι τcορcαιρ cjrjr. do δαοιnιδ.

Ral. Sιoc doρoloċta ʒo n-ιmτíʒτea Loca Єιρeann eδιρ ċoιρ ┐ eaċ.

Ɒeρτaċ Luρca do lορccαδ do Loclannαιδ.

Suιδne mac Rοιclιʒ, αδ Lιρρ moιρ, quιeuιτ.

Coρmac Lαιτραιʒ bριuιn moριτuρ.

Sodomna Єρrcoρ Sláιne do mαρδαδ do loclannαιδ.

Caτaραċ αδ Aρdamacha, moριτuρ.

Luċτ dá ċoδlaċ do Nορmannαιδ do τοιδeaċτ ι ρρeaρann Cheρ-bαιll

barony of Moycashel, county of Westmeath. Ann. F. M. 857; Ann. Ult. 858 (= 859). This entry is out of place here.

ᵃ *Comharba of Finian.*—i. e. Abbot of Clonard.

ᵇ *Loch Cend.*—Now probably Lough Ki-neel, near Abbeylara, county of Longford. This entry is in the Ann. F. M. at 853.

ᵇ *Frost.*—This frost, and the other entries down to Cathasach, Abbot of Ard-Macha, are given in the Ann. F. M. at A. D. 854, and the Ann. Ult. at 855, the true year being 856. They are clearly out

trick, and Suairlech, comharba of Finian^e, to establish peace and tranquillity throughout all Erin; and it was at this meeting that Cearbhall, son of Dunlaing, gave Maelsechlainn his full demand, according to the decision of the Comharba of Patrick, Cearbhall having been for forty nights previously, accompanied by the son of the King of Lochlann, destroying the land of Maelsechlainn.

Aedh Finnliath, son of Niall, accompanied by Flann, son of Conang, King of Cianachta, plundered Meath. And it was Flann that had solicited Aedh to commit this devastation. There was also another cause, for Maelsechlainn had plundered the land of Aedh three years successively. Flann was the son of Niall's daughter. Now, Niall and Flann entered into this war, not knowing what might result from it, and from fear of this confederacy Maelsechlainn made peace with Cearbhall, as we have said before.

The plundering of Loch Cend^a after a very great frost, where one hundred and thirty persons were killed.

[856.] Kal. An intense frost^b, so that the lakes of Erin were traversed both by foot and horse.

The oratory of Lusca^c was burned by the Lochlanns.

Suibhne, son of^d Roichlech, Abbot of Lis-mor, died.

Cormac, of Lathrach Briuin^e, died.

Sodhomna, Bishop of Slaine^f, was killed by the Lochlanns.

Cathasach, Abbot of Ard-Macha, died.

[860.] Two fleets of Northmen^g came into the land of Cearbhall, son

of place here.

^c *Lusca.*—Now Lusk, in the county of Dublin.

^d *Son of.*—Grandson of Roichlech.—F. M. 854. "Nepos Roichlich."—Ult. 855.

^e *Lathrach Briuin.*—Now Laraghbrien,

near Maynooth, in the county of Dublin.

^f *Slaine.*—i. e. Slane, in the county of Meath.

^g *Two fleets of Northmen.*—The arrival of these fleets is not noticed in any of the published Annals. They must have put

baill mic Ōunlaing vá innḟaḋ. Anuaiṗ ṫanguṗ ṫá inniṗin vo Cṡṗḃall aṗ ann ṗo ḃaoi Cṡṗḃall ḟoṗ mṡṗcca. Ra ḃáṫṫuṗ váġḋaoṡne
Oṗṗaiġe ga ṗáḋa piṗ go haloinn ⁊ go ṗocṗaiḋ ga nṡḟicaḋ: Ní háḋ-
ḃaṗ mṡṗga vo ḃeiṫ ḟoṗ ḋuine i n-Oṗṗaiġiḃ vo niaṽ na Loċlonnoig
anoṗa .i. an ṫṡṗ uile vo loṫ. Aṫṫ ċṡna go ṗo coimḃḋa Ōia ṫuṗa,
⁊ go ṗuga ḃuaiḋ ⁊ coṗgaṗ voṫ naimḋiḃ amoil ṗugaiṗ go minic, ⁊
amail ḃéṗa ḃeoṗ. Léig aṗ ṫṗa vo mṡṗga, uaiṗ námá an meaṗga
vo ṡngnam. O vo ċuala Cṡṗḃall ṗa ċuaiḋ a mṡṗga uaiḋ, ⁊ ṗa ġaḃ
a aṗma. Ṫḃinig imuṗṗo ṫṗian na hoṡḋċe an ṫan ṗin. Aṗ amlaiḋ
ṫáinig Cṡṗḃall immaċ aṗ a ġṗianán ⁊ ṗiogċainnel móṗ ṗeime ⁊
ṗaḃoí ṗoilṗi na cainvleṗin go ḟaḋa aṗ gaċ leiṫ. Ra ġaḃ uaman
móṗ na Loċlannaig ⁊ ṗa ṫeiċṗioṫ ḟo na ṗléiḃṫiḃ ḟaigṗiḃ ḋóiḃ ⁊ ḟo
na cailltiḃ. An luċṫ imuṗṗo ṗa ṫaiṗiṗ ṗa hṡngnam víoḃ ṗa maṗḃaḋ uile. O ṫáinig maivin ammucha aṗ na máṗaċ, ṗa ċuaiḋ Cṡṗḃall go no ṗocṗaiḋe na cċṡnn uile, ⁊ ni ṗa ġaḃ uaċa, aṗ maṗḃaḋ a
nveaṗgáiṗ, go ṗa cuiṗiṫ aminaḋmuim, ⁊ go ṗo ṗgaoiliṫ iav ḟoṗ gaċ
leiṫ.

Ra immiṗ Cṡṗḃall ḟéin go cṗuaiḋ iṗin ammuṗ ṗain, ⁊ ṫáinig
ṗiṗ go móṗ a méḋ aṫṫ iḃ an aiḋċe ṗeime, ⁊ ṗa ṗgé go móṗ ⁊ ṫug
ṗonaiṗṫe moṗ voṗum ṗain. Ra gṗeiṗṗ go móṗ a muinnciṗ go
viocṗa ḟoṗ na Loċlannaiḃ, ⁊ aṗ moó na leiṫ an ṫṗlóig ṗa maṗḃaḋ
ann, ⁊ na ṫeaṗna ann ṗa ṫeiċṗiṫ aṗ ammuṗ a longa.

Og aċaḋ mic Eaṗclaiġe ṫugaḋ an maiḋm ṗin. Ro impa Cṡṗḃall iaṗṫṫain go mḃuaiḋ ⁊ go neavául inóiṗ.

Iṗin aimṗiṗ ṗin ṫainic hona ⁊ Ṫomṗiṗ Ṫoṗṗa vá ṫoiṗeac
ṗoiċinelaċ

into Waterford harbour, and passed up | Kilkenny. The victory gained at this
the Barrow to plunder Ossory. | place by Cearbhall over the Danes of Wa-
ʰ *Achadh mic Earclaidhe.*—This is pro- | terford is entered in the Ann. F. M. at the
bably the celebrated place now called | year 858, but 860 was the true year.
Agha, *alias* St. John's, near the city of | ⁱ *Hona and Tomrir Torra.*—There is

son of Dunlang, to plunder it. When messengers came to announce it to Cearbhall, he was intoxicated. The good men of Osraighe said to him gently and kindly, to encourage him : " What the Lochlanns do in Osraighe now is no cause for a person to get drunk, i. e. to destroy the whole country; but may God protect thee, and mayest thou gain victory and triumph over thy enemies, as thou hast often gained, and as thou shalt hereafter. Give up, however, thy drunkenness, for drunkenness is the enemy of valour." When Cearbhall heard this, his drunkenness went off him, and he took his arms. The third part of the night had passed over at this time. Cearbhall came out of his royal chamber with a large, royal candle [carried] before him, the light of which candle shone far on every side. The Lochlanns were seized with great dread, and they fled to the nearest mountains and woods; but such of them as remained through valour were all killed. When the next morning came, Cearbhall set out early in pursuit of them all with his forces, and having dreadfully slaughtered them, he did not leave them until he put them to flight, and until they had dispersed in every direction.

Cearbhall himself acted with great hardihood in this battle, but what he had drunk the night before came much against him; [however], he vomited much, which gave him great relief. He greatly and vehemently incited his people against the Lochlanns, of whom more than one-half their host was killed in the action, and such as escaped fled to their ships.

At Achadh mic Earclaidhe[h] this victory was gained. Cearbhall returned with victory and great booty.

At this time came Hona and Tomrir Torra[i], two noble chiefs (and

no account of the arrival of these chieftains, or of their battles with the Irish, in the published Annals. Their career appears to have been very brief.

ꞃoiċinelaċ (⁊ Ͳꞃuí an ċhona), ⁊ ꝼiꞃ ḃeoḋa cꞃuaiḋe ꝃo mḃlaiṫ moiꞃ iaḋ eiccuꞃ amuinnciꞃ ꝼéin lan ꞃaoꞃclanna ḋna iaḋ ḋeꞃċimiuḋ Loclann. Ͳangaccuꞃ cꞃa an ḋiaꞃ ꞃin gona ꞃoċꞃaiḋe go Luimneaċ, ⁊ ó Luimneaċ go Poꞃc laiꞃge. Aċc éꞃna aꞃ mó ꞃa caiꞃiꞃniꞡꞃic ina mḃꞃioꞡaiḃ ꝼéin iná 'na ꞃoċꞃaiḋe. Ra cionóilꞃic Eoꞡanacc ⁊ Aꞃaiḋ cliaċ ḋóiḃ, ⁊ ꞃa ċuiꞃꞃic cenn i gcenn, ⁊ ꞃa cuiꞃeaḋ cꞃḟꞃ cꞃuaiḋ ꝼccuꞃꞃa, go ꞃa cuiꞃic na Loċlannaig i mbaile bḟg, ⁊ cloċ-ḋaingḟn ime. Ra ċuaiḋ ḋna aṅ ḋꞃaoi .i. hona ⁊ ꝼeaꞃ ba ꞃine ḋíoḃ aꞃ an ċaiꞃiol 'ꞃa ḃél oꞃlaigċe, og acaċ a ḃee, ⁊ og ḋénaṁ a ḋꞃaoig-ꝼċca, ⁊ ga ꝼꞃail aꞃ aṁuinnciꞃ aḋꞃaḋ na nḋee. Ͳainig ꝼeaꞃ ḋꞃeaꞃaiḃ Muṁan cuige go ccug buille ḋo ċloiċ móiꞃ ḋaꞃ ꞃin a ṁanc ḋó, go ccug a ꞃiacla uile aꞃꞃ a ċḟnn. Ra impa iaꞃ ꞃiṅ a aigiḋ aꞃ a ṁuinnciꞃ ꝼén, ⁊ aꞃꞃeḋ ꞃo ꞃáiḋ ag cuꞃ aꞃola cḟꞃꞃaiḋe ḋaꞃ a ḃél amaċ: ḃam maꞃḃꞃa ḋe ꞃo aꞃ ꞃé, ⁊ ꞃa ċuic aꞃ aiꞃ, ⁊ ꞃa ċuaiḋ a anam aꞃꞃ. Ra gaḃaḋ ḋóiḃ iaꞃccain ḋo ċloċaiḃ gona ꞃa ꝼéḋꞃac a ꝼulang, aċc ꞃagḃaiḋ a n-ionaḋ ꞃin, ⁊ ciagaiḋ ꝼoꞃ ꞃḟꞃ-gḟnn ba nḟꞃꞃa, ⁊ maꞃḃcuꞃ annꞃaiḋe ancaoiꞃeċ oile, go maꞃḃac amlaiḋ ꞃin an ḋa ċaoiꞃeaċ .i. hona Luimnig, ⁊ Ͳomꞃiꞃ Ͳoꞃꞃa. Ní ceaꞃna ḋna ḋa maiciḃ aċc ḋiaꞃ namá, ⁊ uaiċeaḋ beg leo, ⁊ ꞃugꞃac ꝼiꞃ Muṁan buaiḋ ⁊ coꞃguꞃ aṁlaiḋ ꞃin.

Iꞃ in bliaḋain ꞃi ḋo ꞃonaḋ móꞃ ꞃluaꞡ la Maoilꞃeaċlainṅ, ꞃig 'Eiꞃeann, ⁊ Ceaꞃḃall mac Ͳunlaiṅg laiꞃ go Maꞡ maċa. Ra gaḃꞃac longꞃoꞃc ann ꞃin. Ḃa ꝼgail imuꞃꞃo la Maoilꞃeaċlainn ammuꞃ longꞃoiꞃc ḋo ċaḃaiꞃc ḋo Aoḋ mac Néill ꝼaiꞃ; ciaḋ álainn

an

ᵏ *Luimnech.*—i. c. Limerick. The word is here used to denote, not the city, but the Lower Shannon, from the city of Limerick to the sea.

ˡ *Port-Lairge.*—This is the present Irish name of the city of Waterford, but the name is hardly so old as the time here referred to, as Lairge, the chieftain from whom the name was derived, flourished in 951. See Ann. F. M., A. D. 858, note ᵖ.

ᵐ *Eoghanacht.*—i. c. Eoghanacht Chaisil.

(and Hona was a Druid); and these were hardy men of great fame among their own people, and fully noble, of the best race of the Lochlanns. These two came with their forces to Luimnech[k] and from Luimnech to Port-Lairge[l]; but, however, they prevailed more by their own vigour than by their forces. The people of Eoghanacht[m] and Ara Cliach[n] assembled against them, and they met face to face, and a hard battle was fought between them, in which the Lochlanns were driven to a small place surrounded by a stone wall. The Druid, i. e. Hona, the elder of them, went up on the wall, and his mouth opened, praying to his gods and exercising his magic, and ordering his people to worship the gods. One of the men of Munster came towards him and gave him a blow of a large stone on the mouth, and knocked all the teeth out of his head. He afterwards turned his face on his own people, and said, as he was pouring the warm blood out of his mouth: "I shall die of this," said he, and he fell back, and his soul went out of him. They were afterwards so plied with stones that they were not able to bear them, and they quitted that place, and repaired to a neighbouring morass, and here the other chieftain was killed; and thus were the two chieftains killed, i. e. Hona, of Luimnech, and Tomrir Torra. Of their chief men, only two escaped with a few forces; and thus the men of Munster gained victory and triumph.

[860.] In this year a great hosting[o] was made by Maelsechlainn, King of Erin, accompanied by Cearbhall, son of Dunlang, to Magh-Macha[p]. They encamped there. Maelsechlainn was afraid that his camp should be surprised by Aedh, son of Niall, though fair was the answer

These were seated in the great plain of Cashel, in the county of Tipperary.

[n] *Ara Cliach.*—A territory in the east of the county of Limerick.

[o] *A great hosting.*—Ann. F. M. 858; Ann. Ult. 859 (= 860).

[p] *Magh-Macha.*—Now the Moy, near the city of Armagh.

an ffeaṡṗa ṗíoḋa tuṡ Aoḋ ṗaiṗ tṗéṗ an ḋuine naoṁ .i. Ḟeẋna, comaṗḃa Ṗaḋṗaicc. Aṗeaḋ ḋo ṗiṡne Maoilṗeaċlainn Laiṡin ⁊ ḟiṗ Mumaṅ ⁊ Connaċta ⁊ Ulaiḋ, ⁊ ḟiṗ ḃḣṗeaṡ ḋo ċaḃaiṗt a ttimċioll a puḃla, ⁊ a n-aiṗm noċta 'na láṁaiḃ; an ṗíṡ ḟéin .i. Maoilṗeaċ- lainn, ṗo ḃaoi ṡo ḟaittṡċ ḟuiṗeċaiṗ ṡan ċoḋlaḋ aṗ ṡla Aoḃa, ṡé ḋo ṗaḋ luiṡe a ḟḟiaḋnaiṗi comaṗḃa Ṗaḋṗaic; ṡiḋeaḋ táinic Aoḋ ṡo na ḟluaṡaiḃ ḋo ċaḃaiṗt ammuṡ Lonṡpuiṗt aṗ Maoilṗeaċlainn, ⁊ ní maṗ ṗa ṗaoilṗit ṗa ḟuaṗattuṗ, uaiṗ ṗo ḃattuṗ a n-aiṗm uile a láiṁiḃ ṗluaiṡ Maoilṗeaċlainn, aṡuṗ ṗa eiṗṡiṗit a naoineaċt ṗan luċt táinic ḋá n-ionnṗoiṡiḋ ṡo ṗo cuiṗṗit amaiḋm iaṗ aṗ maṗḃaḋ a nḋeaṗṡ-áṗ. Ra ṡaḃ ḋna ḋáṗaċt ṗaiṗfin oile ḋfoḃ, ⁊ aṗeaḋ tanṡattuṗ ḋ'ionnṗoiṡiḋ puiḃle Maoilṗeaċlainn, an ḋaṗ leo ṗaḃ iaḋ amuinntiṗ ḟéin; ṗa ḃattuṗ am ṡo ṗo maṗḃait uile iaṗttain; ⁊ aṗ an éitioċ ḋo ṗaḋṗat ḋo ṗiṡne Ḋia ṗin. Ra impu Maoilṗeaċ- lainn ḋ'á tiṡ a haiċle an ċoṗṡuiṗ ṗain. Ra ḃaoi ḋna Aṁlaiḃ i ḟḟaṗṗaḋ Aoḋ 'ṗin maiḋm-ṗa.

Oenaċ Raiṡne ḋo ḋénaṁ la Cṗḃall mac Ḋunlainṡ.

Aṗ la Cṗḃall mac Ḋunlainṡ ṗoṗ muinntiṗ Ṙoḋuilḃ i Sleḃ Maiṗṡe, ⁊ a maṗḃaḋ uile aċt ṗíṡ uaċaḋ téaṗna ḋfoḃ i ccailltiḃ: cṗfċ Leitṡlinne, ⁊ ḋna a ḃṗaiḋ ṗa ḃoí aca aṗ maṗḃaḋ ḋṗéimṡ móiṗ ḋo muinntiṗ Leitṡlinne ḋóiḃ.

Kal. Matoḋan mac Muṗioḋaiṡ, ṗí Ulaḋ, in cleṗicatu oḃiit. Maonṡal aḃ Ṗoḃaiṗ moṗituṗ.

Tṗiaṗ

ᵃ *Amhlaibh was along with Aedh.*—This is not stated in the published Annals.

ʳ *Raighne.*—This was the ancient name of the chief seat of the Kings of Ossory, situated in the barony of Kells, county of Kilkenny. See Ann. F. M., A. D. 859, p. 494.

ˢ *Sliabh-Mairge.*—Now Slievemargue, a barony in the south-east of the Queen's County. There is no mention made of this Rodolph in the published Annals.

ᵗ *Leithglinn.*—Now Old Leighlin, in the county of Carlow. This entry is not in the published Annals.

answer of peace which Aedh had given him through the holy man, Fethghna, successor of Patrick. What Maelsechlainn did was to place the men of Leinster and Munster, and Connaught and of Uladh and Breagh around his tent, with their weapons naked in their hands. The king himself, i. e. Maelsechlainn, remained vigilantly and warily without sleep from fear of Aedh, though he [Aedh] had taken an oath [of fealty to him] before the successor of Patrick. Notwithstanding, Aedh came with his forces to attack the camp of Maelsechlainn, but they did not find it as they expected, for the forces of Maelsechlainn all had their arms in their hands, and they rose out together against the party who came to attack them, and put them to flight after having cut off many of them with great havoc. One party of them, however, were seized with a panic, and came to the tent of Maelsechlainn, thinking it was that of their own people, and remained there until they were all killed. And God did this in consequence of the falsehood which they had told. Maelsechlainn returned to his house after this triumph. Amhlaibh was along with Aedh^q in this discomfiture.

The fair of Raighne^r was celebrated by Cearbhall, son of Dunlang.

A slaughter was made by Cearbhall, son of Dunlang, of the people of Rodolph, at Sliabh-Mairge^s, and he slew them all except very few who escaped to the woods. They had plundered Leithglinn^t, and had [obtained] its spoils after having killed a large number of the people of Leithghlinn.

[857.] Kal. Matudan^u, son of Muiredhach, King of Uladh, died *in clericatu.*

Maenghal, Abbot of Fobhar, died.

Three

^u *Matudan.*—The obits of this prince, and of the Abbot Macnghal, as also the death of the three men killed by lightning, are dated by the Annals of Ulster 856, which ought to be 857. They are therefore out of place here.

Triaṗ do loṗgaḋ do ṫeniḋ ṗaiġnén a tTailten.

Ḱal. Cionaoḋ mac Ailpin peҳ Pictoҏum, moҏicuҏ : conaḋ do ҏo ҏaiḋeaḋ an ҏann :—

Naḋ maiҏ Cionaoḋ ꝼo líon ҏꝼoҏ,
Ҏo óſҏa ꝼol in ꝼaċ taiꝼ
Aon ní a loꝼa ꝼo nim,
Ꝼo bҏuinne Ҏomha ní bҏail.

Cumҏuḋ Eҏſcoҏ ⁊ ҏҏinceҏſ Cluana Ioҏaiҏḋ quieuit.
Tioҏҏaiḋe banban ab tíҏe daꝼlaҏ quieuit.
Maoltuile ab Imlſċa Ioḃaiҏ moҏicuҏ.
Adulphҏi Saҳon Moҏicuҏ. Ceallaċ mac Ꝼuaiҏe ҏi Laiꝼſn Deaҏꝼaḃaiҏ, moҏicuҏ. Cſҏnaċ mac Cionaḋa, ҏi Ua mbaiҏċe tiҏe moҏicuҏ.
Aoḋ mac Néill ⁊ a cliamain .i. Amlaiḃ (inꝼſn Aoḋa ҏo ḃaoi aꝼ Amlaoiḃ) ꝼo ſloꝼaiḃ móҏa Ꝼaoiḃiol ⁊ Loċlann leo ꝼo maꝼ miḋe, ⁊ a ionnҏaḋ leo, ⁊ ҏaoҏċlanna iomḋa do ṁaҏḃaḋ leo.

Maoilҏeaċloinn mac Maolҏuanaiḋ, ҏiꝼ Eiҏeann, í ҏҏiḋ Callan December deҏuncҭuҏ eҏt, unde quiḋam cecinit :

Aҏ iomḋa maiҏꝼ in ꝼaċ ḋu,
Aҏ ſꝼel moҏ la Ꝼaoiḃelu,
Do ҏóҏtaḋ ſíon ſlann ꝼo ꝼlſnn,
Do ҏoḋba aoinҏi 'Eiҏſnn.

Aoḋ mac Néill, deaҏꝼnáṁa Maoilҏeaċloinn do ꝼaḃail ҏiꝼe n-'Eiҏeann taҏ éiſ Maoilҏeaclainn. Cҏaiḃḋeaċ ҏoiċinealaċ aiꝼneaḋ

ˢ *Cinaedh Mac Ailpin.*—Ann. Ult. 857 (= 858). Ogyg., p. 481.

ᵗ *Cumsadh.*—"Cumsuth, Episcopus et anchorita *princeps* Cluana Irairdd *in pace pausavit.* Cinaedh Mac Ailpin, *rex Pictorum*. Adulf *rex Saxan mortui sunt.* Tipraiti Ban, abbas Tire-da-glas."—*Ann. Ult.* 857 (= 858).

ᵘ *Ceallach, son of Guaire.*—Ann. F. M. at 856; but the true year is 858.

Three persons were burned by lightning at Tailten.

[858.] Kal. Cinaedh Mac Ailpin*, King of the Picts, died, on whom this verse was composed :—

That Cinaedh with the number of studs liveth not,
Is the cause of weeping in every house.
Any one king under heaven of his worth
To the borders of Rome there is not.

Cumsadh^y, Bishop and Chief of Cluain Iraird, died.
Tipraide Banbhan, Abbot of Tir-daghlas, died.
Maeltuile, Abbot of Imleach Iobhair, died.

Adolph, King of the Saxons, died. Ceallach, son of Guaire^z, King of South Leinster, died. Cearnach, son of Cinaedh, King of Ui-Bairche-tire, died.

[862.] Aedh^a, son of Niall, and his son-in-law, i. e. Amhlaeibh (the daughter of Aedh was wife to Amhlaeibh), set out with great forces of Gacidhil and Lochlanns to the plain of Meath, and they plundered it and slew many noble persons.

[863.] Maelsechlainn^b, son of Maelruanaidh, King of Erin, died on the day before the Calends of December, of which a certain poet sung :—

There is many a moan in every place,
It is a great cause of grief with the Gaeidhil,
Red wine has been spilled into the valley,
The sole king of Erin died.

[863.] Aedh, son of Niall, the mortal enemy of Maelsechlainn, assumed

---

ᵃ *Aedh, son of Niall.*—F. M. at 860; true year 862.

ᵇ *Maelsechlainn.*—The Ann. Ult. 861, and F. M. 860, tell us that he died on Tuesday, 30th Nov., and this enables us to correct the chronology of these Annals, for the 30th November fell on Tuesday in 863. O'Flaherty, Ogyg., p. 434.

neaḋ Aoḋa: ṡéċ mbliaḋna ḋécc ḋo i ṗiġe ġo ṙioḋaṁail, cia ṗo ġeḃṡḃ imnṡḃ minic.

Ailill banbain, ab bioṗaṗ
Aonġaṗ Cluana Ḟṡṗca Molua, ṡaṗienṗ, moṗicuṗ.
Maoloḋaṗ hUa Cinḋṗiḋ ṡaoi léiġiṗ Éiṗṡnn moṗicuṗ.
Muiṗġiuṗ, anġcoiṗce Aṗomacha, quieuic.
Ḋálaċ ab Cluana mic Noíṡ quieuic.
Ġoṗmlaiċ, inġṡn Ḋonchaḋa, ṗioġan cṡṁṗaċ, in poeniceniia obiic.
Ḟionán Cluana caoin, eṗṗcop ⁊ anġcoiṗe quieuic.
Ḟinnċeallaċ ab Ḟeaṗna moṗicuṗ.
Séġonan mac Conainġ, ṗi Caiṗṗġe bṗaċaiḋe moṗicuṗ. Ḟlan-naġán mac Colmáin moṗicuṗ. Ġuin Aoḋa mic Ḋuibḋaḃaiṗṡnn, ṗí hUa ḟṗioġence, Cṡnṙṗaolaḋ i ṗiġe Muṁan.
Ḋomnall mac Ailpin ṗeẋ ṗiccoṗum moṗicuṗ.
Ḳal. Ḋiṙġáṗ ḋo caḃaiṗc ḋo Chṡṗball mac Ḋunlainġ, ⁊ ḋo Cinnéḋe mac Ġaicine .i. mac ḋeiṗḃṗeacaṗ Cṡṗḃaill ṡoṗ lonġuṗ Ṙoḋlaiḃ, ⁊ ḃá ġaiṗiḋ ṗeime cánġaccuṗ a Loċlann; ⁊ Conall Ulcaċ ḋo ṁaṗḃaḋ ann aġuṡ Luiṗġnen, cum pluṗimiṡ aliiṙ.
Inṗṡḃ bṗṡġ la Loċlannaiḃ, ⁊ ḋul aṗ uaṁannaiḃ ioṁḋaiḃ, ⁊ aṙṡḃ ón na ḋṡṗnaḋ ġo minic ṗeime.

Aṗ

ᵉ *Seventeen years.*—Aedh died 12th Cal. Dec., which fell on Friday, as the Chronicon Scotorum states. This indicates the year 879, and makes the length of his reign 16, not 17 years.—O'Flaherty, *ibid.*
ᵈ *Ailell Banbhan.*—Ann. F. M. 857.
ᵉ *Aenghus.*—Ann. F. M. 858.
ᶠ *Maelodhar O'Tindridh.*—Ann. Ult. 861, where he is called ṗui leiġiṗ ġoiḋeal, "sage leech of the Gael." This is the first notice of an Irish physician to be found in the Irish Annals since the introduction of Christianity. See Ann. F. M., A. D. 860, p. 494, note ᵘ.
ᵍ *Muirghius.*—Ann. F. M. 860; Ult. 861.
ʰ *Of Cluain mic Nois.*—The Four Masters call him Abbot of Cluain-Iraird, A. D. 860.
ⁱ *Gormlaith, daughter of Donnchadh.*—Ann. F. M. 859; Ult. 860.
ᵏ *Finian.*—Ann. F. M. 860.

assumed the kingdom of Erin after Maelsechlainn. The disposition of Aedh was pious and noble. He was seventeen years[c] in the kingdom peaceably, though he often met with annoyance.

Ailell Banbhan[d], Abbot of Biror [died].

Aenghus[e], a sage of Cluain Ferta Molua, died.

[862.] Maeolodhar O'Tindridh[f], chief physician of Erin, died.

Muirghius[g], anchorite of Ard-Macha, died.

Dálach, Abbot of Cluain mic Nois[h], died.

Gormlaith, daughter of Donnchadh[i], Queen of Teamhar, died in penitence.

Finian[k], of Cluain-caein, bishop and anchorite, died.

Finncheallach[l], Abbot of Fearna [now Ferns], died.

Segonan, son of Conang[m], King of Carraig Brachaidhe, died. The killing of Aedh, son of Dubhdabhoirenn[n], King of Ui-Fidhgeinte. Cennfaeladh, in the kingdom of Munster.

Domhnall Mac Ailpin[o], King of the Picts, died.

[863.] Kal. A dreadful slaughter was made of the fleet of Rodlaibh[p], by Cearbhall, son of Dunlang, and by Cincide, son of Gaeithin, i. e. the son of Cearbhall's sister; and they [the crews of the fleet] had arrived from Lochlann a short time before ; and Conall Ultach and Lairgnen were slain there with many others.

The plundering of Breagh by the Lochlanns, and they entered into many crypts[q], a thing not done often before.

[l] *Finncheallach.*—F. M. 860; Ult. 861.

[m] *Seghonan, son of Conang.*—F.M. 857; Ult. 858 (out of place here). Carraig Brachaidhe is in the north-west of the barony of Inishowen, county of Donegal.

[n] *Aedh, son of Dubhdabhoirenn.*—Ann. F. M. 858; Ult. 859.

[o] *Domhnall mac Ailpin.*—He died in 862 (Ann. Ult. 861). Ogyg., p. 484.

[p] *The fleet of Rodlaibh.*—The F. M., at A. D. 860, make it Longphort-Rothlaibh, which may perhaps be a corruption of Longus Rothlaibh, i. e. Rodlaff's, or Rodolph's fleet.

[q] *Crypts.*—See Ann. F. M. 861 ; Ult. 862 ; where this account of the plunder-

'Ap ná ngall la Cṙḃall mac Ďunlaing ag Ḟṙṡa caipeċ, ⁊ a cṙṡc ď'ṗag̃báil.

Muiriogan mac Ďiapmaďa, ṙí Naiṙ ⁊ Laig̃ṡn ciď ďo mapḃaď la gencib, ⁊ pocaide móṙ ďo ṁaiċib Laig̃ṡn.

Ṙal. Ǎoḋ mac Cumupcaig̃, ṗi hUa Nialláin moṙicuṙ. Muiṙeďoċ mac Maoilďuin, ṗi na n-Aiṙċṡṙ iug̃ulacuṙ eṙc ó Ďomnall mac Ǎoḋa mic Néill.

Cṙiḃall mac Ďunlaing ďo innṙṡḋ Laig̃ṡn. Níoṙ bó cian iaṙ ṙin go ṙo cionolṙaď Laig̃in Loclannaig̃ ⁊ iaď ṗéin, go ṙo inďṙiḃṙioď Oṙṙaig̃e na ďíog̃ail ṙin. Ḃa móṙ an cṙuaig̃e! ďoneoċ ṙa ceiċ ď'Oṙnaig̃iḃ im Muṁain ṙa maṙḃaiď ⁊ ṙa haiṙg̃iď uile. Ḃa móď ṙo goṙcaig̃ ṙin mṡnma Cṙiḃaill .i. an luċc ṙogaḃ aig̃e aṁail caiṙiṙi .i. Eog̃anaċc, iaďṙaiďe ďa aṙg̃ain ⁊ ďa ṁaṙḃaď. Ḃṡ g̃ aiṙ imuṙṙo caing̃ṡn na namaď: uaiṙ níoṙ bo iong̃naď laiṙ iaďṙaiďe ďo g̃énam na noṡṙṙac, uaiṙ ṙa ḃlig̃ṙioc. Ro cionol iaṙaṁ ṙloig̃ G̃aoiḃeal ⁊ Loclannaig̃, ag̃uṙ ṙa ṁill na Ṙṡanna compoṙṙaiḋe, ṙa ṁill Mag̃ Ṗeiṁin ⁊ Ṙiṙ muig̃e ⁊ ṙug̃ bṙaig̃ḃe ciniuḋa n-iomḋa laiṙ.

San ḃliaďainṙi, .i. in ceṙcio anno ṙeg̃ni Ǎoḋa Ṗinnléċ, cang̃accuṙ Saxain i mḃṙeacnaiḃ G̃aimuď, ⁊ ṙa inaṙḃaiď na Saxain ḃṙiṡcain aṙ an cíṙ.

Ďallaď

ing of the caves or crypts is given more fully.

' *Ferta Caeirech.*—Now Fertagh, near Johnstown, in the barony of Galmoy, county of Kilkenny.—See Ann. F. M., A. D. 861.

' *Nás.*—Ann. F. M. 861, p. 496, note '; Ult. 862, where is called King of Naas and of Airthir Life.

' *Aedh, son of Cumascach.*—Ann. F. M. 861, of the Niallain, in the Co. Armagh.

" *King of Ui-Niallain.*—Now the Oneillands, two baronies in the Co. Armagh.

' *Airthera.*—Now the baronies of Orior in the county of Armagh. In the Ann. Ult. 862, he is called ṙecnaḃ aiṙď macae ⁊ ṙi na naiṙċeṙ—" Sub-Abbot of Armagh, and King of Orior."

' *Fera-Maighe.*—Now Fermoy, in the county of Cork.—Ann. F. M. 862 (true year, 864).

' *The third.*—Aedh Finnliath succeeded

A slaughter of the Galls at Ferta Caeirech[r] by Cearbhall, son of Dunlang, and they left their prey behind.

Muirigen, son of Diarmaid, King of Nas[s] and of Leinster, was killed by the Pagans, and a great number of the chiefs of Leinster.

[864.] Kal. Aedh, son of Cumascach[t], King of Ui-Niallain[u], died. Muiredhach, son of Maelduin, King of the Airthera[x], was killed by Domhnall, son of Aedh, son of Niall.

Cearbhall, son of Dunlang, plundered Leinster. It was not long after this that the Leinster-men assembled themselves and the Lochlanns, and plundered Osraighe in revenge of this. It was a great pity: such of the Osraighi as fled into Munster were all killed and plundered; and this distressed the mind of Cearbhall the more, that the people he took for friends, namely, the Eoghanachts, should plunder and kill them. He thought little of the doings of the enemies, for he did not wonder at their doing what they did, for they were entitled to it. He therefore assembled an army of Gaeidhil and Lochlanns, and spoiled the neighbouring lands [of the Eoghanachts]; he spoiled Magh Feimhin and Fera Maighe[y], and carried off the hostages of many tribes.

In this year, i. e. the third[z] of the reign of Aedh Finnliath, the Saxons came into Britain Gaimud[a], and the Saxons expelled the Britons from the country.

The in the year 863, so that the third year of his reign was 865 or 866.

[a] *Britain Gaimud.*—Perhaps Gwyned (Guenidotia or Venedotia, i. e. North Wales) may be intended. This seems to be the same expulsion of the Britons which is recorded in the Ann. Ult. at 864, in these words: bpeacan bu inbapbu apa

cip bo paxanaib con po gabab cacc popaib im Maen conain.—"The Britons were driven from their territory by the Saxons, and were put into bondage in Maen Chonain," i. e. Anglesea, called Mona Conain, from Conan, King of Gwynedd. See Ann. Ult. 815; Brut y Tywysogion, A. D. 817.

Dallað Lopcáin mic Catail, ꞃi Miðe, la hAoð mac Néill. Concopaꞃ mac Donnchaða, leiṫꞃi Miðe do báð la hAmlaið ⁊ Cluain Ipaiꞃo. Inꞃſð na nDéiꞃi la Cꞃꞃball mac Dunlaing, ⁊ lánṁilleað hUi n-Aongaꞃa.
Abðaine Ṫiꞃe ða glaꞃ do gaðail do Maoilpeccuiꞃ in hoc anno.
Gaðail Diaꞃmada la gentið.
Eiðgin ðꞃic Eꞃꞃcop Cille ðaꞃa, ꞃcꞃiða et anachoꞃeta cꞅiii°, anno aetatiꞃ ꞃuae quieuit.
Maonac mac Connmaig, ab Roiꞃ cꞃé moꞃicuꞃ.
Domnall hUa Dunlaing, ꞃigðamna Laigꞃn, moꞃicuꞃ.
Cꞃꞃmait mac Cataꞃnaig, ꞃi Coꞃca ðaiꞃcinn, moꞃicuꞃ.
Kal. Tadg mac Diaꞃmada ꞃi hUa Cinnꞃiolaig do ṁaꞃðað ðá ðꞃáitꞃið ꝼéin. 'Aꞃ ꝼoꞃ Loclannaið la Flann mac Conaing ꞃi Cianacṫ. Deaꞃg áꞃ na Loclann, ⁊ a mbuaiðꞃeað uile ꞃan bliað- ain ꞃi la hAoð mac Néill, ꞃig 'Eiꞃeann. Maiðm lán móꞃ la n-Aoð ꝼoꞃꞃ na Loclannaið ag Loc Feaðaill. Inniꞃic ðno na h-eoluig guꞃ ob í a ðꞃn aꞃ moó ꞃo gꞃeiꞃ Aoð i ccꞃnn na Loclann .i. Lanð, ingꞃn Dunlaing : ⁊ aꞃ ꞃiꞃiðe ba ðꞃn do Maoilꞃeacloinn ꞃeiṁe, matt- aiꞃ mic Maoilꞃeacloinn .i. Flaiñ. Ba hí mátaiꞃ Cennéoig mic Gaiṫine í, .i. ꞃi Laigꞃi. Aꞃ móꞃ tꞃa ꞃa ꞃcꞃióðað na ꝼꝼuaꞃac- tuꞃ Loclannaig ð'ulc 'ꞃan bliaðain ꞃi [on g-Cennedigꞃiðe] cið moó ꝼuaꞃꞃattuꞃ ó Aoð Finnliat mac Néill.
Milleað

ᵇ *Lorcan.*—Ann. F. M. 862 ; Ann. Ult. 863.

ᶜ *Uí-Aenghusa.*—i. e. the descendants of Aenghus Mac Nadfraich, King of Munster, slain, A. D. 489. See Ann. F. M., p. 499, note ᵐ, A. D. 862.

ᵈ *Maelpetair.*—He died in 890, according to the F. M., who do not give the year of his accession.

ᵉ *Diarmaid.*—Not in the published Annals. It does not appear who this Diarmaid was.

ᶠ *Eidgin Brit.*—Or the Briton. Ann. F. M. 862. His name was probably Edwin, a Briton. Colgan says that he died on the 18th December, probably confound-

157

The blinding of Lorcan[b], son of Cathal, king of Meath, by Aedh, son of Niall. Conchobhar, son of Donnchadh, half king of Meath, was drowned by Amhlaeibh at Cluain Iraird. The plundering of the Desies, and the total spoiling of Ui Aenghusa[c] by Cearbhall, son of Dunlaing.

The abbacy of Tir-da-ghlas was assumed by Maelpetair[d] in this year.

The taking of Diarmaid[e] by the Gentiles.

Eidgin Brit[f], Bishop of Cill-dara, a scribe and anchorite, died in the one hundred and thirteenth year of his age.

Macnach[g], son of Connmach, Abbot of Ros-Cré, died.

Domhnall, grandson of Dunlaing, royal heir of Leinster, died.

Cearmait, son of Catharnach, King of Corca Bhaiscinn, died.

[866.] Kal. Tadhg, son of Diarmaid[h], King of Ui-Ceinnsealaigh, was slain by his own brothers. A slaughter was made of the Lochlanns by Flann, son of Conang, King of Cianachta. A great slaughter was made of the Lochlanns, who were all disturbed this year by Aedh, son of Niall, King of Erin. A complete and great victory was gained by Aedh over the Lochlanns at Loch Feabhail[i], and the learned state that it was his wife that most incited Aedh against the Lochlanns; i. e. Lann, the daughter of Dunlang, and she had been the wife of Maelsechlainn before, and was the mother of Maelsechlainn's son Flann. She was also the mother of Cenneidigh, son of Gaithin, King of Laeighis[k]. It is written that the Lochlanns sustained great evils in this year [from this Cenneidigh], but more from Aedh Finnliath, son of Niall.

[869.]

ing him with Aedan of Ard Lonain.—
Trias. Thaum., p. 629.

[g] Maenach.—This and the two succeeding entries are given by the F. M. at 862.

[h] Tadhg, son of Diarmaid.—Ann. F. M. 863; Ann. Ult. 864.

[i] Loch Feabhail.—Now Lough Foyle.

[k] Laeighis.—Now Leix.

Milleaḋ ⁊ innṙċḋ Ḃoiṙcṙṙnn la Loclannaib go ṙugrac bṙaigḋe iomḋa leo i ngill ṙe cíoṙ; ṙo báṙ go ṙaḋa iaṙcċain ag caḋaiṙc cíoṙa ḋóiḃ.

Aṙ ṙoṙ Gallaiḃ oc Minḋṙoiċic[m] la Cennéḋig mac Gaicine, ṙi Laigṙi ⁊ la cuaiṙgiṙc n-Oṙṙaige.

Iṙ in aimṙiṙ ṙi cangaccuṙ Aunicer[n] .i. na Daiṅṙiṙ go ṙluagaiḃ ḋiaiṙmiḋiḃ leo go Caeṙ Eḃṙoic[o], guṙ ṙo coglaccuṙ an caéṙaig, ⁊ go noṙéaccuṙ ṙuiṙṙe, ⁊ ba coṙaċ imniḋ ⁊ ḋocṙaċ móiṙ ḋo ḃṙċ-naiḃ ṙin; uaiṙ ní ṙaḋa ḋ'aimṙiṙ ṙeṁe ṙo ṙo ḃaoi gaċ cogaḋ ⁊ gaċ gliṙic i Loċlainn, ⁊ aṙ aṙ ṙo ṙo ṙáṙ an cogaḋ ṙain i Loċlainḋ .i. ḋá ṁac óċca Alḃḋain ṙi Loċlann ṙo ionnaṙḃṙac an mac ṙa ṙine .i. Ragnall mac Alḃḋain, aṙ eagla leo é ḋo gaḃail ṙigi Loċlann caṙ éiṙ a n-aċaṙ; go ccáinic an Ragnall co n-a cṙí macaiḃ go hiṅṙiḃ Oṙc: ṙo ċaṙiṙ iaṙaṁ Ragnall ann ṙin, ⁊ an mac ba ṙoó ḋo cangaccuṙ imoṙṙu na mic ba ṙine go hinnṙiḃ Ḃṙecan go ṙluag moṙ leo, aṙ ccionól an cṙluaig ṙin aṙ gaċ áiṙḋ, aṙ na líonaḋ na mac ṙin ḋo ḋíomuṙ ⁊ ḋo ṁíṙṙaċc um eiṙge i cċṙn Ḃṙangc ⁊ Saxann. Ra ṙaoilṙioḋ a n-aċaiṙ ḋo ḋol i Loċlainn ṙo ċeḋóiṙ ḋaṙ a n-éiṙ.

Ra ṙṙail iaṙam an ḋíomuṙ ⁊ a n-ógḃaḋaca oṙṙa iomṙaṁ ṙíṁṙa ḋaṙ an ocian Cancaiḃṙíċḋa .i. an ṁuiṙ ṙuil eiḋiṙ Eiṙinn ⁊ Eaṙ-ṙáin go ṙangaccuṙ Eṙṙain, ⁊ go noṙṙṙaḋ ulċa iomḋa i n-Eṙṙain eḋiṙ

[1] *Foirtrenn.*—i. c. Pictland.—*Ann. Ult.* 865.

[m] *Mindroichet.*—Now Monadrehid, near Borris in Ossory, in the Queen's County. The Four Masters notice this slaughter of the foreigners at the year 864, but 866 is the true year.

[n] *Aunites.*—This name is perhaps a corruption of *Afnitæ*, or *Hafnitæ*, from Haf-nia (*Höfn*, the haven), called afterwards *Kaupmanna-höfn,* (Merchants' haven), now Copenhagen. But the Editor is not able to quote any other authority for the name of *Hafnites* being applied to the Danes.

[o] *Caer Ebroic.*—i. e. the city of Eboracum or York. See "Annal. Cambriæ" and "Brut y Tywysogion" at 866.

[p] *Albdan.*—The Scandinavian form of

[869.] Foirtrenn[l] was plundered and ravaged by the Lochlanns, and they carried off many hostages with them as pledges for rent: and they were paid rent for a long time after.

A slaughter was made of the Galls at Mindroichet[m] by Cenneidigh, son of Gaithin, King of Laeighis, and by the northern Osraighi.

At this time the Aunites[n], i. e. the Danes, came with countless forces to Caer Ebroic[o], and destroyed the city, which they took, and this was the beginning of great troubles and difficulties to the Britons. For not long before this time every kind of war and commotion prevailed in Lochlann, which arose from this cause; i. e. the two younger sons of Albdan[p], King of Lochlann, expelled the eldest son, Raghnall, son of Albdan, because they feared that he would take the kingdom of Lochlann after their father; and Raghnall came with his three sons to Innsi Orc[q], and Raghnall tarried there with his youngest son. But his elder sons, with a great host, which they collected from every quarter, came on to the British Isles, being elated with pride and ambition, to attack the Franks and Saxons. They thought that their father had returned to Lochlann immediately after setting out.

Now, their pride and youthful ambition induced them to row forward across the Cantabrian Sea[r], i. e. the sea which is between Erin and Spain, until they reached Spain[s], and they inflicted many evils in

this name may probably be Halden, or Halfdane. See Saxon. Chron., A.D. 871; O'Flaherty's Ogyg., p. 485, A. D. 871.

[q] *Innsi Orc.*—i. e. the Orkney Islands.

[r] *Cantabrian Sea.*—i. e. the Biscayan Sea.

[s] *Until they reached Spain.*—Mallet gives an account of an excursion made by a strong force of Scandinavian rovers into Spain in September, 844, which looks very like the one here described, but he does not mention that they crossed the Gaditanean Straits.—"Northern Antiquities," Bohn's Ed., p. 173, note. See also Depping, "Histoire des Exped. Maritimes des Normands," liv. ii., chap. 3 (p. 121, New. Ed., 1844), who cites the Annal. Bertin. for the statement that the Northmen ravaged the coast of Frisia, and infested the Scottish islands in the year 847.

edip opṡain ⁊ innpeú. Ṫanṡaccup iapccain ḋap an Muinċſnn nṠaḋianca,¹.i. ḃail i ccéiḋ muip meḋiceppanian ipin Ocian imſċ- cpaċ, ṡo pánṡaccup an Appaic; ⁊ cuipiḋ caċ pip na Maupio- canuiḃ, ⁊ cuiciḋ ḋeapṡáp na Maupiocana. Aċc ċſna ap aṡ ḋul i ṡcſnn an ċacapa a nuḃaipc an ḋapa mac pip an mac oile: a ḃpáċaip, ap pé, ap mór an míċiall ⁊ an ḋápacc pil popainn ḃeiċ ap ṡaċ cíp a ccíp ap puḋ an ḋoṁuin ṡáp mapḃaḋ, a naċ aṡ cop- naṁ áp n-acapḋa pén acaám, ⁊ piap ap n-acap ḋo ṡénaṁ, uaip ap a aonap acá anopa amuiċ ⁊ imepcin iccíp naċ leip péin, ap map- ḃaḋ an ḋapa mic po paṡpom na pappaḋ, aṁail poillpiṡċeap ḋampa, ṡomaḋ i n-aipLinṡe no poillpiṡċea ḋopoṁ pin: ⁊ po mapḃaḋ an mac oile ḋó a ccaċ pinnbpſċcain ḋno, ma ċéapna an c-aċaip pén ap an caċ pin, que peuepa comppobacum eipc.

In can po ḃaoi ṡa páḋ pin ap ann aḋ ċonnaipc caċ na Maupi- cana ċuca : ⁊ map aḋ ċonnaipc an mac po páiḋ na ḃpiaċpa pſṁ- ainn pin, po Linṡ ṡo hoḃañ 'pan ċaċ ⁊ cáinic ḋ'ionnpoiṡ pí na Mau- picána, ⁊ cuṡ buille ḋo ċloiḃſṁ mór ḋó, ṡo po ṡaḋ a láṁ ḋe. Ro cuipeaḋ ṡo cpuaiḋ cſccup an ḋá lſc 'pan ċaċ pa, ⁊ ní puṡ nſċ ḋſoḃ copṡup ḋa chele 'pan ċaċ pin. Aċc cáiniṡ cáċ ḋſoḃ ḋ'ionnpaiṡ a lonṡpoipc, ap mapḃaḋ poċaiḋe eccuppa. Ra puaṡaip imuppo cáċ áp a ċéle coiḋeacc ap na ṁápaċ ḋo ċum an ċaca. Ro iom- ṡaḋ imuppo pí na Maupicana an lonṡpopc, ⁊ pa éla ipin oíḋċe ap nṡaiḋ a láiṁe ḋe. O cáiniṡ cpa an maiḋin po ṡaḃpac na Loċlañ- aiṡ a n-apma, ⁊ po ċoipiṡpioc iaḋ ṡo cpuaiḋ beoḋa ḋo ċum an caca. Na Maupicana imuppo ó po aipiṡpic a pí ḋ'élúḋ, po ċeiċ- pioḋ ap mapḃaḋ a nḋeapṡáip.

Ro

---

¹ *The Gaditanean Straits.*—i. e. the Straits of Gades, in the south of Spain. The modern Cadiz preserves the name.

ᵘ *The external ocean.*—i. e. the Atlantic.

² *Mauritani.*—i. e. the Moors. Mauritania Proper answers to the modern Morocco.

ʸ *The father himself.*—Meaning, "if our father himself."

in Spain both by killing and plundering. They afterwards crossed the Gaditanean Straits', i. e. where the Mediterranean Sea goes into the external ocean", and they arrived in Africa, and there they fought a battle with the Mauritani*, in which a great slaughter of the Mauritani was made. However, on going to this battle, one of the sons said to the other : " Brother," said he, " it is great folly and madness in us to be going from one country to another throughout the world, killing ourselves, instead of defending our patrimony and obeying the will of our father, for he is now alone away from home, and sojourning in a country not his own; the second son, whom we left along with him, having been killed, as was revealed to me (this had been revealed to him in a dream), and his other son was killed in a battle ! It is wonderful, too, if the father himself" has escaped from that battle, *que² revera comprobatum est.*"

As he was saying these words, they saw the battle array of the Mauritani approaching them; and as the son who said the aforesaid words saw it, he rushed suddenly into the battle, and he came up to the King of Mauritania, and gave him a stroke of a great sword, and cut off his hand. The battle was fought with great hardihood on both sides, although neither party gained the victory in that battle; but both returned to their camps, after many persons had been killed on both sides. They, however, challenged each other to battle the next day. But the King of Mauritania fled from his camp, and fled at night, after having lost his hand. When the morning came, however, the Lochlanns put on their armour, and prepared themselves with hardihood and vigour for the battle. But when the Mauritani perceived that their king had absconded, they fled, after many of them had been cut off with great slaughter".

After

' *Que.*—Read *quod.* The meaning is, that what had been miraculously revealed to him in a dream, was found to turn out true.
 * *Great slaughter.*—The editor has not

Ro cuaccup iappin na Loclonnaiʒ fon cíp ⁊ po aipʒpioc, ⁊ po loipʒpioo an cíp uile; cuʒpao ona pluaʒ móp oíob a mbpaic leo ʒo hEipinn .i. piao pin na pip ʒopma, uaip ip ionann Maupi ⁊ niʒpi: Maupicania ip ionann ip niʒpicuoo. Ap inbfcain má céapna an cpfp ouine oo Loclonnaib eoip in nfc pa mapbaio, ⁊ po báioic oíb pan Muincinn muipioe Ƶaoicanna. Ap paoa ona po báoap na pip ʒopma pin i n-Eipinn. Ap ann aca Maupicania concpa baleapep Inpulap.

Kal. Eclippip polip in Calenoip Ianuapii.

Ceallac mac Ailella, ab Cille oapa, ⁊ ab Iae, oopimiuic in peʒione Piccopum.

Mainchine Eppcop Lecʒline quieuic.

Tuacal mac Apcʒoppa, ppim eppcop Poipcpifnn, ⁊ ab Ouin Caillen, mopicup.

Ƶuin Colmain mic Ounlainʒe, pi Focapc cípe; oo mapbao é oa cloinn féin.

Tiʒfpnac mac Focapca, pi Feap mópeaʒ.

Ip in bliaoain pi cainiʒ Tompap iapla, o Luimnioc ʒo Cluain fepca Opfnainn, (ouine ainopeannoa aʒapb ainoʒio eipioe oo Loclannaib) anoap leip oo ʒebao bpao móp 'pin cill pin, ʒiofo ní map na paoil puaip, uaip cainiʒ peal bʒ fiop peime, ⁊ po ceicfo ʒo maic peime i n-eacpaib, opeam eile i peipcinib, opfm oile 'pin cfmpul. An opfm imuppo fop a puʒpom ap an uplap, ⁊ ip in pelic po mapbpom. Ro baoi ono Copmac mac Elacoiʒ, paoi eaʒna Eipfnn,

been able to find any account of this invasion of Morocco by the Northmen in any other authority.

ᵇ *Blue men in Erin.*—No account of these blue men has been found in any other Annals or history.

ᶜ *Balearic Isles.*—Majorca, Minorca, Cabrera, Iviza, &c.

ᵈ *An eclipse of the sun.*—This eclipse is entered in the Annals of Ulster at the year 864, but the true year is 865.

ᵉ *Ceallach.*—Annals of Ulster, A.D. 864;

After this the Lochlanns passed over the country, and they plundered and burned the whole country; and they carried off a great host of them [the Mauritani] as captives to Erin, and these are the blue men [of Erin], for Mauri is the same as black men, and Mauritania is the same as blackness. It is wonderful if every third man of the Lochlanns escaped, between the numbers who were killed and those who were drowned of them in the Gaditanean Straits. Long indeed were these blue men in Erin[b]. Mauritania is situated opposite the Balearic Isles[c].

[869.] Kal. An eclipse of the sun[d] on the Calends of January.

Ceallach[e], son of Ailell, Abbot of Cill dara and Abbot of I, died in the region of the Picts.

Mainchine[f], Bishop of Leithghlin, died.

Tuathal[g], son of Artgus, chief Bishop of Fortrenn, and Abbot of Dun Caillen [Dunkeld], died.

The killing of Colman, son of Dunlang, King of Fotharta-tire[h] : he was killed by his own children.

Tighernach[i], son of Focarta, King of the men of Breagh [died].

In this year came Tomrar[k] the Earl, from Luimnech to Cluain-fearta-Brenainn[l] (he was a fierce, rough, cruel man of the Lochlanns), thinking that he would find a great prey in that church, but he did not find it as he thought, for intelligence had gone a short time before him, and they fled expertly from him, some in boats, others into the morasses, and others into the church. Those whom he caught on the floor

---

Reeves's "Adamnan," p. 391 ; F. M. 863.

[f] *Mainchine.*—F. M. 863.

[g] *Tuathal.*—F. M. 863; Ann. Ult. 864.

[h] *Fotharta-tire.*—i. e. the inland Fotharta, now the barony of Forth, in the county of Carlow.—Ann. F. M. 863.

[i] *Tighernach.*—Ann. Ult. 864 [= 865].

[k] *Tomrar.*—This Tomrar is not mentioned in any other Annals, unless he be the same as the Tomrar, son of Tomralt, who was slain 923 (F. M.).

[l] *Cluain-fearta Brenainn.*—Now Clonfert. This attack is not mentioned in any other Annals known to the Editor.

Eiŗṡnn, coṁaŗba ŗen Ciaŗáin Saiġŗe ŗin cṡmpal ŗin. Ra ŗaoŗ Dia ┐ bŗénainn iad amlaiġ ŗin. Maŗb imoŗŗu do dáŗacc an Comŗaiŗ 'ŗin bliadain ŗi, aŗ n-imiŗc do bhŗénainn mioŗbal ŗaiŗ. Iŗ in bliaġain ŗin ŗo ċuadaŗ na ŗiġ Loċlonnaiġ im Muṁain ┐ ŗluaġa móŗa leo, ┐ ŗa inoŗiŗio ġo cŗoda an Muṁain. Ġidṡb cṡna cuġad deaŗġ áŗ ŗoŗŗa ann, uaiŗ cainiġ Cinnéciġ mac Ġaicin, ŗí Laoiġŗi (mac éŗide do Laind inġin Dunlainġe, ┐ ŗide dno mataiŗ Ḟlainn mic Maoilŗeaċloinn ┐ aŗ í ba bṡn an canŗa d'Aod mac Néill, ŗiġ Cṡmŗaċ), aŗ é an mac-Ġaicin ba ġaiŗġe, ┐ ba coŗġŗaċa ŗoŗ ġallaib ŗan aimŗiŗ ŗin i n-Eiŗind—cainiġ iaŗam an Cinnéciġ ŗi ┐ Laoiġiŗ ġo noŗeim do Oŗŗaiġib maille ŗiŗ ġo lonġŗoŗc na Loċlann, ġuŗ ŗo maŗbŗac dŗŗġáŗ a ndŗġdaoine aŗ láŗ an lonġŗoiŗc. Iŗ ann ŗin ad ċonnaiŗc Cinnédiġ ŗṡŗ d'á ṁuincīŗ ŗéin, ┐ diaŗ Loċlann aġ cŗiall a ċinn do beim de, cainiġ ġo cŗic ua ŗaoŗad, ┐ ŗo bṡn an da cṡnn do'n dŗŗ ŗin, ┐ ŗo ŗaoŗ a ŗeaŗ muincīŗe ŗéin. Cainic ŗeṁe Cennédiġ ġo mbuaid ┐ coŗġuŗ. Aŗ annŗaide do ŗala an éŗṡċ Loċlannaċ i naiġid Cinnédiġ co n-édalaib moŗa occa. O ŗo ċualacuŗ na maiċe ud do maŗbad ŗo ŗaġŗad a ġcŗeiċ, ┐ a n-édala, ┐ canġaccuŗ ġo cŗuaid, beoda i n-aiġid Cinnéciġ. Ro coġbaid ġoca allṁaŗda baŗbaŗda annŗaide, ┐ ŗcuic iomda badŗŗha ┐ ŗocuide ġa ŗád nūi, nūi. Ro diobaiŗġio iaŗaṁ ŗaiġde iomda ŗcuŗŗa ┐ leċġae ┐ ŗa ġabŗac ŗa deoiġ ŗoŗ a cclóiḃṁib

---

ᵐ *Cormac.*—He was Abbot of Scirkieran, in the King's County. His death is noticed in the Annals of Ulster at the year 868.

ⁿ *Saved them.*—Something seems to have been omitted here. The narrative is probably abridged from some ecclesiastical legend.

º *Died of madness.*—This is probably a mistake, confounding this Tomrar with the Tomrar Mac Ailchi, or Elge, who died, or "went to hell with his pains" in 922, according to the Annals of Clonmacnoise.—See "Leabhar na gCeart," Introd., p. xli.

ᵖ *Predatory party.*—A party who had gone forth from the camp for plunder.

floor and in the churchyard he killed. Cormac[m], son of Elathach, chief of Erin for wisdom, the successor of old Ciaran, of Saighir, was in the church. God and Brenann thus saved them[n]. And Tomrar died of madness[o] in this year, Brenann having wrought a miracle upon him.

In this year the Lochlann kings went into Munster, having great hosts along with them, and they bravely ravaged Munster. They were, however, dreadfully slaughtered, for Cennedigh, son of Gaithin, King of Laeighis, the son of Lann, daughter of Dunlang (who was the mother of Flann, son of Maelsechlainn, and at this time the wife of Aedh, son of Niall, King of Teamhair,—and this son of Gaithin was the fiercest and the most victorious man against the foreigners in Erin at this time), —this Cennedigh came with the Laeighis and a party of the Osraighi to the camp of the Lochlanns and made a slaughter of the best of their men in the middle of the camp. On this occasion Cennedigh saw a man of his people between two Lochlann men who were going to cut off his head, and he came actively to his relief, and beheaded the two Lochlanns, and thus saved his own man. Cennedigh then passed forward with victory and triumph. Then the predatory party[p] of the Lochlanns came against Cennedigh, having great spoils in their hands, and when they heard of the killing of the chiefs aforesaid, they left their plunder and spoils and came vigorously and actively against Cennedigh. They raised foreign barbarous shouts there, and blew warlike trumpets, and many said "nui, nui[q]!" Many darts and half javelins were discharged between them, and at last they took to their heavy, strong-striking swords. But God was assisting the son of Gaithin and his

[q] *Nui, nui.*—Quere, whether this war-cry is not the Norse *noe, noe* (*now, now!*). This account of the conflict between Kennedy, son of Gahan, King of Leix (a territory included in the present Queen's County), must have been taken from some local Annals, preserved, probably, at Clonenagh or Clonfert-Mulloe. No account

ccloíomib troma toitbuilleda. Gideb tra ro baí Dia az furtact
do mac Gaitin co na muinntir, ro ropuairlizfo na Loclannaiz, ⁊
ra fazrat a laeraiz imbualta : ra cuadar arr i maiom ar marbad a nofrzár. Orfm oile ní nféattur i ffad ar a ffainne ar
ffulanz zorta móire dóib, no ar a náire leo teéfo. In¹ uair ad
concattur fluaz mic Gaitin occ tionol an maitiura ro fazrad-
rum leo, tanzattur na nofzaid. Mar ro connaire mac Gaitin
éride, ro zab rota amail raol ro caorcab, zo ro teicriod 'ran
mónaid zur ro márbaid 'ran mónaid uile iad, zo nduattur coin
a ccolla. Ro marbrat ono an luctra .i. mac Gaitin co muinntir
ofrzar aora zrada riz Loclann i n-áird aile rin Mumain .i.
marcfluaz riz Loclann. If na diozail ra marbrat na Loclannaiz fluaz mór cléreé, ra baoi [ina lonzrurt] féin, act ar iar
mbuaid onzta ⁊ aitriže.

If i n-aimfir fin ruz clú mór Maoilciarain² eidir Gaoidealuib
ar a mente buada do breit dó do Loclannaib.

If in bliadainri ba marb Tomrur iarla, náma brénainn do
dáract i rurt Manann, ⁊ ba hfb ad cío brénainn zá marbad.

If in tan ro do rourad Ciarruize forbairi for muinntir an
Tomrair fin, ⁊ ar nattact dóib brénainn ar brú an mara, ro
baoi an coimde az furtact do na Gaoidiolaib : uair baoi an muir
óz bádhad na Loclann, ⁊ na Ciarruize za marbad. Conzal an
Sfnóir ri Ciarruize ruz buaid irin conzail cata ra. Ar uaiteab
tra lomnoct ⁊ zonta tearna do na Loclannaib ; ba mór n-óir ⁊
airzid, ⁊ bancaom ro rázbaid ann fin.

If in bliadain fi ono tanzattur flóiz Loclann ó Phurt Corc-
aiže

of it is given in the published Annals.
¹ *They came.*—i. e. the wounded or wearied Lochlanns rallied, and followed the victorious Irish, to endeavour to recover their spoils.
² *Maelciarain.*—The death of this champion is entered in the Ann. Ult. at 868 ; F. M. 867.

his people, and they prevailed over the Lochlanns, who left the field of conflict and fled routed after having sustained red havoc. Some of them had not gone far, in consequence of weakness, having suffered much from hunger, or who were ashamed to fly; when these perceived the host of the son of Gaithin collecting the spoils which they had abandoned to them, they came[r] after them. When the son of Gaithin saw this, he attacked them as the wolf attacks sheep, so that they fled into a bog, and in that bog they were all killed, and dogs devoured their bodies. This party also, i. e. the son of Gaithin and his people, made a great slaughter of the *aes-gradha* [servants of trust] of the King of the Lochlanns in another direction in Munster, i. e. of the cavalry of the King of the Lochlanns; and in revenge of this the Lochlanns killed a great host of clerics who were in their own camp; but it was after the victory of unction and penance.

At this time Maelciarain[s] obtained great fame among the Gaeidhil from his frequent victories over the Lochlanns.

In this year Tomrar, the Earl, the enemy of Brenann, died of madness at Port-Manann[t], and he saw Brenann[u] killing him.

In this year the Ciarraighi [Kerry-men] made an invading camp against the people of this Tomrar, and having supplicated Brenann on the brink of the sea, the Lord was aiding the Gaedhil, for the sea was drowning the Lochlanns, and the Ciarraghi were killing them. Congal, the senior[x], King of Ciarraighe, gained victory in this battle. The Lochlanns escaped, few, naked, and wounded, leaving behind them much gold and silver, and fair women.

In this year also the hosts of the Lochlanns came from the port of

---

[t] *Port-Manann.*—i. e. the harbour of the Isle of Man.

[u] *Brenann.*—i. e. St. Brendan, of Clonfert. St. Brendan was the navigator of the Irish, and was particularly hostile to the Scandinavians.

[x] *Congal the senior.*—i. e. the aged. There is no account of this destruction of

aiġe d'arġain Ḟſrmaiġe Ḟéne, acc cſna ní ra cſdaiġ Dia dóib, uair iſ an can rin canġaccur na Déri ar crſċaib 'ran ffſrann cécna cṕé rémṕéġad Dé, uair ba ḋearġ-ṅaṁaid reimirin na Déiri 7 Ḟirmaiġe. 'O ro concaccur iaṗam na Déri na Loċlannaiġ oġ orġain 7 oġ innṕad an círe canġaccur d'ionnṕaiġid Ḟearmuiġe, 7 do ronrac ríd daingin ċairiri, 7 ro ċuadar an aonfṕ i ccſnn na Loċlann ġo ġanġ, beoda, commbaġaċ, 7 ra cuiṕſd ġo cṕuaid crodḃa leiċ for leċ ſcuṕra, ġiófd ro mſṁaid forṕ na Loċlaṅaib cṕé miorḃail an ċoimḋheḋ, 7 ra cuiriod a ndearġ áṕ. Ṕá ċuaid imurro a ccaoiriod .i. Ġnimcinnriolaiġ la ainim ġo rainiġ cairċail daingen baoi a ġcomroċraid dóib, 7 ro ſuadair a ġadail, 7 aṕed ba díoṁaoin do, uair ni ra ſéd a ſulanġ ar iomad ſaġa 7 cloċ ġá ndiubṕaġad do. Ireḋ do riġmiriom Cſhnfaolad do ġairm cuiġe, uair ba dóiġ leiṕ ba cara é, 7 airġſda iomda do ġeallad do ar a anacal, 7 a ṕed ba díoṁaoin doroṁ, uair ro cairnġſdroṁ amaċ cria imride na roċaide ro roġnaioriocc do reiṁe, 7 ro marḃad ġo cṕuaġ é, 7 ro marḃaid a ṁuinncer uile. Ba ġairic imurro iarccain ġo ċċanġar do ċum an ċairċeol in ro caiċriom a bſċaid ġo rarċolaċ, 7 ro díorġaoilead uile é. Sic enim placuic Deo.

Ṕal. Diṅſrcaċ, ab Loċhṕa moricuur.

Loċ Ledinn do ṕoud i ffuil, ġo ṕaibe na ṕáircid cró aṁail rġaṁa.

Sriċaiṕ

the followers of Tomrar by field and flood, to be found in the published Annals.

ʸ *Corcach.*—i. e. from the harbour of Cork. There is no account of this transaction given in the published Annals.

ᶻ *Gnim Cinnsiola.*—It is stated in the Ann. F. M. at the year 865, that Gnimbeolu, chief of the Galls of Cork, was slain by the Deisi, and he was, no doubt, the same person as the Gnim Cinnsealaigh here mentioned.

ᵃ *Castle.*—Cairciul. This is the earliest notice of a Danish castle in Ireland. This entry, however, is not to be found in the other Annals.

ᵇ *Lothra.*—Now Lorha, in the barony

of Corcach[y] to plunder Fera Maighe-Feine [Fermoy]. God, however, did not permit them, for at this time the Deisi had come to plunder in the same land by the providence of God, for before this time the Deisi and the Feara-maighe were mortal enemies. When, however, the Deisi saw the Lochlanns plundering and ravaging the country, they came to the Feara-maighe, and they made a firm and faithful peace [with each other], and they went together against the Lochlanns, fiercely, actively, and unitedly, and a fierce and terrible battle was fought between them; however, the Lochlanns were defeated through God's miracle, and they were cut off with great slaughter. But their chief, Gnim Cinnsiolla[z] by name, went to a strong castle[a] which stood near them, and he attempted to take it, but it was a vain effort for him, for he was not able to bear the number of darts and stones shot at him. He then called Cennfaeladh to him, for he thought he was a friend, and promised him many rewards for protecting him; but this was also idle for him, for he was taken out at the request of the hosts who had served him previously, and piteously killed with all his people. Shortly afterwards they came to the castle in which he had passed his time voluptuously, and totally demolished it: *Sic enim placuit Deo.*

[866.] Kal. Dinertach, Abbot of Lothra[b], died.

Loch Leibhinn[c] was turned into blood, so that it was in clots of blood, like *sgama*[d].

Sruthair,

of Lower Ormond, county of Tipperary. See F. M. 864.

[c] *Loch Leibhinn.*—Now Lough Leane, near Fore, in the county of Westmeath. According to the Life of St. Fechin, published by Colgan, Diarmaid, King of Ireland, who died A. D. 664, had lived on

an island in this lake, and, according to the tradition in the country, the Danish tyrant Turgesius had a residence on the same island.—Ann. F. M. 864; Ann. Ult. 865.

[d] *Sgama.*—Scum, dross; the liver, or lights; the scale of a fish. Latin, *squama*.

Sruṫaıṗ, ⁊ Sléḃte, ⁊ Aċaḋ Aṗġlaıṗ ḋ'aṗġaın ḋo ġentıḃ.
Iṗ ın blıaḋaın ṗı .ı. ṗeẋto anno ṗeġıṁıṅıṗ Aoḋa mıc Néıll, maıḋm ṗe Laıġnıḃ ṗoṗ Uıḃ Néıll, ı ttoṗċaıṗ Maolmuaḋ mac Ḋunchaḋa, ⁊ Maolmuıṗċeṁne mac Maoılḃṗıġḋe.
Teaġṁaıl eıḋıṗ 'Oıṗle, mac ṗí Loċlann, ⁊ Aṁlaıḃ a ḃṗáṫaıṗ. Tṗı mıc ḃattuṗ aġ an ṗí .ı. Aṁlaıḃ, ⁊ ıoṁaṗ, ⁊ 'Oıṗle. Oıṗle ba ṗoo a n-aoıṗ ḋíoḃ, ⁊ aṗ é ḃá moó aṗ aoı eanġnama; uaıṗ ṗuġ ḋeaṗṗġuġhaḋ moṗ ınḋıuḃaṗġan ṗoġa ⁊ ınnıoṗtġa ḋo Ġhaoıḋealaıḃ. Ruġ ḋno ḋíṗṗġuġhaḋ ḋo Loċlannaıḃ ın nıuṗt cloıḋım ⁊ ın-ḋıuḃṗaġaḋ ṗaıġṡo. Ro ḃaoı a ḋuḃṗuaċ ġo moṗ ġa ḃṗaıṫṗıḃ. Aṗeḋ aṗ mó ṗo ḃaoı aġ Aṁlaoıḃ. Ní ınıṗın cuıṗı na mıṗċn aṗ a lıḃṗı. Ra ċuaḋaṗ an ḋa ḃṗáṫaıṗ .ı. Aṁlaoıḃ ⁊ Ioṁaṗ ı ġcoṁaıṗle ma caınġın ın mıc óıġ .ı. 'Oıṗle, ġé ṗo ḃattuṗ cúıṗı ḋıċealta occa ḋa ṁaṗḃaḋ, ní hıaḋ tuġṗat aṗ áıṗḋ, aċt cúıṗı eıle ṗo tóġḃattuṗ aṗ áıṗḋ aṗ anḋleṗıoḋ a ṁaṗḃaḋ, ⁊ ṗá ċınṗıot ıaṗaṁ a ṁaṗḃaḋ. 'O ṗo ṗıoıṗ Aṁlaoıḃ ḋál an ḃṗaṫaṗ ba mıoṗġaıṗ leıṗ ḋo ċuıḃeaċt, ıṗṗeḋ ḋo ṗıġne tíċtaıṗeaḋa taıṗıṗı ḋo ċuṗ aṗ cſnn na ṗıtaıṗe ba ṗonaıṗte ⁊ ba ḃeoḋa aıġe, ġo mḃeıttíṗ aṗtıġ aṗ cſnn 'Oıṗle. Táınıc ıaṗam an t'Oıṗlı .ı. an ḋuıne aṗ ḟíṗṗ cṗuṫ ⁊ ſnġnaṁ ḃaoı an tan ṗın 'ṗan ḋoṁan; uaıéſo ḋna taınġ ı ttſċ aḃṗaṫaıṗ; uaıṗ ní ṗaoıl an ní ṗuaıṗ ann .ı. a ṁaṗḃaḋ. Iṗeḋ ımoṗṗo ṗo cuınnıġ ann ní naċ ṗo ṗaoıl. Aṗſo ṗo ıaṗṗ ó ċuṗ ḋıolmaınıuṗ laḃaṗta ḋo taḃaıṗt ḋó. Tuġaḋ ḋoṗoṁ ṗaın. Aṗſo ımoṗṗo, ṗolaḃaıṗṗıoṁ .ı. a ḃṗáṫaıṗ

---

e *Sruthair.*—Now Shrule, on the east side of the River Barrow, near the town of Carlow. See Ann. F. M., p. 562, note.

f *Slebhte.*—Now Sleaty, near the town of Carlow.

g *Achadh arghlais.*—Now Agha, in the barony of Idrone, county of Carlow.

h *By the Gentiles.*—The F. M., at 864, have, "by the Osraighi."

i *Aedh.*—This was the year 869. This entry is not in the published Annals.

k *Amhlaeibh, &c.*—These three princes are mentioned in the Annals of Ulster, at the year 862, as having plundered the an-

Sruthair[e], and Slebhte[f], and Achadh Arghlais[g] were plundered by the Gentiles[h].

In this year, the sixth of the reign of Aedh[i], son of Niall, a victory was gained by the Leinster-men over the Ui-Neill; in the battle fell Maelmuaidh, son of Donchadh, and Maelmuirtheimhne, son of Maelbrighde.

A meeting [took place] between Oisle, son of the King of Lochlann, and Amhlaeibh, his brother. The king had three sons, namely, Amhlaeibh[k], and Imhar, and Oislè. Oislè was the youngest of them in age, but the greatest in point of valour, for he gained great celebrity by excelling all the Gaeidhil in shooting darts and javelins, and he excelled the Lochlanns in strength of sword and in shooting darts. His brothers had a black hatred for him, and Amhlaeibh more than the other. The causes of the hatred are not to be told, on account of their complexity. The two brothers, Amlaeibh and Imhar, consulted together about the cause of the young brother, Oislè; and though they had hidden reasons for killing him, these were not what they brought forward, but they dissembled and brought forward other causes for which they ought to kill him; and they afterwards resolved upon killing him. When Amhlaeibh had learned that the party of the brother whom he hated had arrived, what he did was, to send faithful messengers for the stoutest and most vigorous knights he had, that they might be in the house on Oislè's arrival. Oislè afterwards arrived. He was the best shaped and the most valiant man that was then in the world. He came with a small party to the house of his brother, for he did not expect to meet his death there, as he did. He requested a thing which he did not think would be

cient sepulchral caves, as well as the land of Flann, son of Conaing, chief of Cianachta in Bregia; and the murder of

Oisle, or Flosius, is recorded A. D. 866. "Auisle tertius rex Gentilium dolo et parricidio a fratribus suis jugulatus est."

aḃráċaiṗ (aṗ ṗé) muna ḟṗail ṡṗáḋ ḋo ṁná, .i. inġṡn Cinaoċ aṡaḋṗa, cíḋ na leiṡi ḋaṁṗa uaiṫ í, ⁊ ṡaċ ní ṗo ḋíoṡḃaiṗ ṗia, ḋo ḃéṗṗa ḋuiṫ, 'O ṗo cuala an ṫ-Aṁlaiḃ ṗin, ṗo ġaḃ éḋ móṗ é, ⁊ ṗo noċṫ a ċloiḋṁ, aṡuṗ ṫuṡ buille ḋe i ṡcṡnn 'Oiṗle .i. a ḃṗáṫaṗ, ṡuṗ ṗoṗ maṗḃ. Ro ċoiṁéiṗiṡ cáċ aṗ aṁuṗ a ċéile iaṗṫṫain .i. muinṫṡṗ an ṗí .i. Aṁlaoiḃ, ⁊ muinnṫṡṗ an ḃṗáṫaṗ ṗo máṗḃaḋ ann; báṫṫuṗ ṗṫuic, ⁊ coṁaiṗc maṗṡċ annṗaiḋe. Ro ċuaṗ iaṗṗain ṗa Lonṡṗoṗṫ an ḃṗaṫaṗ ṗo maṗḃaḋ ann, aṗ ccuṗ ḋíṡṡáṗ a ṁuinnṫiṗe. Rob ioṁḋa maiṫioṗ iṗ in Lonṡṗoṗṫ ṗin.

'Sin ḃliaḋain ṗi ḋo ċuaḋaṗ na Ḋanaiṗ ṡo Caeṗ Eḃṗoic ⁊ ḋo ṗaoṗaṫ caṫ cṗuaiḋ ḋo na Saxanaiḃ ann. Ro maiḋ ṗoṗ Saxanuiḃ, ⁊ ṗo maṗḃaḋ ṗiṡ Saxan ann .i. Alle, ṫṗe ḃṗaṫ ⁊ meaḃail ṡiolla óiṡ ḋa ṁuinṫiṗ ṗéin. Ṫuṡaḋ ṫṗa áṗ móṗ iṗ in caṫ ṗin, ⁊ ṗa cuaṗ i aṗ ṗain ṗoṗ Caeṗ Eḃṗoic, ⁊ ṫuṡaḋ ioṁaḋ ṡaċ maiṫiuṗa eiṗṫe, uaiṗ bá ṗaiḋḃiṗ an ṫan ṗin í, ⁊ maṗḃuṗ na ṗṗṗíċ ḋo ḋeaṡḋaoine innṫe. Aṗ aṗ ṗin ṗo ṗáṗ ṡaċ ḋoconaċ, ⁊ ṡaċ iṁneaḋ ḋ'innṗi ḃṗeaṫon.

Iṗ in ḃliaḋain ṗi ṫainiṡ an Cenneḋiṡ aiṗḋiṗc .i. mac Ṡaiṫin, náṁa cluuċ na Loclann ḋ'ionnṗoiṡiḋ Lonṡṗoṗṫ Aṁloiḃ, ṗí na Loclann (⁊ aṗ eṗiḋe ṗṡṁainn ḋo maṗḃ a ḃṗáṫaiṗ) ṡuṗ ṗo loiṗcc . . . . Ṫanṡaṫṫuṗ na Loclannaiṡ na ḋíṡaiḋ, ⁊ maṗ ṫuṡṗoṁ a aiṡhiḋ ṗoṗṗa, ṗo maiḋ ṗeiṁe ḋiḃ ṡo niṡe an Lonṡṗoiṗṫ ⁊ ṗo maṗḃ a nḋeaṗṡáṗ na ṗaoṗclann.

Iṗ in ḃliaḋain ṗi ṫainic ḃaṗṫ iaṗla, ⁊ haimaṗ ḋiaṗ ḋo cinel ṗoicinealaċ

---

¹ *Caer Ebroic.*—i. e. the town of York. See Saxon Chronicle, A. D. 867; Ann. Ult. 866.

ᵐ *Alle.*—The East Anglians (i. e. Northumbrians), says the Saxon Chronicle, "had cast out their king Osbryght, and had taken to themselves a king, Ælla, not of royal blood." The death of Ælla on this occasion is not recorded; but Flor. Wigorn. in his Chron. says, "occisis duobus regibus," viz. Osbryght and Ælla.

ⁿ *The camp of Amhlaeibh.*—In the Ann.

be granted him. He first requested that freedom of speech should be granted him, and what he said was: "Brother," said he, "if thou art not fond of thy wife, the daughter of Cinaedh, why not give her away to me, and whatever dower thou hast given for her, I shall give to thee." When Amhlaeibh heard this, he was seized with great jealously; he drew his sword and dealt his brother Oislè a blow of it on the head, and killed him. The parties of both then rose up to give battle to each other, i. e. the people of the King, Amhlaeibh, and the people of the brother who was killed. Trumpets were blown, and combats were fought between both parties there. The camp of the slain brother was afterwards entered after his peoplē had been dreadfully slaughtered, and many were the spoils found in that camp.

In this year the Danes went to Caer-Ebroic[l] and gave hard battle to the Saxons there. They defeated the Saxons, and killed the Saxon King there; viz. Alle[m], through the treachery and deceit of a young man of his own people. Great havoc took place in that battle. The city of Ebroc was then entered, and much of every kind of riches was carried out of it, for it was wealthy at this time, and all the good people who were found within it were slain. From this arose every kind of misfortune and trouble to the island of Britain.

In this year the famous Cennedigh, son of Gaithin, the celebrated enemy of the Lochlanns, came to the camp of Amhlaeibh[n], King of the Lochlanns (he who murdered his brother, as we have before mentioned), and burned it . . . . The Lochlanns came in pursuit of him, but he turned upon them and routed them back to their camp, and he made a great slaughter of their nobles.

In this year Barith the Earl[o], and Haimar, two of the noble race of

---

F. M., A. D. 865, Ult. 866, Dun-Amhlaeibh, or Amlaff's fort, is said to have been at Clondalkin.

[o] *Barith the Earl.*—The only Barith

roicinealaċ na Loċlann, ṫpé láp Connaċṫ ḋ'ionnroiġiḃ Luimniġ, aṁail na ḋſhnḋaíp ní ḋo Connaċṫaiḃ. Ġioſḃ ní aṁlaiḃ ḋo ṗala, uaip ní 'ran iomaḋ ro ṫaipipniġrioḋ aċṫ na' mḃpiġaiḃ péin. Ro puarpaċ-ṫup na Connaċṫaiġ ṫpia ċelcc a ppopuaipliuġaḋroṁ: uaip ḋo ṗala apeile Muiṁneaċ ronaipṫ, cpuaiḃ, ⁊ ġlic i n-imipṫ apm, ſṫuppa an ṫan pin, ⁊ bá ġlic ḋno a ccomaipliḃ an Muiṁneaċ pin. Ro iopailſṫ-ṫup iapaṁ Connaċṫa paippiḋe ḋola ap amup na Loċlann, map ba ḋo ṫaḋaipṫ eoluip ḋóiḃ, ⁊ ḋo mapbaḋ ḃapiċ. Map panaiġpiḋe ġo niġe an ionaḋ i ṗaba haimap ṫuġ buille ḋó leaṫġa ġo ronaipṫ in haimap, ġo rop mapḃ. Miliḃ imuppo Connaċṫaċ ḋo ċuaiḃ maille pip ap ṫí mapḃṫa an ḃapiċ, ní ṫápla ḋopaiḃe aṁail ba ḋúṫpaċṫ laip, uaip ro ġonaḃ é ṫpe na pliapaiḃ, ⁊ pa cuaiḃ ap ap éiġin iapṫṫain. Ra ġaḃpaṫ ḋno na Connaċṫaiġ po na Loclannaiḃ ġup ċiipioḋ ḋeapġáp na Loċlann, ⁊ ní haṁlaiḃ po ḃiaḃ muna beiṫ an ċaill ⁊ an aḋhaiġ i ppoċpaiḃ. Ireḃ ro ċuaṫṫup iapṫṫain coiniġe an ionaiḃ ap a ṫṫanġaṫṫup, ⁊ ní ḋo Luimneaċ.

Kal. Maolḃúin mac Aoḋa Oipḋniġe, in clepicaṫu oḃiṫ.

Roḃapṫaċ, Epircopur eṫ rapienr Ḟionnġlaipi, mopiṫup.

Copġnach ṫiġe Ṫelle, rċpibniḋe ⁊ anġcoipe, ḋ'écc.

Conall Cille Scípe, epircopur, quieuiṫ.

Copmac hUa Liaċháin, epircopur eṫ anachopeṫa, quieuiṫ.

Oiġſḃċaip, ab Coinḋepe ⁊ Lainneala, quieuiṫ.

Ġuaipe mac Ḋuḃḋaḃaipſhn mopiṫup.

Muipſḃaċ

mentioned in the Irish Annals is Barith, a fierce champion of the Norsemen, who was slain at Dublin in 878, according to the Ann. F. M.; Ult. 880.

^p *Maelduin, son of Aedh.*—A. D. 866 [=867] Ann. Ult. He was the son of Aedh Oirdnidhe, who was King of Ireland A. D. 797–820.

^q *Finnglais.*—Now Finglas, near Dublin. Ann. Ult. 866.

^r *Tigh Telle.*—Now Tihelly, or Tecly, [*the house of St. Telle*, see Mart. Dungal. ad 25 Jun.], near Durrow, in the north of the present King's County. Colgan's Acta SS.,

of the Lochlanns, came through the middle of Connaught towards Luimneach [Limerick], as if they intended to do no injury to the Connaught-men. But this did not happen so, for it was not to numbers they trusted, but to their own vigour. The Connaught-men proposed to cut them off by treachery; for at that time there happened to be a certain Munster-man among them who was brave, hardy, and cunning in the use of arms, and he was also wise in councils. The Connaught-men requested of him to go towards the Lochlanns, as if to guide them, [but in reality] to kill Barith. As he came on to the place where Haimar was, he gave Haimar a strong blow of a half javelin, and killed him. But a Connaught champion, who went along with him for the purpose of killing Barith, did not happen to succeed as he desired, for he was himself wounded through his thigh, and afterwards escaped with difficulty. The Connaught-men, however, attacked the Lochlanns, and made a great havoc of them, but this would not have been the case had not the wood and the night been near them. The Lochlanns then returned to the place from which they had set out, instead of proceeding to Luimneach.

[867.] Kal. Maelduin, son of Aedh[p], King of Aileach, died *in clericatu*.

Robhartach, Bishop and sage of Finnglais[q], died.
Cosgrach, of Tigh Telle[r], scribe and anchorite, died.
Conall, of Cill Scire, a bishop, died.
Cormac Ua Liathain, bishop and anchorite, died.
Oigedhchair, Abbot of Coindeire [Connor] and Lann-Eala [Lynally], died.
Guaire, son of Dubhdabhairenn, died.

Muireadhach,

p. 15, note 10. It is shown on the Ordnance Map under the wrong name of Templekieran. Ann. Ult. 866. The other obits here entered are given in the Annals of the F. M. at 865, and the most of them in the Ann. Ult. at 866, but the true year is 867.

Muirfoaċ mac Caċail, ří hUa Criomċainn, longa papaliri extinctur ert.
Ounchaḋ mac Ounġaile moritur.
Canannan mac Ceallaiġ interrectur ert per oolum ó mac Ġaiċini.
Connmac ab Cluana mic Noir.
Maiom re mac Ġaiċini for Longur Aċa cliaċ, 1 ttorchair Ooolḃ Micle.ˢ
Oubartaċ berraċ raoi fġna quieuit.
Aeoacán mac Fionnacta, ollam leiċe Cuinn, quieuit.ᵗ
Ir in bliaḋain ri .1. in reptimo anno reġni Aoḃa,ᵘ ra ġrennaiġ-riod Laiġin Crḃall mac Ounlainġ um ċaċ. Ra ioplamaiġ ono Crḃall ar amur an caċa rain. Ro comraic oa marcrluaġ ġo norhnrao ofṗaiḃ, ġo ro marḃaḋ roċaiḋe eattupra. In can imurro ro comraic aċt bfġ oon ċaċ cfċċarḃa ar ann cainiġ Sloiġfḃoċ Ua Raitnen, comarba Molairri Leitġlinne, deocain an tan roin é, Errcor imorra, 7 Comarba Ciarain Saiġre iartcain; cainicriḋe ġo na . . . . fġnaiḃ, 7 ġo norhnaḋ rio ċairiri eattorru.
Ir in bliaḋain ri ono ronaḋ morrluaġ la hAoḋ Finnliaċ, mac Néill, riġ 'Eirhn o'ionnroiġiḋ Ciannacta oa n-arġain, 7 oa n-inḋ-raḋ, uair tuġ ri Ciannacta .1. Flann mac Conainġ mac a ofṗb-reaċan féin, oifriom mor for riġ 'Eirhn. Ní raba imurro i n-Erinn

ˢ *Odolbh Micle.*—i. e. Mickle, or the Big. The name is Odulph, Edulph, Adolph, or Adolphus. Frequent mention of a king of Danes of this name occurs in Geffrei Gaimar's "Estoire des Angles."

ᵗ *Aedhacan.*—The scribe has added in the margin the following passage from the F. M., A. D. 865:—Aeoacan mac Finr-neċta tanairi-abbaḋ Cluana 7 ab ċealla n-iomḋa, ḋec 1. Nou. "Aedacan, son of Finsnechta, Tanist-abbot of Cluan [Cloyne], and abbot of many churches, died 1st Nov."

ᵘ *Leth-Chuinn.*—i. e. Conn's half. The northern half of Ireland.

ˣ *Aedh.*—i. e. the year 870. This battle between the Leinster-men and Cearbhall, King of Ossory, is not noticed in

Muireadhach, son of Cathal, King of Ui Creamhthainn, died of long paralysis.

Dunchadh, son of Donnghal, died.

Canannan, son of Ceallach, was slain by treachery by the son of Gaithin.

Connmhach, Abbot of Cluain-mic-Nois, [died].

A victory was gained by the son of Gaithin over the fleet of Ath-cliath; in the battle Odolbh Micle⁸ was slain.

Dubhartach Berrach, a learned sage, died.

Aedhagan‡, son of Finnacht, Ollamh of Leth-Chuinn", died.

[870.] In this year, the seventh of the reign of Aedhˣ, the Leinster-men provoked Cearbhall, son of Dunlang, to battle. Cearbhall prepared for this battle. The two cavalries met together and fought, and many were slain between them. Before, however, much fighting had gone on between them, Sloighedhach Ua Raithnen, successor of Molaisse of Leithglinn (who was a deacon at this time, but afterwards a bishop and comharba of Ciaran of Saighir), came with his . . . . wise, and he made a sincere peace between them.

[868.] In this year a great hosting was made by Aedh Finnliath, son of Niall, King of Erin, against the Cianachtaʸ to plunder them, for the King of Cianachta, i. e. Flann, son of Conang, his own sister's son, had offered a great insult to the King of Erin. There was not in all Erin

the published Annals. Sloighedhach Ua Rathnen, successor of St. Ciaran of Saighir, died in the year 885. F. M.

ʸ *Cianachta.*— i. e. the Cianachta of Bregia. This hosting by King Aedh is noticed by the F. M. at 866, which they make the sixth of the reign of Aedh, and in the Ann. Ult. at 867, but the true year is 868 or 869. The F. M. have quoted several

ancient verses composed on the subject of this battle, which are referred to by the scribe of our MS., who writes in the margin, " Vide carmina de hoc prælio in Ann. Dungal. an. 866." The account here given is the fullest that has yet been discovered. It appears to be perfectly authentic, and seems to have been written immediately after the event had taken

n-Éiriinn uile bá moo enſch na caonṗuaparcaiḃ ionáṛ an Ḟlanora, ⁊ ono ʒen ṗoḃuiḃſc Aoḋ an can pain ḋe, ⁊ Aoḋ na áiporiʒ 'Éireann, ṛo ba maiṫ ʒṙeim Ḟlainn ḋó an can ṛáiniʒ a lſr .i. an can ṛo ḃaoi coʒaḋ ſcoṛṛa ⁊ Maoilrſclainn mac Maolṙuanaiḋ: uair iṛ cṛíſ ṛin ṛo innaṛb Maoilṛeclainn an Ḟlann aṛ a éir. An cṛa imuṛṛo oo ṛaḋ an Ḟlann mac Conainʒ an oiṛṛiomṛi oo ṛiʒ Éirſinn aṛ ann ṛin ṛo boí Ḟlanoa inʒen ṛi Oṛṛaiʒe .i. Ounlainʒ, ⁊ iṛ iṛiḋe ba bſin ḃ'Aoḋ Ḟinnliaṫ ancanṛa, aṛ mbeiṫ ṛeme aʒ Maoilṛeclainn, ⁊ iṛ í ṛuʒ Ḟlann ḋó, an mac ón iṛ ḟſṛr cáiniʒ i n-'Éiṛinn 'na aimṛiṛ, ⁊ ba áiṛoṛí 'Éireann iaṛccain. Aṛi an Lano cécna mácair Cennéoiʒ ſṛoaiṛc mic Ẓaiéíni. Iſ ann aobeiṛim ṛo boi an ṛioʒanṛa aʒ ḋénaṁ cſmṗuil oo naoiṁ Ḃṛíʒio i cCill oaṛa, ⁊ ṛaoiṛ iomḋa aice iṛin caille oʒ cſrʒaḋ ⁊ aʒ ṛnaiḃe cṛann. Ra cuala cṛa an ṛio-ʒanṛa coṁṛaḋ ⁊ uʒa Laiʒſin má ṛſi .i. um Aoḋ Ḟinnliaṫ ⁊ ima mac .i. im Ḟlann mac Maoilṛeclainn, ⁊ ní ṛaḃa aṛ mac oile ṛiaṁ a cló na a allaḋ an can ṛin, ⁊ ó ṛo ḟicir coiṁeiṛiʒe Laiʒſin la Ḟlann mac Conainʒ ṛí Cianṅaċta, cáiniʒ ṛempe ʒo niʒe bail i ṛaḃa a fſr, ⁊ ṛa innir ḋó, ⁊ ṛo nſrc ʒo ṛoſpaiḃe é, im éionól caéa na n-aʒaiḋ. Cuiṛſb cṛa Aoḋ iaṛ ṛin a ṛluaʒ ṛo Cianṅaċta, ⁊ aiṛʒio ⁊ loiṛʒio ʒo n-áṛ móṛ ḋaoine oo maṛbaḋ ḋóiḃ. Ní cáiniʒ imuṛṛo Ḟlann ṛo céḋóiṛ ḋa n-ionnṛoiʒiḋ, uaiṛ ṛaḃaoi coḃlaċ móṛ an can ṛin aʒ inḋſin ḃóinne, ⁊ ṛo cuiṛṛioṁ fioṛ aṛ a n-amuṛ ṛaiḋe ʒo ocíoṛoaoir ḋá róiṛiḃin, ⁊ canʒaccuṛṛom ón, ⁊ ono canʒaccuṛ Laiʒin o'ṛoiṛiʒin an Ḟhlann. Canʒaccuṛ uile iaṛccain i noſʒaiḋ ṛiʒ 'Éiṛeann ⁊ a cṛſca ṛeiṁe. Ro cuaiḃ Aoḋ aṛ áṛo ṛo ḃaoí aʒ ṛſʒaḋ na móṛ ṛoſpaiḃe baoi na oſʒaiḋ. . . . . . ṛé ⁊ a luċc coṁ-aiṛle, ní aṛ líon óʒ bṛiṛceaṛi caṫ, aċt iṛ cṛé fuṛcaċt an coimḃeaḋ,

⁊ cṛé

place, by some Leinster historian who was opposed to the Hy-Niall race; and who may probably have been an eye-witness of the events which he has recorded.

* *Fleet.*—i. e. a fleet of Norsemen or Lochlanna.

Erin, at this time, any one of greater valour or renown than this Flann, and although Aedh was not very thankful to him at this time, he being supreme King of Erin, Flann had afforded him aid when he required it, i. e. when there was a war between him and Maelsechlainn, son of Maelruanaidh, for it was in consequence of this that Maelsechlainn had expelled Flann from his territory. When, however, Flann, son of Conang, offered this insult to the King of Erin, then Flanna, daughter of the King of Osraighe, i. e. of Dunlang, the wife of Aedh Finnliath at this time, she having been previously married to Maelsechlainn, to whom she bore Flann, the best man in Erin in his time, and who was monarch of Erin afterwards. This same Flanna was also the mother of the famous Cennedigh, son of Gaithin. This queen, I say, was then erecting a church to Brigit at Cill-dara [Kildare], and she had many tradesmen in the wood felling and cutting timber. Now, this queen had heard the conversation and talk of the Leinstermen about her husband, i. e. Aedh Finnliath, and her son, i. e. Flann, son of Maelsechlainn, whose fame and renown at this time had never been enjoyed by any son before,—and when she had learned that the rising out of Leinster was going to aid Flann, son of Conang, King of Cianachta, she came forward to where her husband was, and told it to him, and she exhorted him heartily to assemble his forces to give them battle. After this Aedh sent his army throughout Cianachta, which they plundered and burned, and they made a great havoc of the people. Flann himself did not, however, come to attack them immediately, for there was a large fleet[z] at this time in the mouth of the Boinn [Boyne], and he sent for them, requesting that they would come to his relief—and so they did; and the Leinstermen also came to relieve him. They all set out in pursuit of the King of Erin, who had sent his spoils before him. Aedh ascended a hill which commanded a view of the great hosts which were in pursuit

⁊ cpé fípinne plaċa;ª an oíomup ımuppo ⁊ an ıomapcpaıo pluaż, ní hſb ap ıonṁaın pa Oıa, acc ınıplé aıznıo ⁊ cpaıoe oaınzſn. So-ċuıoe ıapaṁ oo'n luċc po, ⁊ ap oíompaċ cſzaıo. Cıonoılíopı uıle ımumpa anopa, ⁊ na bíoo mínma ceıċıo azaıb, uaıp ap paoa uaıb zo n-uıze bap ccıże féın, ⁊ ní capaıo lſnpap pıb, ní hanacal na coızıll pozebċaoı. Oénaıo cpa na noſpnpao báp n-aıċpſċa ⁊ bap pſnaıċpeaċa, puılnzío cpa ppopa ı n-aınm na cpíonoıoe oo ċealzuo ouıb. Mapao a ċıċıpċı mıpı az eıpze, eıpżío uıle ı n-aoınfſċc poċa map paıllpſċup Oıa ouıb. Oıa luaın ap aoı láıċe pſċṁaıne pın. In Flann ımuppo mac Conuınz ıpın paınn eıle, apſb po paıo-pıoe fpıa ṁuınnċıp. Ap uacħao an luċċ úo, ⁊ ap líonṁap aċáımne, ⁊ cpuaıoızıopı ċéım bá n-ıonɥpoızıo, ⁊ oo pızne cpí ċóıpızċe oe .ı. é féın ap ċúp, ⁊ Laızın ıapċcaın, na Loċlannaız pa oeoız; ⁊ po baoı za n-azallao uıle. Cuıcpıo an luċċ úo lıbpı, ap pé, ⁊ bep-ċaoı buaıo ⁊ copzup oíob, ap ní buo pıu leo ceıċeo pſṁaıbpı, ⁊ aċaoıpı líon ap moó. Uaıp ní ap paċ oıle aċúpa az an caċuzaopa, aċċ oo żabáıl pıże Cſṁpaċ,ᵇ no oom ṁapbao. Robċcup áılle cpá na cpí coıpızċı pın, pob ıomoa meıpze álaınn ıoloaċaċ ann, ⁊ pzıaċa zaċa oaċa. Canzaccup ıapuṁ pón ccuma paın o'ıonɥpoızıo pız 'Eıpeann.

Ro baoı ımuppo pí 'Eıpeann za n-ıopnaıoe, ⁊ pé meıpze po baoı aıze, cpoċ an ċoımbſo, ⁊ baċall Iopa.

'O canzaccap cpa na pluaız náıṁoıze ı zcoṁfoċpaıo oo Aoo, pá puıo ⁊ pa copuız uıme pí Ulao oo'n oapa leıċ, ⁊ pí Míoe oon leıċ oıle ⁊ po páıo pıu: Ná h-ıompáıoío ceıċſb, aċċ caıpıpnızıo ıpın coımbſo ó ffuıl copzup oona Cpíopcaıbıb, nap ab banoa bap n-aızſnċa,

ª *Showers.*—i. e. Showers of darts or javelins.
ᵇ *Staff of Jesus.*—This was the celebrated *Baculus Jesu*, said to have been given by our Lord Himself to St. Patrick. See Colgan's Trias Thaum., p. 263, and Dr. Todd's Introd. to the book of "Obits of Christ Church," p. viii., *sq.*

suit of him . . . . and by the advice of his councillors, he said: " It is not by force of soldiers that a battle is gained, but by the aid of God, and the righteousness of the prince. Pride, and superfluous forces, are not pleasing to God, but humility of mind and firmness of heart [are]. These people have great hosts, and they advance proudly. Assemble ye all around me now, and have no intention of flying, for far from you are your own houses, and they are no friends who will follow you; it is not protection or quarter ye shall receive. Do, however, as your fathers and your grandfathers have done; in the name of the Trinity suffer showers[a] to be discharged at you. When you see me rising, rise ye all to attack, as God will show unto you." Monday was the day of the week. Now Flann, son of Conang, on the other hand, said to his people: "These people are few, and we are numerous; harden your steps against them." He then divided his forces into three divisions, in the first of which he was himself, in the second the Leinster-men, in the last the Lochlanns, and he harangued them all, saying: "This people will fall by you," said he, " and ye shall gain victory and triumph over them, for they are too proud to fly before you, and ye are more numerous. I am not engaged in this battle with any other view except to gain the throne of Teamhair, or be killed." These three divisions were indeed beautiful; many were the beautiful parti-coloured standards that were there, and shields of every colour. They afterwards came in this order to meet the King of Erin.

The King of Erin was awaiting them, having six standards, the cross of the Lord, and the staff of Jesus[b].

When the enemies' forces came close to Aedh, he placed and arrayed around him the King of Uladh on the one side, and the King of Meath on the other, and he said to them: " Think not of flight, but trust in the Lord, who gives victory to the Christians; let not your

n-aiġṡiṫa, aċt ɼun ob ḟſnḃa, ⁊ bniſiṫ ɼo hobann caṫ aṅ bun naim-
ḋib, ɼun ṅo maṅa bun cclu ṫṅé bioṫu. Aſſḃ ṅo ṅáiḃſiṫ uile ɼo
nḋionɼnaiḋiſ. Ní ṫáiniɼ imuṅṅo ḋo ṅiɼ 'Ēiṅeann ḋeiṅeaḋ na mbṅia-
ṫan ṅin ḋo ṅáḃ an uaiṅ ṫanɼaṫṫun a námaiṫṫ i ḟṅocun, ⁊ ṅo ḋiu-
bainɼnioḋ ḟṅoṅṅa ḋiomóṅa ḋo ṅaiɼḃiḃ aṅ ṫúṅ ⁊ ḟṅoṅṅa ḋ'ṅaɼaiṅ
iaṅṫṫain, ⁊ an ṫṅiſ ḟṅoṅṅ ḋo leṫɼaiḃ, ionnuṅ ɼun eiṅɼe an ṅiɼ co
naa ṁuinṫiṅ na n-aiɼiḃ, ɼun caiċiɼnioḋ ḋo cṅoḃa ḟṅiu.

Ḟoṅſoṅ ní ṗaɼhum aṅ in ṫṅeinlioḃan aṫá bṅiṅṫe, iomláine na
himṫſéṫa ḋo ṅonṅaṫ caċ 'ṅan caṫṅo Cille hUa nḊaiɼṅe, náiḋ
na bṅiaṫṅa bṅiſɼḃa ḋo laḃaiṅ ṅiɼ 'Eiṅſinn ɼo huilibe ḋo ḋioṅɼaḋ
aṁuiñṫiṅe ṗéin. ɼiḃſḃ ṫáṫam ɼun bṅiṅioḋ leiṅin ṅiɼ aṅ a ná-
ṁaiḋ.

Aɼuṅ annṅin ṅo ṅáiḃ an ṅiɼ (an ṫan baoí an ṁaiḃm ṅé na
ṁuinnṫiṅ): a ṁuinnṫiṅ ionṁain, léɼiḃ ḋo na Cṅſoṅṫaiḋiḃ, ⁊ imṅiḃ
ḟoṅ ioḃalaḋaṅṫaiḃ ó ṫáiḋ a maḋmaimm ṅſṁaiḃ. Níoṅ bó ḋíoṁaoin
ḋoṅoṁ ṅin ḋo ṅáḃ, uaiṅ ḋo ṅónṅaḋ ṅin ṗaiṅṅioṁ, ionnuṅ naċ moḋ
ioná cſcṅamhaḋ ḋioḃ ṅáiniɼ ṅlán. Ṫéṅnaṫṫun Laiɼin iomlán ḋá
n-aṫhaṅḋa ṗéin, uaiṅ ḋo ṅonṅaḋ cine ḃainɼen cſnɼailṫe ḋioḃ ṗéin
ṫṅe coṁaiṅle an ṫaoiṅiɼ ṫṅeaḃaiṅ bui aca, .i. Maolċiaṅáin mac
Rónáin. Ḟlan imuṅṅo mac Conainɼ, ṅo ṫeiċ co na ṗocṅaiḋe, ⁊
ṅuɼṅaṫ muinnṫiṅ an ṅiɼ ṗain, ⁊ ṅo ṅáɼaiḃ a ċſnn, ⁊ ṫuɼaḋ é ḋo
láṫaiṅ aiṅſċṫa an ṅiɼ, ⁊ ṅo baoí an ṅí ann ṅin aɼ iomċaoíńſḃ ṗaiṅ,
⁊ ṅo baoí caċ ɼá ṅáḃa ṅiṅ náṅ bo cóiṅ ḋo a ċáinſḃ ṫṅe ɼoiṅe a
nɼaoil, ⁊ aṅ aḋḃaṅaiḃ eile naċ ḟṅaɼuim aṅ in ṫṅenleaḃaṅ, ⁊c.

Ḳal. Niallán Eṅſcoṅ Sláine, oḃut.

Coṅmac

ᵉ *The old book.*—A marginal note says:
"Sunt verba Firbisii," meaning that this
lamentation over the defects of the old
book was that of Dudley Firbis, the scribe,
who had deciphered "the old vellum
book," and who also adds in the margin
that *Cill Ua nDaighre*, where this battle
was fought, is situated one mile to the
north of Drogheda, "Cill hUa n-Ḋaiɼṅe
mile ó ṫuaiḋ ḋo Ḋṅoiċſṫ Aṫa." It is

your minds be effeminate, but manly, and suddenly put your enemies to flight in the battle, that your fame may last for ever." They all replied that they would do so. The King of Erin had not finished the delivery of these words when the enemy came near him, and first discharged great showers of darts, and afterwards showers of javelins, and thirdly a shower of half javelins, so that the king and his people rose up against them, and fought bravely with them.

Alas! I do not find in the old book[c] which is broken, the whole of the proceedings of both parties in this battle of Cill Ua nDaighre, nor all the fine words which the King of Erin spoke to direct his own people; however, we find that the enemy were defeated by the king.

And then the king said (when the enemy was routed by his people), "Beloved people," said he, "spare the Christians, and fight against the idolaters, who are now routed before you." These words were not spoken by him in vain, for they did this at his bidding, so that not more than one-fourth of them escaped scathless. The Leinster-men escaped in safety to their own patrimony, for they formed themselves into a solid, compact phalanx, by advice of their prudent leader, i. e. Maelciarain, son of Ronan. But Flann, son of Conang, fled with his forces, and was overtaken by the king's party; he lost his head, which was carried before the King's Council, and the king lamented over it then, and all told him that he ought not to lament over it merely on account of the nearness of their relationship, and for other reasons which I cannot get from the old book, &c.

[869.] Kal. Niallan[d], Bishop of Slaine, died.

Cormac,

the place now called Killineer, which is a townland of St. Peter's parish, Drogheda, on the road leading N. W., about half way towards Monasterboice. See the Ordnance Map of Louth, Sheet 24.

[d] *Niallan.*—This and the succeeding obits are given in the Ann. F. M. at 867, and in the Ann. Ult. at 868.

Copmac mac Eloċaiġ, ab Saiġpe, ⁊ pgpiba mopicup.
Ailill Cloċaip, pcpiba et epipcopup et ab Cloċaip. Dubċaċ mac Maoilcuile ᴅoctippimup Latinopum totiup Eupopae in Chpipto quieuit.
Mapcpa Eoḋupa mac Ɖonngaile ó genciḃ i nƊipiupt Ɖiapmaᴅa.
Ɖunlaing mac Muipḃaiġ, pí Laiġſn mopicup.
Maolciapain mac Rónáin, piġ-nia aipċip Eipſnn, mopicup.
Opgain Apᴅmaċa ᴅ'Aṁlaoib, ⁊ a lopccaᴅ co na uſppciġib .i. uſpċaċ mόp mic Anᴅaiġe. Ɖeiċ cceᴅ eiccip bpaiᴅ ⁊ mapḃaᴅ; plaᴅ mόp olċena.
Ɖonnagan mac Céᴅpaᴅa, pi hUa Cenpiolaiġ; Cian mac Cumapgaiġ pi hUa m-baippche tipe mopicup.
Ip in bliaġainpi .i. in octauo anno peġni Aoᴅa Fɪnnleiċ pa ionnapḃpaᴅ Laiġin taoipioċ ᴅa ccaoipioċaiḃ uaċa, uaip ba miopgaipp leo é .i. baoi popmaᴅ aca pip ap méᴅ na ccopgup no beipeᴅ ᴅo na Loċlannaiḃ, no ᴅno, uaip ba tuiliċe aca é, uaip ᴅo Ciappaiḃib Luaċpa a ḃunaᴅ, no ᴅno ap méᴅ a ḃíomaip ba miopgaip leo é; uaip na po péᴅ ᴅin ḃeiċ i ccinn maiċe Laiġſn ⁊ pi Laiġſn, tainig pa ṁuiñcip leip ap ionnapḃa ᴅ'ionnpoiġiᴅ piġ Eipſnn, ⁊ ap méᴅ a blaiᴅe ſngnaṁa po ġaḃ an pí ċuige go honόpuċ é, ⁊ tug a ingin ᴅό ᴅo ṁnaoi .i. Eiċne. Ro bé méᴅ imuppo an pmaċta ⁊ anmpt tappaiᴅ pé pop Loclannaiḃ, conaċ lamᴅaoip naċ gníoṁ moġᴅa ᴅo ᴅénaṁ ip na ᴅomnaiġib: po ba pgel mόp pia innipin na ttaḃpaᴅaoip ᴅo ciupa
ᴅό

^e *Clochar.*—" Clochar mic nDaimen."—*Ann. Ult.*, A. D. 869.

^f *Eodhus.*—No mention of this Eodhus, or of the circumstances of his martyrdom, is found in the Irish Martyrologies.

^g *Died.*—"Moritur." This should be, "was slain," as in the F. M. The Ann. Ult. have "jugulatus est."

^h *Ard-Macha.*—Ann. Ult. 868; F. M. 867. But neither Annals mention the "Oratory of Mac Andaighe."

ⁱ *The eighth.*—i. e. 871. The chieftain

Cormac, son of Elothach, abbot of Saighir [Scirkieran], and a scribe, died.

Ailell of Clochar, scribe, and bishop and abbot of Clochar[a]; Dubhthach, son of Maeltuile, the most learned of the Latins of all Europe, in Christo quievit.

The martyrdom of Eodhus[f], son of Dunghal, by the Gentiles at Disert-Diarmada.

Dunlaing, son of Muireadhach, King of Leinster, died.

Maelciarain, son of Ronan, royal champion of the East of Erin, died[g].

The plundering of Ard-Macha[b], by Amhlaeibh, and its burning with its oratories, i. e. the great oratory of Mac Andaighe. Ten hundred persons were taken captives or killed; a great plunder also.

Donnagan, son of Cédfad, King of Ui-Ceinnsclaigh; [and] Cian, son of Cumas-cach, King of Ui-Bairrche-tire, died.

[871.] In this year, the eighth[i] of the reign of Aedh Finnliath, the Leinster-men expelled one of their chieftains because they hated him, that is, they envied him in consequence of the many victories which he had gained over the Lochlanns, or else they regarded him as illegitimate, for he was of the Ciarraighi-Luachra as to his origin, or they hated him in consequence of his great pride. When therefore he could not be at the head of the chiefs of Leinster, he came with his followers in banishment to the King of Erin, and in consequence of the fame of his valour the King of Erin received him honourably, and gave him his daughter Eithne to wife. So great was the control and the sway which he gained over the Lochlanns, that they durst not perform any servile work on Sundays. It was great news to

here referred to was Maelciarain, son of Ronan, whose obit has just been given (Ann. Ult. 868). He commanded the Leinster-men in their retreat from the

dó . . . . Ir ar tnut ⁊ ar formad ro ionnarbrad Laiġin uata féin é, ⁊ dno ar a beit dr(r)uib Muṁan.

Táiniġ tra iar rin ġo roérairde leir i Laiġnib, ġo nū(r)na airġne ⁊ ionnrada iomda, ⁊ loirġte ⁊ marbta inntib. Act cīna ata a ffáġbaluib naoṁ, ná báð péið do tí no paġad a Laiġnib amac ar ionnarba tuibfct ar ccula do coġad intib do riġini na bad péið, do . . . . rír rfr no coṁlann dó, act ro ġabad do ar ġac airð do ġaib ⁊ do tuaġaib, ⁊ do cloidmib, ġo nūfnrat mionta bfcca be, ⁊ ġur ro bfnad a cfnn be. Ro marbait din a muimtir uile. Ruġad a cfnn iarrin do cum na Loclann, ⁊ ro cuirriodraide for cuaille é, ⁊ ro ġabrat real fora a diubarġan, ⁊ ro cuirriot 'rin muir iarttain é.

Kal. Suairlfć Ineidnein, Ερrcop ⁊ anchoire, ⁊ ab Cluana Iorairð, ortimur doctor reliġionir totiur hibernae, quieuit.

Ġeran mac Diocorca ab Saiġre.

Diarmuid ab Ffrna quieuit.

Dubdatuile, ab léit Mocaoṁoġ.

Maolodar ερrcop ⁊ ancoire, ab Daiṁinri, quieuit.

Cumrud, ab Dirirt Ciarain bealaiġ duin, ερrcop et rcriba quieuit.

Comġan Fota, ab Tamlatta, quieuit.

Coḃtac mac Muirfdoiġ, ab Cille dara, rarienr et doctor, de quo dicitur:—

Coḃtac

battle of Cill Ua nDaighre the year before.

ᵏ *Curses.*—Fáġbala, i. e. things left fixed and immutable by the saints. St. Patrick left success of fish and curse of drowning on several rivers; for example, the curse of drowning on the River Dineen in Idough, &c. St. Columbkille left it as a curse on the family of Maguiggan, in Ulster, that there should never be a priest of the name; which caused them to change it to Goodwin. St. Nia left success of fish and curse of drowning on the River Silecce, in Fermanagh.

ˡ *Suairlech of Inedhnen.*—These obits

to be related all the rents which they paid him . . . . It was out of envy and hatred the Leinster-men expelled him away from themselves, and because he was of the men of Munster.

After this he came with an army into Leinster, and committed many plunders and depredations, many conflagrations and slaughters therein. But, however, it is among the curses[k] of the saints that it will not be safe for one banished out of Leinster to come back to make war therein again. This was the case with him . . . . They observed not the rights of men, or combat towards him, but they attacked him on every side with javelins, and axes, and swords, so that they hacked him into small pieces, and cut off his head. They also killed all his people. His head was afterwards brought to the Lochlanns, who placed it on a pole, and continued for some time to shoot at it, and afterwards cast it into the sea.

[870.] Kal. Suairlech of Inedhnen[l], bishop and anchorite, and abbot of Cluain-Iraird [Clonard], the best doctor of religion in all Erin, quievit.

Geran, son of Dicose, Abbot of Saighir, quievit.

Diarmaid, Abbot of Fearna [Ferns], quievit.

Dubhdathuile, Abbot of Liath Mochaemhog, [quievit].

Maelodhar, bishop and anchorite, Abbot of Daimhinis [Devenish], quievit.

Cumsudh, Abbot of Disert Chiarain of Bealach-dúin [Castlekieran, in Meath], bishop and scribe, quievit.

Comhgan Fota, Abbot of Tamhlacht, quievit.

Cobhthach[m], son of Muireadhach, Abbot of Cill-dara [Kildare], a sage and doctor [dormivit], of whom is said:—

Cobhthach

are given in the Ann. F. M. at 868, and in the An. Ult. at 869, but the true year is 870.

[m] *Cobhthach.*—" Princeps cille daro."— *Ann. Ult.* 869. Comp. F. M., 868, where the following verses are also given.

Cobċaċ Cuirriġ cuirſtaiġ,
Daṁna riġ Life lſnnaiġ :
Durran mac mór Muirſbaiġ
baliaċ hua caoiṁrionn Ceallaiġ.
Cleṫe Laiġſn leiġniḃe,
Saoi rlan reġainn roċlaċ,
Recla ruirſċ réiṁriġe
Comarba Conlaiṫ Cobċaċ.

Maongal, Errcop Cille ḋara, quieuit.

Iſ in bliaġainri ṫainiġ Aoḋ mac Néill illaiġniḃ, ġo maḋ ḋo ḋioġal an óġlaoiċ a ḋubramur romuinn, ḋo marḃaḋ ḋo Laiġniḃ, no ḋno ġo maḋ ḋo ṫoḃaċ cíora. Ro iṁrirtar Laiġne o Aṫ cliaṫ ġo Ġaḃrán. Ṫainiġ ḋno Cſrball mac Ḋunlaing, ri Orraiġe ⁊ Cennéḋiġ mac Ġaiṫin, ri Laoiġri ḋo'n leiṫ oile ḋo Laiġniḃ, ⁊ an méḋ ro réḋaḋar eḋir lorġaḋ ⁊ arġain ⁊ marḃaḋ ḋo ronrattur, ġo rarġattur Ḋun mbolġ, ⁊ ro ġabrat longrort annrain, .i. Cſrball ⁊ Cenneṫiġ.

Ra ṫionolrad Laiġin iartṫain 'má riġ .i. má Muirſbaċ mac mḃrain, ⁊ ciḋ erṫiḋe ba ri cruaiḋ, corġraċ, ġlic, uair ar raḋa ro baoi ror ionnarba a n-Albain, ba aiċintiḋe ḋo cruar ⁊ ſnġnaṁ, ⁊ arſo ro ſmuainreaḋar aca ġur ab córa ḋóiḃ ḋol a ccſnn Laiġri ⁊ Orraiġe báttur i nDún bolġ ionár ḋola i ġcſnn riġ 'Eirſnn baoi oġ bealaċ Ġaḃráin, ⁊ ḋola 'rin aiḋċe ron longrort. Tſġaiḋ iarſm Laiġin, ⁊ a ri maille riu, ġo cruaiḋ ronairt na ccorruġaḋ ġo Ḋun mbolġ, bail a raḃattur a námaiḋ. Borb a meṫ ! Iſ ionġnaḋ an cuinġioll

---

ⁿ *Cuirrech.*—Now the Curragh of Kildare.

º *The youth.*—viz. Maelciarain, son of Ronan. See p. 184, n. ˢ.

ᵖ *Dunbolg.*—In the margin of the MS. the scribe has written toġail ḋuin bolġ, "Destruction of Dunbolg." This was the name of a fort near Donard, in the county

Cobhthach of Cuirrech[n] of races,
Heir apparent of the King of Liffe of tunics:
Alas for the great son of Muireadhach,
Ah! grief: the descendant of the fair Ceallach.
Chief of scholastic Leinster,
A perfect, comely, prudent sage,
A brilliant shining star,
Was Cobhthach, the successor of Connlath.

Maenghal, Bishop of Cill-dara, died.

Aedh, son of Niall, came into Leinster to avenge the youth[o] whom we have mentioned before as killed by the Leinster-men, or indeed it was to levy rent. He plundered Leinster from Ath-cliath [Dublin] to Gabhrún [Gowran]. On the other side of Leinster came Cearbhall, son of Dunlang, King of Osraighe, and Cennedigh, son of Gaithin, King of Laeighis, and did all they could effect by burning, plundering, and killing until they arrived at Dun-Bolg[p], where they encamped, i. e. Cearbhall and Cennedigh.

The Leinster-men afterwards gathered round their king, i. e. round Muiredhach, son of Bran, who was a hardy, victorious, prudent king, for he was for a long time in exile in Alba [Scotland], where he distinguished himself by his hardihood and bravery. And they thought among themselves that they should rather go against the men of Laeighis and Osraighe, who were at Dunbolg, than against the King of Erin, who was at Bealach Gabhráin[q], and to enter their camp at night. The Leinster-men then proceeded, with hardihood and courage, along with their king, arrayed in regular order, to Dunbolg, where their enemies were fierce and numerous! Prodigious was their

of Wicklow. Ann. F. M. 868; Ult. 869.
[q] *Bealach Gabhráin.*—i. e. the road or pass of Gowran, in the county of Kilkenny.

cuingioll daonda, uaip po cuaccup Laigin i muinigin Naoiṁ bpigide go pugdaoip buaid ⁊ copgup do Oppaigib ⁊ do Laoigip. Ro cuaccup dno Oppaige i muingin Naoiṁ Ciapáin Saigpe ma buaid ⁊ copgup do bpeit do Laigniḃ. Ro baccap Laigin go díocpa og atac Naoiṁ bpigide, gup po mapbdaoip a náiṁde . . . . Ipeḋ cpa cangaccup Laigin don leit a paḃa mac Ƶaicíni don longpoṗc. Ni a n-imgabail do pigne mac Ƶaicin, act ap na n-agaid go cpuaid feocaip caimig, amuil ba bép dó. Do gníchep cpa cacugaḋ cpuaid cpoda let pop let anni pin. Ap cian po clop gáip na ffṡ og imipc diocumaing foppa, ⁊ fogap na pcoc ndeaḃca, ⁊ po gaḃ an calaṁ cpiocnugaḋ go ndṡcaccup a n-ṡpaḋa ⁊ a n-iomáince i ngealcact, ⁊ ba caipmṡpg móp d'ṡgnaṁ na laoc pin, act cṡha an lucc po boí don cpluaġ i pcailpib cappag, cangaccup anaigid na n-iumáinci, go po popaccup móp díoḃ. Ba móp an muipn pin, ⁊ ba móp a ffogup 'pin aeip uapca. Imipn po baoi Cepḃall og cṡgapg a ṁuinncipe, uaip ba copac oídci faip, ⁊ po páid; gibeḋ ó ccíopaḋ na naṁaid cugaiḃ, na glupaḋ nṡ uaiḃ ap a inad cacaipi, ⁊ congbaḋ piḃ go cpuaid pip na naiṁdiḃ. Ro cuaidpioṁ Cṡpḃall ⁊ pocpaide laip d'ionnpoigid ṁic a fṡcaṗ .i. Cennedig, po baoí i n-éigṡn móp edip a náiṁdiḃ, ⁊ po cogbuiḃ a gut cpuaid ap áipd, ⁊ po baoi ag nṡpcaḋ a ṁuinncipe a cṡṡhn Laigen (⁊ pa cualaccup Laigin pin) ⁊ dno po báccup an muinncip ga nṡpcaḋ poṁ. Ro ṡpb pa dip dá ṁuincip faipe dpopcoiméd do. Ro diubaipg pí Laigin leitġa foṡapide gup po mapḃ an dapa fṡ did .i. Foloctac, pecnab Cille daipe. Ap móp cpa an coipm ⁊ an foṡpom baoi fcuppa anuaip pin, ⁊ pa cógaiḃ banḃ cṡhn fcuppa, ⁊ baoi mapḃaḋ móp fcuppa pán cán. Ro pcuiṡpioc cpa Laigin on longṗopc, ⁊ po báccup ag bpeit

---

¹ *The clamour.*—bamop an muipn pin. See a similar expression used by the F. M. at the year 1504, p. 1278.

² *Badhbh.*—This was the name of a sort of fairy goddess of war, the *Bellona* of Irish mythology. But the name was also given

their number ! Wonderful was the human condition ! for the
Leinster-men placed all their hope in St. Brighit that they should
gain victory and triumph over the men of Osraighe and Laighis,
and the men of Osraighe placed their hope in Ciaran of Saighir,
for gaining triumph and victory over the Leinster-men. The Leinster-men fervently prayed to St. Brighit that they might kill their
enemies . . . . . The side of the camp to which the Leinster-men
came was that in which the son of Gaithin was. The son of Gaithin did not avoid them, but he opposed firmly and fiercely, as
was his wont. A stubborn, fierce battle was fought there between
them. Far were heard the cries of men suffering discomfiture, and
the sound of the martial trumpets, and the earth shook, so that their
horses and cattle ran terrified, which was a great hindrance to the
valiant deeds of heroes. But, however, such of the host as were
in the clefts of the rocks came down to the cattle and stopped many
of them. Great was the clamour[r], and great was the noise in the air
over them. Therefore Cearbhall was instructing his people, for it
was the beginning of the night, and he said : " Wherever the enemy
come from us to you, let not one of you move from his place of battle, and keep firmly to the enemy." Cearbhall went with a force to
his sister's son, Cennédigh, who was in great jeopardy among his enemies, and he raised his firm voice aloud, and encouraged his people
against the Leinster-men (and the Leinster-men heard it), and his
people were encouraging him. He ordered two of his people to keep
watch for him. The King of Leinster aimed a half javelin at them,
and killed one of them, i. e. Folachtach, vice-abbot of Cill-dara. Great
indeed was the din and tumult that prevailed between them at this
time, and Badhbh[s] showed herself among them, and there was a great

massacre

to the Royston, or carrion crow ; so that
the meaning may, perhaps, be that birds
of prey began to appear on the field of battle, attracted by the dead bodies.

bpeit a pi leo, ⁊ ó nap péd an pí a pluag d'poptad na pappad po ling ap a eac ⁊ táinig andaig a muinnpipe. Ap deimin linn gonad tpe miopbail naoim bpigde ⁊ Sein Ciapáin po pgaoilpiot amlaid pin; ⁊ cia po mapbad paopclanna ftuppa, ní paba áp mòp ann. Ní pa léig Cfpball ná Cennédig ba muinntip lfmmuin Laigfn ap paitciup. Ro mapbad 'pan ló ap na mápac dpfm do Laignid po báctup pop pfcpán. Tángattup Cfpball ⁊ Cennédig na ccat cfngailte cópaigte tpé láp a námad go Gabpán, d'ionnpoigid pi 'Eipfnn .i. Aoda Pinnléit, (deipbpiup Cfpbail a bfipaide, ⁊ mátaip an Cennédig f) ⁊ innipid do pí 'Eipfnn amail do pala dóib .i. longpopt do gabail poppa ⁊ca. Do popad compád taipipi, ⁊ po deigliriod iapttáin.

Rí Laigfn ní hfd do pigne pplfgpa mait do tabaipt pop pí 'Eipfnn, act ip cuimniugad na ndfpnpad pip do pigne, ⁊ ni tapad cíop no gall.

Ip in bliadain pi do ponpad na pig Loclann popbaipi pop Spait¹ Cluaide i mbpeatnaib; pé cetpe míopaid ag popbaipi dóib puippe, pa deoig tpa iap ppoppiac an locta po baoi innte do gopta ⁊ d'íotaid, ap ttpagad go hiongnad an tobaip po baoi aca ap médon: po cuap poppa iapttain. Rugad tpa ap túp gac maitiup po buí innte. Rugad plóg mòp eipte i mbpaid [Oupaltac¹¹ Pipbipigh po pgpiob 1643] inquit tpanpcpiptop ppimup.

Kal. Maongal, ab bfnncaip, quieuit.

Oubtac,

---

¹ *Srath-cluaide.*—This is the Irish name for Strathclyde in Scotland, but it is evidently a mistake for Ailech Cluathe, which was the old name of Dunbarton. This entry is given in the Annals of Ulster at the year 869 [870] as follows :—" Obsessio Ailech Cluathe, a Norddmannis, i. e. Amlaiph et Imhar duo reges Norddmannorum obsederunt arcem illum et distruxerunt in fine .iiii. mensium arcem et predaverunt."—*Dublin MS*. So also the Welsh Annals, e. g. the Annales Cambriæ, A. D. 870, " Arx Alt-Clut a gentilibus fracta est."—Brut y Tywysogion, A. D. 870, ac y torret Kaer Alclut y gan y Paganyeit; "and Caer Alclut was demolished by the Pagans."

¹¹ *Dubhaltach Firbisigh*.—The meaning

massacre between them to and fro. The Leinster-men slipped away from the camp, and were carrying off their king, and when the king could not stop his men from flying, he mounted his horse and followed after his people. We are certain that it was through a miracle of St. Brighit and the Old Ciaran that they separated in this manner; for although nobles were slain between them, there was no great slaughter. Neither Cearbhall nor Cennédigh permitted their people to pursue the Leinster-men, through fear. On the next day some of the Leinster-men who had gone astray were slain. Cearbhall and Cennédigh came in a solid arrayed phalanx through the middle of their enemies to Gabhran [Gowran] to meet the King of Erin, i. e. Aedh Finnliath (the sister of Cearbhall was his wife, and she was the mother of Cennédigh), and they told the King of Erin what had happened to them, i. e. how their camp had been entered, &c. They conversed affectionately, and then separated.

The King of Leinster did not give the King of Erin a good answer, but reminded him of all they had done to him, and gave him neither tribute nor hostages.

In this year the Lochlann King laid siege to Srath-cluaide[t] in Britain, and they continued the siege for four months; at length, however, after having wasted the people who were in it by hunger and thirst, having wonderfully drawn off the well they had within, they entered [the fort] upon them. At first they carried off all the riches that were within it, and afterwards a great host of prisoners were brought into captivity. [Dubhaltach Firbisigh[u] wrote this, 1643] Inquit transcriptor primus.

[871.] Kal. Maenghal[x], Abbot of Beannchar [Bangor], died.

Dubhthach,

is, that the note, "Dubhaltach Firbisigh ꝓ ꞃepoιꞃ 1643," was made by Mac Firbis's, the first *transcriber* of these Annals,

from whose autograph the Brussels copy wasmade. See "Introd. Remarks," pp. 1, 2.

[x] *Maenghal.*—Ann. F.M 869; Ult. 870;

Dubṫaċ, ab Cill Aċaiḋ epircopur, rcpiba et anchopita quieuit.
Ailill, ercop ⁊ ab Foḃair, quieuit.
Curui, ab Inri Cloṫrann, raoi rṡṅċura 'Eirṡṅ, quieuit.
Aṁlaoiḃ ⁊ Imar do ṫoiḃeċt arí́ḃri a hAlbain go- h-'Aṫcliaṫ, ⁊ brad mór ḃríctan ⁊ Alban, ⁊ Saxon leó, ḋá ċéd long a líon.
Toġail Ḋhuin Soḃairġe, quod antea nunquam factum ert.
Ailill mac Dunlaing, ri Laiġṡn ⁊ Norṫhmann interreċtur ert.
Maolmuaḋ mac Finnaċta rí Airṫir Life moritur. Flaiṫṡṁ mac Faolċair do ḃáḋaḋ do ṁuinntir Leiṫġlinne.
Inrṡḃ Connaċt la Crḃall ⁊ Dunċaḋ, i ttorċair buaċail mac Dunaḋaiġ. Inrṡḃ Muṁan dna la Crḃall ḋar Luaċair riar.
Aṁlaoiḃ do dol a h-'Eirinn i Loċlainn do ċogaḋ ar Loċlandaiḃ ⁊ do ċongnaṁ rá a aṫair .i. Gofriḋ, uair no Loclannaiġ aġ cogaḋ na ċṡnnraiḃe ar ttiaċtain ó a aṫair ar a ċṡnn, ⁊ ara ba fada ra inirin ċúir a ċogaiḋ ⁊ ara laiġṡd ṫremḃírġṡr cuġainn cid aġainn no beiṫ a fior, fáġḃam gan a rgriḃṡnn, uair atá ár n-obair im neoċ ar d''Eirinn do rcriḃṡnn, ⁊ cid ní iadraiḃe uile, uair ní namá fuilngid na h'Erṡnnaiġ uile na Loċlann, aċt fuilngid uile iomḃa uaṫa féin.
Ir in ḃliaḋain ri .i. an ḋṡmaḋ bliaḋain flaṫa Aoḋa Finnléiṫ, ro inḃertṫar Iomar mac Gofraiḋ, mic Raġnaill, mic Gofraiḋ Conung, mic Gofraiḋ, ⁊ mac an fir ra ċuaiḋ a h'Eirinn .i. Aṁlaoiḃ, Eire o iarṫur go hairṫear, ⁊ ó ḋerġeart go tuirġeaat.
Ral.

but the true year is 871.
ʳ *Cill-achaidh.*—Now Killeigh, a village in the barony of Geashill, King's County.
ˢ *Amhlaeibh and Imhar.*—Ann. Ult., A. D. 870 [871].

* *Family.*—i. e. the monks of Leighlin.
ᵇ *From Erin to Lochlann.*—There is no account of this in the published Annals.
ᶜ *The tenth.*—i. e. the year 873. This plundering is not noticed in the published Annals.

Dubhthach, Abbot of Cill-achaidh[y], bishop, scribe, and anchorite, died.

Ailell, Bishop and Abbot of Fobhar [Fore], died.

Curui, Abbot of Inis Clothrann [in Loch Ribh], the most learned of all the Irish in history, died.

Amhlacibh and Imhar[z], came again from Alba [Scotland], to Ath-cliath [Dublin], having a great number of prisoners, both British, Scottish, and Saxon. Two hundred ships was their number.

The demolition of Dún-Sobhairce [Dunseverick], which was never done before.

Ailell, son of Dunlang, King of Leinster and of the Norsemen, was slain.

Maelmuadh, son of Finnachta, King of Airther-Liffè, died. Flaithemh, son of Faelchar, was drowned by the family[a] of Leithglinn.

Connaught was plundered by Cearbhall and Dunchadh, on which occasion Buachail, son of Dunadhach, was slain. Munster was also plundered beyond Luachair westwards by Cearbhall.

Amhlacibh went from Erin to Lochlann[b] to wage war on the Lochlanns, and to aid his father Goffridh, for the Lochlanns had made war against him, his father having come for him; but as it would be tedious to relate the cause of the war, and besides it appertains but little to us, though we have a knowledge of it, we forbear writing it, for our business is not to write whatever may belong to Erin, nor even all these; for the Irish suffer evils, not only from the Lochlanns, but they also suffer many injuries from one another.

[873.] In this year, the tenth[c] of the reign of Aedh Finnliath, Imhar, son of Godfraidh, Conung, son of Godfraidh, and the son of the man who went away from Erin, i. e. Amhlaeibh, plundered all Erin from west to east, and from south to north.

[872.]

Kal. Gnia ab Daimliaġ Cianain, epircopur et rcriba et ana-
choreta, quieuit :—

Uair Gnia ġrian ar ccaomélainne.
Cfnn crabuiḋ inri 'Emir
Do ġaḃ naraḋ naomrainne,
Comarba Cianain caliġ.
Céin máir ramaḋ rorċaiḋe
Dia mba cfnn céim ġan cina
Dirran minḋ mór molḃéaiġe
'Ar cara caoimrionn Gniaa.

Cfnnraolaḋ Ua Muicéiġfrna, rí Cairil, ⁊ comarba Ailḃe,
Ffruomnaċ ab Cluana mic Noir.
Loinġrioċ mac Poillen, rrincerr Cille Auraille, t. m.
Robartaċ Dfrmaiġe, rcriba morícur.
Orġain fir na trí maiġe ⁊ na g-Comanḋ ġo Sliaḃ blaḋma
do rioġaiḃ Gall i rnfċta na rele briġde.

Ir in bliaġain ri .i. undecima anno reġni Aoḋa, ra ċairrinġ
báirié, ⁊ dna aitte é do mac an ríġ, longa iomḋa ó muir riar ġo
Loċ Ri leir, ġo ro mill ailéna Loċa Rí eroiḃ, ⁊ na feranna com-
roċruiḃe, ⁊ Maġ luirġ. Ir anrain ro faor Dia comarba Coluim
a lámaiḃ na Loċlann, ⁊ mar ro ċuaiḋ ar a lámaiḃ, an dar leo ba
coirée cloiċe é.

'Eġ

ᵈ *Gnia.*—The death of this bishop and the succeeding obits are entered in the Ann. F. M. at 870; Ann. Ult. 871. The verses on the death of Gnia are also quoted, with some variations of reading, by the Four Masters.

ᵉ *Emhir's Island.*—i. e. Ireland, the island of Emhir, Eber, or Heber, the celebrated Milesian chieftain.

ᶠ *Of Ailbhe.*—i. e. Bishop of Emly.

ᵍ *Three plains.*—This entry is given in the Ann. F. M. at 870 : where, see note.

ʰ *The eleventh.*—i. e. the year 874.

ⁱ *Barith.*—There is no account of this

[872.] Kal. Gnia[d], Abbot of Daimhliag-Cianain [Duleek], bishop, scribe, and anchorite, died.

> For Gnia was the sun of our fair race,
> Head of the piety of Emhir's Island[e],
> He celebrated the festivals of the saints,
> The successor of the wise Cianán.
> For a long time the bright congregation,
> Of which he was head, had dignity without obscurity.
> Alas! for the great precious gem,
> Our fair, bright friend, Gnia.

Cennfaeladh Ua Muichtigherna, King of Caisel, and successor of Ailbhe[f] [died].
Ferdomhnach, Abbot of Cluain-mic-Nois [died].
Loingsech, son of Foillen, chief [abbot] of Cill Ausaille [Killossy], died.
Robhartach, of Dearmhach [Durrow], a scribe, died.

[872.] The plundering of the men of the Three Plains[g], and of the Comanns as far as Sliabh Bliadhma [Slieve Bloom], by the Kings of the Galls in the snow of Bridgetmas.

[873.] In this year, the eleventh[h] of the reign of Aedh, Barith[i], who was tutor to the King's son, drew many ships from the sea westwards to Loch Ri[k], and he plundered the islands of Loch Ri out of them, and the neighbouring lands, and also Magh Luirg[l]. On this occasion God saved the successor of Columb from the hands of the Lochlanns, and when he escaped from their hands they thought that he was a pillar-stone.

The

Barith, or his expedition, in the published Annals.

[k] *Loch Ri.*—Or Loch Ribh, now Lough

Ree, an expansion of the Shannon between Athlone and Lanesborough.

[l] *Magh Luirg.*—Moylurg, i. e. the baro-

'Eɼ ɲiɼ Loċlann, .i. ɡoṫɼɼaiḃ, ꝺo ṫeꝺmaimm ɼɲána oɲonꝺ, ɼic enim Ꝺeo placuiṫ.
Imnɼḃa ḃɲɼṫan in hoc anno.
Ꝺeeɼṫ ciɼciṫeɲ ab anno 871 aꝺ ann. 900.
Ꝃal. Inꝺɲɼċṫaċ mac Ꝺoḃailén, ab ḃɼñċaiɲ quieuiṫ.

Ṫɲí céꝺ bliaɼain caꝺa cuiɲ
O éiṫɲioċṫ Comɼaill ḃɼñċaiɲ,
ɡo ɲé ɲo maiḃ ɲuaṫaɲ nɼle.
Inꝺɲɼċṫaiɼ aiɲꝺ oiɲꝺniḃe.

Maolpóil, ɲɲinceɲɲ Sɲuṫɲa ɡuaiɲe, moɲiṫuɲ.
Ƒuɲaꝺɲán maċ ɡaɲḃáin, ɲeċnab Cille aċaiḃ, moɲiṫuɲ.
Céle mac Ioɲṫuile, ɲecnab Aċaiḃ bó Cannix, moɲiṫuɲ.
Ƒlann mac Ꝺoṁnaill, ɲiɼḃamna an ṫuaiɲɼiɲṫ, moɲiṫuɲ.
Eccnɼcan mac Ꝺálaiɼ, ɲí Cinel Conaill moɲiṫuɲ.
Ciaɲmac hUa Ꝺunaḃaiɼ, ɲí ɡaḃɲae, moɲiṫuɲ.
ɡuin Muiɲɼḃaiɼ mic Ꝺoṁnaill, ɲioɼḃamna Laiɼɼ̃.
Ciaɲoḃaɲ mac Cɲunnmaoil, ɲi hUa ƒƒelmɼḃa moɲiṫuɲ.
Moɲɲ ɡlaiɲine mic Uiɲine, ɲí hUa Maccaile. Aɲ ꝺo ḃaɼ
Eiccneċáin, Inꝺɲɼċṫaiɼ, Ƒlainn. ⁊ Ciaɲmacáin, aṫ ɲuḃɲaꝺ :—

'Ecc aɲ eiṫiɼ ƒoɲaccaiḃ
Sluaɼa ɲaiɼɼɼ iaɲ ɲɼṫṫaiḃ

Maɲo

ny of Boyle, in the county of Roscommon.
ᵐ *The King of the Lochlanna.*—The death of this King is noticed in the Ann. F. M. at 871, Ult. at 872 ; but no mention is made of the ugly disease. The Ulster Annals say : " Imhar *Rex Normannorum totius Hiberniæ et Britanniæ vitam finivit.*"—*Dublin MS.*

ⁿ *A chasm.*—The words " Deest circiter," &c., are a note by the transcriber in the margin of the MS.
ᵒ *Indrechtach.*—These entries are given in the Ann. F. M. at 901 ; Ult. 905 ; but the true year is 906.
ᵖ *Ui-Felmedha.*—i. e. the barony of Ballaghkeen, in the county of Wexford, now

The King of the Lochlanns[m] died of an ugly, sudden disease, *sic enim Deo placuit*.
Britain was much annoyed this year.
A chasm[n] from about the year 871 [873] to the year 900.
[906.] Kal. Indrechtach[o], son of Dobhailen, Abbot of Beannchar [Bangor], died.

> One in three hundred fair revolving years,
> From the death of Comhghall of Beanchar,
> To the period of the happy death
> Of the great illustrious Indrechtach.

Maelpoil, chief [i. e. abbot] of Sruthair Guaire, died.
Furadhran, son of Gabhrán, Prior of Cill-achaidh, died.
Ceile, son of Urthuile, Prior of Achadh bo Cainnigh [Agabo], died.
Flann, son of Domhnall, royal heir of the North, died.
Egnechan, son of Dálach, King of Cinel Conaill, died.
Ciarmac Ua Dunadhaigh, King of [Ui Conaill] Gabhra, died.
The killing of Muiredhach, son of Domhnall, royal heir of Leinster.
Ciarodhar, son of Crunnmhael, King of Ui-Felmedha[p], died.
The death of Glaisin, son of Uisin, King of Ui-Maccaille[q]. It was of the death of Eignechán, Indrechtach, Flann, and Ciarmacan, was said :—

> Death has left destitute[r]
> The hosts[s] who seek after precious gifts;

If

called the Murchoos, or O'Murphy's country.
[q] *Ui-Maccaille.*—Now Imokilly, Co. Cork.
[r] *Destitute.*—These verses are also quoted by the F. M. at A. D. 901, whose chronology is about five years antedated at this period.
[s] *The hosts.*—viz. the poets.

Maro cloí den rí réicreć,
Món liać Eccneć i n-éccaib.
Eccnać ba vodaing v'óccaib
Rí ceiniuil Conaill cftaiġ,
Oirran ṡnúir crevbar mibenv
Fo tuinn íreṅn iar n-éccaib.
Inorfétać bfnvćuir buiónig,
Ciarmac Ṡabra ṡairmroḃraiġ,
Flann Feabail rial rri vodaing,
'Eccnet ril Conaill caingniġ.

Irce erc crigerimur annur reṡni Flann mic Maoilreclonn. Ctnni Oomini vcccc. Ra cionalav morfluaġ ffſr muṁan lar in dír cébna .i. la Flaitbfrać, ⁊ la Corrmaic v'iarraib bráiġiv Laiġfn ⁊ Orraiġe, ⁊ ra báccur rin muṁan uile i n-aonlongroirc. Oo rala Flaitbeartać ar a euć ar ruv rraici 'rin longrorc: corćair a eać i gclair nvoṁain raoi, ⁊ ba cel olc vorom rain. Soćuibe va ṁuinźir rén, ⁊ von crluaġ uile vo nár b'áil vol an crluaġta ar a haiéle rin; uair bá cél vuaibrioć leo uile an cuicimri an vuine naoiṁ. Cangaccar cra cfćta uairle ó Laiġnib, ó Chfrball mac muirfṡain, v'ionnroiġib Chormaic ar cúr, ⁊ ra labraccar

¹ *Thirtieth year*.—Flann succeeded in the year 879, and the year here intended in 908.

" *A. D.* Dcccc.—This is a mistake for Dccccviii.

ˣ *The same two*.—No reference is made to these two great ecclesiastics in any previous part of these Annals, which shows that there is a chasm of some years here.

ʸ *Flaithbhertach*.—i. e. Flaithbhertach Mac Inmhainen, Abbot of Inis-Cathaigh, now Scattery Island, in the Shannon, near the town of Kilrush.

ᶻ *Cormac*.—That is, Cormac Mac Cuilemain, King of Munster and Bishop of Cashel. This battle is given by the F. M. at A. D. 903, and in the Ann. Ult. at 907, but the true year was 908. The scribe writes in the margin of our MS.: "*De morte Cormaci filii Culennani, regis Mo-*

If it has changed the colour of a potent king,
Great grief that Eignech has died.
Eignech, who was the sternest of youths,
King of the populous Cinel Conaill,
Alas! that his face, shrivelled, colourless, is left
Beneath the surface of the clay in death.
Indreachtach of populous Beannchar,
And Ciarmhac of Gabhra, of great fame,
Flann Feabhail, generous, resolute against difficulty,
Egnech of the race of Conall of goodly councils.

[908.] This is the thirtieth year[t] of the reign of Flann, son of Maelsechlainn.

[908.] A. D. DCCCC[u]. The great host of Munster was assembled by the same two[x], i. e. by Flaithbhertach[y] and Cormac[z], to demand the hostages of Leinster and Osraighe, and all the men of Munster were in the same camp. Flaithbhertach went on horseback through the streets of the camp; his horse fell under him into a deep trench, and this was an evil omen[a] to him. There were many of his own people, and of the whole host, who did not wish to go on the expedition after this, for they all considered this fall of the holy man as an ominous presage. But noble ambassadors came from Leinster, from, Cearbhall, son of Muirigan, to Cormac first, and they delivered a message of peace from the Leinster-men, i. e. one peace to be in all Erin

moniæ, Archiepiscopi *Casseliensis et Martyris*." Dr. Hanmer says that Cormac was killed by the Danes, but Dr. Keating, in his "History of Ireland," from the historical tract called *Cath Belaigh Mughna*, i. e. the Battle of Ballaghmoon, states that King Cormac was not slain by the Danes, but by the Leinster-men.

[a] *An evil omen.*—Cel olc. The scribe glosses the word cel by ꝑdiꞃcine, in the margin. Dr. Lynch, in his translation of Keating's "History of Ireland," translates it *malum omen*. See Ann. F. M., p. 566, note.

rattar tsttairstt ríoḃa, im méiḋe aḋ éṫṫ ḋo ó Laiġniḃ, .i. aoin
riḋe ḋo beiṫ i n-'Eirinn uile ġo bealtaine ar a ccionn, uair coic-
tiġsṫr ḋ'ṗoġṁar an tanrain, a braiġḋe ḋo taḃairt an sṫláiṁ
Maonaiġ, an ḋuine naoiṁ sġnaiḋ ċraiḃḋiġ, ⁊ ḋaoine eile ċraiḃ-
ḋeċa; reoiḋ ⁊ maiṫiura iomḋo ḋo taḃairt ḋo Plaitḃeartaċ ⁊ ḋo
Cormac. ḃá railiḃ ġo mór la Cormac an tríórin ḋo taipġrin
ḋo, ⁊ táinig iarrin ḃá innirin ḋo Plaitḃeartaċ, ⁊ ra innir ḋo-
raiḋe aṁail tugaḋ ċuige ó Laiġniḃ. Aṁail ro ċuala Plaitḃeartaċ rin, ro ġaḃ aḋuaṫ mór ⁊ areḋ ro ráiḋ: Paillriġiḃ, ar ré, ḋo
ḃsġmsnnamnaiḋe, ⁊ ḋsroile ḋo ċineoil treoḋ, uair mac comaitiġ
ṫu; ⁊ ra raiḋ briatra iomḃa rearḃa tarcarlaċa ar raḋa re
n-innirin.
    Ar é frsġra tuġ Cormac fairriom : Ar ḋeṁin lṁra ḋno, ar
Cormac, an ní ḃiar ḋe rin .i. caṫ ḋo ċur, a ḋuine naoiṁ, ar Cormac, ⁊ biara ro ṁalaċtain ḋe, ⁊ ar ḋoċa bár ḋraġail ḋuit. Aġur
ó ḋuḃairt rin, táinig ḋa puball féin, ⁊ ré tuirrioċ ḋoḃrónaċ, ⁊ ó ro
ruiḋ ro ġaḃ ríotal uḃall tugaḋ ḋó, ⁊ ro ḃaoi ġa rroḋail ḋá ṁuinntir, ⁊ areḋ ro ráiḋ: A ṁuinntir ionṁain, ar ré, ní ṫioḋnaṫaiḃ-ri
uḃla ḋuiḃ ón uairri amaċ ġo bráṫ. Anḋeḋ a ṫiġearna ionṁuin
talmanḋa, ar a ṁuinntir, ciḋ 'ma noṫrnair brón ⁊ ḋuḃa ḋuinn? Ir
minic ḋo ġní mioċélmuine ḋúinn. Areḋ ḋno ro ráiḋriom; ciḋ óṅ,
'a ṁuinntir ionṁuin, cá ní ḋuḃrioċ ro ráiḋiar? Uair bsġ a n-ioṅġ-
naḋ ġen ġo ttuġainnri uḃla ḋuiḃ ar mo láiṁ féin; uair biaiḋ nsṫ
éiġin uaiḃri um rarraḋ tioḋnaicrsṫ uḃla ḋuiḃ. Ro órḋaiġ for-
aireḋ iarttam. Ro ġairmḃ cuiġe annrin an ḋuine naoṁta, craiḃ-
ḃsṫ sġnaiḋ (Maonaċ mac Siaḋail), arḋċoṁarḃa Comġaill, ⁊ ḋo
                                                                riġne

ᵇ *Séds.*—i. e. jewels, precious stones.
ᶜ *Apples.*—Keating has the same artless words, but Dr. Lynch, in his Latin trans-
lation of Keating, improves the style thus: " Nunquam posthac (inquit) *quidquam* inter vos, O charissimi, distri-

Erin until May following (it being then the second week in Autumn), and to give hostages into the keeping of Macnach, a holy, wise, and pious man, and of other pious men, and to give séds[b] and much property to Cormac and Flaithbhertach. Cormac was much rejoiced at being offered this peace, and he afterwards came to tell it to Flaithbhertach, and how it was brought to him from Leinster. When Flaithbhertach heard this, he was greatly horrified, and said: "This shows," said he, "the littleness of thy mind, and the feebleness of thy nature, for thou art the son of a plebeian;" and he said many other bitter, insulting words, which it would be tedious to repeat.

The answer which Cormac made him was: "I am certain," said Cormac, "of what the result of this will be; a battle will be fought, O holy man," said he, "and Cormac shall be under a curse for it," and it is likely that it will be the cause of death to thee." And when he said this, he came to his own tent, being afflicted and sorrowful, and when he sat down he took a basinful of apples which was brought him, and he proceeded to divide them among his people, and he said: "Beloved people," said he, "I shall never present you with apples from this hour henceforth." "Is it so, O dear earthly lord," said his people; "why dost thou exhibit sorrow and melancholy to us? It is often thou hast boded evil for us." "It is what I say; but, beloved people, what ominous thing have we said, for it is no great wonder that I should not distribute apples among you with my own hand, for there shall be some one of you in my place who will present you with apples"[c]. He afterwards ordered a watch to be set, and he called to him the holy, pious, and wise man (Maenach[d], son of Siadhal), the chief Comharba of Comhghall, and he made his confession and his will

buam."

[d] *Maenach.*—He was abbot of Disert-Diarmada, now Castledermot in the county of Kildare, which was one of the monasteries founded by Diarmaid, coarb of St. Comgall, of Bangor.

ɼıɡne a ḟaoıɼıḃın ⁊ a ťıomna na ḟıaḋnaıɼı, ⁊ ɼo ċaıť Coɼɼ Cɼíoɼť
aɼ a láıṁ, ⁊ ḋo ɼaḋ láıṁ ɼıɼ an ɼaoɡal 'na ḟıaḋnuɼe ın Ṁaonaıɡ,
uaıɼ ɼo ḟıťıɼ ɡo maıɼɼıťe 'ɼın cať é, aċť níoɼ ḃáıl ḋo ɼoċuıḋe ḋá
ḟıoɼ ḟaıɼ. Ro ḃaoı ḋno ɡá ɼáḃa a ċoɼɼ ḋo ḃɼeıť ɡo Cluaın uaṁa
ḋa mbeıť a ɼɼoıɼḃe, muna beıť ḋno, a ḃɼeıť ɡo ɼelıc Ḋıaɼmaḋa
ınıc Aoḋa Róın, baıl ı ɼaḃa aɡ ɼoɡluım ɡo ɼaḋa. ḃa lánɼaınť leıɼ
ımuɼɼo a aḋṅacal ı cCluaın Uaṁa aɡ mac Lénın. ḃa ɼeɼɼ ımuɼɼo
la Ṁaoṅaċ a aḋṅacal ıɼ ın Ḋıɼıoɼť Ḋıaɼmaḋa; uaıɼ ba baıle la
Comɡall Ḋıɼıoɼť Ḋıaɼmaḋa, ⁊ ɼa Coṁaɼba Coṁɡaıll Ṁaonaċ.
Aɼ é aɼ ſɡnaıḋe ɼo ḃaoı na aımɼıɼ, .ı. Ṁaonaċ mac Sıaḋaıl, ⁊ ba
móɼ ɼa ɼaoťɼaıɡ an ťan ɼa aɡ ḋénaṁ ɼíoḋa eıḋıɼ Laıɡnıu ⁊ ɼıoɼa
Ṁuṁan ḋa ɼɼéḋaḃ. Ro ımťıɡſťťaɼ ɼoċoıḋe ḋo ɼluaɡ Ṁuṁan ɡo
nſṁċumḋaıɡťe. Ro ḃaoı ḋno ɡlóɼ móɼ ⁊ ɼeɼťan ı lonɡɼoɼť ɼɼſɼ
Ṁuṁan an ťan ɼa, uaıɼ ċualaḋaɼ Ḟlann mac Ṁaoılɼeaċloınn ḋo
ḃeıť ı lonɡɼoɼť Laıɡſn ɡo ɼlóɡ móɼ ḋo ċoıɼ ⁊ ɼoɼ eoċ.
Aɼ an ɼın ɼo ɼaıḋ Ṁaonaċ : A ḋaɡḋoıne Ṁuṁan, aɼ ɼó, ba cóıɼ
ḋuıḃ na ḃɼaıɡḋe maıťe ťaɼɡuɼ ḋuıḃ ḋo ɡaḃáıl ı nſɼláıṁ ḋaoıne
ɼɼaıḋḃſċ ɡo bealltoıne, .ı. mac Cſɼḃaıll ɼıɡ Laıɡſn, ⁊ mac ɼıɡ
Oɼɼaıɡe. Ra báťťuɼ ɼıɼ Ṁuṁan uıle ɡá ɼáḃa ɡuɼ oḃ é Ḟlaıċ-
ḃeaɼťaċ mac Ionmaınen, a aonaɼ, ɼo coıṁéɡnıɡ ıaḋ ım ċoıḃſċť ı
Laıɡnıḃ.
A haıċle an ɡſɼáın móıɼ ḋo ɼonɼať ťanɡaḋaɼ ťaɼ Slıaḃ
Ṁaıɼɡe ımaɼ ɡo Ḋɼoıċſḋ Leıťɡlınne. Ro ċaıɼıɼ ımuɼɼo Ťıoḃ-
ɼaıḋe,

^e *Cluain Uamha.*—Now Cloyne, in the county of Cork, of which St. Colman Mac Lcinine was the founder and patron.

^f *Diarmaid.*—i. e. to the cemetery of the church of Diarmaid. This Diarmaid was grandson of Aedh Roin, King of Uladh, and founded the Church of Disert Diar- mada, now Castle Dermot, which he dedicated to St. Comgall of Bangor about A. D. 800. He died A. D. 824 (Ann. Ult.). The Macnach here referred to was the successor of Diarmaid rather than the successor of St. Comgall, who does not appear to have ever been at the place.

will in his presence, and he took the body of Christ from his hand, and he resigned the world in the presence of Maenach, for he knew that he would be killed in the battle. But he did not wish that many should know this of him. He also ordered that his body should be brought to Cluain Uamha[e], if convenient; but if not, to convey it to the cemetery of Diarmaid[f], son [*read*, grandson] of Aedh Roin, where he had studied for a long time. He was very desirous, however, of being interred at Cluain Uamha of Mac Lenin. Maenach, however, was better pleased to have him interred at Disert-Diarmada, for Disert Diarmada was one of Comhghall's towns[g], and Maenach was successor of Comhghal. This Maenach, son of Siadhail, was the wisest man in his time, and he exerted himself much at this time to make peace (if he could), between the men of Leinster and Munster. Many of the forces of Munster went away without restraint. There was great noise and dissension in the camp of the men of Munster at this time, for they had heard that Flann, son of Maelsechlainn, was in the camp of the Leinster-men with great forces of foot and horse.

It was then Maenach said: "Good men of Munster," said he, "ye ought to accept of the good hostages I have offered you to be placed in the custody of pious men till May next; namely, the son of Cearbhall, King of Leinster, and the son of the King of Osraighe." All the men of Munster were saying that it was Flaithbhertach, son of Ionmainén, alone, that compelled them to go into Leinster.

After this great complaint which they made, they came over Sliabh Mairge[h] from the west to Leithghlinn Bridge. But Tibraide, successor of Ailbhe [of Emly], and many of the clergy along with him, tarried

[g] *Towns.*—i. e. monasteries. See Dr. Todd's Book of Hymns, p. 136.

[h] *Sliabh Mairge.*—This name is still preserved in that of Slievemarague, a ba-rony forming the south-east portion of the Queen's County, but the original Sliabh Mairge extended so far into the county of Kilkenny as to embrace the old church of

paiδe, caṁaṗba Ailḃe, ⁊ ṗoċaiδe δo ċléiṗciḃ ime i Leitġlinn, ⁊
Ġiollaδa an tṡlóiġ, ⁊ a ccaṗoill lóin illeitġlinn. Ro ṗenniδ iaṗ
ṗin ṗcuic ⁊ caiṗmṡṗca aġ ḟṡṗaiḃ Muṁan ⁊ taṅġattuṗ ṗṡṁṗa ġo
Maġ n-Ailḃe. Ro ḃattuṗ imuṗṗo ⁊ a noṗuim ṗa coille noaiṅġin
oġ ioṗnaiδe na náṁaδ. Do ṗonṗat ḟiṗ Muṁan tṗí caṫa commoṗa
coimméiδe δíoḃ: Plaitḃeaṗtaċ mac Ionmainen, ⁊ Ceallaċ mac
Cṡṗḃaill ṗí Oṗṗaiġe ṗeṗ in ċéδ ċaṫ; Coṗmac mac Cuilṡnáin ṗí
Muṁan ṗe caṫ mṡδoin Muṁan. Coṗmac mac Moṫla ṗí na
nDéiṗi, ⁊ ṗí Ciaṗṗaiġe ⁊ ṗiġ ciniuδ eile iomḃa, iaṗċaṗ Muṁan iṗ
in tṗṡṗṗ caṫ. Taṅġattuṗ iaṗaṁ aṁlaiδ ṗin aṗ Maġ n-Ailḃe.
ḃa ġṡṗánaċ iaδ aṗ iomaδ a náṁaδ, ⁊ aṗ a n-uaitṡċt ṗéin. Aṗeδ
inniṗiδ eoluiġ .i. an luċt ṗo ḃaoi ṡtuṗṗa ġo ṗaḃaδaṗ Laiġin có n-a
ṗoċṗaiδiḃ tṗi cuδṗuma no ceitṗe cuδṗumo, no aṗliu ṗe ḟṡṗaiḃ
Muṁan δo ċum an ċaṫa. ḃa tṗuaġ móṗ annuall ṗo ḃaoi iṗ in ċaṫ,
aṁail iniṗiδ ealuiġ .i. an luċt ṗo ḃaoi iṗin ċaṫ .i. nuall an δaṗa
ṡluaiġ ġá maṗḃaδ, ⁊ nuall an tṡloiġ eile aġ commaoiδim an
maṗḃta ṗin. Dá ċúiṗ imuṗṗo ṗo iomṗolaiṅġ maiδm oḃann aṗ
ḟṡṗaiḃ Muman .i. Celṡċaiṗ, ḃṗátaiṗ Ciṅġeġain, δo leim ġo hoḃann
aṗ a eaċ, ⁊ maṗ δo liṅġ aṗ a eaċ aṗeδ ṗaiδ: A ṗaoṗċlanna Muman, aṗ ṗé, teiċiδ ġo hoḃann on ċaṫ aδuaṫmaṗ ṗo, ⁊ léiġiδ eiδiṗ
na cléiṗciḃ ṗéin na ṗo ġaḃṗaδ coṁnaiδe eile aċt caṫ δo ṫaḃaiṗt;
⁊ ṗo ṫeiċ iaṗttáin ġo hoḃann, ⁊ ṗoċaiδe moṗ maille ṗiṡ. Aġaṗ
δno ṗaṫ eile an ṁaδma : Ceallaċ mac Cṡṗḃaill, maṗ at ċonnaiṗc-
ṗiδe an caṫ i ṗaḃattuṗ maiṫe muinnciṗe ṗiġ 'Eiṗṡn aġ tuaṗġain
a caṫa

Toach Scoithin, now Tiscoffin.

¹ *Magh-Ailbe.*—This was the name of a large plain in the south of the county of Kildare. *Bealach Mughna,* where this battle was fought, still preserves that name, in the anglicized form Ballaghmoon. It is situated in the south of the county of Kildare, and about two miles and a half to the north of the town of Carlow. The site of the battle is still shown, and the stone on which King Cormac's head was cut off by a common soldier is not yet for-

ried at Leithghlinn, and also the servants of the army and the horses that carried the provisions. After this, trumpets were blown and signals for battle were given by the men of Munster, and they came before them to Magh-Ailbhe¹. Here they remained with their back to a fast wood, awaiting their enemies. The men of Munster divided themselves into three equally large battalions: Flaithbhertach, son of Inmainen, and Ceallach, son of Cearbhall, King of Osraighe, over the first division^k; Cormac, son of Cuilenán, King of Munster, over the middle division; Cormac, son of Mothla, King of the Deisi, and the King of Ciárraighe, and the kings of many other septs of West Munster, over the third division. They afterwards came in this order on Magh Ailbhe. They were querulous on account of the numbers of the enemy and their own fewness. The learned, i. e. [the scholars] that were among them, state that the Leinster-men and their forces amounted to three times or four times the number of the men of Munster, or more. Unsteady was the order in which the men of Munster came to the battle. Very pitiful was the wailing which was in the battle, as the learned who were in the battle relate, i. e. the shrieks of the one host in the act of being slaughtered, and the shouts of the other host exulting over that slaughter. There were two causes for which the men of Munster suffered so sudden a defeat, i. e. Céilechar, the brother of Cingégan, suddenly mounted his horse, and said: "Nobles of Munster," said he, " fly suddenly from this abominable battle, and leave it between the clergy themselves, who could not be quiet without coming to battle." And he suddenly fled afterwards, accompanied with great hosts. The other cause of the defeat was: when Cealach, son of Cearbhall, saw the battalion in which were the

gotten by tradition.

^k *Division.*—This agrees with the account of this battle given by Keating from the *Cath Bealaigh Mughna.* It is very probable that both accounts have been epitomized from the same original work.

a cata féin, ro ling ar a eac ⁊ ro raiḋ re a ṁuinntir féin; Eirġiḋ ar ḃar n-fċaiḃ, ⁊ ionnarḃaiḋ uaiḃ an luċt fuil in ḃar n-aiġiḋ, ⁊ ge aḋrubairtrim rin, ní ḋo ċatuġaḋ aḃunaḋ aḋuḃairt, aċt ar ḋo teiċfm; aċt trá ro fár ḋo na cauiriḃ rin, teiċfḋ i nainfċt ḋo na cataiḃ Muiṁnfċaiḃ. Uċ tra, ba truaiġ ⁊ ba mór an t-ár ar fuḋ Maiġe Ailḃe iartain. Ní coiġiltea cléirfċ rfċ laoċ ann rin. ḋa coimméḋ ra marḃ ḋaoir, ⁊ ro ḋiċfṅḋaoir; an tan ra hainctea laoċ no cléireċ ann, ní ar trócaire ḋo nítea, aċt raint ḋa impulang ḋ'fagḃail fuarlaigte uaḋaiḃ, nó ḋá mḃreit aġ fognam ḋóiḃ. Terna tra Cormac an ri attoraċ an ċéḋ ċata. Aċt ro ling a eac i cclair, ⁊ ra tuitriom ḋon eoċ : óro ċoncattur orfm ḃ'á ṁuinntir rin, ⁊ riaḋ a maiöm, tangattur ḃ'ionnroiġiḋ an rí, ⁊ ra ċuirfttar ar a eac é. Ar ann rin aḋ ċonnairriom ḋaltu ḋó féin, raorclanḋa ḋ'Eoganaċt é, Aoḋ a ainm, raoi eagna ⁊ ḃreiéfṁnaċta ⁊ rfnċara é, ⁊ laiḋne; areḋ ro ráiḋ an rí frir: A ṁeic ioṁainn, ar ré, na lfn ḋiom-ra, Aċt noḋ ḃeir ar aṁail ar fenn cotniocfa. Ro innirrura ḋuit-ri reṁe ro go muirriḋe miri 'rin ċat ro. Ro ċairir uaittfḋ i ffarraḋ Chormaic, ⁊ táinic reṁe ar a fuḋ na rliġfḋ, ⁊ ba hiomḋa fuil ḋaoine ⁊ eaċ ar fuḋ na rliġfḋ rin. Scitlit ḋno corra ḋeirréḋ a eićriom ar an rliġiḋ rleaṁain, i rlioċt na fola rin, tuitiḋ an teaċ ar a hair riar, ⁊ ḃrirfḋ a ḋruim ⁊ a ṁuinél ar ḋó, ⁊ ro ráiḋ aġ tuitim : In manur tuar, Domine, commenḋo rririttum meum ; ⁊ faoiḋiḋ a rriorraḋ, ⁊ tfgaiḋ na meic mallaċtan eccraiḋḃfċa, ⁊ gaḃaiḋ gaae ḋá colainn, ⁊ gaḃaiḋ a cfnn ḋá ċolainn.

ġér

[1] *Spared.*—Keating has nearly the same words, which Dr. Lynch has improved upon in his Latin translation, quoted in a note to the Annals of the F. M., A. D. 903. "Siquidem in illo conflictu, sacri et profani homines promiscuâ interneccione mactabantur, nullâ ordinis aut dignitatis habitâ ratione."—*O'Donovan's Four Masters*, vol. i., p. 568, note.

[m] *His head.*—The F. M. state that it was

the chieftains of the people of the King of Erin cutting down his own battalion, he mounted his horse, and said to his own people : "Mount your horses, and drive the enemy before you." And though he said this, it was not to fight really he said so, but to fly. But, however, it resulted from these causes that the Munster battalions fled together. Alas! pitiful and great was the slaughter throughout Magh-Ailbhe afterwards. A cleric was not more spared[l] than a layman there; they were equally killed. When a layman or a clergyman was spared, it was not out of mercy it was done, but out of covetousness to obtain a ransom for them, or to bring them into servitude. King Cormac, however, escaped in the van of the first battalion, but his horse fell into a trench, and he fell off the horse. When a party of his people who were flying perceived this, they came to the king and put him up on his horse again. It was then he saw a foster-son of his own, a noble of the Eoghanachts, by name Aedh, who was an adept in wisdom and jurisprudence, and history, and Latin, and the king said to him : "Beloved son," said he, "do not follow me, but escape as well as thou canst. I told thee before now, that I should fall in this battle." A few remained along with Cormac, and he came forward along the way on horseback, and the way was besmeared throughout with much blood of men and horses. The hind feet of his horse slipped on the slippery way in the track of blood, and the horse fell backwards, and broke his [Cormac's] back and neck in twain, and he said, when falling, "In manus tuas, Domine, commendo spiritum meum," and he gave up the ghost; and the impious sons of malediction came and thrust darts through his body, and cut off his head[m].

Though

Fiach Ua Ugfadain, of Denlis, that cut off King Cormac's head, but the name of the place, as well as that of the family, is unknown to tradition, and the identification of them has hitherto escaped the ken of our topographical investigators.

Gér ba iomba an marbaḋ ar Maiġ Ailḃe, ra ḃerḃa a nair, nír bo raitťċ croiḃaċt Laiġſn ḋe rin, ġur ro lſnrat an ṁaiḋm tar Sliaḃ Mairġe riar, ⁊ ro ṁarḃрat raorċlanna iomḋa ḋon lſnṁain rin.

I ррortoraċ an ċata ro ċéḋóir ro marḃaḋ Ceallaċ mac Cſrḃaill, ri Orrraiġe, ⁊ a ṁac. Ar rġaoilteaċ imurro ro marḃaiḋ ó rin amaċ erir laoċ ⁊ cléiреaċ : ar mór ḋo cléiрċiḃ maite ro marḃaḋ irin ċat ro, ⁊ ar mór ḋo ríoġaiḃ, ⁊ ḋa taoiriоċuiḃ. Ro marḃaḋ ann Foġartaċ mac Suiḃne, in ruí reallromḃaċta ⁊ ḋiaḋaċta, ri Ciarraiġe, ⁊ Ailill mac Eoġain, an tairоfġnaiḋ óċċ ⁊ an t-árоrґаorсlann, ⁊ Colman, ab Cinnetiġ, árо ollaṁ ḃreitſṁnaċta Eirſnn, ⁊ roċuiḋe ar ċſna, quor longum ert rеriḃere.

Na laoiċ imurro, Cormac rí na nḋéiri, Ḋuḃaġán, ri fFſr niaiġe, Cſnfaolaḋ, rí hUa Conaill, Conn ḋar ⁊ Ainerlir ḋ'Uiḃ Tairḋealḃaiġ, ⁊ Eiḃean ri Aiḋne, ro ḃaoi ar ionnarḃaḋ a Muṁain, Maolmuaḋ, Maḋuḋán, Ḋuḃḋaḃairſnn, Conġal, Cataрnaċ, Fſraḃaċ, Aoḋ, rí hUa Liatáin, ⁊ Ḋomnall ri Ḋúin Ceaрmna.

Ar iaḋ ḋno ra ḃrir an ċat ro .i. Flann mac Maoilreċloinn, Riġ Eirſnn, ⁊ Cſrḃall mac Muirfġan rí Laiġſn, ⁊ Taḋġ mac Faoláin rí hUa ġCionnriolaġ, Témenan, rí hUa nḊfġa, Ceallaċ ⁊ Loрċán ḋa rí feaр Cualann, Inḋeiрġe mac Ḋuiḃġiolla, rí hUa n-Ḋrōna

---

ⁿ *Many good clergymen.*—This seems to imply that the clergy were wont to go on military expeditions so late as 908. Fothadh na Canoine had induced the monarch Aedh Oirdnighe (A. D. 804) to release the clergy from this barbarous duty, and Adamnan had made greater exertions, to the same effect, about a century earlier. But the union of the kingly with the episcopal dignity would appear to have encouraged the continuance of this custom to the time of Cormac Mac Cullenan, though, perhaps, not in the northern parts of Ireland, where the influence of the law of Adamnan and Fothadh prevailed at this time.

º *Cenn-Etigh.*—Now Kinnitty in the King's County.

Though extensive was the slaughter on Magh Ailbhe, to the East of the Bearbha [Barrow], the prowess of the Leinster-men was not satiated with it, but they followed up the route west across Sliabh Mairgè, and slew many noblemen in that pursuit.

In the very beginning of the battle, Ceallach, son of Cearbhall, King of Osraighe, and his son, were killed at once. Dispersedly, however, others were killed from that out, both laity and clergy. There were many good clergymen[n] killed in this battle, as were also many kings and chieftains. In it was slain Fogartach, son of Suibhne, an adept in philosophy and divinity, King of Ciarraighe [Kerry], and Ailell, son of Eoghan, the distinguished young sage, and the highborn nobleman, and Colman, Abbot of Cenn-Etigh[o], Chief Ollamh of the judicature of Erin, and hosts of others also, of whom it would be tedious to write.

But the laymen were, Cormac, King of the Deisi, Dubhagan, King of Fera-Maighe [Fermoy], Cennfacladh, King of of Ui-Conaill [Connilloe], Conodhar and Aneslis, of the Ui-Toirdhealbhaigh[p], and Eidhen, King of Aidhne[q], who was in exile in Munster; Maelmuadh, Madudan, Dubhdabhoirenn, Congal, Catharnach, Feradhach; Aedh, King of Ui-Liathain[r], and Domhnall, King of Dun-Cearmna[s].

But the persons who gained this battle were Flann, son of Maelseachlainn, King of Erin; and Cearbhall, son of Muirigen, King of Leinster; and Tadhg, son of Faelan, King of Ui-Ceinnsealaigh; Temhenan,

[p] *Ui-Toirdhealbhaigh.*—A tribe seated in the S. E. of the county of Clare, near Killaloe.

[q] *Aidhne.*—A territory coextensive with the diocese of Kilmacduagh, in the S. W. of the county of Galway. The Eidhen here mentioned was the progenitor of the famous family of O'Heyne.

[r] *Ui-Liathain.*—A tribe and territory nearly coextensive with the barony of Barrymore, county of Cork.

[s] *Dun-Cearmna.*—The ancient name of a fort situated on the Old Head of Kinsale, county of Cork.

n-Ορόna, Pollaṁan mac Oilella ní Ϝοτaρτa Ϝea, Ͳuaτal mac Uӡaiρe ní hUa Muiρḟoaiӡ, Uӡρan mac Cinnéoiӡ, ρi Laoiӡρi, Maolċallann mac Ϝḟӡaile, ní na ϜϜορτuaċ, Cleiρċén ní hUa mbaiρce. Ͳáinӡ iaρτan Ϝlann, ní 'Eiρḟn, maρcṗluaӡ móρ ριοӡḃa, ӡuρ ρo ioḃnaic Diaρmaiο mac Cḟibaill i ριӡe Oρρaiӡe.

Aρρ ann ρin τanӡaττaρ orḟm a n-aiӡiḃ Ϝlainn, ⁊ cḟnn Coρ-maic an Rí aca: aρeο ρo ράiοριοο ρe Ϝlann: " bḟτa ⁊ ρláinτe, a Rí ċumaċτaiӡ ċorӡρaiӡ, ⁊ cḟnn Coρmaic aӡaiñ ouiτ; ⁊ aṁail aρ béρ oo na ρíoӡaib, τóӡaib oo ṗliaρaο, ⁊ cuiρ an cḟnn ρo ρoiτe, ⁊ ρoρòinӡ é oo ṗliaρaiο. Aρ olc, imuρρo, aoρubaiρτ Ϝlann ριuριοṁ, ní buiḃḟċaρ oo ρao òóib. Móρ an ӡníoṁ, aρ ρé, a cḟnn oo ӡoio oon Eρrcoρ naoṁ, a onóiρ imuρρo, aρeò oo ӡénρa, ⁊ ní a ṗoiρòinӡ. Ra ӡaḃ Ϝlann an cḟnñ 'na láiṁ, ⁊ ρο ρόӡ é, ⁊ oo ρao na τimċioll ρo τρí an cḟnn coiρρeaca, [an naoiṁ eρrcoiρ], ⁊ in ρíορmaiρτíρeċ. Ruӡaò uaò iaρτcain an cḟnn ӡo honóραċ oionnρoiӡiò an ċuiρρ, bail a ρaḃa Maonaċ mac Siaòail, coṁaρba Coṁ-ӡaill,

¹ *Ui Deaghaidh.*—A territory in the N. W. of the county of Wexford, nearly coextensive with the present barony of Gorey.

ᵘ *Feara-Cualann.*—A territory in the north of the county of Wicklow.

ˣ *Ui-Drona.*—Now Idrone, county of Carlow.

⁷ *Fotharta-Fea.*—Now the barony of Forth, county of Carlow.

ᶻ *Ui-Muireadhaigh.*—A territory comprising the southern half of the present county of Kildare.

ᵃ *Laeighis.*—Now Leix, in the Queen's County.

ᵇ *Fortuatha.*—A territory in the county of Wicklow, comprising Glendalough and the neighbouring districts.

ᶜ *Ui Bairche.*—A territory comprising the present barony of Slievemargue in the S. E. of the Queen's County, and some of the adjoining districts of the county of Carlow.

ᵈ *With thy thigh.*—Keating has: "Here is the head of Cormac, King of Munster, for thee, sit upon it, as is the custom of [conquering] kings; but the monarch, far from complying with their request, reprimanded them, and said that it was very wicked to have cut off the head of the holy bishop; and he refused to treat it with any indignity. He took up the head in his hand, kissed it, and passed it thrice

nan, King of Ui-Deaghaidh[t]; Ceallach and Lorcan, two Kings of Feara-Cualann[u]; Inneirghe, son of Duibhgilla, King of Ui-Drona[x]; Follamhan, son of Oilell, King of Fotharta-Fea[y]; Tuathal, son of Ugaire, King of Ui Muireadhaigh[z]; Ughran, son of Cennedigh, King of Laeighis[a]; Maelchallann, son of Ferghal, King of the Fortuatha[b]; Clercén, King of Ui-Bairche[c].

Flann, King of Erin, came with a numerous royal body of horse, and he escorted Diarmaid, son of Cearbhall, into the kingdom of Osraighe.

Then a party came up to Flann, having the head of Cormac with them, and what they said to Flann was: "Life and health, O powerful, victorious king! We have the head of Cormac for thee, and, as is customary with kings, raise thy thigh, and put this head under it, and press it with thy thigh"[d]. Flann, however, spoke angrily to them instead of giving them thanks. "It was an enormous act," said he, "to have taken off the head of the holy bishop; but, however, I shall honour it instead of crushing it." Flann took the head into his hand, and kissed it, and had carried round him thrice the consecrated head [of the holy bishop], and of the true martyr. The head was

around him in token of respect and veneration." Dr. Lynch, in his Latin Translation of Keating's History, improves the style thus :—"Invictissime Rex simul et felicissime, En regis in prælio cœsi caput ad tuos pedes projicimus, ei tu inside et totâ corporis mole innitere, (superioribus enim Hiberniæ regibus solemne fuit hostici regis in prælio cœsi caput femori suppositum duriori sessione premere). Itane orationem et munus non gratulatione aliquâ, sed acerbissimâ deferentium increpa-

tione rex excepit, nec solum sacrum caput tam contumeliose tractare renuit, verum etiam in percussores acriter invectus quòd sacrato episcopo violentas manus afferre ausi fuerint. Deinde caput ipsum reverenter exceptum osculatus tribus sibi vicibus circumdatum honore debito prosecutus, Mainacho Siadhulli filio, Comgelli successori deferendum dedit, qui caput unà cum trunco corpore justis pro dignitate ritè persolutis, Deserti Diermodi humari curavit."

ξaill, ⁊ ρuξραιδε coρρ Coρmαιc ξo Oιριoρτ Oιαρmατα, ⁊ ρo [hαδnαιceαδ ξo] honoραċ ann ρ¹nn é, bαιl α nδénαnn ρſρτα ⁊ mιoρbαιlle.

Cια τρα nαċ τιξ cριδe ⁊ noċ cι αn ιn ξníom móρρα, .ι. mαρδαδ ⁊ τſρcαδ (δ'αρmαιδ αδéτċιδιb) αn δυιne nαοιm αρ mo ſnξnαm τάιnιξ ⁊ τιοcρα δρſραιδ 'Eιρſnn ξo bραċ Sαοι nα Ζαοιδιlξe, ⁊ nα Lαιδne, αn τ-άιρδeρſcoρ láncραιδbſc, láιn-ίοδαn, mſoρbulδα, ιn-ξſnuρ, ⁊ ιn-ſρnαιξċe, αn ραοι ρſċταρδαcτα, ⁊ ξαċ ſξnα, ξαċ ρſρρα, ⁊ ξαċ eolαιρ, ραοι ριlιδαċτα ⁊ ρoξluma, cſnn δéρeιρce, ⁊ ξαċ ρuαlċα, ⁊ ραοι ροιρċſbαιl, αιρδρí δá ċoιξſδ Mumαn uιle ρe ρé.

Ro ιοmρα τρα Flαnn, Rí 'Eιρſnn αρ ρρáξbαιl Oιαρmαδα ι ρυξe Oρραιξe, αρ αρ nδénαm ρ¹οδα αcomαιρ ſτυρρα ⁊ α bραιċρe. Ra ιοmρατταρ δnο Lαιξιn ξo mbuαιδ ⁊ coρξuρ.

Τάιnιξ Cſρbαll mαc Mυιρſξαn, ρι Lαιξſn, ρeme ξo Cιll δαρα, ⁊ buιδne moρα ι nſρξαδαιl αιξe, ⁊ Flαιτbeρταċ mαc lοnmαιnén ſττορραραιδe. Nα n-ſρbαιlτ αρoιle ρcοluιξe Lαιξnſċ δ'uιlc ρα Flαιτbeαρταċ, αρ nάρ ρe α ιnnρ¹n, ⁊ nι ċοιρ α ρcρ¹bſnn.

Τυξαιδ ιαρττaιn Flαιτbeαρταċ ξo Cιll δαρα, ⁊ τυρξαδ clέιρ¹ξ Lαιξſn αċċoραn móρ δó; uαιρ ρo ρſδαττυρ ξυρ ob é α αοnαρ ρα nſρτ αn ρluαιξſδ, ⁊ ξυρ αρ α n-αιξιδ α ċοιle τάιnιξ Coρmαιc. Aρ n-écc ιmυρρo Cſρbαιll, ρι Lαιξſn ρα léιccſδ Flαιτbeαρταċ αρρ, ⁊ ξo mαδ ι ccιοnn bliαδnα ρ¹n ιαρ ρραιρ¹nn. Ro ιοδnαιc Mυιρſnn comαρbα bρ¹ξδe é, ⁊ ρluαξ móρ clέιρſċ ιιmρe ⁊ mιοnδα ιοmδα, ξo ράιnιξ ξο Mαξ Nαιρb; ⁊ ó ράιnιξ Mumαιn δο ρoιne ρ¹δ ιnnτe.

Ra

` *Improper to be written.*—The author of these calumnies (here spoken of as "a certain scholar of Leinster"), as well as the unmentionable crimes themselves, attributed to the royal abbot of Inis-Cathaigh, are unknown.

' *Muirenn, successor of Brighit.*—i. e. abbess of Kildare. She died A. D. 917.—*Ann. Ult.*

⁸ *Magh Nairbh.*—This was the name of a plain in the barony of Crannagh, county of Kilkenny. See Ann. F. M., p. 856.

was afterwards carried away from him honourably to the body, where Maenach, son of Siadhal, Comharba of Comhghall, was, and he carried the body of Cormac to Disert-Diarmada [Castledermot], where it was honourably interred, and where it performs signs and miracles.

Why should not the heart repine and the mind sicken at this enormous deed, the killing and the mangling, with horrid arms, of this holy man, the most learned of all who came or will come of the men of Erin for ever? The complete master of Gaedhlic, and Latin, the archbishop, most pious, most pure, miraculous in chastity and prayer, a proficient in law, in every wisdom, knowledge, and science; a paragon of poetry and learning, head of charity and every virtue, and head of education; supreme king of the two provinces of Munster in his time.

Flann, King of Erin, returned home, after having left Diarmaid in the kingdom of Osraighe, and after having ratified an amicable peace between him and his brethren. The Leinster-men also returned home after victory and triumph.

Cearbhall, son of Muirigen, King of Leinster, proceeded directly to Cill-dara [Kildare], carrying with him great troops into captivity, and among the rest, Flaithbhertach, son of Inmainén. What a certain scholar of Leinster has ascribed of evil to Flaithbheartach is shameful to be mentioned, and improper to be written[e].

They afterwards brought Flaithbheartach to Cill-dara [Kildare], and the clergy of Leinster gave him great abuse, for they knew that he alone had invited the expedition and the battle, and that Cormac came against his own will. On the death of Cearbhall, King of Leinter, however, Flaithbheartach was set at liberty, which, according to some, was after the expiration of one year. Muirenn[f], successor of Brighit, accompanied by a great number of clerics, escorted him to Magh Nairbh[g], and when he arrived in Munster he made peace there.

He

Ra cuaib iapttain bá maimptip go hInip Catais, 7 po baoi peal go cpáibbíc inti, go ttáinig amac bopíbipi bo gabail pige Caipil, go paba ba bliagain tpiocab i pige Muman. Ap bo'n cat po pa can Oallán (mac Moipe) ollam Chepbaill pí Laigín :—

Copmac Peimin Pogaptac
Colmán, Ceallac cpuaib n-ugpa,
Go pé mile bo pocpattap
I ccat bealuig muaib Múgna.
Ainepíip, bín bopuma,
Fípgal péig iomon pcpiblinn,
Copmac pionn a Pemíhmaig
7 Cennpaolab a Fpigpinn.
Connobap bin Abapmaig
7 Eibín a h-Aibne,
La Cípball bo pocpattap
Oia maipt ap Maig Ailbe.
Maolmuab 7 Mabubán,
Uc pob alainn an paipínn,
Oubacan ó Abainn Móip,
Oublaec 7 Oubbaboipínn,
Congal 7 Catappac
7 Fípabac papaib,
Oomnall

[h] *Dallan, son of Mor.*—Keating says that he was poet to Cearbhall, King of Leinster, quoted by the F. M., A. D. 903, but their chronology is five years antedated.

[i] *Aneslis, shelter of Borumha.*—Now Beal-Borumha, a fort on the west side of the River Shannon, about one mile to the north of Killaloe. This was the residence of the chief of the Ui-Toirdhealbhaigh. This Aneslis was not the ancestor of any line of the Dalcais whose pedigree is known.

[k] *Frighrenn.*—This was the name of the chief seat of the Ui-Conaill-Gabhra, now

He afterwards went to his monastery on Inis-Cathaigh [Scattery Island], and spent some time there piously, but he came out afterwards to assume the kingdom of Caisel, and he was in the [enjoyment of] the kingdom of Munster for thirty-two years. Of this battle, Dallan, son of Mor[h], Ollamh of Cearbhall, King of Leinster, sang:—

> Cormac of Feimhin, Foghartach,
> Colman, Ceallach, of hard battles,
> With six thousand, fell
> In the famous battle of Mughain.
> Aneslis, shelter of Borumha[i],
> Fearghal the sharp, of the straight stream,
> Cormac the fair, of Magh Feimhenn,
> And Cennfaeladh, of Frighrenn[k],
> Conodhar, too, of Magh Adhair[l],
> And Eidhen, of Aidhne[m].
> By Cearbhall all were slain
> On Tuesday on Magh Ailbhe.
> Maelmuadh and Madudhan;
> Alas! fair was the host!
> Dubhagan, of Abhainn Mor[n],
> Dubhlach and Dubhdabhoirenn.
> Congal and Catharnach,
> And Feradhach, of the wilderness,

Domhnall,

the baronies of Upper and Lower Conillo, county of Limerick.

[l] *Magh Adhair.*—A level plain in the barony of Tulla, county of Clare. This Conodhar is not the ancestor of any known line of the Dal-Cais.

[m] *Eidhen, of Aidhne.*—He was the an-

cestor of the O'Heynes of Aidhne, a territory in the S. W. of the county of Galway.

[n] *Abhainn Mor.* —Avonmore (or the Great River), now the Blackwater River in the county of Cork. This Dubhagan was the ancestor of the O'Dubhagans [O'Dugans] of Fermoy, county of Cork.

2 F

Domnall a Dun Cfrmna caom,
⁊ Aoð ó Chapn Tapaiʒ.
Plann Tímpa do'n Taillтfnmaiʒ,
If Cfpball Dúin Capmain citać.
I pept December cloipiodap
Cat ʒo céduiƀ iolać,
Tadʒ mac Paoláin, Temenan,
Ceallać if Lopcán Lópʒlan;
Indeipʒe mac Duiƀʒiolla,
Ro diongƀattup cóiʒ nonƀaip.
Maolcallann mac Pfpʒaile,
Domnoll if Lopcán Liamna,
Uʒaipe no Tuatal a Dún Ofpmaiʒe,
Noćap cfépap tiamƀa.
Uʒpan Maipʒe mópʒlonnać,
Cleipćen ó Inif Pailƀe,
Pollaman mac Aillella,
Duƀdaƀoipfhn adaimne.
Tadʒ an tpiać a Ofʒaƀaip,
Ʒo puptaiƀ bpute bopppŕlat,
Ar ŕé cać po ŕpcomail,
Do clóð cat pop Copmac. Copmac.
Ro ba ʒníom ʒo ttiumapʒain
⁊ Ar lop pap mfopann

Rob

º *Dun Cearma.*—i. e. the old head of Kinsale.

ᵖ *Carn Taisigh.*—This was the residence of the chief of Ui-Liathain, now the barony of Barrymore, county of Cork; but its situation or modern name has not been yet determined.

ᑫ *Flann, of Teamhair.*—i. e. of Tara and Teltown in Meath.

ʳ *Dun Carman.*—This was the name of an ancient seat of the kings of Leinster, the site of which is now occupied by the

Domhnall, of Dun Cearma[o], the fair,
And Aedh, of Carn Tasaigh[p],
Flann, of Teamhair[q], of the plain of Tailltin;
And Cearbhall of the showery Dun Carman[r].
On the seventh[s] of September they joined
Battle with exulting hundreds,
Tadhg, son of Faelan, Temenan,
Ceallach and Lorcan the comely;
Indeirge, son of Duibhgilla,
They discomfited five times nine persons:
Maelcallann, son of Fearghal,
Domhnall and Lorcan of Liamhain[t],
Ugaire, of Dun-Dearmhaigh[u].
They were not a gloomy four;
Ugran, of Mairge[v], the great-deeded,
Cleircen, of Inis-Failbhe,
Follamhan, son of Ailell,
Dubhdabhoirenn we acknowledge,
Tadhg, the lord of Desgabhair[x],
With crushing flails of strong rods,
It is he that discomfited,
That gained the battle over Cormac.
It was a deed of dark plunder,
And it was enough to confuse us,

'Twas town of Wexford.

[s] *The seventh.*—The scribe writes in the margin of the MS., "17 Sept.," which agrees with the F. M.

[t] *Liamhain.*—Otherwise called Dun Liamhna, and now anglicized Dunlavan, county of Dublin.

[u] *Dun-Dearmhaigh.*—Probably fort of Durrow, on the border of Laeighis and Osraighe.

[v] *Mairge.*—Now Slievemarague, Queen's County.

[x] *Desgabhair.*—i. e. South Leinster, i. e. Ui-Kinsellagh.

Rob uaḃur, ro iomarcraiḋ,
Tuiḋfét na érí ar Cŕḃall.
In-terrcor, an tanméara
An raoi roiéſna (no ba roéla) rorḃarc
Rí Cairil, ri Iarmuṁan,
A Ḋé, oirran oo Chormac.

       Cormac.

Comalta comaltroma ⁊ coimléiġinn Cormac mac Cuilennáin
⁊ Cŕḃall mac Muirſgan, unoe Cormac cecinit:—

Taile ḋam mo tiompán, go nofrnar a heirŕinm,
Tre rainŕearc oo Ǵhelŕeirc inġin Oerill.

i. e. Ǵelŕearc inġĕn Oerill, ri Franġc, ra ail iao maraon
unoe Forou Ǵeilŕeirce.

Ral. Cŕḃall mac Muirigén, ri Laiġĕn moricur; unoe Oallan
cecinit:—

Mor liach Lire longach,
Ǵan Cŕḃall cuḃaiḋ ceileaċ;
Fŕr rial foraiḋ forḃaraċ,
Oia rroġnaḋ Eire éiṁeaċ.
Liaċ lĭmra cnoc Almaine,
⁊ Aillĭn ġan óġa,
Liaċ liom Carman, noċa cél,
⁊ fér oara róoa.
Níor bo cian a ŕaoġalŕom
A aitle Cormac ro cuillfo,

           Lá

' *Gelsherc.*—Keating makes no mention of this royal foster-mother of Cormac and Cearbhall.

' *Forod-Geilsheirce.*—*Quære*, whether this is intended for Foradh Goilsheircc, i. e. Geilsherc's seat or bench? It was

'Twas pride, 'twas intolerance,
Their coming into his territory against Cearbhall.
The bishop, the confessor,
The famous, (or renowned) illustrious doctor;
King of Caisel, King of West Munster.
O God! alas for Cormac!
                              Cormac.

Cormac, son of Cuilenan, and Cearbhall, son of Muiregan, were foster-brethren and school-fellows; hence Cormac sung :—

Bring me my tympan, that I may play on it,
For my ardent affection for Gelsherc, daughter of Deirill.

i. e. Gelsherc^y, daughter of Deirill, King of the Franks, nursed them both, unde Forod Geilsheirce^z.

[909.] Cearbhall[a], son of Muirigen, King of Leinster, died; hence Dallan sung :—

Great grief that Life of ships
Is without Ceallach, her befitting spouse;
A generous, steady, prolific man,
To whom submissive Erin was subservient.
Sorrowful to me the hill of Almhain,
And of Aillen, to be without soldiers;
Sorrowful to me is Carman—I conceal it not—
As the grass is growing over their roads.
Not long was his life
After the dishonouring of Cormac;
                                        A day

probably the name of a place in Ireland where she resided.

[a] *Cearbhall.*—The death of Cearbhall, son of Muiregen, is noticed in the Ann. F. M. at 904; Ann. Ult. 908 [909]. The verses which follow are quoted by F. M.

Lá go leiṫ, ní maoilpiaġail,
Ir aoin ḃliaġain gan ḟuillṡ.
Ermaċ riġe roġlaine,
Rí Laiġṡ liniḃ laoċraḋ,
Durran all nárb nAlmaine,
Do ḋul iréḋ rṡḃ raoċráċ.
Saoṫ la reoḋa ronċaiḋe,
Ḟlaiṫ nár Náir noiṫċ iarrma,
Ra ċroṫ ḋrunga ḋorċaiḋe,
Moo liaċaiḃ an liaċro. Mór.

Goirmḟlaiṫ inġṡ Ḟloinn cecinit:—

ba roḃraiġ Ceaṙball do ġnér,
ba roḃraiġ a ṫér go bár
An ro ḃaoi ḋa ċiorṫ gan cior
Taiṙċeall ar a niorṫ ḟri Nár.
Olc ormra cumaoin ḋa ġall
Maṙbraṫ Niall ⁊ Ceaṙball
Cṡḃall la hUlṫ comall ngle
Niall Glúnḋuḃ la h-Amlaiḋe.

Orṡm gu ráḋa ar aṁlaiḋ ro loiṫṡ Cṡḃall .i. ag ḋola ḋó i cCill ḋara an ḟuḋ ḟráiḋe in céime cloiċi rair, ⁊ eaċ ḋiomraċ ḟaoi, inuair ṫainig airḋ an arḋ re cṙḋcae ciorṁaire, ann rin uair rin ro ċuir an ciorṁaire a congna amaċ, ⁊ an ṫṡ na urċoṁail

---

[b] *Gormflaith, daughter of Flann.*—She was daughter of Flann Sinna, monarch of Ireland, and had been married to Cormac Mac Cullenan, King of Munster, afterwards to Cearbhall, King of Leinster, and after his death to Niall Glundubh, monarch of Ireland. She was the daughter of a king, and had been the wife of three kings. It is stated, nevertheless, in the Annals of Clonmacnoise, that "after all

A day and a half, no wrong calculation,
And one year without addition.
Ruler of a noble kingdom,
King of Leinster, of numerous heroes.
Alas! that the lofty chief of Almhain
Has died in a bitter, painful, manner;
Sorrowful for brilliant jewels,
To be without the valiant, renowned King of Nás.
Although dense hosts have fallen,
Greater than all the sorrows is this sorrow.

Gormflaith, daughter of Flann[b], sung :—
Cearbhall was always vigorous;
His rule was vigorous till death;
What remained of his tributes unpaid,
He brought by his strength to Nás.
Evil towards me [was] the compliment of the two Galls.
They slew Niall and Cearbhall;
Cearbhall was slain by Ulbh, a great deed,
Niall Glundubh, by Amhlaeibh.

Some say that the manner in which Cearbhall was slain was this: As he was going through the street of the stone step eastwards at Cill-dara [Kildare], having a proud steed under him, when he came opposite the shop of a fuller, there the fuller[c] sent the Congna[d] out, the horse

these royal marriages, she begged from door to door, forsaken of all her friends and allies, and glad to be relieved by her inferiors."—See Ann. F. M., A. D. 903, 917, 941.

[c] *Fuller.*—Cιοpṁaιpe. The scribe glosses this word in the margin by pú-caιpe, which is still a living word, meaning, "a fuller."

[d] *The Congna.*—This word is used in the Ann. F. M., A. D. 1499 and 1597, in the sense of a machine or instrument.

mail amaiṫ, ꝛo ꝛceinn an tṡé ᴅiomꝛaċ ᴅaꝛ a haiꝛ, ṡo ttaꝛla a ṡa
ꝼén alláiṁ a ṡiolla ꝼén baoi na óꝼṡaiᴅ (ṡo mbaᴅ é ainm an ṡiol-
laꝛain Uille, no ainm an ċioꝛmaiꝛe) ba maꝛb tꝛa Cꝛꝼball ᴅon loc
ꝛin i ccionn bliaᴅna, ⁊ ꝛo aᴅnaicṡ é inteꝛ paꝛtꝛeꝛ ꝛuoꝛ i ꝛelicc
Náiꝛ, unᴅe ᴅicituꝛ :—

Pailṡ naoi ꝛíoṡ ꝛeim naṡa,
I ccill Naiꝛ ꝛo neiṁ niaṁᴅa;
Muiꝛṡan maoin ṡan mṡꝛball,
Cꝛꝼball, iꝛ Ceallaċ cialloa.
Colman, bꝛan beoᴅa,
Pionn, Paolán, Dúnċaᴅ ᴅána,
I cCill Coꝛbain, ꝛo ċuala,
Ro claoitte a n-uaṡa aṡa.

bécc hUa Leċlobaiꝛ ꝛi Ohail Aꝛaiᴅe moꝛituꝛ; unᴅe ᴅicituꝛ :—

'Aꝛᴅ ꝛṡél ꝛṡaoilte lonṡ liꝛ
O ꝛo ꝛuaiꝛ moꝛ n-imniᴅ
Naᴅ maiꝛ óꝛṡaꝛ ᴅꝛuaċ oil
Cloṫꝛuiꝛe tuaċe inbiꝛ.

Caitill mac Rutꝛaċ ꝛi bꝛṡtan; Caiꝛeoṡ mac Dunoṡ, ꝛí
hUa Pꝛꝼṡuꝛa .i. i n-Uib Cinnꝛiolaiṡ; Muṡꝛon mac Soċlaċáin, ꝛí
hUa Maine, moꝛituꝛ.

Ro inniꝛiomuꝛ ꝛeiṁe ꝛo .i. ꝛin cṡꝼꝛamaᴅ bliaṡain ꝛiṁainn na
ꝛluaiṡ

ᵉ *Cill Naas.*—Now Kill, a church near Naas, in the county of Kildare, dedicated to St. Corban.

ᶠ *Becc Ua Leathlabhair.*—i. e. Beg O'Lalor. His death is noticed in the Ann. F. M. at 904, where these verses are also quoted, Ann. Ult. 908 [909].

ᵍ *Tuath-Inbhir.*—The ancient name of the mouth of the River Bann, near Coleraine.

ʰ *Cadell, son of Roderick.*—He died in the year 909, according to the Annales Cambriæ; 907, according to the Brut y Tywysogion.

horse being opposite it outside; the proud steed started back, so that he [the king] struck against his own javelin, which was in the hand of his own horseboy (whose name was Uillè, or this was the name of the fuller), and Cearbhall died of that wound at the end of a year, and he was buried among his fathers in the cemetery of Nás; hence is said:—

> There are nine kings of famous career
> In Cill-Nais^e, of shining lustre:
> Muiregan, a hero without mistake,
> Ceallach and Cearbhall the sensible,
> Colman, Braen, and Bran the lively,
> Finn, Faelan, Dunchadh, the bold,
> In Corban's church, I have heard,
> Their warlike graves were made.

Becc Ua Leathlabhair^f, King of Dal-Araidhe, died; hence was said:—

> Awful news that disperses the ships of the sea,
> Which have braved great dangers,
> That no longer lives, the beloved golden scion,
> The renowned prince of Tuath-Inbhir^g.

Cadell^h, son of Roderick, King of Britain; Caireog, son of Dunog^j, King of Ui Fergusa, in Ui Ceinnsealaigh; and Mughron, son of Sochlachán^k, King of Ui-Mainè, died.

We have related before now, i. e. in the fourth year before us^l, how

---

^j *Caireog, son of Dunog.*—This obit is not in the published Annals.

^k *Mughron, son of Sochlachán.*—A. D. 908 [909]. "Mugron mac Sochlachán, rex Nepotum Mainé *defunctus* est."—*Ann.*

Ult. "Tribes and Customs of Hy Many" (Irish Arch. Society), p. 98.

^l *The fourth year before us.*—i. e. before the present date. There is no account of the expulsion of the Danes from Ireland

ṗluaiᵹ Loċlannċa ḃ'ionnaṙba a h-'Eiṙinn ṫṙe ṗaċ aoine ⁊ ſṙ-
nuiᵹṫe an ḃuine naoiṁ .i. Chéle Daḃaill, uaiṙ ba ḃuine naoṁ
cṙaiḃḃſċ éṙiḋe, ⁊ éċ móṙ aiᵹe mana Cṙíoṙḃaiᵹḃiḃ, ⁊ ṙa ċaoḃ nſṙ-
ċaḃa ḃo laoċ n-Eiṙionn i ᵹcſṅn na ṗáᵹanḃa ṙo ṙaoċṙaiᵹ ṙén ṙe
heṙṙaiᵹṫe, ⁊ ṙo ċuinᵹiḃ ṙaoiṙe ḃ'ſᵹailṙiḃ 'Eiṙſnn, ⁊ ḃo ċuṙ ḟeiṙᵹe
an ċoimḃheḃ uaċa, uaiṙ aṙ aṙ ḟeiṙᵹ an ċoimḃheḃ ḃo ḃeiċ ḟṙiu
ċuᵹaḃ ſċċaiṙċinſḃaiᵹ ḃa millſḃ .i. Loċlannaiᵹ ⁊ Danaiṙ ḃo inṙiḃ
na h'Eṙenn ioiṙ ċill ⁊ ċuaiċ. Ra cuaḃaṙ ċṙa na Loċlannaiᵹ a
h-Eiṙinn, amuil a ḃuḃṙamuṙ, ⁊ ba ċaoiṙioċ ḃóiḃ hinᵹamunḃ, ⁊ aṙ
ann ṙa ċuaḃaṙ a n-iniṙ ḃṙſċan [i mḃṙſċnuiḃ]. Aṙ é ba ṙi ḃṙſċan
an ċan ṙin .i. mac Caiċill mic Ruaḃṙaċ. Ro ċionoilṙiḃ ḃṙſċain
ḃoiḃ, ⁊ ċuᵹaḃ ċaċ cṙuaiḃ ṙonaiṙċ ḃoiḃ, ⁊ ṙa cuiṙio aṙ éiᵹin a
cṙíoċaiḃ ḃṙſċan iaḃ.

Ċainiᵹ iaṙ ſin hinᵹamunḃ co n-a ṗluaᵹaiḃ ḃ'ionṙaiᵹiḃ Eḃel-
ḟṙiḋa, ḃainṙioᵹan Saxan; uaiṙ boí a ḟſṙṙiḋe an ċan ṙa i nᵹaloṙ .i.
Eḃelḟṙiḃ (na hincṙſċaḃ nſċ mé ᵹé ṙa innṙiuṙ ṙeaṁam écc Eḃelḟṙiḋ, uaiṙ ċaoiṙioċa ṙo ionáṙ écc Eḃelḟṙiḋ, ⁊ aṙ ḃon ᵹaloṙṙa aṙ
maṙḃ Eḃelḟṙiḋ, aċċ nſoṙ ḃáil ḃaṁ a ṗáᵹḃáil ᵹan a ſcṙíḃſṅn na
nṅſṙṅṙaḃ Loċlannaiᵹ aṙ noul a h'Eṙinn). Ro ḃaoi iaṙaṁ hinᵹa-
muṅḋ

under the fourth year prior to this, nor in any other part of this Fragment, from which it is clear that some portion of the matter immediately preceding has been lost. The printed Annals are very meagre at this period.

ᵐ *Cele-Dabhaill*.—The scribe writes in the margin, "Cele Daḃaill ab ḃeann-ċoiṙ ⁊ Comaṙba Comᵹaill ṙo Eiṙinn, obiit Romæ anno Christi 927 die 14. Septembris Ann. Dung.," i. e. according to the Ann. of Donegal (or F. M.), "Cele-Dabhaill, Abbot of Bangor, and successor of Comhgall, throughout Erin, died at Rome on the 14th of September, in the year of Christ 927." See Ann. of Ult., A. D. 927.

ⁿ *Hingamund*.—We do not find any mention of Hingamund in any previous portion of these Fragments; nor does the name occur in the Saxon Chron., or other English historians of the period. But the Brut y Tywysogion mentions "Igmond," who, in the year 900, "came [apparently

how the Lochlann hordes were expelled from Erin through the merits of the fasting and prayers of the holy man, Cele-Dabhaill[m], for he was a holy and pious man, and had great zeal for the Christians, and, besides strengthening the heroes of Erin against the Pagans, he laboured himself by fasting and prayer, and he sought freedom for the churches of Erin, and he strengthened the men of Erin by his strict service to the Lord, and he removed the anger of the Lord from them; for it was in consequence of the anger of God against them that it was permitted that foreign hordes should come to destroy them, i. e. Lochlanns and Danes, to destroy Erin, both church and state. The Lochlanns went away from Erin, as we have said, under the conduct of Hingamund[n], their chieftain, and where they went to was to the island of Britain. The King of Britain at this time was the son of Cadell[o], son of Roderick. The Britains assembled against them, and a hard and spirited battle was given them, and they were forcibly driven from the territories of the Britons.

After this Hingamund and his forces came to Ethelfrida[p], Queen of the Saxons, for her husband was at that time in a disease, i. e. Ethelfrid. (Let no one criticise me, because I have mentioned the death of Ethelfrid before, for this [fact, which I now relate] was before the death of Ethelfrid, and it was of this disease he died, but I did not like to leave unwritten all that the Lochlanns did after leaving

from Ireland] to Mona, and fought the battle of Ros-meilon," now Penros, near Holyhead.—*Ann. Cambr.*, A. D. 902.

º *Cadell.*—Clydaug, or Clydog, son of Cadell, son of Rodri Mawr, was slain by his brother Meuruc, A. D. 917.—*Brut y Tywysog.*, or 919, *Ann. Cambr.*

ᵖ *Ethelfrida.*—This was the celebrated Æthelflæd, daughter of Ælfred the Great,

who was married to Æthelred, Ealdorman of the Mercians, who, after her husband's death, defended her territories with great success against the Danes. She died at Tamworth, 19 Kal. Julii, 919.—Henr. Hunting. A double entry of her death occurs in the Sax. Chron. at 918 and 922. The Ann. Ult. give 917 or 918; Ann. Cambr. 917; Brut y Tywys. 914; Lap-

munꝺ aᵹ iappaiꝺ ꝼꞅꞃaiñ aꞃ an ꞃioᵹain acccaiꞃiꞃꝼeꝺ, ⁊ i nꝺinᵹneꝺ cꞃoaꝺ ⁊ cꞃꞅꝟaꝺ, aꞃ ba cuiꞃꞃioċ é an can ꞃin ꝺo ċoᵹaꝺ. Cuᵹ iaꞃam Eꝺelꝼꞃiꝺa ꝼꞅꞃainn a ꝼꝼoᵹuꞃ ꝺo Caꞃcꞃa ꝺó, ⁊ ꞃo an ꞃeal ann ꞃin. Aꞃeꝺ ꞃo ꝼáꞃ ꝺe ꞃin, ó ꝺo ċonaiꞃc an caṫꞃaiᵹ lán ꞃaiꝺꝟiꞃ, ⁊ an ꝼꞅꞃann coᵹaiꝺe impe, cuᵹaꝺ mian a cꞅċcaꝺa ꝺó. Cainiᵹ hinᵹa-munꝺ iaꞃ ꞃin ꝺ'ionnꞃoiᵹiꝺ caoꞃioċ Loċlonn ⁊ Ꝺanaꞃ, ⁊ ꞃo baoi oᵹ ᵹꞅꞃán móꞃ na ꝼꝼiaꝺnuiꞃe, ⁊ aꞃeꝺ ꞃo ꞃáiꝺ, naċ maiṫ ꞃo ḃáꝺaꞃ ᵹan ꝼꞅꞃann maiṫ aca, ⁊ ᵹuꞃ bo cóiꞃ ꝺóiꝟ uile coiꝟeċc ꝺo ᵹaḃáil Caꞃ-cꞃa, ⁊ ꝺá cꞅċcaꝺ co na maiċiuꞃ ⁊ co n-a ꝼꞅꞃannaiꝺ. Ꝛá ꝼáꞃ cꞃíꝺ ꞃin caṫa ⁊ coᵹaꝺ iomꝺa, móꞃa. Aꞃeꝺ ꞃo ꞃáiꝺ; ᵹuiꝺꞅin ⁊ aicċꞅm iaꝺ ꞃén aꞃ cúꞃ, ⁊ muna ꝼꝼaᵹam iaꝺ aṁlaiꝺ ꞃain aꞃ aiꞃ, coꞃnaṁ iaꝺ aꞃ éiᵹin. Ꞃo ꞃaoṁꞃaccuꞃ uile caoiꞃiᵹ Loċlonn ⁊ Ꝺanaiꞃ ꞃin. Cainic Inᵹamunꝺ iaꞃccain ꝺa ċaiᵹ iaꞃ nꝺál cionóil 'na ꝺꞅᵹaiꝺ. Cꞅꝺ ꝺeiꞃꞃiꝺ ꝺo ꞃonꞃaꝺꞃoṁ an coṁaiꞃle ꞃin, ꝼuaiꞃ an ꞃioᵹan a ꝼioꞅ. Ꞃo ċionoil an ꞃioᵹan iaꞃam ꞅlóᵹ móꞃ impe ꞃan cán, ⁊ ꞃo líon an caṫꞃaiᵹ Caꞃcꞃa ó na ꞅlóᵹaiꝺ.

Aꞃ bꝼꞅ naċ iꞅ na láiṫiꝟꞃi ꞃo cuiꞃꞃꞅꝺ Ꝼoiꞃcꞃꞅnnaiᵹ ⁊ Loċlonnaiᵹ caṫ. Aꞃ cꞃuaiꝺ imuꞃꞃo ꞃo cuiꞃꞃioc ꝼiꞃ Alban an caṫ ꞃo, uaiꞃ baoi Colum Cille aᵹ conᵹnaṁ leo, uaiꞃ ꞃo ᵹuiꝺꞃioꝺ ᵹo ꝺioċꞃa é, uaiꞃ ba hé a n-aꞃꞃcol é, ⁊ aꞃ cꞃíꝺ ꞃo ᵹaḃꞃaꝺ cꞃeiꝺꞅṁ. Uaiꞃ ꝼꞅcc oile anuaiꞃ ꞃo baoi Imaꞃ Conunᵹ na ᵹiolla óᵹ, ⁊ cáiniᵹ ꝺ'inꞃꞅꝺ Alban, cꞃí caṫa móꞃa a líon, aꞃeꝺ ꝺa ꞃonꞃaꝺ ꝼiꞃ Alban eiꝺiꞃ laoċ ⁊ cléiꞃċ, beiṫ ᵹo maiꝺin i n-aoine, ⁊ a n-ioꞃnaiꝺe ꞃa Ꝺia, ⁊ ꞃa

penberg's Hist. of England (Thorpe's Transl.), ii., p. 95.

⁹ *Chester.*—York was sometimes called Ceastre, or Ceastrum (Sax. Chron., A. D. 763), and it is possible that our author may intend the treaty made at York between the Danes and Æthelflæd, Queen of the Mercians, in the year 918 (*recte*, 919), according to the Saxon Chron., but we read there also (Petrie's Edit., at the same date), that Queen Æthelflæd also got into her possession the town of *Legra-ceastre*, which may be either Chester or Leicester.

ʳ *Almost.*—The whole of this paragraph

ing Erin.) Hingamund was asking lands of the queen, in which he would settle, and on which he would erect stalls and houses, for he was at this time wearied of war. Ethelfrida afterwards gave him lands near Chester[q], and he remained there for some time. What resulted from this was: as he saw that the city was very wealthy, and the land around it was choice, he coveted to appropriate them. After this, Hingamund came to meet the chieftains of the Lochlanns and Danes; he made great complaints before them, and said that they were not well off without having good lands, and that they all ought to come to take Chester, and to possess themselves of its wealth and lands. From this many and great battles and wars arose. What he said was: Let us ask and implore themselves at first, and if we do not obtain this by their will, let us contend for them by force. All the chiefs of the Lochlanns and Danes approved of this. Hingamund afterwards returned to his house, a host having followed after him. Though they held this consultation secretly, the queen received intelligence of it. The queen collected great hosts about her from every direction, and the city of Chester was filled with her hosts.

Almost[r] at the same time the men of Fortrenn[s] and the Lochlanns fought a battle. Vigorously, indeed, did the men of Alba fight this battle, for Colum Cille was assisting them, for they prayed to him fervently, because he was their apostle, and it was through him they had received the faith. On a former occasion, when Imhar Conung[t] was a young man, he came to plunder Alba with three large battalions. What the men of Alba, both laity and clergy, did, was,

to

has been quoted by Dr. Reeves, in his Edition of Adamnan, p. 332 sq., where, see his notes and references.

[s] *Fortrenn.*—i. e. the country of the Picts. Ann. Ult. 917 (or 918).

[t] *Imhar Conung.*—i. e. Ivor, the king. This is a digression, for he was slain in the year 904, by the men of Fortrenn.— Ann. Ult.; Reeves's Adamn., pp. 333, 392. But the present battle was fought

ra Colam Cille, ⁊ éiġme móra do dénaṁ rir in coimḋheḋ, ⁊ almrana iomḋa bíḋ ⁊ eḋaiġ do taḃairt dona hiġalraiḃ, ⁊ do na boc-
taiḃ, ⁊ corp an coimḋheḋ do caitṁ alláṁuiḃ a raġart ⁊ ġeallaḋ
ġac maitiura do ġénaṁ amail ar rṡir no iopalraioir a ccléirig
ropra, ⁊ comaḋ eaḋ ba meirġe ḋóiḃ i ġcṡn ġac cata, bacall Cho-
laim Cille, ġonaḋ aire rin audeṡar Catḃuaiḋ fria ó rin alle; ⁊ ba
hainm cóir, uair ir minic ruġraḋroṁ buaiḋ a ccataiḃ lé; aṁail do
ronrat iaram an tan rin dola a muiniġin Colaim Cille. Do ron-
raḋ an moḋ céḋna an tan ra. Ra cuirioḋ iaraṁ an catra ġo
cruaiḋ feocair; ruġraḋ na h-Albanaiġ buaiḋ ⁊ corġar; ro marḃaiḋ imurro na Loclonnaiġ ġo h-iomḋa ar maiḋm ropra, ⁊ marḃtar a riġ ann, .i. Oittir mac Iarnġna. Ar cian iartain na ro
raiġrioḋ Danair na Loclonnaiġ orra, act ro buí ríḋ ⁊ coṁranaḋ
doiḃ; act iomram don rġeol ro tionrġnamar.
Ro tionolrat rluaiġ na nDanar ⁊ na Loclonn d'ionroiġiḋ Car-
tra, ⁊ ó nac fruartur a fraoṁaḋ tre atac no ġuide, ro ṡṁua-
ġrattur cat ar ló ḋairite. Tanġadar 'ran lo rin d'ionroiġiḋ na
catrac; ⁊ ro ḃaoi rlóġ mór ġo n-iomaḋ raorclann 'ran ccatraiġ
ar a ccionn. 'O ro concattur na rluaiġ raḃattur irin catraiġ,
da ṁúr na catrac, rlóiġ iomḋa na nDanar ⁊ na Loclonn ḋá n-ion-
roiġiḋ,

about the year 918, according to Ann. Ult. See their account, Reeves, ib. p. 332.

" *Cathbhuaidh*.—i. e. battle-victory. In like manner the name of Cathach [præliosum] was given to the ornamented box of the O'Donnells of Tirconnell, containing a Psalter supposed to have been written by the hand of St. Columba, which was carried before their armies in battle. This valuable relic, through the public spirit of its owner, Sir Richard O'Donnell, is now deposited in the Museum of the Royal Irish Academy.

ˣ *On this occasion*.—i. e. on the occasion of the battle between the men of Fortrenn and the Lochlanns, in 918—the history of the battle with Imhar Conung, in 904, having been introduced merely to record the precedent for the use of the *Cathbuaidh*, or victory-giving crozier of St. Columkille.

ʸ *Otter, son of Iargna*.—Or son of Iargn; Iargna may be the gen. case. The Ann.

to remain untill morning fasting and praying to God and to Colum
Cille, and they cried out aloud to the Lord, and gave many alms of
food and clothes to the churches, and to the poor, and to take the
body of the Lord from the hands of their priests, and to promise to
do every good, as their clergy would order them, and that they would
have as their standard, at the head of every battle, the crozier of
Colum Cille, for which reason it is called the Cathbhuaidh[u] from that
time forth, and this was a befitting name for it, for they have often
gained victory in battles by means of it, as they did afterwards at that
time, when they put their trust in Colum Cille. They acted in the
same way on this occasion[x]. This battle was afterwards fought fiercely
and vigorously. The Albanachs gained victory and triumph. The
Lochlanns were slain in great numbers, and defeated, and their king
was slain, i. e. Otter, son of Iargna[y], and it it was long after this until
either Danes or Lochlanns attacked them, but they enjoyed peace and
tranquillity. But let us return to the story which we commenced.

The hosts of the Danes and the Lochlanns collected to Chester,
and when they did not get themselves complied with by entreaty or
supplication, they proclaimed battle on a certain day. On that day
they came to attack the city, and there was a large host, with many
nobles, in the city to meet them. When the hosts, who were within
the city, saw, from the wall of the city, the many hosts of the Danes
and Lochlanns [coming] to attack them, they sent messengers to the
King of the Saxons[z], who was in a disease, and on the point of death
at

Ult., in their account of this battle, mention this chieftain as Ottir, without giving the name of his father.

[z] *King of the Saxons.*—This was Æthelred, Ealdor of the Mercians, whose Queen was Æthelfled, sister of King Edward,

and daughter of Alfred the Great. He died in 912.—Sax. Chron. and Flor. Wigorn. in anno; Lappenberg's Hist. of England, ii., p. 90. Therefore, the event here described must have taken place in or before that year. But our author's chrono-

roiȝiṫ, ṗa ċuiṗṛioṫ ṫfċṫa ṫ'ionṛoiȝiṫ ṗi Saxan, ṗo ṫaoi a nȝaloṗ, ⁊ aṗ ṫṛú ecca an uaiṗ ṛin, ṫ'iaṗṗaiṫ a coṁaiṗliṛioṁ, ⁊ coṁaiṗle na ṗioȝna. Aṛí coṁaiṗle cuȝṛaiṫe caṫuȝaṫ ṫo ȝénaṁ a ṗṛoȝuṛ ṫo'n caṫṗaiȝ allamaiȝ, ⁊ ṫoṗaṛ na caṫṛac ṫo ṫeiṫ aiṫela, ⁊ ṛloȝ ṗiṫ-aiṗe ṫo ṫoȝa, ⁊ a mṫeiṫṛiṫe i ṗṛolaṫ alla anall, ⁊ man ṫuṫ ṫṗeiṛi ṫo luṫṫ na caṫṛaṫ aȝ an caṫuȝaṫ, ṫeiṫheṫ ṫoiṫ ṫaṗ a n-aiṛ iṛin ṫaṫṗaiȝ muṗ ba i maiṫm, ⁊ anuaiṗ ṫo ṫioṫṛaiṫíṛ ṛṗṁóṗ ṛlóiȝ na Loṫ-lonn ṫaṗ ṫoṗuṛ na caṫṛac aṛṫíṫ, an ṛlóȝ ṫiaṛ a ṗṛolaṫ ṫall ṫo ṫúnaṫ an ṫoṗuiṛ ṫaṗ éiṛ na ṫṗeimi ṛin, ⁊ ȝan ní aṛ moo ṫo léȝfn oṗṗa; ȝaṫáil ṛon ṫṛeim ṛin ṫioȝṛaiṫ iṛin ṫaṫṗaiȝ, ⁊ a maṗṫaṫ uile. Do ṗonaṫ uile aṁlaiṫ ṛin, ⁊ ṗo maṗṫaṫ ṫfṗȝ-áṗ na nDanaṗ ⁊ na Loṫlonn aṁlaiṫ. Ciṫ móṗ ṫna an maṗṫaṫ ṛin, ní hfṫ ṫo ṗonṛaṫ na Loṫlonnaiȝ ṛáȝṫail na caṫṛaṫ, uaiṗ ba ṫṛuaiṫ ainṫȝiṫ iaṫ, aṫṫ aṛfṫ aṫṛuṫṛaṫṫuṗ uile ṫliaṫa iomṫa ṫo ȝénaṁ aca, ⁊ ȝaṫla ṫo ṫuṗ ṛoṫa, ⁊ ṫollaṫ an ṁuiṗ ṛoṫa; ⁊ aṛfṫ ón ná ṛa ṛuiṗ-ȝfṫ, ṫo ṗónaṫ na ṫliaṫa, ⁊ ṛo ṫáṫaṗ na ṛlóiȝ ṛoṫa aȝ ṫollaṫ an ṁuiṗ, uaiṗ ba ṛainṫ leo ȝaṫáil na caṫṛaṫ, ⁊ ṫioȝail a muinnṫiṗe.

Iṛ ann ṛin ṛa ċuiṗ an ṗí (⁊ é i ṛoċṛaiṫ ṫo ṫáṛ) ⁊ an ṗioȝan ṫfċṫa uaṫa ṫ'ionṛoiȝiṫ na nȜaoiṫiol ṛo ṫaṫṫaṗ eiṫiṗ na Ṗáȝá-naiṫ (aṛ ba h-iomṫa ṫalṫa Ȝaoiṫealaṫ aȝ na Ṗáȝánaiṫ), ṫa ṛáṫ ṗiṛ na Ȝaoiṫealuiṫ: ṫfṫa ⁊ ṛláinṫe ó ṗi Saxan aṫá a nȝaloṗ, ⁊ ó n-a ṗióȝain, ȝá ṛṛuil uile nfṗṫ Saxan, ṫuiṫṛi, ⁊ ṛo ṫeiṁniȝṛioṫ conaṫ

logy is probably wrong.

* *Gaeidhil.*—i. e. the Irish, or Dano-Irish, called above the Gall-Gaeidhil. See p. 128, note ᵐ.

ᵇ *Over all the Saxons.*—In Powell's Hist. of Wales, by W. Wynne (Lond., 1697, pp. 45, 46), this attack upon Chester is referred to in the following words:—"After the death of Anarawd (A. D. 913), his eldest son, Edwal Foel, took upon him the government of North Wales, Howel Dha holding the principality of South Wales and Powis. At what time a terrible comet appeared in the heavens. The same year the city of Chester, which had been destroyed by the Danes, was, by the pro-

at that time, to ask his advice, and the advice of his queen. The advice which he gave was, to give [them] battle near the city outside, and to keep the gate of the city wide open, and to select a body of knights, and have them hidden on the inside; and if the people of the city should not be triumphant in the battle, to fly back into the city, as if in defeat, and when the greater number of the forces of the Lochlanns should come inside the gate of the city, that the hosts who were in ambuscade should close the gate of the city after this party, and not to pretend to any more, but to attack the party who should come into the city, and kill them all. This was all done accordingly, and a red slaughter was accordingly made of the Danes and Lochlanns. Great, however, as was that slaughter, the Lochlanns did not abandon the city, for they were hardy and fierce, but they all said that they should make many hurdles, and that posts should be placed under them, and that they should perforate the wall under [the shelter of] them. This project was not deferred; the hurdles were made, and hosts were [placed] under them to pierce the wall, for they were covetous to take the city, and to avenge their people.

Then the king, who was on the point of death, and the queen sent ambassadors to the Gaeidhil[a] who were among the Pagans (for the Lochlanns, then Pagans, had many a Gadelian foster-son), to say to the Gaeidhil : " Life and health from the King of the Saxons, who is in disease, and from his Queen, who has sway over all the Saxons[b], to

curement of Elfleda, new built and repaired, as the ancient records of that city do testify. This, in the ancient copy, is called Leycester, by an easy mistake for Legecestria or Chester, called by the Romans *Legionum Castra*. The next summer the men of Dublin cruelly destroyed

the island of Anglesey." The "ancient copy" here referred to is probably the Anglo Saxon-Chron., which calls the place *Legraceastre*, A. D. 918. There is great confusion between Chester and Leicester in the Saxon Chron. The former name is written Legaceaster, Leiceaster, Leg-

conaḋ ṗíoṗċapaıḋ caıpıpı ḋóıḃpıoṁ pıḃpı: ap amlaıḋ pın ap ᵹaḃċa
ḋuıḃpı ıaḋpoṁ; uaıp ᵹaċ óᵹlaċ, ⁊ ᵹaċ cléıpſċ Ƶaoıḃealaċ cáınıᵹ
cucapoṁ a h-'Єıpınn, ní cuᵹpacpom a ıomapcpaıḋ onópa ḋ'óᵹlaċ
no cléıpeċ Saxon; uaıp ap coıṁméc ap náṁaıḋ ḋuıḃ maılle an
cıneḋ náıṁḋıḃıpı na Paᵹánḋḋa. Ipeḋ ḋın ap lıḃpı aṁaıl ap capaıḋ
caıpıpı pıḃ, a ṗpopcaċc poṁ an ċuaıpcpı. Aṁlaıḋ po ón a páḋ
pıupom, ᵹonıḋ ó ċaıpḋıḃ caıpıpıḃ ḋuıḃ canᵹamap-ne ḋa ḃap naᵹal-
laṁ, ḋo páḋ ḋuıḃpı pıp na Danapaıḃ, cıḋne comaḋa ṗſpaınn ⁊
ıonnṁaıp ḋo ḃepḋaoıp ḋon luċc nó ḃpaıċpſḋ an caċpaıᵹ ḋóıḃ. Ma-
popoemaḃaıcpıoṁ paın, a mḃpeıċ ḋo ċum luıᵹe ı ṗpaıl ı mḃıa
poıpḃe a mapḃċa, ⁊ map ḃeıopıoṁ aᵹ caḃaıpc an luıᵹe pa cclaıḋ-
mıḃ, ⁊ pa pᵹıaċaıḃ, aṁuıl ap ḃép ḋóıḃ, cuıpᵹıcc uaċa an uıle apm
poıḋıoḃpaıᵹce. Do pıᵹnſḋ uıle aṁlaıḋ pın, ⁊ po ċuıppıoc a n-apma
uaċa, ⁊ ap aıpe ıp pıp na Danapaıḃ ḋo ponpaḋ na Ƶaoıḃıl pın,
uaıp ḃa luᵹ ḃa capaıḋ ḋóıḃ ıaḋ ıonáıḋ na Loċlonnaıᵹ. Sochaıḋe
ıapaṁ ḋíoḃ pa mapḃaḋ aṁlaıḋ pın, ap lécaḋ cappaᵹ móp ⁊ paḃaḋ
móp 'na ᵹcſnn: Soċuıḋe móp oıle ḋo ᵹaıḃ, ⁊ ḋo paıᵹḋuıḃ, ⁊ ó uıle
acmoınᵹe mapḃċa ḋaoıne.
 Ro ḃaccap ımuppo an ploᵹ oıle, Loċlonnaıᵹ póc na cliaċaıḃ
aᵹ collaḋ na múp. Apeḋ ḋo ponpaḋ na Saxoın ⁊ na Ƶaoıḃıl, po
ḃaccap ſcoppa, caıpᵹe ḋíoṁópa ḋo lécuḋ anuap ᵹo ccpapᵹpaıoíp
na cliaċa na ccſnn. Apeḋ ḋo ponpaḋpum na aıᵹıḋ pın, columna
mópa ḋo ċup po na cliaċaıḃ. Apeḋ ḋo ponpaḋ na Saxoın na
ṗpuapaḋap ḋo lıonn ⁊ ḋ'uıpᵹe pın ḃaıle ḋo ċup ı ccoıpıḃ an ḃaıle,
⁊ pıuċaḋ poppa a léᵹan ı mullaċ ın luċc po ḃaoı po na cliaċaıḃ,
ᵹo po pcoṁa ı lſċap ḋíoḃ. Apé ṗpeaᵹpaḋ cuᵹpaḋ na Loċlonnaıᵹ
                                                            aıppın

ccaster (Caer-Llcon, or Caerleon, in the Bret y Tywysogion, *Lleon* being a corruption of *Legionum*); the latter, Legraceastcr, Lcogereccaster, Ligcraccaster, Leyces-tre, &c. The fortification of Chester (Ligccaster), by Queen Æthelflœd, is recorded in the Saxon Chron. at A. D. 907.

to you, and they are certain that you are true and faithful friends to them. It is therefore meet that you should adhere to them, for they gave to every Gadelian soldier and clergyman who had come to them out of Erin, as much honour as they did to any Saxon soldier or clergyman, for this inimical race of Pagans is equally hostile to you both. It then behoves you, as ye are faithful friends, to relieve them on this occasion." This was the same as if it was said to them: We have come from faithful friends of yours to address you, [to request] that ye should ask the Danes, what gifts in lands and chattels they would give to those who would betray the city to them. If they would consent to this, to bring them to swear, to a place where there would be a facility of killing them; and when they shall be swearing on their swords, and on their shields, as is their wont, they will put away all kinds of missile weapons. They all did accordingly, and they put away their arms; and the reason that the Gaeidhil acted so towards the Danes was, because they were less friends to them than to the Lochlanns. Many of them were killed in this manner, for large rocks and large beams were hurled down upon their heads. Great numbers also were killed by darts and javelins, and by every other kind of apparatus for killing men.

The other hosts, however, were under the hurdles, piercing the walls. What the Saxons and the Gaeidhil who were among them did, was to throw down large rocks, by which they broke down the hurdles over their heads. What the others did to check this was, to place large posts under the hurdles. What the Saxons did next, was to put all the beer and water of the town into the cauldrons of the town, to boil them, and spill them down upon those who were under the hurdles, so that their skins were peeled off. The remedy which the Lochlanns applied to this was to place hides outside on the hurdles. What the Saxons did next was, to throw down all the beehives in

aippin ṗeiċṗo oo pgaoileo ap na cliaċaiḃ anuap. Ap ṗo oo pónpao na Saxoin gaċ a paḃa oo cliaḃ bṗċ ipin ḃaile oo pgaoilṗo po luċc na coglu, na po léig ḃóiḃ copa na láṁa o'iomluao pa hiomao na mbṗċ ga ccṗpcao. Ro léigpioo iapccan oon ċaṫpaig ⁊ po ṗágpao í. Ní cian iapccain co ccángacap apipi oo caṫuġhao.
Ip in ḃliaḃainpi cáinig cionol mop ḃpeipne ap cpṗċaiḃ. Ra hinnipioo pin oo píg 'Eipṗnn, ⁊ oo ṁaccaiḃ. Ap annpin po páio pí 'Eipṗnn: ap oeipṗo n-aimpipe ann, ap pé, an can láṁuio coṁaicig mup po eipgio a n-aigio paopċlann. Oo pónao cionól oipṗpgna po céoóip la pí n-Eipṗnn ⁊ la ṁaccoiḃ, ⁊ cangaccap pṗmpa go opuim ċpiaiċ, ⁊ po baccup og péccao cionól na mbpéṗnṗċ ann pin. Ní pacup peṁe pin cionol oo aiċṗcuiḃ. Oo cuippioo cṗnn i gcṗnn iapccain, ⁊ gen go paḃa pi pṗmpa oo puaḃpaoap go cpuaio pig n-'Eipṗnn. Ro coñaccup meic pí 'Eipṗnn caċ pealao ó ċáċ amaċ ; cangaccup oá ionpoigioopioe, ⁊ po cuippioo ppiu. Ro ṁaiḃ pe macaiḃ an pí ap an ċaṫpin, ⁊ pomaio ap na caċaiḃ oile po céoóip, po cuippo a noṗpg áp, ⁊ po gaḃao pochaioe oíoḃ gup cṗnnaigic iao oo ċionn ionnṁaip.
Cáinig an pí go mbuaio ⁊ copgup oo ḃpeiċ o na aiċṗḃaouiḃ, ap mapḃao pí na mbpeipnṗċ .i. Plann mac Cigṗpnáin.
Ral. Annup xxxi.up. Plainn, Oiapmaio pí Oppaige, ⁊ Aoḃ mac Ouiḃgiolla,

Druim-criaich.—Now Drumcree, a townland in the parish of Kilcumny, barony of Delvin, and county of Westmeath.

Attacotts.—The meaning of this is very doubtful. The term *aithech tuatha* (attacot) is applied by the old Irish writers to the enslaved descendants of the Firbolgs, and to all those who were not of the royal line of the Milesians or Scoti ; but the chiefs of the men of Breifne were descended from as royal a line as the monarch of Ireland himself. The probability, however, is, that the monarch of Ireland spoke in derision on account of the motley appearance presented by these hordes of plunderers. This defeat of the men of Breifne is recorded in the Ann. Ult., A. D. 909 [910]—Caṫpoṁio pe Plonn mac Maelpcṅnall cum suis filiis pop pipu ḃpeipne ubi ceciderunt Flann

the town upon the besiegers, which prevented them from moving their hands or legs from the number of bees which stung them. They afterwards desisted and left the city. It was not long, however, until they came to fight again.

[909.] In this year there came a great muster of the Brefnians [into Meath] to commit depredations. This was told to the King of Erin and to his sons. Then the King of Erin said, "It is the end of the world that is come," said he, "when plebeians like these dare to attack noblemen." An irresistible muster was immediately afterwards made by the King of Erin and his sons, and they came forward to Druim-criaich[e], and [thence] they reconnoitered the assembled forces of Breifnè. They had never before seen a muster of Attacotts[d]. They met each other face to face, and though they had no king[e] at their head, they attacked the King of Erin with hardihood. The sons of the King of Erin saw a battalion at some distance out from the rest; they came towards it, and attacked it. The sons of the king defeated that battalion, and the other battalions were likewise at once defeated and dreadfully slaughtered, and many of them were taken prisoners, who were afterwards ransomed by prices.

The King returned after having gained victory and triumph over the plebeians, after the King of the Brefnians, i. e. Flann, son of Tighernan, had been killed.

[910.] Kal. The thirty-first year of Flann[f]. Diarmaid, King of Osraighe,

Mac Tigernain et alii nobiles multi interfecti. " An overthrow of the men of Brefne, by Flann, son of Maelsechlain and his sons, where Flann, son of Tighernan, fell, and many other nobles were slain." The same passage occurs in the Ann. Clonm. at 902, and F. M. at 905 (the true year is 910). But there is no mention of

Attacoti or plebeians in any of these Annals.

[e] *No King.*—This looks very strange, for it is stated in the next paragraph that their King Flann, son of Tighernan, was killed. Perhaps there was a body of Attacotts, who were without a king, acting as auxiliaries to Flann and his Breifnians.

[f] *Of Flann.*—i. e. of Flann Sionna (son

Ouibġiolla, ní Ua nOpona oo millfo oeipġipc Maiġe Raiġne, ⁊ millfo oóib Cill na gCailleaċ .i. Pinchi, ⁊ Rectín, ⁊ muinncip Aoba oo mapbao paġapc an baile, ⁊ apeb ón po oioġail Dia pop Aob mac Ouibġiolla pain, uaip po mapbpao apaile comaitiġ o'Oppaigib é ag iompóo oa éiġ. Rí hUa nOpóna an tAob pin, ⁊ na ttpí maiġe, ⁊ piġoamna hUa Cinnpilaiġ, unoe oicitup:

A óġa Ailbe aine,
Caoimio piġ Slaine paoipe,
Epebaio Aob mbuionfċ mbeapba,
Go po puio Pfpna paoine.
Peapna mop milib ooġnaċ,
Nippaine apmao cuimnfċ,
Mapbán buo fpgna allao,
O po bit bpan Oub buionfċ.
Ro paoib mo oíon mo oicte,
Rí na píoġ peoiġ pooa.
Ap puaiċniġ pop paiċ 'Eoain,
Aob i n-éccaib, a óġa.

Uallaċán mac Caċail, piġoamna hUa Pailġe moriċup.
Uġaipe mac Oilella oo pioġao pop Laiġnib.
buaoaċ mac Moċla piġoamna na nOéipi moriċup.

Ral.

of Maelsechlainn), King of Ireland, who began his reign A. D. 879, so that his thirty-first year was 910. See O'Flaherty, Ogyg., p. 434.

ᵍ *Ui-Drona.*—A tribe inhabiting the present barony of Idrone, county of Carlow. See Book of Rights, p. 212, n.

ʰ *Cill-na-g Cailleoh.*—i. e. the church of the nuns. The founders of this church were the holy virgins Finech and Rechtin.

It is the church now called Killinny [Cill Phineċa, Ch. of S. Finech], in the parish and barony of Kells, county of Kilkenny. See F. M., A. D. 859, note ⁱ, p. 494.

ⁱ *Ailbhe.*—i. e. Magh Ailbhe, a plain on the east side of the Barrow, near Carlow.

ᵏ *Slainé.*—i. e. the River Slaney.

ˡ *Bearbha.*—i. c. the River Barrow.

ᵐ *Fearna.*—i. c. Ferns, in the county of Wexford.

raighe, and Aedh, son of Dubhghioll, King of Ui-Drona[g], destroyed the east of Magh Raighne, and they destroyed Cill-na-gCaillech[h] [i. e. of the nuns] Finech and Rechtin, and the people of Aedh killed the priest of the place, which God afterwards revenged upon Aedh, son of that Dubhghioll, for some plebeians of the Osraighi killed him as he was returning to his house. This Aedh was King of Ui-Drona, and of the Three Plains, and royal heir of Ui-Ceinsealaigh. Unde dicitur:—

> O youths of pleasant Ailbhe[i],
> Mourn ye the King of noble Slaine[k].
> Slain is Aedh of hosts of the Bearbha[l],
> The just king of the land of peaceful Fearna[m],
> To great Fearna, of the thousand noble graces,
> There came not, if I well remember,
> A corpse of more illustrious fame
> Since Bran Dubh[n] of troops was slain.
> My shelter, my protection has departed;
> May the King of kings make smooth his way.
> It is easily known by Rath-Aedhain[o]
> That Aedh is dead, O youths!

Uallachan[p], son of Cathal, royal heir of Ui-Failghe [Offaley], died. Ugaire, son of Oilell[q], was made King of Leinster. Buadhach, son of Mothla[r], royal heir of the Deisi, died.

[911.]

[n] *Bran Dubh.*—A famous King of Leinster, who was slain A. D. 601. See Ann. F. M., pp. 228, 229, 576.

[o] *Rath-Aedhain.*—i. e. Aidan's Fort, another name for Ferns. So called from St. Aedh or Aidan, alias Mogue, [i. e. mo Aeḋ óᵹ].

[p] *Uallachan.*—His death is entered in the Ann. Clonm. at the year 902, F. M. 905, but the true year is 910.

[q] *Ugaire, son of Oilell.*—He died in 915, according to the Ann. F. M.

[r] *Buadhach, son of Mothla.*—Ann. F. M. 905.

Ḳal. Airḋe ioñgnaḋ .i. na ḋí grén ḋo pioṫ maille in uno ḋie. 1 pṙiḋ. noin Maii. Ḋunlang mac Coirḃre, rigḋaṁna Laigſn, moritur. Ḋoṁnall mac Aoḋa, ri Ailig ḋo gaḃail baċla.
Maolmórḋa, princepſ [.i. airċinneċ] Ṫíre ḋa glaſ, moritur.
Gaíṫin mac Ugrain, rigḋaṁna Laoigiri, moritur. Ḃuaḋaċ mac Gorrain, rigḋaṁna hUa mḃairrċe, moritur. Ḋianim ingſn Ḋuiḃ-giolla, bſn Ḋunluing, moritur; unḋe ḋiċitur :—

Ḋianim ḋíon ar nḋaoine, porċaċt greim Rig na nḋúile,
Ḋurran ċaoḃ rḋa ruaiṫnig, ḋo ḃeiṫ 1 n-uairṫig úire.

Inrſḋ Orraige la Cormac rig na nḊéiri, ┐ ċealla iomḋa [ḋo] milleḋ ┐ ċeall manaċ. Ro marḃṫaċ Orraige ḋearḃraċair an Choṙmaiċ .i. Cuilſnnan; an ċan ro ḃaoi Cormac ag milleḋ Orraige, ċainig Maolruanaiḋ mac Néill, mac an rí ro ḃaoi reṁe ṙorſ na Ḋéiriḃ, ┐ orſm ḋo Orraigiḃ leiſ, ḋaréiſ Cormaiċ go ḋúnaḋ an Cormaiċ, ┐ ċainig an Cuileannán a ḋrurramur rſṁainn na n-aigiḋ, ┐ ḋo raḋ ḋeaḃaiḋ ḋoiḃ, ┐ ro marḃaḋ Cuileannán ran ḋeaḃaiḋrin. Ag iomróḋ ḋo Cormac ro ċuala an ſgéliſin, ┐ aḋ ċonnairċ ſén éḋaċ a ḃráċair a láiṁ an loċċa ro marḃ é. Ḃa ḋuḃaċ, ḋoḃrónaċ iarċċain Cormac.

Iſ in mḃliaḋain ri ro marḃaḋ mac Ḃraonáin, mic Cſrḃaill go ċruag ar lár a ḋaingin ſén, ┐ gér raoil Ḋiarmaiḋ go maḋ

ferrḋe

* *A wonderful sign.*—This wonder is entered in the Ann. Clonm. at 902, but in the Ann. Ult. at 910 [911].
† *Dunlang.*—Ann. F. M. 906.
u *Domhnall.*—Ann. F. M. 906; Ann. Ult. 911. He was the eldest son of Aedh Finnliath, monarch of Ireland, and the ancestor of the family of O'Donnelly.
x *Maelmordha.*—Ann. F. M. 905.
y *Gaeithin.*—Ann. F. M. 906.
z *Buadhach.*—Ann. F. M. 906.
a *Dianimh.*—Ann. F. M. 906, where these lines are quoted.

[911.] Kal. A wonderful sign*, i. e. two suns moving together during one day, i. e. prid. non. Maii. Dunlang^t, son of Cairbre, royal heir of Leinster, died.

Domhnall[u], son of Aedh, King of Ailech, took the [pilgrim's] staff.
Maelmordha[x], princeps (i. e. erenach) of Tir-da-glas, died.
Gaeithin[y], son of Ughran, royal heir of Lacighis, died.
Buadhach[z], son of Gossan, royal heir of Ui-Bairrche, died.
Dianimh[a], daughter of Duibhghill, wife of Dunlang, died; unde dicitur :—

Dianimh, shelter of our people, is fettered by the power of the King of the elements.
Alas! that her tall and beautiful person is in a cold house of clay.

The plundering of Osraighe by Cormac, King of the Deisi[b], and many [secular] churches and monastic churches were destroyed by him. The Osraighi killed the brother of Cormac, i. e. Cuilennan. When Cormac was plundering Osraighe, Maelruanaidh, son of Niall, the son of the king who was before him over the Deisi, having a party of the Osraighi with him, pursued Cormac to Cormac's own residence, and the Cuilennan whom we have mentioned before came to oppose them, and gave them battle, and Cuilennan was killed in that battle. On Cormac's return he heard this news, and he saw the clothes of his brother in the hands of those who had slain him, and he was melancholy and sorry in consequence.

In this year the son of Braenan, son of Cearbhall, was piteously slain in the middle of his own fortress, and though Diarmaid[c] thought that

[b] *Cormac, King of the Deisi.*—This entry is not in the published Annals. This Cormac is mentioned by the F. M. at 915, and his death is recorded by them at 917.
[c] *Diarmaid.*—This Diarmaid, King of Ossory, was uncle to the murdered chief-

ꝼeṙṙve vó maṙbav mic a bṙáṫaṙ, ní aṁlaıv vo ṗála vó, uaıṙ vo eıṙġſccuṙ Clann Ounġaıle uıle cṙıv ṙın ı ccſnn Oıaṙmava, ⁊ aṁaıl na eıṙġſv Ceallaċ aıṙ, aṙ aṁlaıv ṙo eıṙġe Maolmóṙva mac bṙáṫaṙ vó na cſnn, ⁊ ṙé cuımneċ ın aıncṙıve vo ṙıġne Oıaṙmaıv ṙe a a aṫaıṙ, ⁊ ṙé na ṙſnóıṙ ann: ⁊ ṙo eıṙġe an Maolmóṙva ṙın ġo ꝼeoċaıṙ beava ı ccſnn Oıaṙmaca, ṙónaıc vá Oṙṙaıġe v'Oṙṙaıġıv cṙéṙ an ċoġav ṙın: ṙo baoı maṙbav móṙ ſccaṙṙa. Caınıġ ona mac Coba mic Ouıḃġıolla, mac ón ınġıne Cſṙbaıll mıc Ounlaınġ, ı n-aıġıv Oıaṙmava, aṙ ba ġoıṙc leıṙ mac bṙáṫaṙ a ṁáṫaṙ ⁊ a vala vo ṁaṙbav la Oıaṙmaıv. Móṙ ṙaoṙċlann ṙo maṙbaıc ṙan ċaġavṙa, ⁊ móṙ ceall ṙó ꝼáṙaıġıc.

Ḳal. Saṙuġhav Cṙvmacha vo Cſṙnaċán mac Ouılġen, ſvon, cımıv [.ı. bṙıaıġe] vo Bṙeıċ eṙce, (.ı. aṙ ın ccıll) ⁊ a báváġ Illoċ Cıṙṙ. Cſṙnaċán ıaṙ ṙın vo bavaġ vo Nıall Ġlúnvub ın eovem lacu, ı noíoġaıl ꝼáṙaıġċe Cṙvmaċa.

Maoılbṙıġve ımuṙṙo mac Maoılvoṁnaıġ, ab. Liṙ móıṙ moṙıcuṙ.

Flann mac Laoıġe, ab Coṙcaıġe moṙıcuṙ.

Coṙmac eṙſcop Saıġṙe.

Cıobṙaıve ab Imleaċa moṙıcuṙ.

Maolbṙıġve mac Coṙnáın, comaṙba Ṗávṙaıcc ⁊ Colum cılle, ġo n-ıomav cléıṙeaċ 'Eıṙeann leıṙ, ım Muṁaın v'áċċuınġıv ıonṁaıṙ aṙ maıċıv Muṁan va ċabaıṙc ı ꝼuaṙlaġav bṙaıve bṙſcon; ⁊ ꝼuaıṙṙıoṁ ṙaın; ⁊ cuġ laıṙ an mbṙaıv ccṙuaġ ṙın aṙ mbávav a long,

tain, and is mentioned by the F. M. at the years 900, 914, 917; but this passage, which was evidently preserved in some Ossorian collection of Annals, is nowhere given by them.

ᵈ *Cearnachan, son of Duilgen.*—This entry is given by the F. M. at the year 907, but in the Ann. Ult. at 911 [912]. The situation or modern name of Loch Cirr is now unknown.

ᵉ *Maelbrighde.*—Ann. F. M. 907; Ann. Ult. 911 [912].

that he would be the better of the killing of his brother's son; it did not turn out so to him, for in consequence of this all the Clann Dunghaile rose up against Diarmaid, and, as if Ceallach would not rise against him, Maelmordha, the son of a brother of his, rose up against him, being mindful of the cruelty which Diarmaid had exercised against his father when he was an old man; and this Maelmordha rose up fiercely and vigorously against Diarmaid, and they divided Osraighe into two parts by that war. There was great slaughter between them. The son of Aedh, son of Duibhghilla (who was the son of the daughter of Cearbhall, son of Dunlaing), came also against Diarmaid, for it was bitter to him that the son of his mother's brother, and his *alumnus*, should have been killed by Diarmaid. Many nobles were killed during this war, and many churches were wasted.

[912.] Kal. The plundering of Ard-Macha by Cearnachan, son of Duilgen[d], i. e. by taking a prisoner out of it [i. e. out of the church], and drowning him in Loch Cirr. Cearnachan was afterwards drowned by Niall Glundubh in the same lake, in revenge of the profanation of Ard-Macha.

Maelbrighde[e], son of Maeldomhnach, Abbot of Lis-mor, died.
Flann, son of Laegh[f], Abbot of Corcach, died.
Cormac[g], Bishop of Saighir [Serkieran], [died].
Tibraide[h], Abbot of Imleach [Emly], died.
Maelbrighde, son of Tornan[i], successor of Patrick and Colum-Cille, with many ecclesiastics, [went] into Munster to solicit gifts from the men of Munster to ransom the prisoners of the Britons, and he obtained them, and he brought with him the miserable prisoners, their

[f] *Flann, son of Laegh.*—Ann. F. M. 907.
[g] *Cormac.*—Ann. F. M. 907.
[h] *Tibraide.*—Ann. F. M. 908.
[i] *Maelbrighde, son of Tornan.*—Some-

thing like this is entered by the F. M. at 908, and Ann. Ult. at 912 [913] thus: "Maelbrighte mac Tornain came into Mounster to release pilgrims of the British."

Loinʃ, ⁊ aη na ccuηηιoṁ ι ττίη, ⁊ aη ττοιὁίττ όόιὅ aη ιοnnʃaὅáιl Οαnaη ⁊ Loclann.

Ḱal. Maolmoeόóc ρηιncepη Onoma móιη moηιτυη.

Tιoὅηαιὁe eηγcoη Cluana eὁnίc moηιτυη.

Cατηαοιneαὅ ή Maoιlmιchιὁ mac Flannaʃáιn ⁊ ηe nOonn-chaὁ hUa Maoιlηeacloιnn foη Loηcán mac nOunchαιὁ, ⁊ foη Foʃaηταc mac Tolαιηʃ, ὁu ι ττοηcαιη ιle. Lacτnán mac Cίηnαιʃ, ηί Oúιn Naιηn Laoιʃηι, moηιτυη. Maolpaoηαιc mac Flaτηοe, ηί Rατα Oomnαιʃ, moηιτυη. Ετalὅ, ηι Saχοιn ττυαιηʃιητ moηιτυη. Flαιτὅeαηταὁ mac Ιonmαιnen ι ηιʃe Cαιηιl.

Coὅlaὁ lánmóη Loclann [oo] ʃαὅαιl aʃ Poητ Lαιηʃe, ⁊ focla Oηηαιʃe .ι. τυαιηʃίητ Oηηαιʃe, o'ιoηηηαὁ ὁόιὅ; ὅηαὁ móη ⁊ ιomαὁ ὅό, ⁊ eallαιʃ oo ὅηeιτ ὁόιὅ ʃo nuιʃe α loηʃα.

Tanʃαττυη 'ηαn ὅlιαὁαιn ηιn γlόιʃ móηα Ouὅʃall ⁊ Fιonnʃall ooηιὁιηι o'ιοnηοιʃτc Saχοn aη ηίοʃaὅ Sιτηιuca hUí Ιοmαιη. Ro fuαʃηαττυη cατ foη Saχοιn, ⁊ aηίὁ ón na ηο fuιηʃίττυη Saχοιn acτ τanʃαττυη fo ὁeὁυαιη o'ιoηηοιʃιὁ na ὅPáʃánaὁ. Ro cuιηίὁ cατ cηυαιὁ feocαιη eατττοηηα, aʃυη ὅα móη ὅηιʃ, ⁊ ὅηυτ ⁊ coηnαm cίττaηnae. Ro τοὁαιleὁ móη fola ηαοηὁlann 'ηαn ὁατ γα; ʃιὁίὁ ιγ ιaὁ Saχοιn ηυʃ ὅυαιὁ ⁊ coηʃαη aη mαηὅαὁ οίηʃáιη na ὅPαʃáναὁ, uαιη oo ʃαὅ ʃαloη ηί να ὅPαʃáναὁ, ⁊ ηυʃαὁ aη ιν ὁατ é ʃo

---

¹ *Maelmaedhóg.*—His death is entered in the Annals of F. M. at 909.

ˡ *Tibraide.*—Ann. F. M. 909.

ᵐ *Maelmithidh.*—Ann. F. M. 909.

ⁿ *Dun-Nair in Laeighis.*—A place in the Queen's County. This entry is not in the published Annals.

º *Rath-domhnaigh.*—Now Rathdowney, a small town in the barony of Upper Ossory, Queen's County. It is called Rath-Tamhnaigh.—F. M., A. D. 909.

ᵖ *Ethalbh.*—Æthulf, or Æthelwulf.

ᵠ *Flaithbhertach, son of Inmainen.*—He was Abbot of Inis-Cathaigh, and had been the chief cause of the Battle of Bealach Mughna, in which Cormac Mac Cuillenain was killed. He became King of Munster A. D. 908, and died 944.

ʳ *Lochlanns.*—This entry is given in the Ann. F. M. at 910, but the true year is 913.

their ships having been swamped, and themselves cast ashore, having come to shun the Danes and Lochlanns.

[913.] Kal. Maelmaedhóg[k], princeps [i. e. abbot] of Drum-mor, died.

Tibraide[l], Bishop of Cluain-eidhnach [Clonenagh], died.

A battle was gained by Maelmithidh[m], son of Flannagan, and Donnchadh Ua Maelsechlainn, over Lorcan, son of Donchadh, and Fogartach, son of Tolarg, in which many fell: Lachtnan, son of Cearnach, King of Dun-Nairn in Laeighis[n], died. Maelpatraic, son of Flathrai, King of Rath-domnaigh[o], died. Ethalbh[p], King of the North Saxons, died.

Flaithbhertach, son of Inmainen[q], [was installed] in the kingdom of Caisel.

A very large fleet of Lochlanns[r] settled at Port-Lairgè [Waterford], and plundered the north of Osraighe: they carried off a great number of prisoners, and many cows and small cattle to their ships.

There came in this year great hosts of Black Galls[s] and Fair Galls[t] again into Saxonland, after setting up Sitric, grandson of Imhar, as king. They challenged the Saxons to battle. And the Saxons did not indeed delay, but they came at once to meet the Pagans. A stubborn and fierce battle[u] was fought between them, and great was the vigour, and strength, and emulation on both sides. Much of the blood of nobles was spilled in that battle, but it was the Saxons that gained victory and triumph, after having made great havoc of the Pagans,

---

[s] *Black Galls.*—Or dark foreigners, i. e. Danes.

[t] *Fair Galls.*—Or fair-haired foreigners, i. e. Norwegians.

[u] *Fierce battle.*—This is perhaps the same battle described in the Saxon Chron.

at the year 911, in which Otter the Earl and many other Danish chieftains were slain, but the two narratives do not agree in every particular; nor does the Saxon Chronicle mention Sitric, grandson of Imhar, as the leader of the party.

é go coill baoi compocpaib dóib, ⁊ ba mapb ann pin é. Oittip dno an t-iapla ba moó muipn 'pan caé pa, ó po connaipc áp a muinntipe do cup do na Saxonaib, apeo do pigne, teicfb po caillib nolúit baoi i compocpaib do, ⁊ in neoc po maip da muinntip leip. Tangattup dponga díomópa Saxon 'na bfghaio, ⁊ po gabpat mun gcaille maccuapt. Ro iopail imuppo an piogan oppa an caill uile no éfpgab da cclaibmib, ⁊ ba ttuagaib : ⁊ apfb on do pigneo amlaio. Ro tpapgpab an caill ap túp, ⁊ pa mapbad uile na Pagánaig, po battup pan ccaile. Ra mapbaio tpa amlaio pin na Pagánoa lapin píogan go po lít a clu ap gac leit.

Do pigne Edelopioa tpia na gliocap péin pío ppia piopa Alban, ⁊ pe bpeatnuib, gibé tan tiugpaioíp an cinfb ceona ba hionpoighib, gup po eipgioippin do congnam lé. Damao cucapom no taopoaoip, gup po eipgeópi leopum. Céin po bap ime pin, po lingpiot pip Alban ⁊ bpftan po bailib na Loclonn, pa millpio, ⁊ pa aipgpiod iad. Taimg pí Loclann iaptain, ⁊ pa aipg Spait cluaide, .i. pa aip an típ, act ní po cumaing namaio [ní] do Spait cluaide.

* *Etheldrida.*—See above, p. 227, note ᵇ, and comp. Lappenberg's History of England (Thorpe's Transl.), vol. ii., p. 93 *sq.* From the manner in which "the Queen" is here mentioned, it would seem that the transactions here recorded must have taken place after the death of Æthelred in 912, or during the illness which incapaci-

Pagans, for the King of the Pagans had contracted a disease, and he was carried from the battle to a neighbouring wood, where he died. But when Otter, the most influential Iarl that was in the battle, saw that his people were slaughtered by the Saxons, he fled to the dense woods which were in his neighbourhood, carrying with him the survivors of his people. Great parties of Saxons followed in pursuit of them, and they encompassed the wood round about. The Queen ordered them to cut all the wood down with their swords and axes. And they did so accordingly. They first cut down the wood, and [afterwards] killed all the Pagans who were in the wood. In this manner did the Queen kill all the Pagans, so that her fame spread abroad in every direction.

Etheldrida[x], through her own wisdom, made a treaty with the men of Alba and the Britons, that whenever the same race should come to attack her, they would rise up to assist her; and that should they come to them, she would assist them. While they were thus joined, the men of Alba and Britain attacked the towns of the Lochlanns, which they destroyed and pillaged. The King of the Lochlanns afterwards arrived, and plundered Srath Cluaide[y], i. e. he plundered the country, but the enemy was not able to take Srath Cluaide.

tated him from taking any part in public affairs.

[y] *Srath Cluaide.*—i. e. Strathclyde, in North Britain.

GENERAL INDEX.

ABHAIN Mor, or Avonmore, 217, *n.*
Achadh arglais, or Agha, 171.
Achadh mic Earclaidhe, 145.
Adamnan, when a school-boy, story of, 75, *seq.*; relics of, 55; assumes abbacy of Ia, 89; ransoms captives, 89; comes to Ireland, 93; promulgates " Law of Innocents," 97; his contention with Irgalach, 101; his rule for celebration of Easter, 111; death of, 115.
Adolph, king of the Saxons, 151.
Aedh, son of Ainmire, 8, *n.*, 9.
—— Allan, 12, *n.*, 23, 29, 42, *n.*, 45, 59.
—— king of Ailech, 129.
—— of Carn Tasaigh, 219.
—— son of Cumascach, 155.
—— son of Duibhghilla, 239, 243.
—— son of Dluthach, 95.
—— son of Dubhdabhoirenn, 153.
—— Finnliath, 155, 157.
—— Laighean, 42, *n.*, 50, *n.*, 51.
—— son of Maelduin, 99.
—— Menn, 41.
—— Finnliath, son of Niall, 141, 143, 147, 151, 157, 159, 171, 177, 189.
—— Roin, king of Uladh, 59.
—— bishop of Sleibhte, 99.
—— Uairidhnach, 11, 12, *n.*
—— king of Ui-Leathain, 211.
Aedhagan, son of Finnacht, 177.
Aedhan the leper, 37.
Aedhgen Ua Maithe, 49.
Æthelred, king of the Saxons, 231, *n.*
Aenghus, king of Fortrenn, 55.
—— son of Faelchu, 55.
—— a sage of Cluain Ferta Molua, 153.
—— the high wise man, 141.
—— son of Bec Boirche, death of, 57.
—— Uladh, death of, 65.
Ailbhe. *See* Magh Ailbhe.
Aidhne, territory of, 211, *n.*

Ailech, destruction of, by Finnachta, 71.
Ailech-Frigrinn, 23.
Aileran the wise, death of, 65.
Ailen, the two sons of, 51.
Ailgenan, son of Dunghal, king of Munster, 129, 135.
Ailell Banbhan, abbot of Biror, 153.
—— bishop and abbot of Fore, 195.
—— son of Bodhbhcha, 53.
—— of Clochar, 185.
—— son of Conall Grant, 51.
—— son of Cu-gan-mathair, 103.
—— son of Domhnall, death of, 67.
—— son of Dunghal, 98.
—— son of Dunlang, 195.
—— son of Eoghan, 211.
Aillinn, battle of, 57.
Aindli, wise man of Tir-da-ghlas, 135.
Ainge, river, 118, *n.*
Aircelltair, or Ailcelltra, battle of, 71, 77.
Airghialla, 34, *n.*
Airiur-Gaeidhel (or Argyle), 14, *n.*
Airmeadhach of Craebh, 89.
Airthera, or Orior, 155.
Albain, or Scotland, 40, *n.*
Albanachs, the, 231.
Albdan, king of Lochlann, 159.
Alle, king of the Saxons, 178.
Almhain, or Allen, hill of, 82, *n.*; kings slain in battle of, 49–51, 221.
Amlaeibh, 223.
—— Coning, 127.
—— son of king of Lochlann, 135, 149, 151, 157, 171, 173, 185, 195.
Anastasius, 21.
Aneslis, or Beal-Borumha, 216, *n.*
Anglesea, or Mona Conain, 155.
Aodhan Mac Gabrain, 7.
Ara Cliach, 147.
Aradh Tire, 141.

2 K

Arcadians of Cliach, 131.
Ard-Macha, burning of, 69, 185, 243.
—— plundered, 127.
Argyle, ancient name of, 14, *n*.
Aunites, or Danes, 159.
Attacotts, the word, 237.
Ath-muiceadha, 131.

Badbh, 191.
Baedan, abbot of Cluain-mic-nois, 65.
Baeth-galach, 45.
Baithin, abbot of Benchair, 67.
Balearic Isles, 163.
Banbhan, scribe of Cill-dara, 89.
Barith the Earl, 173, 197.
Bealach Chonglais, 131.
—— Gabhrúin, 189.
—— Lice, battle of, 53.
Bec Boirche, 87.
Beccan, abbot of Cluain-Iraird, 93.
Bece Ua Leathlabair, king of Dal Araidhe, 225.
Bede, date of his work, 56, *n*.; death of, 65; reference to, 113, 115.
Beg Boirche, slayer of Congall Cennfoda, 71.
Bennchair, deaths of four abbots of, 65.
—— burning of, 69.
Berbha, or the Barrow, 85, 239.
Black men of Erin, 163.
Blathmac, son of Aedh Slaine, 63, 65.
—— son of Maelcobha, 69.
Blue men of Erin, 163.
Bodhbhchar, son of Diarmaid Ruanaidh, 111.
Bogbaine, 48, *n*.
Boinn, or Boyne, 10, *n*., 101, *n*.
Boirinn, battle of, 55.
Boromean tribute, 22, *n*., 33, 34, *n*.
Borumha, the tax so called, 76, *n*.; remission of, 93.
—— book so called, 78, *n*.
—— Laighen, 82.
Braen, 225.
Breenan, son of Cearbbally, 241.
Bran, 225.
—— son of Conall Beg, 97, 109.
—— Dubh, 239.
—— king of Leinster, 40.
—— son of Maeluchtraigh, 69.
Breagh plundered by the Lochlanna, 153.
—— Magh, 21, 118, *n*.
Breassal Breac, ancestor of chiefs of Osraighe, 8, *n*.
Breifnians, attack on Meath by, 237.
Brenann, 165, 167.
—— of Biror, 6, *n*., 7.
Brendan, St., 6, *n*.
Brigit, St., 17, 40, *n*.
Britain Gaimud, 155.

Bruide, son of Deril, 111.
—— son of Bile, 89, 93.
Buachail, son of Dunadhach, 195.
Buadhach, son of Gossan, 241.
—— son of Mothla, 239.
Buan of Albain, 41.

Cadell, son of Roderick, 225, 227.
Caer Ebroic, or York, 159, 171.
Caireog, son of Dunóg, 225.
Calatros, battle of, 87.
Caltruim, 65.
Cana, son of Gartnan, 91.
Cantabrian Sea, 159
Carn Lughdhach, 137, 139.
Carrleagh, 14, *n*.
Carlingford Lough, 120, *n*.
Casan, scribe of Lusca, 97.
Cathal (son of Aedh), battle of, 60, *n*., 61.
—— son of Fingaine, king of Munster, 21, 157.
Catharnach, 211, 217.
Cathasach, abbot of Ard-Macha, 143.
—— son of Luirgne, 69.
—— son of Maelduin, 87.
Cathbualdh, 231.
Carthach, abbot of Tir-da-ghlas, 135.
Ceallach, son of Cearbhall, 207, 211.
—— abbot of Cill-dara and I, 163.
—— King of Feara-Cualann, 213, 217, 219, 225.
—— son of Guaire, 151.
—— son of Raghallach, 105.
Ceannmaghair, 28, *n*.
Cearbhall, son of Dunlaing, 129, 131, 135, 139, 141, 143, 147, 153, 155, 157, 177, 189.
—— son of Maelodhra, 95.
—— son of Muirigen, 201, 211, 215, 217, 221, 223, 225.
Cearmait, son of Catharnach, 157.
—— son of Cinaedh, 151.
Cearnachan, son of Duilgen, 243.
Ceile, son of Urthuile, Prior of Aghabo, 199.
Ceilochar, brother of Ciugógan, 207.
Ceallach, son of Faelchair, 57.
Cele-Christ, 55.
Cele-Dabhaill, 227.
Cenndeilgtin, or Cenndelgtben, battle of, 53, 109.
Cennedigh, son of Gaithin, 157, 159, 165, 170, 173, 189.
Cenn-Etigh, or Kinnitty, 210, *n*.
Cennfaeladh, son of Colgan, 87.
—— son of Crunmhael, 71, 77.
—— son of Maelbresail, 93.
—— son of Suibhne, 87.
—— king of Ui Conaill, 211.
—— Ua Muichtigherna, King of Caisil, or Munster, 153, 169, 197.

Cer of Cera, 51.
Cetamun, 57.
Cethernach, son of Nae Ua Ceallaigh, 55.
Chester, 228, n., 233.
Children, mortality of, 89.
Cian, son of Cumascach, 185.
Cianachta, of Meath, or of Bregia, the territory called, 32, n., 116, n., 125, 177.
Cianachta Glinne Gaimhin, 87.
Ciar, daughter of Duibhrea, 87.
Ciarmacan, 199.
Ciarmach Ua Dunadbaigh, king of Ui Conaill Gabhra, 199.
Ciarraighi, or Kerry-men, 167.
Ciarodbar, son of Crunnmhael, 199.
Cicaire, king of Osraighe, 85.
Cill Ausaille, 197.
Cillene Fota, abbot of Ia, 53.
Cill-na-gCaillech destroyed, 239.
—— Nais, 224, n.
—— ruaidh, 53, n.
—— Ua nDaighre, battle of, 177.
Cinaedh, Caech, son of Irgalach, 51, 53, 55, 57, 109.
—— Mac Ailpin, king of the Picts, 151.
—— Cinaeth, son of Conaing, 117, 119.
Cineide, son of Gaeithin, 153.
Cinel-Cairbre, 50, n.
Cinel-Conaill and Cinel-Eoghain, 30, n., 35.
Cinel-Conaill, sovereignty of Erin separated from, 59.
Claenadh, battle of, 109.
Clane, round hill of, 39, n.
Clercén, king of Ui-Bairche, 213.
Clergy, presence of the, in warlike expeditions, 210, n.
Clonard, ancient name of, 14, n.
Clothna, son of Colgan, 49.
Cluain-Dobhail, 36, n.
—— eidhneach, 11.
—— fearta-Brenainm, 163.
—— Iraird, 14, n.
—— Uamha, or Cloyne, 205.
Cobhthach, abbot of Kildare, 187.
Cobhthach-Cael-mBreagh, 39.
Cochall-Odhar, death of, 57.
Coibhdenach, son of Fiacha, 49.
Colga, son of Blathmac, 87.
Colgu, son of Eochaidh, 57.
—— son of Failbho Flann, 85.
—— son of Domhnall, death of, 65.
Colman Banbain, 53.
—— Beg, 7.
—— son of Fergus, 11.
—— abbot of Benchair, death of, 87.
—— Cas, death of, 65.
—— abbot of Cenn-Etigh, 211, 217, 225.

Colman, son of Dunlang, 163.
—— son of Finnbhar, 105.
—— Ua Altain, 57.
—— Ua Cluasaigh, 61 ; his sailing to Inis-bofinne, 67 ; his death, 71.
—— Uamach, 53.
Colum-Cille, his story respecting death of Feradhach, 9 ; his death, 11 ; patron of Cinell Conaill, 40, n. ; his manner of tonsuring, 21, 113 ; his relics brought to Ireland, 125, n. ; crozier of, 231.
Comanns, plundering of the, 197.
Comhgall of Beanchar, 199.
Comhgan Fota, abbot of Tamlacht, 187.
Compama, the word, 40, n.
Conacan, son of Colman, 129.
Conaing, son of Congal, 61, 63.
Conall of Cill Scire, 175.
—— Crau, 49.
—— Men, king of Cinel-Cairbre, 51, 107.
—— son of Domhnall, death of, 65.
—— Gabhra, 107.
—— son of Niall of the Nine Hostages, 30, n.
—— Ultach, 153.
Conchadh, king of the Cruithnigh, 59.
Conchobhar Aired, King of Dal Araidhe, 99.
—— son of Donnchadh, 157.
Convail, the word, 26, n.
Condail of the kings, 44, n.
Congal, 211, 217.
—— Caech, 17, 18, n.
—— Cennfoda, son of Dunchadh, 71.
—— the Senior, king of Ciarraighe, 167.
—— son of Fergus of Fanaid, 26, n., 33.
—— son of Lorchine, 69.
—— son of Maelduin, 93.
Congalach, son of Conain, 49, 95, 97.
Conmael, 36, n.
Connaught plundered by Cearbhall and Dunnchadh, 195.
Conneire, or Connor, 66, n.
Connell, Old, 44, n.
Cunnga, the, 223.
Connla, son of Breasal Breac, race of, 8, n., 9.
Connmach, abbot of Cluain-mic-nois, 177.
Conodhar of the Ui-Toirdealbhaigh, 211, 217.
Coning, son of Godfraidh, 195.
Corann, battle of, 89, 107.
Corban's church, 225.
Corca-Laighde, 8, n., 9 ; interchange of kings of, with those of Osraighe, 8, n., 9 ; O'Driscoll, chief of, 8, n.
Corcach, or Cork, 169.
Cormac, son of Cuilenan, 201, 207, 221.
—— king of the Deisi, 211, 213, 217, 241.
—— son of Dunlang, 139.
—— son of Elathach, 165.
—— son of Elothach, 185.

General Index.

Cormac of Lathrach Briuin, 143.
—— son of Mothla, 207, 209.
—— son of Maelfothartagh, 69.
—— bishop of Saighir, 243.
—— Ua Liathain, 175.
Corrbile, 41.
Cosgrach of Tigh Telle, 175.
Crannacht, battle of, 97.
Crimhthann, son of Cellach, 53.
Critan, abbot of Benchair, 67.
Crohane, Co. Tipperary, ancient name of, 134, n.
Cronan Mac Ua Cualna, abbot of Benchair, 93.
—— the Dwarf, abbot of Cluain mic nois, 95.
Cruachan Claenta, 39.
Crufait, or Croboy, 125.
Cruachain, in the Eoganacht-Chaisil, or Cruachan Maighe Ramhna, 134, n., 135.
Cruithne, or Cruithnigh, Picts, 59, n., 87.
Cu, names compounded with, 36, n., 37, n.
Cubretan, 36, n., 45.
Cuganmathair, king of Munster, death of, 65.
Cuilennan, brother of Cormac, 241.
Cuimin Finn, abbot of Ia, 67.
—— Foda, death of, 61.
Cuindles, abbot of Cluain-mic-Nois, 53.
Culoingsi, the son of, 51.
Cumar-na-tri-n-uisce, 139.
Cumascach, son of Ronan, 69.
Cummeni of Mughdhorna, 97.
Cumsudh, abbot of Castlekieran, 187.
—— bishop of Cluain-Iraird, 151.
Curui, abbot of Inis Clothrann, 195.
Cuthbertus, bishop, 91.

Dachonna, bishop of Conneire, 53.
Dalach, abbot of Cluain mic Nois, 153.
Dallan, son of Mor, 217.
Danes, the, 131, 133, 173.
—— and Lochlanns, the, 117, 159.
—— See Lochlanns
Darerca, St., extract from life of, 9, n.
Deilginis-Cualann, 59.
Deisi, the 169.
Desgabbair, or South Leinster, 219, n.
Desies, the, plundered, 157.
Dianimh, daughter of Duibhgbilla, 241.
Diarmaid, 127, 157, 169, n.
—— cemetery of, 205.
—— son of Aedh Slaine, death of, 65.
—— son of Cearbhall, 213.
—— abbot of Cluain-Iraird, 17.
—— abbot of Ferns, 187.
—— Midhe, son of Airmheadbach Caech, 93.
—— king of Osraighe, or Ossory, 241, 237.
Dicuill, son of Eochaidh, 69.
Dinertach, abbot of Lothra, 169.

Dinn-Canainn, 39.
Dinnrigh, 38, n.
Disert-Diarmada, or Castledermot, 203.
Dochuma Chonoc, abbot of Gleann-da-locha, 89.
Doer, son of Maeltuile, 71.
Domhnall, son of Aedh, 155, 241.
—— Breac, son of Eochaidh Buidhe, 87, 89.
—— king of Connaught, death of, 57.
—— king of Dun Cearmna, 211, 217, 219.
—— grandson of Dunlaing, 157.
—— Mac Allpin, King of the Picts, 153.
Doiriadh, son of Conla, 51.
Dongalach Ua Aenghusa, 51.
Donnagan, son of Cedfad, 185.
Domichadh, son of Murchadh, 41, 52, n.
—— Ua Fiachrach, 51.
—— Ua Maelsechlainn, 245.
Donnbo, 34, n., 38, 47.
Donnsleibhe, son of, 21.
Druim-Coepis, battle of, 69.
—— Corcain, battle of, 57.
—— criaidh, or Drumcree, battle of, 237.
—— Fornacht, battle of, 55.
Drust, King of Alba, 55.
Duach, King of Osraighe, death of son of, 7.
Dubhaltach Firbisigh, or Mac Firbisigh, 1, 193.
Dubhartach Berrach, 177.
Dubbdabhoirenn, 211, 217, 219.
Dubbdachrioch, son of Dubhdabhoirenn, 51.
Dubhdainbher, King of Ard Cianachta, 91.
Dubhdathuile, abbot of Liath Mochaemhog, 18.
Dubhdibhderg, son of Dunghal, 107.
Dubhghlaise, or Douglas, 85.
Dubhagan, King of Fera-Maighe, 211, 217.
Dubhlach, 217.
Dubhthach, abbot of Cill-achaidh, 195.
—— son of Maeltuile, 185.
Dudley Firbisse, 1.
Duibhduin, 69.
Duncannon, 39, n.
Dunbolg, or Donard, 189.
Dun Carman, 218, n., 221.
—— Cearmna, 211, n.
—— Ceithirn, or Giant's Sconce, 87.
Dunchadh, 225.
Dunchadhs, the two, 105.
Dunchadh, son of Cormac, slain, 57.
—— son of Donngbal, 177.
—— Muirisge, son of Maeldubh, 89.
—— son of Murchadh, 57.
—— Ua Ronain, 69.
Dun Dearmbaigh, 219, n.
Dungaile, son of Maeltuile, 69.
Dunghal, King of the Cruithni, or Picts, 87.
Dun-locha, battle of, 87.
Dun-Sobhairce, or Dunseverick, 66, n., 195.

General Index. 253

Dunlaing, son of Cairbre, 241.
—— son of Muireadhach, 185.
Dun-Neachtain, battle of, 89.

Easter, the celebration of, 111.
Ecbertus, death of, 57.
Eclipse of the sun, 163.
Ederscel, king of Bregia, 53.
Egnechan, son of Dalach, 199.
Eidgin Brit, bishop of Cill-dara, 157.
Eidhen, King of Aidhne, 211, 217.
Eignech, son of Conaing, 49.
Elodhach, son of Flann O'Sgigi, 51.
Emhir's Island, i. e. Ireland, 197.
Eochaidh Iarlaithe, king of Dal-Araidhe, death of, 65.
Eochaidh Leamhna, 107.
Eodhus, son of Dunghal, 185.
Eodus, son of Ailell, slain, 57.
Eoghan, race of, 18.
—— son of Niall of the Nine Hostages, 30, *n.*
Eoganacht Chaisil, 134, *n.*, 147, 155.
Erannan, son of Criomhthan, 37.
Eecra, a silver drinking vessel, 9, *n.*
Etheldrida, St., daughter of Anna, 91.
Ethelfrid, King of Northumbria, 91.
Ethelfrida, Queen of the Saxons, 227, 247.
Etholo, King of North Saxons, 245.

Faelan, 225.
—— son of Colman, 87.
—— king of Leinster, 55, 69.
—— son of Murchadh, 57.
—— Senchustal, king of Ui-Ceinnsealaigh, 85.
Faelchu, abbot of Ia, 53.
Faelcobhar of Clochar, 103.
Faha, 11, *n.*
Fahan, 20, *n.*
Fail, name of Ireland, 48, *n.*
Failbhe, abbot of Ia, death of, 87.
Falchar, king of Osraighe, 93, 95.
Feara-Cualan, 212, *n.*
Fearchair, son of Maelduin, 97.
Fearna, or Ferns, 239.
Fechin of Tobhar, death of, 65.
Feidhlimidh, son of Maelcothaigh, 103.
Feimhin, battle of, 7.
Feradhach, 211, 217.
—— Finn, death of, 7, 11.
Fera Maighe, 155, 169.
—— Ros, 35, 72, *n.*
Ferdomhnach, abbot of Cluain-mic-Nois, 197.
Ferdoragh, baron of Dungannon, 31, *n.*
Fergal, king of Erin, 40, *n.*
—— Glut, 49.
—— hill of, 41, *n.*
—— Ua Aithechta, 49.

Fergal Ua Tamnaigh, 49.
Ferghal Aidhne, king of Connaught, 97.
—— son of Maelduin, 21, 23, 29, 49, 89.
Fergus, son of Aedan, 93.
—— of Fanaid, 26, *n.*
—— Forcraidh, 107.
Fernmhagh, battle of, 57, 99.
Fersat, battle of, 69.
Ferta Cairech, or Fertach, 155.
Fethghna, comharba of Patrick, 127, 141, 149.
Fiachna, 17.
Fiach Ua Ugfadain, of Denbis, 208, *n.*
Fianambail, son of Maeltuile, king of Leinster, 87, 95.
—— son of Maenach, 97.
Fiannamhail, son of Oisen, 99, 101.
Fidhgal, son of Fithchellach, 51.
Fidh-Gaible, wood of, 48, *n.*
Fincheallach, abbot of Fearna, 153.
Finech and Rechtin, 239.
Finguine, son of Cu-gan-mathair, 97.
Finian of Cluain-caein, 153.
Finn, 225.
Finnachta, son of Dunchadh, 23 ; victor in battle of Aircelltair, 71 ; beginning of his reign, *ib.* ; stories told respecting, 71, *seq.* ; battle between him and Bec Boirche, 87; his murder, 95.
Finnglais, 175.
Finnian, festival of, 38, *n.*
Finntan Ua Eachach, 11.
Firbisse, Dudley, 1.
Fithchellach, son of Flann, 93.
Flaithbhertach, abbot of Inis-Cathaigh, 201.
—— son of Inmainen, or Ionmainén, 205-7, 215, 245.
—— son of Loinsech, 55, 57, 59.
—— son of Niall, 129.
Flaitheamhail, son of Dluthach, 51.
Flaithemh, son of Faelchar, 195.
Flaithir, a poet, 67.
Flannu, daughter of king of Osraighe, 179.
Flann, son of Aedh Odhbha, 51.
—— abbot of Benchair, 55.
—— king of Cianachtu, 141, 143,157, 171.
—— son of Conaing, 177.
—— son of Domhnall, 199.
—— king of Erin, 213, 219, 237.
—— Fiona, son of Ossa, 111.
—— son of Irghalach, 51.
—— son of Irthuile, 55.
—— son of Laegh, 243.
—— son of Maelsechlainn. *See* Flann Sionna.
—— Sinna Ua Colla, abbot of Cluain-mic-nois, death of, 59.
—— Sionna, son of Maelsechlainn, 165, 201, 205, 211, 237.

Flann, son of Tighernan, 237.
Fochard-Muirtheimhne, 59.
Fogartach, son of Geirtide, 109.
—— son of Niall, 51.
—— son of Tolarg, 245.
—— Ua Cernaigh, 20, n., 21, 53.
—— son of Suibhne, 211, 217.
Foichsechan, 95.
Follamhan, son of Oilell, 213.
Forannan, abbot of Ard-Macha, 127.
—— abbot of Cill-dara, 99.
Forbasach, 49.
Forod Geilsheirce, 221.
Fortuatha, 212, n.
Foirtrenn, or Pictland, 159, 229.
Fothain, 11, n.
Fotharta-Fea, 212, n.
—— -tire, 163.
Frighrenn, 217.
Frigrinn, Ailech, 23, n.
Frosach, Niall, 21.
Frosta, remarkable, 143.
Furadhran, prior of Cill-achaidh, 199.

Gabhorchenn, 91.
Gabhrán, or Gowran, 137, 191.
Gaditanean Straits, 161.
Gaeidhil, or Scoti, 125.
Gaeithing, son of Ughran, 241.
Gaimide of Lughmhagh, 97.
Gaithin, son of, 177.
Gall Craibhtheach, 43, n.
Gall-Gaoidhil, or Dano-Irish, 129, 139, 141, 233.
Gall of Lilcach, 57.
Galls of Erin, 135, 157, 159.
—— the Black and the Fair, 245.
Gelshere, daughter of Deirill, 221.
Gerald, Pontifex of Mayo, death of, 59.
Geran, son of Diocose, 187.
Gilla-na-naemh, or Nehemias, 1, n.
Glais Chuilg, 109.
Glaisiu, son of Uisin, 199.
Gleann na nGealt, 41, n.
Glifit, 131.
Gnathnat, abbess of Cill-dara, 93.
Gnia, abbot of Daimhliag-fianain, 197.
Gnim Cinnsiolla, 169.
Goffridh, 195.
Gormflaith, daughter of Flann, 223.
Gormlaith, Queen of Teamhar, 153.
Greallach-Dollaidh, 95.
Greenan Ely, 23, n.
Gregory the Great, 62, n.
Guaire Aidhne, death of, 63.
Guaire, son of Dubhdabhoirenn, 175.
Gwyned, 155.

Haimar, the Lochlann, 173.
Hingamund, 227.
Hona, chief of the Lochlanns, 145.
Horm, lord of the Danes, 121, 131.
Hugh of Leinster, 42, n.
Huidhrine of Maghbile, 95.

Ia, family of, 21.
Iargna, chief of the Lochlanns, 119, 123.
Imblech-Phich, or Imleach Fich, battle of, 91, 103.
Imhar, 127, 171, 195.
—— Conung, 229.
Imleach, or Emly, 139.
Immolate, signification of the word, 16, n.
Inis-bo-finne, 67, n.
—— Breoghain, battle of, 55.
—— an Ghaill, 44, d.
—— mac Nesain, or Ireland's Eye, 105.
—— Tarbna, 139.
Indrechtach, abbot of Hy, 125, 127.
—— son of Dobhailen, abbot of Bangor, 199.
—— son of Tadhg, 51.
—— son of Muiredbach, 53.
Inneirghe, son of Duibhgilla, 213, 219.
Innis-Fail, ancient name of Ireland, 35, n.
Innsi Orc, 159.
Irgalach, son of, slain, 57.
Irgalach, son of Conaing, 101, 133, 105.

Jakes, meaning of the word, 12, n.
Jewels. See Valuables.
Justinian II., 99, n.

Killineer, near Drogheda, 183.
Kill-Luaithrinne, 32, n.
Kinnaweer, 28, n.
Knockfarrell, 41, n.

Lachtnan, son of Cearnach, 245.
Laeighis, or Leix, 212, n.
Laidhgnen, king of Ui Cinnselaigh, 53.
Lairgnen, 153.
Lann, daughter of Dunlaing, 129, 139, 157, 165.
Legionum Castra, 233, n.
Leicester, confounded with Chester, 232, n.
Leinster devastated by the Ui Neill, 22, n.
Leithglinn, or Leighlin, 149.
Leix, the territory called, 165, n.
Leo the emperor (i. e. Leo III.), 21; died, 55, 56, n.
Leoghain (or Ua Eoghain) Fergus, 51.
Letaithiech, son of Cucarat, 49.
Lethchaech, 50, n.
Leth-Chuinn, 34, n.
Liag-Maclain, battle of, 87.
Liamhain, or Dunlavan, 219, n.

General Index.

Lilcach, 43, n.
Linn-Duachaill, 120, n.
Loch Cend, 143.
—— Cime, 109.
—— Eachach, or Loch Neagh, 99.
—— Feabhail, or Loch Foyle, 157.
—— Gabhair, 71, n.
—— Laeigh, 127.
—— Leibhinn, or Lough Leane, 169.
—— Ri, or Ribh, 197.
Lochlanns, or Norwegians, 115, n., 129, 131, 133, 145, 153, 155, 157, 159, 163, 165, 167, 185, 195, 197, 199, 227, 233, 245, 247.
Loichine Menn, abbot of Kildare, 97.
Loingsech, son of Aengus, 33, 97, 105, 107.
—— son of Foillen, 197.
—— victor in battle of Tulach-árd, 69.
Lorcan, king of Feara Cualann, 213, 219.
—— son of Cathal, 157.
—— son of Donchadh, 245.
Luaithrin, the virgin, 32, n.
Luan, meaning of the word, 85, n.
Luchrinna, St., 32, n.
Luimnech, or Limerick, 147.
Lunatics in Ireland, belief respecting, 41, n.
Lusca, oratory of, 143.
Lynch, Rev. John, 1.

Mac Ailerain, of Cill-ruaidh, 53.
—— Andaighe, great oratory of, 185.
—— Concumbri, death of, 57.
—— Conmella, Laidhcenn, 55.
—— Erca, son of Maelduin, 51.
—— Feimhin, 6, n.
—— Giallain, 135.
—— Onchon, death of, 57.
—— Radgund, 109.
Madudan, 211, 217.
Maelbrighde, son of Macdomhnach, 243.
—— son of Tornan, 243.
Maelcaich, son of Scandal, death of, 67.
Maelchallan, son of Ferghal, 213, 219.
Maelciarain, 167, 183, 185.
Maelcobha, 16, n.
Maelcron, son of Muireadhach, 139.
Maelduin, son of Aedh, 175.
—— Beg, son of Fergus Conainn, 61.
—— son of Feradach, slain, 57.
—— son of Maelfithrigh, 87.
Maelfeichine, 125.
Maelfothartaigh, king of the Airghialls, 97.
—— son of Ronan, 65.
—— son of Suibhne, 69.
Maelguala, king of Munster or Cashel, 137, 141.
Maelmaedhóg, chief of Druin-mor, 245.
Macl-mic-Failbhe, 36, n.

Maelmithidh, son of Flannagan, 245.
Maelmona, the son of, 51.
Maelmordha, chief of Tir-da-glas, 241–3.
Maelmuadh, 211, 217.
—— son of Finnachta, king of Airthir-Liffé, 195.
—— son of Donchadh, 171.
Maelmuirtheimhne, son of Maelbrighde, 171.
Maelodhar, abbot of Devenish, 187.
—— O'Tindridh, chief physician of Erin, 153.
Maelpatraic, son of Flathrai, 245.
Mael-petair, abbot of Tir-da-ghlas, 157.
Maelpoll, chief of Sruthair Guaire, 199.
Maelruanaidh, son of Niall, 241.
Maelrubha, son of, 21.
Maelsechlainn, son of Maelruanaigh, 115, 116, 123, 127, 129, 135, 141, 147, 151, 179.
Maeltuile, abbot of Imleach Iobhair, 151.
Maenach, son of Connach, 157.
—— son of Fingbin, death of, 63.
—— son of Siadhal, 203, 215.
Maenghal, abbot of Bangor, 193.
—— bishop of Kildare, 189.
—— abbot of Fobhar, 149.
Magh Ailbhe, or Ballaghmoon, battle of, 207, 239.
—— Adhair, 217.
—— Breagh, 21, 23.
—— Cuillinn, 109
—— Feimhin, 155.
—— Luirg, 197.
—— Macha, or the Moy, 147.
—— Muirtheimhne, 97.
—— Nairbhi, 214, n.
—— Raighne, east of, plundered, 239.
—— Leine, 38, n.
Mainchine, bishop of Leithghlin, 163.
Mairge, or Slievemarague, 219, n.
Maistin, battle of, 55.
Manuan, the Isle of Man, battle of, 7, 7, n.
Matodan, king of Uladh, 123, 127, 149.
Mauritani, or Moors, 161, 163.
Meath plundered by Aedh, 151.
Mennbairenn, abbot of Achadh-bo, 97.
Meucossach, son of Gammach, 51.
Mindroichet, 159.
Mochua of Balla, 95.
Modichu, son of Amairgin, 43.
Molaisse of Leithglinn, 177.
Moling Luchra, 23, 33, 34, n., 77, seq., 97.
Mona Conain, or Anglesea, 155.
Mughain, lines on battle of, 217.
Mugbron, son of Sochlachán, 225.
Muireadbach, son of Cathal, 177.
—— son of Bran, 189.
—— son of Domhnall, 199.
—— son of Indrechtach, 59.

Muiroadhach, son of Maelduin, 155.
Muiregan, or Muirigen, son of Diarmaid, king of Naas, 155, 225.
Muirenn, successor of Brighit, 215.
Muirghes, son of Conall, 49.
—— son of Maelduin, 99.
Muirghius, anchorite of Ard-Macha, 153.
Mura Othna, St., 12, n., 15, n., 40, n.
Murchadh, son of Bran, king of Leinster, 21, 23, 41, 45, 49, 55.
Muredhach, the sons of, 51.

Nanny Water, the, 118, n.
Nás, now Naas, 155, 223, 225.
Nehemias Mac Egan, 1.
—— son of Cearuach, 103.
Nia, son of Cormac, 51.
Niall Frosach, 21, n., 23.
—— Glundubh, 223, 243.
—— son of Murghes, 51.
—— of the Nine Hostages, 15, n.
Niallan, bishop of Slaine, 183.
Niar, 141.
Northmen, or Gall-Gaeidhil, 129, 139, 143.
Norwegians, or Lochlanns, 115, n.
Nuada, son of Dubhdunchuire, 51.
Nuada Uirc, king of Gull and Irgull, 49.
Nuadhat, the grandsons of, 51.
Nui, the Danish war-cry, 165, n.

Odhbha, 50, n.
Odolbb Micle, 177.
O'Driscoll, chief of Corca-Laighde, 8, n.
Oeghedchar, bishop of Oendruim, death of, 61.
O'Gaman, battle of, 63.
Oigedhchair, abbot of Coindeire (Connor), 175.
Oilell, son of Feradbach, 49.
Oisle, son of, king of the Lochlanns, 171.
Osraighe, or Ossory, plundered by the Deisi, 241; by the Lochlanns, 155, 245; by Rodolph, 129.
—— Duach, king of. See Duach.
—— extent of diocese of, 86, n.
Ossa, king of the Saxons, 69.
Othain Mura, or Othain mor, 11, 20, n.
Otter, Earl of the Pagans, 247.
—— son of Iargna, 231.
Owen, race of, 15, n.

Paganism, relapses into, 127.
Pagans and Saxons, battle between, 245.
Patrick, St., invoked by the Danes, 121.
Peter the apostle, tonsure of, 21, 111.
Picts of Dalaradia, 87, n.
Plague, deaths of Blathmac and Diarmaid by, 65.
Pope of Rome, never an Irishman, 62, n.
Port-Lairge, 147.

Port-Manann, 167.
Prediction, Ferghal's, concerning his sons, 23.
R. E., meaning of the letters, 71, n.

Rath-Aedha, or Rahugh, 141.
Ráth-Aedhain, or Ferns, 239.
Rathmor of Magh-line, battle of, 87.
Raghnall, son of Albdan, 159.
Raighne, fair of, 149.
Rechtabbra, son of Cumascach Ua Maine, 51.
Rechtin, 239.
Regner Lodbrok, 124, n.
Riagail of Bennchair, 111.
Robbartach, bishop of Finnglais, 175.
—— of Dearmhach, 197.
Roderick, king of the Britons, 135.
Rodlaibh, the fleet of, 153.
Rodolph, 129.
Roisene, abbot of Corcach, or Cork, 89.
Ronan, king of Leinster, story of his wife, 65.
Ross, diocese of, 8, n.
Rumann, 53.

Saxons, the, 89, 130, n., 155, 173, 233, 245.
Scandinavian nations, ferocity of, 123, n.
Scotland, Albain a name of, 40, n.
Sebhdan, daughter of Corc, 59.
Sechnasach, son of Blathmac, 67, 69.
Segine, bishop of Ard-macha, 91.
Segonan, son of Conang, 153.
Seigine, abbot of Benchar, 63.
Sgama, the word, 169.
Shields, appearance of miraculous, 99.
Showers, miraculous, 21.
Simon Magus, tonsure of, 21, 113.
Sinainn, or Shannon, 76, n.
Sitric, grandson of Imhar, 245.
Slainè, or Slaney, 239.
Slebhte, or Sleaty, 99, 171.
Sliabh-Mairge, or Slievemarague, 149, 205.
Slighe-Asail, 76, n.
Sloighedach Ua Raitbnen, 177.
Snànah Aighnech, or Carlingford Lough, 120, n.
Snoring, 24, n.
Sodhomna, bishop of Slaine, 143.
Spain, incursion into, by Scandinavians, 159.
Srath-cluaide, siege of, 193; plundered, 247.
Sruthair, or Shrule, 171.
Star, miraculous, seen, 16, n.
Steersman, Irish word for, 116, n.
Suairlech, comharba of Finian, 143.
Suairlech, 127.
—— of Inedhnen, 187.
Suibhne, abbot of Ard-Macha, death of, 57.
—— son of Conghalach, 49.
—— abbot of Lis-mor, 143.

General Index. 257

Suibhne, son of Maelumha, 89.
—— Menn, 17, 18, n.
Suitheman, son of Arthur, 141.
Sundays, no work performed by Lochlanns on, 185.

Tadhg, son of Aigtbide, 51.
—— son of Diarmald, 157.
—— son of Faelan, 211, 219.
—— son of Failbhe, 97.
—— king of Munster, 32, n.
Tailltin, 20, n.
Tairchealtach Mac na Cearta, 137.
Teamhair, the king of, and Horm, 135.
Teltown, 20, n.
Temhenan, king of Ui-Deaghaidh, 213, 219.
Theodosius III., 21.
Three Plains, plundering of the men of the, 197.
Tiberius Apsimarus, 105.
Tibraide, successor of Ailbhe of Emly, 205, 243.
—— bishop of Cluain-eidhnach, 245.
Tighernach, king of Breagh, 119, 163.
Tigh Telle, 175.
Tipraide Banbhan, abbot of Tir-da-ghlas, 151.
Tir-Chonaill, whence named, 30, n.
Tir-da-ghlas, abbacy of, 157.
Tir-Eoghain, whence named, 30, n.
Tonsure of Peter the apostle, 21, n., 111.
Tonsuring of clerks in Erin, 111.
Tomrar the Earl, 163, 165, 167.
Tomrir Torra, chief of the Lochlanns, 145.
Tribute, Boromean, 22, n.
Tualm-snamha, king of Osraighe, 85.
—— Tenbath, 38, n.
Tualaith, daughter of Cathal, 57.
Tuath Inbhir, 225.
Tuathal, abbot of Dun Caillen, 163.
—— son of Morgan, death of, 65.
—— Techtmhar, imposes Borumha, 77, n.
—— son of Ugaire, 213.
Tuenoc, son of Fintan, death of, 65.
Tulach-árd, battle of, 69.
Turgesius, 124, n., 169, n.

Ua Aithechta, Fergal, 49.
—— Altain, Colman, 57.

Ua Brachaidhe, Suedhgus Derg, 55.
—— Cluasaigh, Colman, 61.
—— Colla, Flann Sinn, 59.
—— Daimine, Duibhdil, 51.
—— Domhnaill, Focarta, 51.
—— Eoghan (or Leoghain), Fergus, 51.
—— Fiachrach, Donnchadh, 51.
—— Cernaigh, Fogartach, 20, n.
Uallachan, son of Cathal, 239.
Ua Maelcaichs, the two, 51.
—— Maighleine, 43.
—— Maithe, Aidhgen, 49.
—— Tamhnaigh, 49.
Ugaire of Dun Dearmhaigh, 219.
—— son of Oilell, 239.
Ughran, son of Cennedigh, 213, 219.
Ui Aengbusa, 157.
—— Bairche, 212, n.
—— Deaghaidh, 212, n.
—— Drona, 212, n., 239.
—— Felmedha, or Ballaghkeen, 199.
—— Liathain, 211, n.
—— Maccaile, or Imokilly, 199.
—— Muireadhaigh, 213, n.
—— Niallain, 155.
—— Neill, northern, race of the, 15, n.; devastate Leinster, 22, n.
—— Neill, southern, Colman Beg, chief of, 7.
—— Tuirtre, the tribe of the, 68, n.
—— Toirdealbhaigh, the tribe, 212, n.
Uillè, 225.
Uladh, plundering of, by Aedh, 129.
Ulbh, 223.
Ultan, son of Dicolla, 87.
—— son of Ernin, 63.
Umhaill, 127.
Urchralthe Ua hOssin, 91.

Valuables, Feradhach's, 9, 10, n.
—— meaning of the word, 9, n.
Vessels, silver drinking, 9.

Wonders, three, in Irish romantic stories, 47, n.

Zain, chief of the Lochlanns, 119, 123.

2 L

www.ingramcontent.com/pod-product-compliance
Lightning Source LLC
Chambersburg PA
CBHW032147230426
43672CB00011B/2473